Rxpert SERIES
Student's Companion

Drug Delivery Systems

RXpert SERIES
Student's Companion

Drug Delivery Systems

Dulal Krisha Tripathi

Deependra Singh

Manju Rawat Singh

Amber Vyas

Pharma Med PRESS
An Imprint of BSP Books Pvt. Ltd.

PharmaMed Press

An imprint of BSP Books Pvt. Ltd.

4-4-309/316, Giriraj Lane,

Sultan Bazar, Hyderabad - 500 095.

Drug Delivery Systems

***by* Dulal Krishna Tripathi, Deependra Singh, Manju Rawat Singh and Amber Vyas**

Published by

PharmaMed Press

An imprint of BSP Books Pvt. Ltd.

4-4-309/316, Giriraj Lane, Sultan Bazar, Hyderabad - 500 095.

Phone: 040-23445688; Fax: 91+40-23445611

E-mail: info@pharmamedpress.net

www.bspbooks.net/www.pharmamedpress.net

ISBN: 978-93-48734-82-2 (Hardback)

Preface

In the new curriculum for Master in Pharmacy, introduction of Drug Delivery system courses by the Pharmacy Council of India, is really a revolutionary work. In this course Sustained Release (SR) and Controlled Release (CR) formulations, Polymers, Dosage Forms for Personalized Medicine, Rate Controlled Drug Delivery Systems, Gastro-Retentive Drug Delivery Systems, Buccal Drug Delivery Systems, Ocular Drug Delivery Systems, Transdermal Drug Delivery Systems, Protein and Peptide Delivery, and Vaccine delivery systems have been introduced as a result the students or the reader will know the essential information about these types of dosage form.

Based on the knowledge, skill, attitude and the values that are necessary for the successful practice of the profession have been derived. The competencies developed through the courses of the curriculum based on the expected outcomes. The pharmacists thus produced are expected to serve the industries with desired strength of knowledge.

The book has been prepared by various authors, Dr. Bina Gidwani, Dr. Vishal Jain, Dr. Shib Shankar Shukla, Dr. Ravindra Pandey, Dr. Kapil Agrawal, Priya Namdev, Sakshi Tiwari, Dr. Sanjib Bahadur, Dr. Amber Vyas, Dr. Deependra Singh, Dr. Manju Rawat Singh, and Dr. DK Tripathi. The authors strongly feels and believes that the ER-2020 regulations, curriculum and syllabus will definitely improve the knowledge and skills of the students on par with the contemporary and future professional requirements and can make them successful practitioners in the particular field of pharmacy.

The theory course of Drug Delivery System primarily explains the various types of dosage forms, their manufacture, components, advantages, etc. so that the students can correlate between the concepts. Through this theoretical knowledge the students can identify the problems in the real life situations.

Therefore, this course has been designed to impart the basic knowledge on manufacture of different types of dosage forms.

The book has been prepared with simple language so that the reader can easily understand each topic quite easily. The authors have taken sufficient precaution to make the book free from mistake. Even then, if anybody finds any mistake please inform the authors directly for rectification.

- Authors

Preface

Content

CHAPTER - 3

Dosage Forms for Personalized Medicine

Dr. Deependra Singh, Dr. Manju Rawat Singh, and Dr. D.K. Tripathi

CHAPTER - 4

Rate Controlled Drug Delivery Systems

Dr. Bina Gidwani, Dr. Vishal Jain, Dr. Shiv Shankar Shukla, and Dr. Ravindra Pandey

CHAPTER - 5

Gasto-Retentive Drug Delivery Systems

Dr. Kapil Agrawal, Dr. Deependra Singh, Dr. Manju Rawat Singh, and Dr. Amber Vyas

CHAPTER - 6

Buccal Drug Delivery Systems

Dr. Kapil Agrawal, Dr. Bina Gidwani, Dr. Vishal Jain, Dr. Shiv Shankar Shukla, Dr. Ravindra Pandey, and Dr. Amber Vyas

CHAPTER - 7

Ocular Drug Delivery Systems

Priya Namdev, Sakshi Tiwari, Dr. Kapil Agrawal and Dr. Amber Vyas

CHAPTER - 8

Transdermal Drug Delivery Systems

Priya Namdev, Sakshi Tiwari, Dr. Sanjib Bahadur, Dr. Amber Vyas

CHAPTER - 9

Protein and Pepide Delivery

Dr. Vishal Jain, Dr. Bina Gidwanim, Dr. Sanjib Bahadur and Dr. Kapil Agrawal

CHAPTER - 10

Vaccine Delivery Systems

Dr. Sanjib Bahadur, Dr. Deependra Singh, Dr. Manju Rawat Singh, and Dr. DK Tripathi

CHAPTER - 1

Sustained Release (SR) and Controlled Release (CR)

Dr. DK Tripathi, Dr. Deependra Singh, and Dr. Manju Rawat Singh

Introduction, Basic Concept, Biopharmaceutical Classification System of Drugs, Classification of Sustained Release Products, Factors Influencing, Approaches for SR/CR Formulation, Mechanism of Drug Release From SR/CR Formulation

INTRODUCTION

Pharmaceutical products prepared for oral delivery of a drug which is of immediate release type. These are called conventional drug delivery systems. These are intended for maximum drug release and absorption. But these dosage forms suffer from some limitations such as:

- Frequent administration of drugs with short half-life is required, which can increase the chances of missing dose of drug leading to poor patient compliance.
- The plasma concentration-time profile obtained shows a typical peak-valley; thus, attainment of steady state condition becomes difficult.

To overcome the drawbacks of such conventional delivery systems of drug, various advancements have been made in techniques of preparing drug delivery systems, such as controlled or sustained release delivery systems of drug and multiple dosing could have been avoided in many cases.

Probably in 1938 Lipowski of Israel made a patent in sustained release dosage forms. Coated pallets were prepared for prolonging the release of drug and it was probably the first work for development of the coated particle approach to prepare sustained release tablet that was prepared in the early 1950s[1] by Howard Press, in Hoboken, NJ in his methodology patent were known as "Nitroglyn" which was manufactured under licence by Key Corp. in Florida.

Any delivery system of drug is developed to deliver a therapeutic dose of drugs to the desired location in the body in order to get rapid results and then maintain the desired drug concentration[2]. The novel drug delivery systems (NDDSs) have been developed over a period of time to improve patient compliance and to optimize the dosage regimen without compromising the therapeutic efficacy. The sustained release dosage forms intended for oral administration have gained greater attention because of more flexibility in dosage form design[3]. Thus, the need for a sustained or controlled release formulation comes out of the following reasons:

- Due to undesirable properties of the drug, such as short biological half-life, local irritation, extensive metabolism, and narrow therapeutic index, etc.
- The nature of the disease state, or
- Patient compliance.

The most important among all these reasons is the need to improve the therapeutic efficacy of the drug and the safety of the patients. Before considering a drug for this type of formulation, the drug must be examined and evaluated for its physicochemical, pharmacokinetic and pharmacodynamic characteristics. Each property of a drug there is a range of values those are suitable for making a sustained or controlled-release dosage form. Outside the range, it is really difficult to design such dosage forms; sometimes, in the extreme, it becomes impossible. For example, extremes of aqueous solubility, oil/water partition coefficients, binding, extensive metabolism or degradation of the drug during movement from the site where it is delivered to the site where it is to work (target site), therapeutic index are some of the factors that limit the designing a successful sustained or controlled release product.

However, because of all these limiting factors, a sustained or controlled release product is designed. Theoretically, each of these limiting factors can be overcome by physical, chemical, biological and biomedical engineering methods alone or in combination for the successful design of sustained or controlled release delivery of drug.

The modified release oral dosage forms can be classified as shown below:

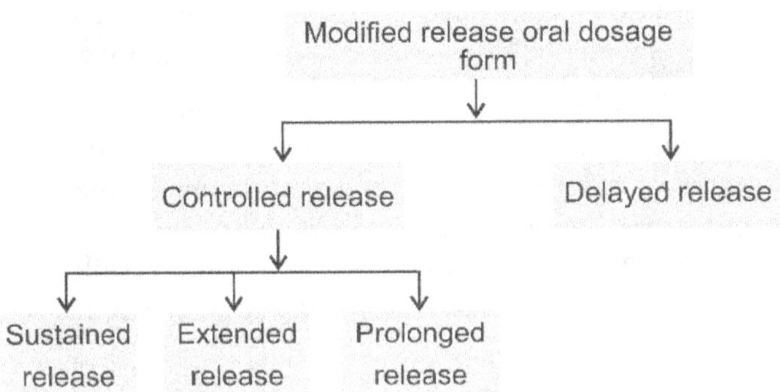

Such modified release formulations have been given different names for differences in their design.

- **Repeat action**

  In this type of dosage form, a dose of the drug is initially released just after administration, usually almost equivalent to a single dose of the drug. After a certain period, a second single dose is released[4].

- **Sustained release**

  This is a specific type of modified release dosage form which can reduce at least two-fold in the dosage frequency compared to conventional drug delivery system[5].

- **Controlled release**

  The dosage form in which the drug is released in a predictable manner but slower than conventional dosage form[6,7].

- **Delayed release dosage form**

  This is a specific type of modified release dosage form that releases the drug at a particular time, such as enteric coated tablet[8].

- **Extended release**

  Pharmaceutical dosage forms that release the drug slower than normal manner at a predetermined rate and necessarily reduce the dosage frequency by two folds[9].

- **Prolonged release system**

  These are designed to release the drug slowly and to provide a continuous supply of drugs over an extended period. These prevent very rapid absorption of the drug, which could result in extremely high peak plasma concentration of drug[10].

- **Timed release drug delivery system**

  Timed release drug delivery system is used to achieve the drug release after a lag time of about 4-5 hrs. For example, enteric coated dosage forms using cellulose acetate phthalate are designed to protect the drug from the acids in the stomach. A thick coat delays the drug release in the small intestine and thus, drug release is delayed. The time-controlled drug release maybe retarded up to 5 hrs. This targets the drug to the colon[11].

- **Site-specific release**

  These are designed and developed to target the drug directly to a certain biological location or site. In the case of site-specific release, the drug directly reaches a certain organ or tissue.

Objectives of oral sustained released dosage form

The objectives or purposes of the design and development of sustained release dosage forms intended for oral administration are:

➢ To maintain the drug concentration at a reasonably constant level for a considerable period.

- To minimize the frequency of doses administrated as compared to conventional dosage form
- To deliver a drug directly to site of action, minimizing or eliminating side effects.
- To deliver the drug directly to specific receptors or to localized cells or to specific areas of the body.
- The safety margins of potent drugs can be increased.
- To reduce both local and systemic adverse side effects in sensitive patient[12, 13].

BASIC CONCEPT

It is understood that duration of action of a drug is more related to the design of a controlled release dosage form. Duration of action is either less or not an inherent kinetic property of the drug molecule itself. Thus, it is necessary to understand the pharmacokinetic and pharmacodynamic properties of the drug molecule. Principal concept behind biopharmaceutical classification system (BCS) is that if two drug products produce the same concentration profile within the gastrointestinal (GI) tract, they should produce the same plasma concentration profile after oral administration. This concept can be summarized by applying the Fick's first law in the following equation

$$J = P_w C_w \quad .....(1.1)$$

Where, J is the flux across the gut wall,

P_w is the permeability of the gut wall to the drug, and

C_w is the concentration profile at the gut wall

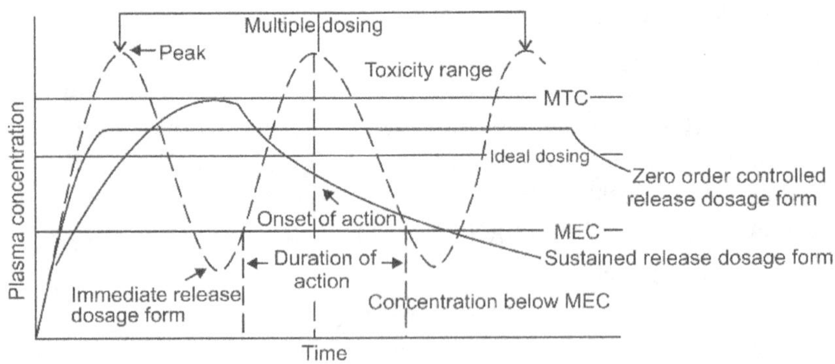

Fig.1.1 Plasma concentation-time profile of a drug.

In terms of bioequivalence, it is assumed that highly permeable, highly soluble drugs housed in rapidly dissolving drug products will be bioequivalent. Unless major changes are made to the formulation, dissolution data can be used as a substitute for pharmacokinetic data to demonstrate bioequivalence of two drug products. This has been mentioned earlier that the basic purpose of developing sustained or controlled release dosage form are safety of the patient and improvement of therapeutic efficacy, and patient's compliance. In case of conventional dosage forms, the dose (D) and dosing interval (τ) can be varied as per therapeutic requirement. As shown in Figure 1.1 each drug has a specific therapeutic window, plasma concentration below the lower limit is not therapeutically effective and the concentration in plasma above the upper limit shows toxic side effects. Therapeutic window can be quantitatively expressed as therapeutic index (TI) can be defined as the ratio of LD_{50} (median lethal dose) to ED_{50} (median effective dose); it can also be defined as the ratio of maximum tolerable drug concentration in the blood (C_{max}) to the minimum concentration of drug in the blood (C_{min}) required to produce an acceptable therapeutic response;

$$\text{Therapeutic index, TI} = \frac{C_{max}}{C_{min}}$$

The drugs which dispose quite linearly, their one compartment characteristics can be expressed as;

$$t_{\frac{1}{2}} \frac{\ln TI}{\ln 2} > \tau$$

Where, $t_{\frac{1}{2}}$ is the half-life of the drug. Since the therapeutic index, TI of most of the drugs is almost 2 and it would necessary to administer the drug at an interval of less than the half-life of the drug. In fact, due to such frequent dosing patient compliance becomes a poor and inadequate treatment result. In general, the dosing interval can be increased either by modifying

(1) The drug molecule to decrease the rate of drug elimination (k_{el}), or

(2) The rate of release of the drug from the dosage form to decrease the rate of absorption (k_a) of the drug.

Both the concepts require to reduce the fluctuation in plasma concentration during multiple dosing, to extend the dosing interval without over-dosing or under-dosing.

The conventional dosage forms release the active ingredients atthe site of absorption immediately. This is demonstrated in the following simple kinetic scheme. The absorption pool represents a solution of the drug at the site of absorption, Kr, Ka and Ke - the first order rate-constant for drug release, absorption and overall elimination respectively. Immediate drug release from a conventional dosage form implies that Kr>>>>Ka. For non-immediate release dosage forms, Kr<<<Ka; that is, the release of drug from the dosage form is the rate limiting step. The drug release from the dosage form should follow the zero-order kinetics, as shown by the following equation:

$$Kr^{\circ} = \text{Rate of incoming of the drug} = \text{Rate of outgoing of the drug}$$

$$= Ke \times C_d \times V_d \qquad .....(1.2)$$

Where,

Kr° is the Zero-order rate constant for drug release-Amount/time

K_e is the First-order rate constant for overall drug elimination-time

C_d is the desired drug level in the body – Amount/volume

V_d is the Volume space in which the drug is distributed in litter

For selecting of the drug, several physicochemical and pharmacokinetic parameters are to be considered for formulation of sustained release dosage form shown in table 1. This mostly includes the knowledge on the absorption mechanism of the drug from the GI tract[14]. Sustained or zero-order drug release has been achieved by following classes of sustained drug delivery system[15].

Table 1.1 Physicochemical and pharmacokinetic parameters for drug selection.

Physicochemical Parameters	
Parameters	***Selection criteria***
Molecular size	>1000 Daltons
Aqueous solubility	More than 0.1mg/ml at pH 1 – 7.8
Apparent partition coefficient	High
Absorption mechanism	Diffusion
General absorbability from GI	Release does not depend on pH and enzyme
Pharmacokinetic Parameters	
Elimination half-life	$(t_{1/2})$2 – 8 hr
Absolute bioavailability	75% or more
Absorption rate constant (K_a)	Must be more than the rate of release
Apparent volume of distribution (V_d)	Larger V_d and MEC, larger would be the required dose
Total clearance	Independent of dose
Elimination rate constant	Depends on the design
Therapeutic concentration (Css)	Lower C_{ss} and smaller V_d, lower amount of drug required
Toxic concentration	Depends on MTC and MEC, safer dose is required

BIOPHARMACEUTICAL CLASSIFICATION SYSTEM OF DRUGS

Based on aqueous solubility and based on aqueous solubility, and intestinal permeability drugs can be classified into four categories – class I, class II, class III, and class IV.

Class* I *drugs: *High Solubility and High Permeability*

The drugs in this class exhibit a high absorption number and a high dissolution number. Bioavailability anddissolution are very rapid. In other words, the drugs of this class have high solubility and high permeability. Bioavailability and bioequivalence studies are unnecessary for such product. These compounds are highly suitable for design of SR and CR formulations. Examples include Propranolol, Metoprolol, Diltiazem, Verapamil etc.

Class* II *drugs: *Low Solubility and High Permeability*

Drugs of this class have a high absorption number but a low dissolution number. Drugs put in class II category have low solubility but high permeability. This drug exhibited variable bioavailability and need the enhancement in dissolution for increasing the bioavailability. These compounds are suitable for design the SR and CR formulations. For example, Phenytoin, Danazol, Ketoconazole, Mefenamic acid, Nifedipine, Felodipine, Nicardipine, Nisoldipine, etc

Class* III *drugs: *High Solubility and Low Permeability*

The drugs having high solubility and low permeability are classified as class III. Thus, permeability of these drugs is found to be rate limiting step for their absorption. These drugs exhibit a high variation in the rate and extent of drug absorption. Since the dissolution is rapid, the variation is attributable to alteration of physiology and membrane permeability ratherthan the dosage form factors. These drugs are problematic for controlled release development. These drugs showed the low bioavailability and need enhancement impermeability. For example, Acyclovir, Alendronate, Captopril, Enalapril, and Neomycin.

Class* IV *drugs: *Low Solubility and Low Permeability*

This class of drugs show poor and variable bioavailability because they have low solubility as well as low permeability. Several factors such asdissolution rate, permeability, and gastric emptying form the rate limiting steps for the drug absorption. These are not suitable for developing controlled release formulation. For example, Chlorothiazide, Furosemide, Tobramycin, Cefuroxime, etc

Difference between sustained release dosage form and conventional dosage form

Therapeutic efficacy and safety of drugs, administered by conventional dosage forms, can be improved by administering the drug through sustained release dosage forms. Therefore, there are differences between sustained release and conventional dosage forms in terms of drug release, therapeutic efficacy, and safety. The major differences are presented in table 1.2.

Table 1.2 Difference between sustained release dosage form and conventional dosage form[16].

Sustained release dosage forms	Conventional dosage form
The total dose of drug and frequency of dosing is reduced by SR dosage form and therefore, it improves the patient compliance and efficiency of a treatment.	Frequency of dosing is more in conventional dosage forms as a result, total amount of drug administered is large, but efficiency of the treatment is also poor.
The plasma concentration of the drug in blood is maintained at steady level and prolonged therapeutic action of the drug is achieved.	In multiple dosing of conventional dosage forms, the plasma concentration of the drug shows variations in blood; hence, prolonged action cannot be achieved.
By using matrix system SR tablet dosedumping can be avoided and toxicity due to overdose can be reduced.	In case of conventional dosage forms, probability of dose dumping is more due to fast release of drug and multiple dosing.
The overall cost of treatment is less because, the number of doses is less, but cost of production of single unit SR dosage formwould bemore due to requirement of costly processes and equipment.	In case of conventional dosage forms, the cost of production is less; but total cost of treatment would increase because of multiple dosing.
The *in-vitro* and *in-vivo* correlations are excellent as compared to the conventional dosage forms.	*In-vitro* and *in-vivo* correlation may be poor.

ADVANTAGES

- It can improve patient compliance and convenience[17].
- Reduces dosing frequency[18].
- Reduces fluctuations in circulating drug levels[19].
- It exerts uniform effect[20].
- Total amount of drug required is less[21].

- It can minimize or eliminate local side effects[22].
- It can minimize or eliminate systemic side effects.
- It can minimize accumulation of drug with chronic dosing[23].
- It obtains less potentiating or reduction in drug activity on chronic use.
- Safety margin of potent drug can be increased by excellent designing the formulation[24].

DISADVANTAGES

- It requires immediate change during the therapy or if any significant adverse effect is noted and immediate termination of therapy is required, sustained release does not permit immediate termination of therapy[25].
- These require more costly process and equipment for manufacturing of the sustained release drug delivery systems (SRDDSs).
- There is less flexibility in adjusting the dosage regimen since the dose is fixed during designing of the dosage form.
- Risk of dose dumping may be there, because the SRDDS contains a drug amounting 3-4 times more than the conventional dosage form. Sometimes this large quantity of drug may get rapidly released and causes toxicity.
- It reduces the absorption of drug that may delays the onset of action. The effect of food can influence the absorption of drug.
- Kinetics may differ markedly from one SR formulations to another.
- SRDDS cannot be formulated with the drug that can be absorbed at specific time in the GIT.
- It can increase the potential for first pass clearance.
- For oral SRDDS, effective drug release is influenced and limited by GI residence time.
- SRDDSs are designed for normal population that is based on the biological half-lives. Since, the disease state alters the drug dispositions as well as inter-patient variability in pharmacokinetic parameters is not accommodated.
- Drugs which are acted upon by enzymes in intestine undergo significant enzymatic breakdown as the drug remains in the body for longer time.
- In case of accidental failure of the product, the effective antidote may be difficult to be used.

CLASSIFICATION OF SUSTAINED RELEASE PRODUCTS

➢ Based on the mechanism of controlling the drug release, the SRs are classified as follows:

1. Chemically controlled systems

2. Biodegradable system
3. Drug polymer conjugates
4. Diffusion-controlled systems
5. Matrix diffusion
6. Polymer erosion
7. Polymer swelling
8. Geometry

Based on drug release from the SRDF is as follows:

(a) Continuous release system: this includes.
    i. Dissolution controlled release systems.
    ii. Diffusion-controlled release systems
    iii. Dissolution and diffusion-controlled release systems
    iv. Ion exchange resin drug complex
    v. Slow dissolving salts and complexes
    vi. pH dependent formulations
    vii. Osmotic pressure-controlled systems
    viii. Hydrodynamic pressure-controlled systems

(b) Delayed transit and continuous release systems
    i. Altered density systems
    ii. Mucoadhesive systems
    iii. Size based systems

(c) Delayed release systems
    i. Intestinal release systems
    ii. Colonic release systems.

FACTORS INFLUENCING

There are number of criteria that must be considered for designing and developing sustained or controlled release dosage forms. The important factors that can influence the rate of release of drug from a sustained release drug delivery system can be classified into two categories:

1) Physicochemical, and
2) Biological

Physicochemical Properties of Drug

These include stability, solubility, partition coefficient, charge, protein binding. All these properties play important role in the design and performance of a sustained or controlled release dosage forms.

1) Aqueous solubility
2) Partition coefficient ($P_{o/w}$)
3) Drug pKa and ionization at physiological pH
4) Drug stability
5) Molecular weight and diffusivity
6) Protein binding
7) Dose size.

1) ***Aqueous solubility***

For absorption, a drug must be present in solution state at the site of absorption. Thus, the drugs having low aqueous solubility and poorly absorbed after oral administration due to less transit time of the undissolved drug in the gastrointestinal tract. This is most surprising that the site of the gastrointestinal tract where the drug is least soluble is its site of absorption. For example, solubility of tetracycline is more in stomach than in intestine, and intestine is the major site of absorption for tetracycline. Such drugs are not suitable for making their SR/CR dosage form. However, such a drug becomes suitable for making SR/CR formulation, if the system can retain the drug in the stomach and gradually release it to the small intestine; or if the solubility of the drug is modified in such a way that the solubility is independent of the external environment (acidic pH) but the drug is gradually released in the intestine.

Since most of the drugs are either weak acids or weak bases; it would be difficult to prepare SR forms of drugs having very low water solubility or greater solubility. Because a drug having greater water solubility and rapid dissolution rate, it is quite difficult to retard its rate of dissolution. A drug with greater water solubility can readily dissolve in water or in gastro-intestinal fluid and its dosage form tends to release the drug from its dosage form at a faster rate. Thus, the drug is absorbed quickly resulting a sharp increase ofits concentration in the blood compared to less soluble drug. Hence, it becomes difficult to incorporate a highly water-soluble drug in the dosage form and retard the drug release, particularly when the dose is high. The pH-dependent solubility, chiefly in the physiological pH range, would be another problem for making SR formulation. Thus, water-solubility of a drug appears as an obstacle and if 10 mg of drug solubilizes perml of water presents difficulties in solubilization of dosage form. In general, highly soluble drugs are undesirable for formulation into an SR product[26].

The most observed that a drug is released from its oral sustained/controlled release dosage form following its aqueous solubility. The delivery systems which follow diffusion mechanism fails to work satisfactorily if it contains a poorly soluble drug; because the driving force for diffusion is the concentration of drug in solution is low. In such cases, bioavailability of the drug would not be consistent and complete. The absorption/ bioavailability of drug shall be dissolution rate limited. If such drugs are formulated as matrix systems, these work satisfactorily.

Therefore, the aqueous solubility of a drug must be considered when suitable polymer is being selected for making SR/CR dosage form by coating. Some antibiotics and drugs of high molecular weight have reasonably good to excellent aqueous solubility, but their dissolution rate is not good. Their slow dissolution rate can be utilized while making their SR/CR dosage form by incorporating the drug in a suitable matrix system.

Moreover, aqueous solubility may become a constraint for efficient drug-loading into various carriers such as liposomes, erythrocytes, and other microparticles. Most observed that many of the water-soluble drugs leak out from such carriers.

2) *Partition coefficient* ($P_{O/W}$)

The partition coefficient is defined as the ratio of the drug soluble in an oil phase to the drug soluble in an adjacent aqueous phase. Permeation of the drug across the biological membranes depends not only on the partition coefficient, but also on the diffusion across the rate controlling membrane when a drug is administered. When the drug is eliminated from the body; it must diffuse through a variety of biological membranes that primarily act as lipid-like barriers. A major criterion in evaluation of the ability of a drug to penetrate these lipid membranes; that are its membrane permeability. Its apparent oil and water partition coefficient can be defined as;

$$K = \frac{C_o}{C_w} \qquad .....(1.3)$$

Where,

K is the partition coefficient,

C_o = Equilibrium concentration of all forms of the drug in an organic phase at equilibrium,

C_w = Equilibrium concentration of all forms in an aqueous phase.

In general, the drugs with an extremely large value of K are very oil soluble and will partition into the membranes quite readily. The relationship between tissue permeation and partition coefficient for the drug is generally defined by the Hansch correlation, which indicates a parabolic relationship between the logarithms of its partition coefficient as shown in Figure 1. 2[27, 28].

The ability of a drug to diffuse through a membrane (diffusivity) depends on the molecular size of the drug. The relation between the diffusivity and molecular size of a drug can be expressed as;

$$\text{Log } D = -s_V \log V + k_V = -s_M \log M + k_M \qquad \text{.....(1.4)}$$

Where,

D = the diffusivity of the drug,

M = molecular weight of the drug,

V = molecular volume of the drug, and

s_V, s_M, k_V and k_M = constants in a particular medium.

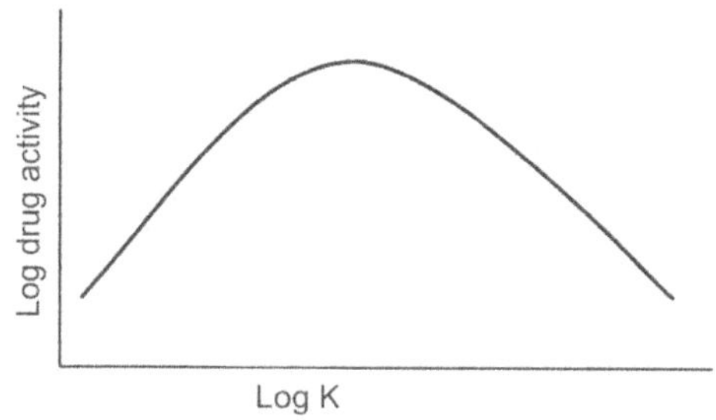

Fig.1.2 Relation between drug action and partition co-efficient.

3) ***Drug pKa and ionization at physiological pH***

Drugs which are primarily present in an ionized form are poor candidates for oral SR drug delivery system. Usually, the drugs are well absorbed in their unionized forms; whereas permeation of ionized drug is negligible because the absorption rate of the ionizeddrug is 3-4 times less than that of the unionized drug. The pKa-range for an acidic drug whose ionization is pH sensitive is within 3.0 - 7.5; similarly, the pKa-range for a basic drug whose ionization is pH sensitive is within 7.0-11.0 are ideal for optimum positive absorption. In fact, the drug should remain in unionized form at the site of absorption to an extent 0.1-5.0%[29].

4) ***Drug stability***

The stability of a drug in the environment it is placed is another important factor to be considered during development of its sustained/controlled release dosage form. For example, when a drug product is administered orally, gastric and intestinal pH and contents become its environment. A drug hydrolyses both in acid or base medium and drugs also undergo enzymatic degradation when administered orally. Drugs that are unstable in gastric pH can be formulated as slow-release dosage form and the release of drug can be delayed until the dosage form reaches the intestine. Drugs that undergo metabolism in the gut wall and show instability in the small intestine are not suitable for SR system and this could be realized by examining their bioavailability. Their bioavailability will be decreased. However, if the drug is modified chemically to form prodrug, having different physicochemical properties can be administered through different route of administration[30]. For example, controlled release nitroglycerine. On the other hand, if the drug is metabolized by the enzymes present at the site of administration or along the pathway of the drug, this can be utilized for formulating controlled/sustained release dosage form of the drug for example, prodrug.

5) ***Molecular weight and diffusivity***

Diffusion as such is a concentration gradient phenomenon. Drug diffusivity is the ability of a drug to diffuse through the membrane. Diffusivity depends on size and shape of the cavities of the membrane. The diffusion co-efficient of intermediate drug molecular weight is around 100 – 400 Daltons; through flexible polymer range is 10^{-6}–10^{-9} cm^2/second. Molecular size or weight is indirectly proportional to the diffusibility. Drugs with larger molecular size are not preferred candidate for oral SR system.

6) ***Protein binding***

Protein binding of drugs is a known phenomenon to all. Many drugs bind to plasma proteins and can influence the duration of drug action. The proteins are re-circulated in the blood and not eliminated. If the drug binds with the protein up to a reasonably high degree, the drug-protein complex can be usedas the depot and for prolonged releases of the drug. The literature review suggests this approach. The rate and extent of oral absorption can be influenced if the drug interacts and binds with mucin-like protein[31, 32]. There are other drug-protein interactions that exert effects on the performance of the drug. In 1961, R.R. Levine investigated this and demonstrated that quaternary ammonium compounds bind with mucin present in GI tract. If the bound drug acts as a depot, absorption of the drug will increase. If the drug undergoes degradation and/or washing at the further lower part of the GI tract, binding of the drug to mucin may result in a reduction of availability of free drug for absorption.

7) ***Dose size***

There is an optimum limit of bulk size for the dose that can be given. This is applicable to the formulations intended for oral administration. Usually, a single dose containing 0.5 – 1.0g of drug is considered as maximum strength for a conventional dosage form. This is equally applicable for the sustained-release dose formulations. The drugs that require large dosing size can sometimes be given in multiple amounts or formulated into liquid system. In this case, the margin of safety is a point of concern particularly when the drug possesses narrow therapeutic range which is involved in the administration of large amounts of a drug[23].

Biological Properties of Drug

The design of a controlled or sustained release drug-product should be based on complete information about the disposition of the drug. This involves complete characterization and examination of absorption, distribution, metabolism, and elimination (ADME) of the drug following multiple dosing. But most unfortunately, this is available. In general, decisions on the design are taken because of incomplete information. For design of a controlled or sustained release drug-product depends on every pharmacokinetic property and biological response-parameter. The biological factors generally influence the design of a SR/CR dosage forms are:

1) Absorption
2) Distribution
3) Metabolisms
4) Biological half-life/duration of action
5) Margin of safety/therapeutic index
6) Side effect
7) Disease state
8) Route of administration
9) Target sites
10) Acute or chronic therapy
11) Patient

1) Absorption

Almost constant concentration of drug in blood or tissue can be maintained from the orally administered SR dosage form when uniform amount of the drug is released at a consistent rate and equivalent amount of the drug is absorbed. It is desirable that the amount of drug released must be absorbed. In fact, delivery of the drug from a sustained/controlled release system depends on the rate at which the drug is released from dosage form (rate-limiting step). It is expected that the drug once released would be absorbed immediately. But it is not always true, variation in rate and extent of drug absorbed occur commonly, particularly if the dosage form is administered orally. The quality of the sustained release dosage form would be considered as desirable when it could release the drug at predetermined rate and the drug released is completely absorbed. Generally, the release of the drug from the dosage form is the rate limiting step, the rate of drug-absorption (Ka) depends on the rate of release (Kr); that is, Kr << Ka. If the transit time of dosage forms in the absorptive areas of GI tract is assumed to be about 8-12 hr, the maximum half-life for absorption should be approximately 3-4 hrs. The drugs with lower absorption rate constants are poor candidates for making SR dosage form. The possible reasons for the lower rate of absorption are

- Poor water solubility,
- Small partition co-efficient,
- Protein binding,
- Acid hydrolysis, and
- Metabolism or site specific or dose-dependent absorption.

Drugs having the high apparent volume of distribution can influence the rate of elimination of the drugs. Such drugs are poor candidates for oral SR drug delivery systems. Similarly, a drug which capable of inducing metabolism, metabolized at the site of absorption is not suitable for SR drug delivery system. A drug capable of inducing first-pass effect is also a poor candidate for SR delivery, as it could be difficult to maintain constant blood level. Drugs that are metabolized before absorption, either in the lumen or in the tissues of the intestine, indicate decreased bioavailability from the sustained release systems[23].

The fraction of the traditional dose of a drug absorbed from a single dose administered orally may be found sometimes quite low due to various reasons such as degradation of drug due to solvolysis, metabolism, binding of drugs with proteins, physical loss, etc. It has been stated earlier that the drug should be completely absorbed, but complete absorption of drug is not essential. Solution of this type of problem can be best explained by development of a controlled release ocular drug delivery system (ocusert). Pilocarpine administered through ocular route is absorbed across the cornea only up to 1% of the delivered dose. The huge loss of drug is mainly due to drainage and absorption of drug into non-target tissues. This low bioavailability problem of the drug can be solved by developing a controlled release formulation and a constant level of drug concentration in target tissues can be maintained for extended period of time.

Significant loss of drug after oral administration occurs mainly due to (1) hydrolytic degradation of the drug in the contents of GI tract, (2) metabolism by intestinal flora, and (3) metabolism during its transit across the GI wall. For all routes of administration, metabolism at the site of administration like hydrolytic degradation is a major problem. However, in all the routes, the quantities of metabolizing enzymes are not same; for example, more in the GI tract and few in precorneal portion of the eye. Both hydrolytic and metabolic degradations are first order reactions with respect to concentration. It is to know that drug only in dissolved state is susceptible to hydrolytic degradation; thus, solid drug or drug present in solid dosage forms is not hydrolytically degraded.

When the drug is absorbed erratically, such as the GI tract, it becomes difficult to design a controlled release product. In case of oral route, different segments of the GI tract have different absorptive properties. Thus, these segments can influence the rate and extent of absorption of some drugs from GI tract. For example, the rate and extent of absorption of drugs such as dicumarol, and aminoglycosides such as gentamicin, kanamycins are different in different segments of GI tract. Dicumarol, quaternary ammonium compounds such as hexamethonium and decamethonium is an oral anti-coagulant drug. Similarly, there are some drugs which are absorbed in GI tract either by specialized transport mechanism or at special sites of the GI tract. These drugs are not suitable candidate for developing sustained or controlled release dosage form. For example, riboflavin is absorbed by an active transport process and preferentially absorbed at the upper part of the GI tract. However, riboflavin has been formulated in various sustained release multivitamin formulations.

Iron is another drug which is not uniformly absorbed throughout the length of the GI tract. At the upper part of the duodenum, relatively greater absorption of iron takes place, while the lower end of the duodenum has the lower absorptive capacity.

2) Distribution

The distribution of drug molecules into the tissues and cells is one of the primary factors particularly in drug elimination kinetics. The concentration of drug circulating within the system is reduced by this process; simultaneously, the elimination process can also become rate limiting in the attainment of equilibrium drug-concentration with blood and extravascular tissue. The drug-distribution within the body depends on the extent of binding of the drug to the tissues and plasma proteins. The drug molecules bound with proteins are considered as inactive and cannot permeate biological membranes, but a high degree of protein binding can prolong the therapeutic action. In fact, the apparent volume of distribution is one of the important parameters of the drug that can explain the magnitude of distribution as well as the extent of protein binding within the body. The apparent volume of distribution is a proportionality constant of the plasma concentration of the drug to the total drug amount within the body. The driving force behind the rate processes is concentration of the drug, not the amount and it is the quantity which is of interest. Therefore, to design a sustain release formulation, the information about the disposition of drug is very necessary[32]. Interpretation of apparent volume of distribution is difficult not only in one-compartment kinetic system but in multi-compartment kinetics it is more difficult to interpret. Since, definite studies cannot be conducted, it is considered as the proportionality constant or *fudge factor* rather than a specific physiological parameter. Thus, depending on the time course of drug disposition, apparent volume of distribution can accept different values. However, the numerical values of apparent volume of distribution should be carefully interpreted.

The complete information or as much information about drug disposition as possible should be collected before designing a controlled/sustained release formulation; because in most cases, decisions are taken based on the information about apparent volume of distribution. The apparent volume of distribution can influence the concentration and the amount of drug either in circulating blood or in target tissues. It can influence the elimination kinetics of a drug. But the extent of influence cannot be predicted because it is not possible to interpret the apparent volume of distribution completely.

At steady state the total apparent volume of distribution for a drug can be calculated by using the following equations;

$$V_d^{ss} = [(k_{12} + k_{21})/k_{21}]\ Vp \quad .....(1.5)$$

$$V_d^{extrap} = [(\alpha - \beta)/k_{21} - \beta)]\ Vp \quad .....(1.6)$$

$$V_d^{area} = V_d^{ss} + [k_{el} - \beta)/k_{21}]\ Vp \quad .....(1.7)$$

Where,

V_d^{ss} = apparent volume of distribution at steady state,

V_d^{extrap} = apparent volume of distribution, obtained from extrapolation method,

V_d^{area} = apparent volume of distribution, obtained by area method.

V_p = volume of central compartment,

α = fast disposition constant,

β = slow disposition constant,

k_{el} = elimination rate constant (from central compartment),

k_{12} = first order drug distribution constant from central to peripheral compartment,

k_{21} = first order drug distribution constant from peripheral to central compartment.

This has been found that among V_d^{ss}, V_d^{extrap}, and V_d^{area}, the value of V_d^{ss} gives almost correct estimate.

To avoid ambiguity in apparent volume of distribution, it would be better to use T/P ratio as explained below for calculation of the amount of drug in central (P) and peripheral compartments (T) at steady state. If the value of P is known, the value of T can be calculated as indicated below (eqn.1.7);

$$\frac{T}{P} = \frac{k_{12}}{(k_{21} - \beta)} \quad .....(1.8)$$

It is to be noted that the physical state of the drug (such as the extent of binding) cannot be said from the T/P ratio. The distribution characteristics of a drug can be described by the volume of distribution at steady state and the

T/P ratio. The basic difference between these two parameters: the V_d^{ss} indicates the extent of drug distribution in the body, while T/P ratio indicates the relative distribution of drug between compartments. Prediction of the value of $V_d^{ss}$from T/P ratio and vice versa is not possible. Table 1.3 below shows the values of T/P and V_d^{ss}. This indicates that the two parameters behave independently.

Table 1.3 The values of T/P and V_d^{ss} for some drugs.

Drug	T/P	V_d^{ss} litres	Drug	T/P	V_d^{ss} litres
Amoxicillin	1.04	22	Furosemide	0.96	5
Diazepam	2.85	130	Pentobarbital	1.30	63
Procainamide	14.35	62	Trimethoprim	1.24	12
Tolbutamide	0.27	24	Theophylline	0.97	40
Digoxin	4.31	500	Meperidine	2.04	289

The total body clearance at steady state can be calculated as follows (eqn.1.8):

$$\text{Total body clearance at steady state} = V_d^{ss}\left(0.693/t_{1/2,\beta}\right) \quad .....(1.9)$$

Recently, it is recognized that disposition of many drugs follows multi-compartment kinetics; but dose calculation is based primarily on one-compartment kinetics. For a given therapeutic concentration of drug, the dose would be similar for drugs with similar volume of distribution. This assumption is found true only when the relative distribution of the two drugs between compartments is similar. The error which may be reduced by incorporating T/P ratio into sustaining dose considerations for drugs exhibiting multicompartment kinetics.

Finally, this can be said that the parameters, T/P ratio and volume of distribution at steady state, provides the insight aspect of drug disposition.

3) Metabolisms

Metabolism of the drug includes either of the two processes – (1) transformation of active form of drug to its inactive form, (2) conversion of an inactive drug to an active metabolite.

Metabolism of the drug takes place in various tissues containing enzymes. Drugs that are significantly metabolized before absorption are either metabolized in the lumen or inthe tissue of the intestine. As a result, the bioavailability of such drugs is reduced from slower-releasing dosage forms. Most of theenzyme-systems present in the intestinal wall are saturable. If the drug is released at a slower rate at these regions, lesser amount of total drug is exposed to the enzymatic process during a specific time-period; as a result, relatively more complete conversion of the drug to its metabolites occurs. A better and practical solution to such problem is formulating prodrugs of these enzyme-susceptible compounds. There are some drugs that can either induce or inhibit the enzyme synthesis. These types of drugs are the poor candidates for making SR delivery system because it is difficult to maintain their uniform blood levels. Drugs having variation in bioavailability due to the first-pass effect or intestinal metabolism are not suitable for making SR drug delivery system[30]. When the biological activity of a drug is partly or completely due to a metabolite, the design of SR/CR dosage form becomes more difficult; for example, isosorbide 2, and 5-dinitrate. There are two areas of metabolism that restrict the design of SR/CR dosage form – (1) if a drug induces or inhibits the synthesis of enzymes during its use for a prolonged period, the drug is not suitable for designing of SR/CR dosage form because it becomes difficult to maintain a uniform plasma concentration of the drug, (2) if due to intestinal metabolism or -first-pass effect, the plasma concentration of a drug becomes widely fluctuating, the design of a SR/CR dosage form becomes difficult. Depending on the size (amount) the fraction of the dose would be lost. As a result, the bioavailability of the drug would be reduced significantly, provided the drug is released from its dosage form slowly. For example, hydralazine is metabolized at the intestinal wall and/or the liver during absorption. However, hydralazine is well absorbed. On the other hand, bromocriptine is incompletely absorbed. Its ultimate bioavailability is only 6% due to first pass metabolism at the liver. Similarly, only about 25% of the oral dose of levodopa is absorbed, the loss of drug is mainlydue to first-pass metabolism in the liver and metabolism by gut microbial flora. In fact, studies showed that sustained release dosage form of levodopa is not better than its standard dosage form. Another study showed that about 41% of the oral dose of propoxyphene can reach the systemic circulation due to first-pass effect, if the drug is completely released, absorbed, and not metabolized during its transportation through intestinal wall. The study also showed that the bioavailability of the drug depends on the dose administered. Salicylamide also demonstrated its dose-dependent bioavailability. The drug is metabolized when it passes through the intestinal wall. Maximum of about 60% of the orally administered dose can be observed in blood as glucuronide form, provided the dose is small. The most interesting observation lies with nitroglycerin. Nitroglycerin has been commonlyadministered as sublingual tablet. The purpose of the study was to assess the effectiveness of the oral route of administration as opposed to the sublingual route. The usually the logic in support of the sublingual route was that nitroglycerin is extensively metabolized during its first pass through the liver. In fact, oral doses of 2 mg of nitroglycerin given 4 times a day failed to produce any observable effect in angina pectoris. Other indicated that nitroglycerin was absorbed sufficiently from GI tract to bring about peripheral vasodilatation.

Based on the above discussion, it can not be accepted that it is possible to formulate the controlled release systems for drugs which are extensively metabolized if the rate of metabolism is not too much high nor does the metabolism vary with the oral and other routes. It is logical to accept that a controlled release product can be preparedtill the metabolism remains predictable.

4) Biological half-life/duration of action

The objective of developing an oral sustained-release product is to maintain a constant therapeutic blood levels over an extended period. The duration of action of a drug significantly influences the design of oral SR delivery system. It depends on the biological half-life. The factors influencing the biological half-life of a drug include its

- Elimination,
- Metabolism, and
- Distribution patterns.

To minimize fluctuations in the blood levels, drugs having short half-lives are to be administered frequently. With such drugs, it is desirable to prepare SR dosage forms. For a given steady state plasma-drug concentration, it is necessary that the zero-order rate of release of a drug from its dosage form should be directly proportional to its rate of elimination. Thus, faster rate of release is required for drug having very short half-life, for a moderate duration of time, while the dosage form requires large dosage. Generally, drugs with half-lives less than 2 hr are not good candidates for making sustained-release preparations. Again, drugs having long half-lives, more than 8 hr, are also not suitable for making sustained release dosage forms, because theireffect is already sustained[30].

It should be noted that the duration of action of many drugs, such as monoamine oxidase inhibitors[33] and corticosteroids[34], is longer than that suggested by their biological half-lives. However, corticosteroid for its anti-inflammatory effects is being administered on alternate day which is not related to its biological half-life. Thus, from the standpoint of therapy, it would be justified to say that Sustained release formulation of corticosteroids is not necessary. In fact, sustained release formulation of prednisolone sodium phosphate and methylprednisolone has been found equally effective as their conventional tablets[35]. However, the numerical value of biological half-life which makes a drug a good candidate for controlled release has not been established. In 1961, K.R. Heimlich and his colleagues quoted a value of about 4 hr so that for a drug with such a half-life, the ratio of sustaining dose to immediate release dose becomes approximately 2 if the duration of action of sustained release drug is 12 hr. To extend the release of the drug, having biological half-life of about 4 hr, up to 12 hr, about 1 g of the drug should be the controlled release dose with immediate release dose is of 325 mg.

Sustained release formulations of procainamide are available in the market and have been shown to be capable of either maintaining therapeutic plasma level or minimizing the fluctuations in plasma level over a period of 8-hr. On considering the above discussion, this can be said that a duration of release is extended to 6, 8, or 12 hr for a drug with half-lives between 4 and 6 hr and whose minimum effective dose ranges from 125 mg to 325 mg will enforce little problem as dose size is concerned.

It should be noted that the duration of action of many drugs, such as monoamine oxidase inhibitors and corticosteroids, is longer than that suggested by their biological half-lives. The anti-inflammatory effects of corticosteroids have been considered as the basis for alternate-day dosing schedule and this is not related to the biological half-life. The advantage of this dosage regimen is that it can minimize the adrenal suppression side effects sometimes associated with chronic corticosteroid therapy. Thus, making of sustained release corticosteroid preparation is not justified. In fact, sustained release formulations of prednisolone sodium phosphate and methyl prednisolone have been found to be equally effective as traditional tablets, no benefit is found over the latter.

Similarly, there is hardly any advantage of making sustained release formulations of drugs having long biological half-lives. It has been stated that if there are no appreciable differences in effectiveness when a drug is given as a single large dose per day or in several smaller doses throughout the day, the therapeutic need for a prolonged action dosage form would be doubtful; for example, phenylbutazone is such a drug. The table 4 shows the biological half-lives of various drugs.

Table 1.4 Half-lives of some common drugs.

Drug	Half-life	Drug	Half-life
Ampicillin	1.67 hr	Methylprednisolone	3.3 hr
Cephalexin	0.9 hr	Prednisolone	1.0 hr
Cloxacillin	1.5 hr	Diazepam	20 hr
Furosemide	0.491 hr	Phenytoin	22 hr
Levodopa	0.75 hr	Warfarin	52 hr
Penicillin G	0.75 hr	Meprobamate	11.3 hr
Propylthiouracil	1.05 hr	Guanethidine	9 – 10 days

5) Margin of safety/therapeutic index

Margin of safety of a drug can be described by considering therapeutic index, which is the ratio of median toxic dose and median effective dose.

$$\text{Therapeutic index} = \frac{\text{Median Lethal/Toxic Dose}}{\text{Median Effective Dose}} = \frac{LD_{50}}{ED_{50}}$$

A drug is considered to be relatively safe with therapeutic index more than 10. However; the value of this ratio gives no information about

a) The nature of the distribution of toxicity and effectiveness,

b) The size of the doses producing therapeutic and toxic effects, and

c) Plasma or serum drug concentrations corresponding to toxic and therapeutic levels.

It can only be used as a rough estimate of the relative safety of a drug. The table 5 shows wide variation in the therapeutic index of various drugs. If the ratio is more, the drug is safer. Since the therapeutic index is relative not absolute, the toxic and therapeutic effect must be clearly defined.

Table 1.5 Therapeutic indices of some common drugs.

Drug	Therapeutic Index	Drug	Therapeutic Index
Aprobarbital	5.3	Chlorpheniramine	1400
Digitoxin	1.5 – 2.0	Penicillin	>100
Diphenhydramine	2300	Phenobarbital	2.6
Paracetamol	~10	Tripelennamine	19000

Based on therapeutic index and therapeutically effective and safe range of plasma concentration, the decision on margin of safety of a drug should be determined. It indicates the range of plasma concentration in which the drug is safe and therapeutically effective. The drugs with lesser therapeutic indices, the release pattern becomes more precise to maintain the plasma concentration within the narrow therapeutic and safety range. The unfavorable therapeutic index of a drug can be overcome by suitable use of the SR mechanisms[36].

Based on the properties, drugs can be categorized into two classes. The properties of drugs to be considered before designing a sustained release formulation are tabulated below:

Drugs suitable	Drugs not suitable
Physicochemical properties 1. Compounds with low molecular weight 2. Good aqueous solubility, pH independent (Penotoxyphylline) 3. With non-aqueous solubility (for Parenteral; Steroids) 4. Unionized (at least 0.1-5%) in GI tract 5. Very weak bases pKa< 5.0 (Theophylline pKa=0.7, Diazepam pKa = 3.7)	1. Large molecular size/weight (proteins and peptides for oral) 2. Very low aqueous solubility 0.1 mg/ml) (Nifedipine, Griseofulvin) 3. Largely in ionized form in the G.I. tract 4. Strong bases (pKa> 11.0) such as Guanethidine

Table *contd...*

6. Very weak acids pKa> 8.0 (Pentobarbital pKa =8.1) Unionized at all pH, absorb well 7. Moderately weak acids pKa 2.5-7.5 Aspirin (3.5), Ibuprofen (4.4). 8. Moderately weak bases (pKa 5.0-11.0), Codeine (8.2) Ionization depends on pH	5. Strong acids (pKa< 2.5) such as Cromolyn sodium
Pharmacokinetics 1. Short $t_{½}$ (2 – 5hr) such as Theophylline (4 hr), Sodium diclofenac (2 hr), Nifedipine (2.5 hr), Diltiazem (3.5 hr), Glipizide (3.4hr) 2. Well absorbed from all regions of GI tract	1. Drugs that exhibit slow absorption 2. Carrier mediated transport such as several vitamins 3. Site specific absorption such as vit B_{12} 4. Degradation in the GI tract such as Nitroglycerin, Penicillin G, Erythromycin 5. First pass hepatic metabolism such as Nitroglycerin, Propranolol 6. Induces or inhibits metabolism such as Rifampicin, Barbitu-rates, PAS
Pharmacodynamic 1. Therapeutic range of blood conc. wide enough 2. Response ∞ blood concentration	1. Having large dose 2. Drugs whose metabolites are also active

6) Side effect

The side effects of some drugs are mostly observed with the fluctuations in the plasma concentrations. The occurrences of side effects can be reduced by controlling the plasma concentration of drug within therapeutic range at any given time. The SR dosage form is the most widely used when the drug has the local side effects (at the GI tract) rather than a systemic side effect. The properties of a drug which induce local or systemic side effect can be modified by formulating them in a suitable oral SR dosage form that uses a specific controlled release mechanism[37]. It has been demonstrated that the toxic effects of valproic acid can be altered by administering the drug as a constant infusion than as a bolus. It is reported that brocadepatemtab, a controlled release product of levodopa, lowered the frequency of drug induced dyskinesis and the patients in the study could tolerate the larger daily dose of the drug. On the other hand, a sustained release prednisolone tablet produced adrenocortical suppression to similar extent produced by same dose in conventional tablets.

An attempt was made to reduce the frequency of drowsiness after taking chlorpheniramine maleate in form of porous matrix tablets. This was found unsuccessful. The success or failure of these products the side effect is related to the type and success of preparing a controlled release product.

The technique of making controlled release products has been widely used to reduce the frequency of gastro-intestinal side effects than that of systemic side effects. Drugs prone to cause gastric irritation are aspirin, ferrous sulphate, potassium chloride, nitrofurantoin, etc. It is assumed that by slowing the rate of release of such drugs, the chance of GI irritation could be reduced; because at any time, smaller amounts of the drug are being exposed to the gastro-intestinal mucosa. Similar observations were found in case of sustained release products of ferrous sulphate and aminophylline. However, after ingestion of time-release tablets of aspirin (Bayer's product) gastric bleeding was reported. Thus, preparation of controlled release products cannot be considered as a fool proof technique for reducing GI side effects.

Gastric irritation is one of the common side effects of potassium therapy. To avoid this problem, enteric coated tablets are usually used; but this creates another problem, called intestinal erosion and stenosis due to increase of potassium ions locally. Wax-matrix controlled release formulation of potassium chloride can resolve this problem satisfactorily. Such formulation releases potassium over 4 – 6 hr.

Similarly, by using sustained release sodium chloride tablet the occurrence of side effects such as nausea and vomiting has been reduced.

Thus, the properties of drugs can cause local and systemic side effects which can sometimes be avoided by using a suitable controlled release system. The specific controlled release mechanism used depends on the drug property causing the side effects.

7) Disease state

Disease state and circadian rhythm are not the properties of a drug. They become important when drug considered for formulating SR dosage form. For example, aspirin is a drug of choice for rheumatoid arthritis but, it is not suitable for SR dosage form. Even then, aspirin SR dosage form can be advantageous to maintain its therapeutic concentrations, particularly throughout the night, thus alleviating morning stiffness. Similarly, asthma attacks usually occur before bedtime, due to a low cortisol level. The highest cortisol level occurs between 12 midnight and 4 a.m. These variations involve the design an oral SR delivery in accordance to circadian rhythm.

During the treatment, pathological changes play an important role in designing a suitable drug delivery system. For example, while designing an ocular controlled-release product, for an external inflammation, the time course of changes in protein content in ocular fluids and in the integrity of the ocular barriers should be considered. Sometimes, the manifestations of the disease state may be used as an advantage. For example, higher tyrosinase level in melanoma cells can be targeted for preferential bioconversion of 2,4-dihydroxyphenylalanine in these cells[38].

Alkaloids of Belladonna and synthetic anticholinergics are among the drugs used in the treatment of peptic ulcer. Since the use of this type of drugs in this disease state is controversial, these drugs are prescribed as adjuncts to therapy because they can decrease gastric secretion of acid and pepsin induced by vagal stimulation. Belladonna alkaloids are relatively short-acting; its sustained release dosage form can help to control the secretion of gastric acid and pepsin. A study assessed the duration of action of belladonna alkaloids released from its spansules and reported that the therapeutic concentration of the alkaloids could be extended up to 8 to 12 hr. Unfortunately, gastric acid and pepsin secretion was not measured. Although similar extension of therapeutic concentration was not found in all sustained release preparations, the reason for such difference might be the design of the products concerned.

Another disease state is angina pectoris which would be benefited by sustained release medications. Although the efficacy of orally administrable, traditional dosage form of nitroglycerin is controversial, its sustained release dosage forms are available. In fact, therapeutic benefit of sustained release nitroglycerin administered by oral route is also controversial. In another study, the benefits of using sustained release formulation of pentaerythritol tetranitrate in angina pectoris was found to be controversial. No satisfactory justification could be made by anyone. In 1959, A. Wilson stated that prophylaxis carries with it the danger of concealing the warning symptoms of pain, eventually resulting to over-exertion with potentially harmful results.

8) Route of administration

The therapeutic efficacy of a drug greatly depends on the route of administration of the drug. In designing a controlled/sustained release dosage form, the oral and parenteral routes have been acknowledged the most attention. However, recently the transdermal route is gaining attention. Based on technological achievement of a suitable sustained or controlled release dosage form, the area of the body where the drug would be administered can hinder. Sometimes, the drug delivery, through certain routes of administration, can exert a negative influence on drug efficacy, particularly in case of chronic administration. Hence, other routes of administration should also be considered. The effects of sustained or controlled release systems may also be influenced by physiological conditions depending on the route of administration, such as first-pass, GI motility, blood supply, and appropriation of small foreign particles by the liver and spleen.

Advancement in biotechnology has increased the number of peptides and proteins, and has made specific demands on the route of delivery and on the design of the delivery systems. Thus, for certain drugs, the routes of administration are very important. Moreover, route of administration is selected because of treatment requirement. Various route of administration through which drugs can be administered are buccal, sublingual, oral, ocular, nasal, pulmonary, intrauterine, skin, vaginal, rectal, etc.

9) Target sites

To reduce the unwanted side effects, it is necessary to maximize the fraction of applied dose reaching the target organ or tissue. By local administration or by using suitable carrier systems, this can be partially achieved. However, absorptive surfaces of most of the routes are impermeable to macromolecules or other targeted delivery systems. Thus, it requires either intravascular or intra-arterial administration of drug. There are two approaches to achieve drug targeting – (1) the first approach is the chemical modification of the parent compound to a derivative which is activated only when it reaches the target site. (2) This approach uses the carriers such as liposomes, microspheres, nanoparticles, antibodies, cellular carriers (erythrocytes and lymphocytes), and macromolecules to direct the drug to its site of action.

There are various methods to modify the chemical structure of drug molecules. The most common method is the making the prodrug and the most sophisticated is the chemical delivery system approach.

A prodrug is an inactive chemical derivative of a particular drug substance and becomes converted in vivo into the active drug molecule when exposed to a required environment. But it cannot provide site specific delivery, of course with few exceptions. On the other hand, in a chemical delivery system transformation of the active drug takes place by synthetic means into an inactive derivative. When this derivative is placed in the body, will undergo several predictable enzymatic transformations primarily at the site of action. For local delivery of drug in eye, brain and testes, this approach has proven successful.

Most of the macromolecules are impermeable to the GI tract and most of the drug-carrier complexes are not stable in the hostile environment of the GI tract. Thus, administration of large drug-carrier complex is restricted to intramuscular, intravenous, or intraarterial injection, or to direct injection into the target tissues such as a tumor. If macromolecular and particulate carrier is administered intravascularly sequestration by mononuclear phagocytes of the reticuloendothelial system takes place rapidly. Presently this is the major problem in drug targeting. Since, these drug-carrier complexes are rapidly eliminated from the body, very small fraction of the injected carrier ultimately reaches the target.

A second method is to impart specificity to the drug carrier by joining specific ligands to its external surface. These include erythrocyte membrane glycoproteins, heat aggregated immunoglobulins, monoclonal antibodies, and native immunoglobulins. None of these techniques has been found to be successful because of the difficulties in preserving the *in vivo* recognition ability and avoiding activation of any immunological response.

Vascular system itself is another problem in targeting drug carriers. To recognize the target, a drug-carrier must first extravasate. The vascular endothelium of most tissues and organs is essentially impermeable to molecular assemblages such as liposomes (0.025 – 5.0 μm) and nanoparticles (< 1μm). The tissues and organs are continuous with an effective pore diameter of 2 nm. Under certain conditions, impermeability of the capillary endothelial lining may be a useful property: (1) confinement of drug within a physiological compartment, (2) use of particles whose direction or release characteristics are under external control, and (3) delivery of drug to the lung, liver, and spleen.

Two forms of external control have been discovered. Liposomes can be made from lipids with release characteristics. These are a function of a temperature gradient due to either local inflammation or localized heating through collimated radiation. Drug is released from circulating liposomes as they pass through the target region.

Microspheres have also been used for passive targeting to organs such as the liver, spleen, lung and kidney. Intravenous injection of particles between 7 to 12 μm leads to mechanical filtration by the lungs, whereas particles between 2 to 12 μm leads to blockage in the first capillary bed encountered. Such blockage can lead to first order targeting of, for example, the liver and kidney, and second-order targeting to tumor-bearing organs.

10) Acute or chronic therapy

The duration of drug therapy depends on whether complete cure or control of disease state is desired. Hence, during designing a sustained or controlled release system, the length of drug therapy becomes an important factor. For example, designing of a contraceptive implant which can work for one year and designing of an analgesic formulation which works for a day would be different. In general, long-term toxicity of rate-controlled drug delivery system is different from that of conventional dosage form.

11) Patient

The design and development of a controlled or sustained release dosage form depends on whether the patient is ambulatory or bedridden, young, or old, obese or gaunt, etc. For example, an implant or intramuscular injection can perform differently when administered to a bedridden patient and administered to an ambulatory patient. However, such variation includes individual patient variation. Variation in performance due to individual patient variation cannot be controlled by a research scientist. Rest of the variations are controllable and should be considered during design. For example, a single unit-controlled release oral product is prone to intra- and inter-patient variation due to variation in GI motility[39].

APPROACHES FOR SR/CR FORMULATION

Methods for Preparation of Controlled Release tablets.[40]

1) ***Wet Granulation Technique***
   a) Milling and gravitational mixing of drug, polymer, and excipients
   b) Preparation of binder solution
   c) Wet massing by addition of binder solution or granulating solvent
   d) Screening of wet mass
   e) Drying of the wet granules
   f) Screening of dry granules
   g) Blending with lubricant and disintegrant to produce "running powder"
   h) Compression of tablet
2) ***Dry Granulation Technique***
   a) Milling and gravitational mixing of drug, polymer and excipients
   b) Compression into slugs or roll compaction,
   c) Milling and screening of slugs and compacted powder
   d) Mixing with lubricant and disintegrant
   e) Compression of tablet
3) ***Sintering Technique***
   a) Sintering is defined as the bonding of adjacent particle surfaces in a mass of powder, or in a compact, by the application of heat.
   b) Conventional sintering involves the heating of a compact at a temperature below the melting point of the solid constituents in a controlled environment under atmospheric pressure.
   c) The changes in the hardness and disintegration time of tablets stored at elevated temperatures were described because of sintering.
   d) The sintering process has been used for the fabrication of sustained release matrix tablets for the stabilization of drug release.

MECHANISM OF DRUG RELEASE FROM SR/CR FORMULATION

The most of the oral controlled release systems depend on dissolution, diffusion, or a combination of both mechanisms to achieve a slow release of drug in the gastrointestinal tract. To assess drug release kinetics, some of the *in vitro* systems can be considered and various systems have been designed and used also[41, 42]. On the basis of mechanism followed the release of drug from a sustained or controlled release product can be classified into following types.

1. Dissolution-controlled products
2. Diffusion-controlled products
3. Diffusion and dissolution-controlled system
4. Ion exchange resins
5. pH-independent product
6. Osmotically controlled release
7. Altered density formulations

1. Dissolution-controlled products

In this type of systems, dissolution is controlled as rate limiting step and such systems are very simple to prepare. A sparingly soluble drug is having slow dissolution characteristics; hence would be inherently beneficial for preparing sustained release dosage form; for example, digoxin, griseofulvin, salicylamide, ferrous sulphate, etc. On the other hand, the drugs which are highly soluble in water can be transformed into suitable salts or derivatives for decreasing their solubility. Unfortunately, these drugs fail to meet the criterion of constant bioavailability rate because their surface area decreases with time.

The rate of dissolution of the drug is controlled by slowly soluble polymers which surrounds the drug or remains as a thin coat in a micro encapsulation. If the coating polymer is dissolved, the drug becomes available for dissolution. Hence, by varying the thicknesses of the coat and/or by changing the composition of the polymer system, the rate of drug release can be modified.

If the process of dissolution is controlled by the diffusion layer and if the rate of diffusion from the solid surface through an unstirred liquid layer to the bulk solution is rate limiting, the flux J, the rate of flow of material (dm/dt) through a unit area (A) can be expressed as:

$$J = \frac{1}{A}\frac{dm}{dt} = -D\frac{dc}{dx} \qquad (.....1.10)$$

Where,

D is the diffusion coefficient, and

$\frac{dc}{dx}$ is the concentration gradient from the solid surface to the bulk solution.

If the thickness of the diffusion layer is assumed to be h and the concentration gradient is linear; then,

$$\frac{dc}{dx} = \frac{C_b - C_s}{h} \qquad (.....1.11)$$

Where,

C_s is the concentration of the drug at the solid surface and

C_b is the concentration of the drug in the bulk solution

By combining the equation 1 and 2, the flow rate of the material can be expressed as;

$$\frac{dm}{dt} = -(DA/h)(C_b - C_s)$$

$$= kA(C_s - C_b) \qquad .....(1.12)$$

Where,

k is the intrinsic dissolution rate constant.

According to the equation 3, the rate of dissolution remains constant when, the surface area, diffusion coefficient, thickness of the diffusion layer, and concentration difference are kept constant. As dissolution process continues, all of the parameters particularly the surface area changes.

The rate of dissolution of the drug from a dosage form of various geometrical shapes can be expressed as:

$$Mt/M\infty = 1 - [1 - K_o t/c_o a]^n \qquad .....(1.13)$$

Where,

Mt is the amount of drug released in time t,

M∞ is the amount of drug released at infinite time a is the half-thickness of a slab or the radius of a sphere or of a cylinder, and n is equal to 3 for a sphere, 2 for a cylinder, and 1 for a slab.

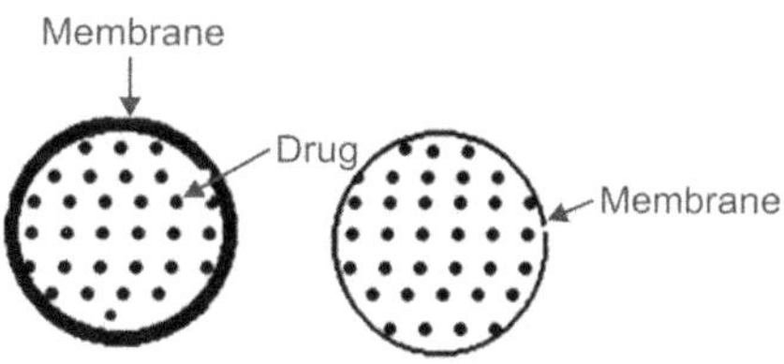

Fig.1.3 Schematic diagram of dissolution controlled drug release. (effect of membrane thickness).

Most of the dissolution control products are classified into two categories:

a) Encapsulation Dissolution controls.

b) Matrix Dissolution control.

In some of the preparations a fraction of the total dose, for immediate release, is provided to provide a pulse dose soon after administration.

a) *Encapsulation Dissolution control*

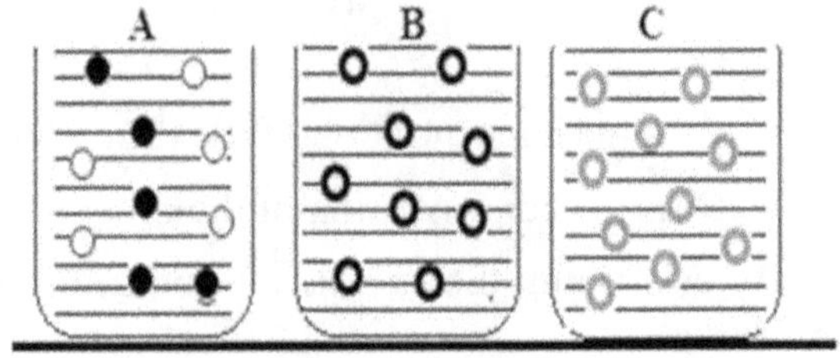

Fig. 1.4 Schematic representation of microencapsulation.
A. Establishing three-phase system,
B. Deposition of coating material
C. Solidification of coating material

In this method, individual particle or granule of drug is coated with a slow dissolving material. The coated particles can be compressed into tablets or filled in the capsules. The rate of dissolution of the drug (and thereby bioavailability for absorption) is controlled by micro encapsulating polymer or polymer system. Once the coating dissolves in the surrounding fluid such as gastric fluid, the drug becomes available for dissolution. By changing the thicknesses of the coat and composition of the polymer system used, the rate of drug release can be varied. These products should not be chewed because the coating may be damaged. One of the advantages of encapsulated or pelleted products is that the onset of absorption is less sensitive to or independent of the stomach emptying. The entrance of the pellets into the small intestine (where the majority of drug are absorbed) is usually more uniform than with non-disintegrating sustained-release tablet formulations. The time required for dissolution of the coat depends on its thickness and aqueous solubility. Spansule sustained release product was first introduced into the market in early 1950s and various studies have been conducted to assess its *in-vivo* performance[44-47] and clinical effectiveness[48]. This type of products can be prepared either by coating (Fig 1.3) or by microencapsulation method (Fig 1. 4).

- **Seeds or Granule coated products**

Various drugs have been formulated as sustained release coated granules and compressed into tablets. For example, combination of anti-spasmodic-sedative drugs, anti-cholinesterase and aspirin. In various ways drug-coated beads or granules are prepared. Commonly nonpareil seeds are coated with drug followed by a coat of slowly dissolving material such as carbohydrate sugars and cellulose, polyethylene glycol, polymeric material, and wax.

Usually one-quarter to one-third of the seeds is used to prepare non-sustained form for immediate drug release. Rest of three quarters or two-third seeds are divided into groups and polymeric coating of different thicknesses are applied. Depending on the duration of time these coats slowly dissolve and release the drug to maintain a steady level. Rosen et al [49,50]have illustrated this method with relevant example and described the release pattern of the drugs.

They have demonstrated how the release rate of the coated drug varies with change of coating material and thickness of the coat.[51, 52]

Capsules can be filled with coated granules to administer to the patients. *In vivo* photographs [53, 54] shows how the coated particles disintegrate in GIT and remain dispersed even after 10 – 12 hr. In case of compressed tablets there are some additional factors such as excipients used, effect of compression, extent of fracture of the coated particles during compression, etc. which influence the sustained action of the drug. Green[55] reported that fractured microcapsule of aspirin releases the drug immediately.

- **Microencapsulation**

Like coated particles, the rate of release the drug from microcapsules depends on the thickness of the coating and the type of polymer used. Microencapsulation process can be used to encapsulate solids, liquids, and gases. However, other forms of microencapsulation can be used for pulsed dosing or for supplying the drug through diffusion process. The microencapsulation processes are classified as shown in table 1.6.

Table 1.6 Classification of microencapsulation processes.

Process of microencapsulation	Type of material used for coating
Coacervation/phase separation	Water-soluble polymer
Interfacial polymerization	Water-insoluble and water-soluble monomers
Electrostatic method	Oppositely charged aerosols
Precipitation	Polymers soluble in water or other solvents
Hot melt	Low molecular weight lipids
Salting out	Water soluble polymers
Solvent evaporation	Polymers soluble in solvents

Out of all the microencapsulation processes, coacervation seems to be the oldest one. In *coacervation* process interaction between two oppositely charged polyelectrolytes in water is utilized to form a polymer-rich coating solution called a coacervate[56]. The solid or liquid encapsulated by the coacervate is called embryo capsule. After cooling of the system, the coating solution forms a polymer network and transform into gel. Then the gelled coacervate is crosslinked and the capsule wall is formed. By this method, both water soluble and insoluble drugs can be microencapsulated using gelatin-gum arabic coacervate system. However, for such coating the drug should be coated with carnauba wax[57] or ethyl cellulose or cellulose acetate phthalate. The Fig 1.5 shows such microencapsulation process.

In case of *interfacial polymerization method*, the drug is dissolved in an organic solvent which is immiscible with water and suitable monomers are dissolved in water. The organic phase is then dispersed in aqueous phase. The monomers react at the liquid-liquid interface and form a capsule wall[58, 59]. For complete polymerization a suitable cross-linking agent should be present in the continuous phase. Drugs having low melting point and soluble organic liquids can be encapsulated by this process.

The *electrostatic method* is found suitable when the drug to be encapsulated and the coating material are oppositely charged[60]. Both drug and coating material are atomized and sprayed in form of aerosol. Microcapsules formed are cooled and appropriately collected.

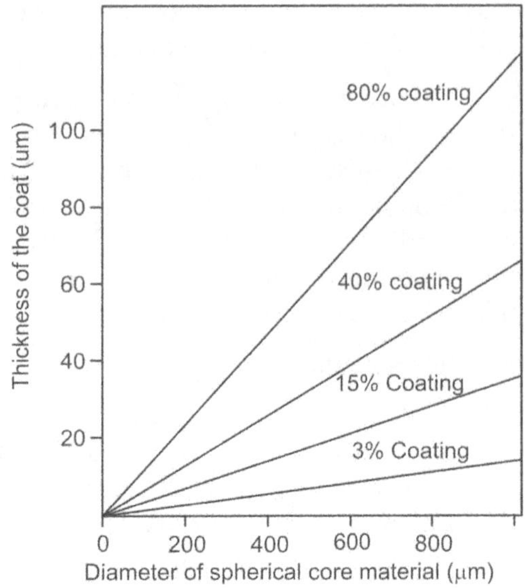

Fig. 1.5 Coating thickness vs. particle size.

There are many ways which can be brought together under *precipitation method.* In this method the polymer is either precipitated or congealed around the drug particles and forms microcapsules. For example, ethyl cellulose can be precipitated from cyclohexane by cooling, sodium alginate forms gel when meets aqueous solution of calcium chloride. Similarly, desolvation of water-soluble polymers with water-miscible solvents.

In *hot melt method*, the suitable polymer is melted first, the drug is mixed thoroughly. The hot mixture is sprayed. The molten mixture form drops which on cooling solidify. Thus, the drug to be encapsulated should be thermally stable. The coating material usually used for this purpose contains relatively low molecular weight lipids and the melt should have low viscosity even after mixing with drug.

In the *salting out* method, a suitable salt is added to the aqueous solution of polymer. By addition of salt, the polymer gets separated from the solvent (water). During this process of separation, the polymer forms a coat over the drug particles. In this method, there may be good possibility of incorporation of salt into the walls of the microcapsule formed.

In *solvent evaporation* technique, the drug and the polymer are dissolved in a water miscible organic volatile solvent. This solution is then dispersed into an aqueous solution, so that an emulsion is formed. Once the solvent is evaporated, solid microcapsules formed are left.

By changing the amount of coating material from 3 to 30% of the total weight, the thickness of the microcapsule coat can be varied from 1μm to 200μm. The thickness of the coat can be calculated theoretically from capsule size. Among different polymers (synthetic and natural) appropriate polymer is selected based on drug to be coated, desired release characteristics, and stability of the polymer in the gastric fluid.

b) *Matrix Dissolution control*

In this system an alternative approach is used. The drug is thoroughly mixed with a slow dissolving carrier (polymer or polymer mixture) and then compressed to make tablets. The rate of drug release of the drug from this type of formulation is controlled by the (1) rate of penetration of the dissolution fluid into the matrix, (2) porosity of the surrounding layer, (3) presence of hydrophobic additives and by the (4) the wettability of the polymer system and surface of particle.

Although zero-order release from most of the systems is desired, there are some systems that would give more advantage from release controlled by the composition of the releasing medium such as pH. The erosion of the methyl vinyl ether/maleic anhydride copolymer synthesized by Heller and Trescony[49]is very much sensitive to the pH of the aqueous medium. Thus, the rate of release of the drug is also dependent on the pH of the medium. These polymer systems are completely soluble at pH above certain value and are completely insoluble at pH below that value.

There are two general methods for preparation of wax-drug particles. In one method, the drug particles are dispersed in distilled water and the system is heated gradually up to 90°C with agitation. For a particular formulation wax is added to system with continuous stirring at the same temperature for 10 min. The wax is melted and starts engulfing the dispersed drug particles and forms spherical agglomerates. The system is stirred continuously and cooled to room temperature. The agglomerates become hard. Then the particles are filtered and dried for 24 hr at 40°C. The average size of the particles is reduced if the speed of stirring is increased. Although the aqueous dispersion method shows higher release rates of all waxes; however, no method is adequate to define the release characteristics.

Compression of spray-congealed particles releases the drug through erosion, solubilization, and leaching from the tablet. However, no model can produce the desired release characteristics. Although zero-order release is desired from most of the systems, there are systems that have more advantages from release that is controlled by the composition of the releasing medium, such as pH. Each polymer system shows a characteristic pH above which the polymer is completely soluble and below which it is completely insoluble. The pH depends on the size of the alkyl group in the copolymer ester. Thus, dissolution of the polymer and release of drug strictly depend on the pH of the medium.

2. Diffusion–Controlled products[43]

These systems are prepared with water– insoluble polymer which controls the flow of water and the subsequent release of dissolved drug from the dosage form. Diffusion occurs when a drug passes through the polymer that actually makes the controlled release device. The diffusion can occur through pores in the polymer matrix or by passing between polymer chains. Theseare broadly classified into two categories:

A. Reservoir Devices

B. Matrix Devices

The basic mechanisms of drug release from these two systems are primarily different.

A. Reservoir Devices

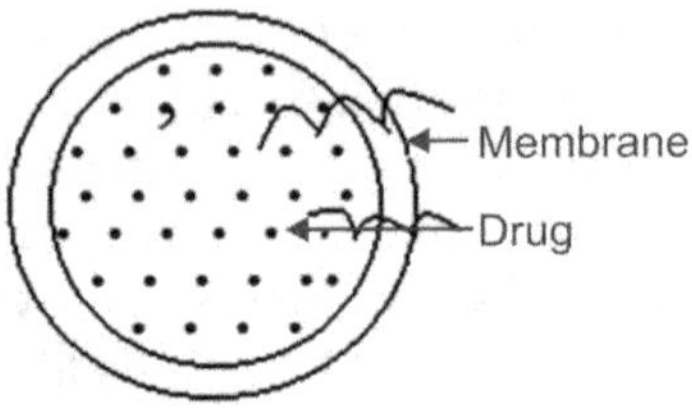

Fig.1.6 Diffusion control of drug release by a water-insoluble polymer.

In this system, a drug is enclosed by water-insoluble polymeric material; the drug is remained in the core of the particle. The drug partitions itself into the membrane and exchanges with the fluid surrounding the particles. The active agent or the drug is released into the surrounding environment by diffusion process through the rate limiting membrane. In the reservoir systems the drug delivery rate remains constant. Additional amount of drug will enter the membrane, diffuse to the periphery, and exchange with the surrounding media. A schematic diagram as shown in Fig.1.6 represents release of drug from a reservoir device.

The flux of drug, J (amount/area-time), across a membrane in the direction of decreasing concentration is expressed by Fick's law:

$$J = -D\,dC/dx \qquad .....(1.14)$$

Where, D is the diffusion coefficient in area/time and dC/dx is the change of concentration, C with distance, x. After attainment of steady state, the eqn. 5 can be integrated and written as;

$$J = -D\Delta C/l \qquad .....(1.15)$$

If the rate of release of the drug is expressed as dM/dt, then

$$dM/dt = ADK\,\Delta C/l \qquad .....(1.16)$$

Where, A = area

D = diffusion coefficient

K = partition coefficient of the drug between the membrane and core of the drug

l = diffusional pathlength, that is the ideal thickness of the coat, and

ΔC = concentration difference across the membrane.

When the partition coefficient is high, the core will be exhausted of drug within a short period and zero order release would be observed only over a short period of the time course of the drug release.

In fact, to achieve a constant rate of drug release from the reservoir, it is necessary to maintain constant area, diffusional path length, concentration, and diffusion coefficient; that is all the terms on the right-hand side of the eqn. 1.7 should remain constant. Commonly, many oral sustained release products, one or more terms changes in the product; as a result, zero-order release of drug is not observed. Methods used to develop reservoir type formulation are (1) press-coating[50, 51], and (2) air suspension methods[52-55]. These methods have been used to apply insoluble polymers to coat the drug in cores of the tablets. The microencapsulation process is commonly used to coat drug particles to incorporate into tablets or capsules[56-60]. Generally, drug is incorporated in the coating film and in the core of the microcapsule to provide the initial and sustaining doses respectively. Pan coating or polymerization technique is commonly used for coating. The coated pellets, granules or microcapsules thus produced, is then compressed into tablets. However, sufficient care should be taken during tableting so that no or minimal fracture or fusion of granules take place that can alter the release characteristics[61]. Several studies have been conducted to evaluate potential application of polymers and/or copolymers as coating materials for diffusion-controlled encapsulated dosage form[62-63]. For example, the release of phenobarbital, and salicylic acid from cast film of HPC (Hydroxypropylcellulose) by a diffusion-controlled process. Good *in vitro* release profile has been observed by laminating a blank film to the releasing side of the film. The Fig.1.7 shows the release characteristics of salicylic acid from the film of HPC.

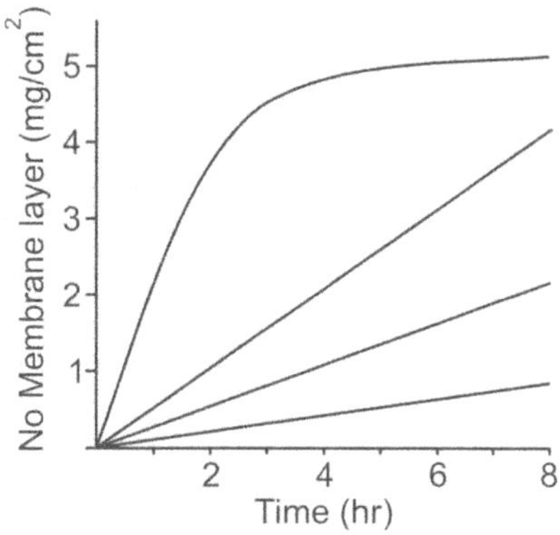

Fig.1.7 Drug release from film containing salicylic acid.

The important factors influencing the release rate of drug are:

- ***Polymer ratio in the coating***

By increasing the proportion of polyethylene glycol (PEG) in the film, the rate of release of the drug can be increased, keeping the amount drug constant. This is because PEG leaches out of the system very rapidly and the sizes of the pores are increased. As a result, the drug comes out of the system easily. Hence, by incorporating a leachable polymer in the coat, the release rate of the drug can be improved.

- ***Thickness of the film-coat***

It is expected that by decreasing the thickness of the coat, the rate of release of drug can be increased. Studies indicated the same when microcapsules of clofibrate prepared by coacervation using gelatin-sodium sulphate for coating. The Fig 1. 8 shows that the rate of drug release can be increased to more than 12 hr by increasing the thickness of the coat.

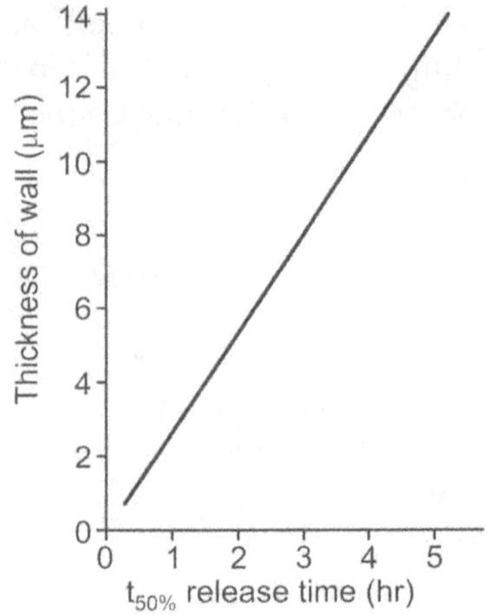

Fig.1.8 Relation between wall thickness and release rate.

- ***Hardness of the microcapsules***

*B*y increasing the hardness of the microcapsules, the rate of release of the drug can be prolonged. The effect of hardness of the tablets of sodium pentobarbital on the release of drug has been investigated and found true. The tablets were prepared using nylon. The mechanism of delayed release of sodium pentobarbital from the tablet might be leaching of the drug though network of nylon fiber constituting the microcapsules. In releasing the drug from microcapsules both dissolution and diffusion can be involved. If the coating material is properly selected, diffusion control system can be obtained.

B. Matrix Devices

In the matrix system, a solid drug or active substance is dispersed in the polymer matrix system to form a homogeneous mixture known as *matrix system*. The drug passes from the polymer matrix into the external environment through the process called diffusion. As the drug-release continues, the rate of release of the drug usually decreases with this type of system. This happens since the active agent has a progressively longer distance to travel and therefore, requires a longer diffusion time for release. Thus, the rate of drug release depends on the rate of diffusion, not on the rate of dissolution of the drug. The rate of release of the drug from such system can be expressed by an equation derived by T. Higuchi.

$$Q = [D\varepsilon/T\ (2A - \varepsilon Cs\ Cs\ t]^{1/2} \qquad .....(1.17)$$

Where,

Q is the amount of drug (g) released per unit surface area,

D is the diffusion coefficient of the drug in the release medium,

ε is the porosity of the matrix,

T is the tortuosity of the matrix,

Cs is the solubility of the drug in the releasing medium, and

A is the concentration of the drug in the tablet.

The assumptions behind the equation 8 are

- A pseudo-steady state is maintained during release
- Cs << A; that is, excess of solute is present,
- C = 0 in solution at all the times (perfect sink condition)
- Drug particles are much smaller than those in the matrix,
- Diffusion coefficient remains constant, and
- No interaction between the drug and the matrix occurs.

For treatment of data obtained, the equation 8 can be reduced to

$$Q = kt^{\frac{1}{2}} \quad .....(1.18)$$

Therefore, according to the equation 9, the amount of drug released from the matrix is plotted against the square root of the time required for the release; a straight line would be obtained, if the release is diffusion controlled. However, the rate of release of the drug from a uniform matrix system can be controlled by controlling the following parameters:

- Initial concentration of the drug in the matrix,
- Solubility of the drug,
- Porosity
- Tortuosity
- Leaching solvent composition, and
- Polymer system constituting the matrix.

When such systems are used *in vivo*, zero-order release is not commonly obtained. The reason behind this observation is most probably changing of the diffusional pathlength.

As per the expected release pattern from this type of system, a portion of the drug should be released immediately after administration (initial dose for immediate absorption) and thereafter in portions (for sustained action). This is usually done by placing the initial dose in coat of the tablet. The coated or matrix formulation can be tableted by press coating. The uncoated tablets are prepared by compressing initial dose with sustaining dose.

There are three major types of matrix diffusion control system:

- Insoluble plastics,
- Fatty, and
- Hydrophilic matrices.

Considerable basic researches have been conducted to develop insoluble matrix systems for sustained release of drug. However, some problems may be found while developing oral matrix system. For example, this has been reported that sometimes a matrix sustained release tablet is chewed after oral administration. This can bring about serious problem if the drug has narrow therapeutic window, because the drug will immediately be absorbed. Such problem can be resolved if the drug is dissolved directly in plastic matrix. As a result, the drug will not be released into the gastric fluid even after mastication. The Fig.1. 9 show such type of formulation.

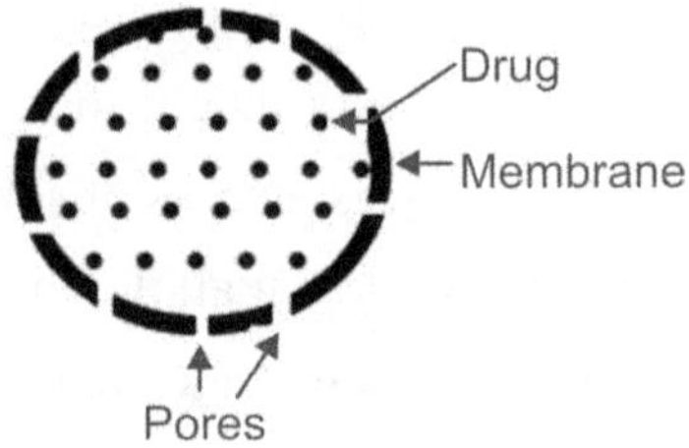

Fig.1.9 Diffusion control drug release by partially soluble polymer.

The fatty matrices are waxes which are melted, and the drug is dispersed and mixed thoroughly. The hot mixture is then cooled normally and allowed to congeal. The congealed mass is then granulated and compressed into cores. These cores are coated as per the method described previously.

In 1962, hydrophilic gums were first used to prepare sustained release products. According to this method, the drug is mixed thoroughly with nondigestible hydrophilic gum such as HPMC or sodium-CMC and then the mixture is compressed into tablets. After oral administration, the initial dose of the drug is released immediately into a medium, either water or gastric fluid. Then, hydration and gelation of the gum takes place at the interface between the tablet and medium. This produces a viscous gel which works as a barrier and retards the release of the drug into the medium. Studies indicate that release of drugs from some of the matrices follows the Higuchi's model for diffusion-controlled system[64].

3. Diffusion and dissolution-controlled system

The main feature of this system is that a partially soluble membrane encloses the drug. The Fig.1.10 shows a schematic diagram of such system. In this system a part of the membrane dissolves and allows the drug, present inside the core, to diffuse through the pores in the polymer coat. From this type of product, the release profile of the drug can be described by the equation 10.

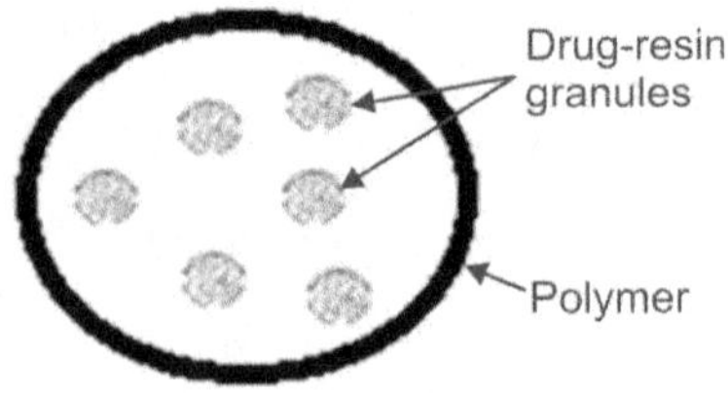

Fig. 1.10 Polymer coated drug resin system.

$$\text{Rate of release} = AD(C_1 - C_2)/l \quad .....(1.19)$$

Where, A = surface area

D = diffusion coefficient of the drug through pores,

l = diffusion pathlength,

C_1 = concentration of the drug in the core,

C_2 = concentration of the drug in the dissolution medium.

Here, the rate of release of the drug depends on the fraction of soluble polymer forming the coat. The zero-order release of KCl can be produced by such system. Such tablets of KCl decrease the gastric irritation caused by conventional tablet of KCl.

Use of lipase-lipid-drug system to provide sustained release, can demonstrate a dissolution-diffusion controlled system. In this case the erosion of matrix is due to thee lipolytic action of the lipase on the substrate. If the lipase activity accelerator such as calcium carbonate or glyceryl monostearate is added to the formulation, the rate of release of drug can be flexible. In drugs, the tablets containing lipase could produce consistently higher and more uniform blood level of the drug than those without having lipase.

4. Ion-exchange Resins

For a long time, the concept of ion exchange has been used in analytical and protein chemistry. For sustained release drug delivery system formulation, it is a preferred method because theoretically drug release characteristics depend on the ionic environment of the resin-drug complex. Hence, it is less susceptible to environmental conditions such as enzyme content and pH at the site of absorption. This method of sustained release needs the presence of ions in the solution. However, it is applicable to the skin, external ear canal, or any areas where available eluting ions are limited. This approach would be more suitable where the pool of available ions is more, such as in the subcutaneous or intramuscular route. The resin may biodegrade with an attendant alteration in the programmed release rate. In the GI tract, a constant ionic environment is present but it may vary with intake of diet, water intake, etc. Oral products using this principle can provide prolonged drug release (Fig.1.10).

Resins are water-insoluble compounds that contain anionic or cationic groups in repeating position on the resin chain. The resin can be mixed with the drug solution either by repeated exposure of the resin to the drug in a chromatographic column or by keeping the resin in contact with drug solution for a longer period. The drug-resin complex thus prepared is then washed to remove contaminant ions and dried to prepare beads or particles.

If a high concentration of an appropriately charged ion is kept in contact with the ion-exchange group, the drug molecule is exchanged and diffuses out of the resin to the bulk solution as per the scheme shown below:

Resin [N $(CH_3)]^+X^- + Z^- \rightarrow$ Resin [N $(CH_3)]^+Z + X^-$

Or

Resin (SO_3^-) $A^+ + B^+ \rightarrow$ Resin (SO_3^-) $B^+ + A^+$

Where X^- and A^+ are the drug ions

The factors that influence the rate of diffusion of drug from resin-drug complex are

- The area of diffusion,
- Diffusion pathlength,
- Amount of solvent in the matrix of the resin, and
- Cross-linking of the resin (structural rigidity of the resin).

Hence, the porosity of the resin and particle or bead size must be controlled during formulation process. The rate of release of drug can be further controlled by coating the drug-resin complex using any one of processes described previously. Mixture of coated and uncoated drug-resin complexes in a definite ratio can be filled in capsule and can be used to obtain a desired release profile. The drug-resin complex of phenylpropanolamine when administered once in 12 hr for 2 weeks has been found to provide the same plasma concentration similar to a solution of the drug administered 5 hrly.

5. pH-independent product

There are some unusual features in the gastro-intestinal tract, which are not found in other routes of administrations. The short transit time in the GI tract reduces the length of prolongation; this is a problem for dosage form design.

The pH of various zones of GI tract varies from 7 in the mouth, to 1 – 4 in the stomach, to 5 – 7 in the small intestine. Since most of the drugs are weak acids or weak bases, their sustained release formulations depend on pH. For example, papaverine HCl being highly soluble in the upper part of GI tract is found to be released in the gastric region than in the intestine. However, to achieve pH-independent drug release, suitable buffer can be added to a formulation. Buffers used are salts of amino acids, citric acid, phthalic acid, phosphoric acid, or tartaric acid. The rate of availability of propoxyphene from a buffered controlled release formulation can show a significantly increased reproducibility[65].

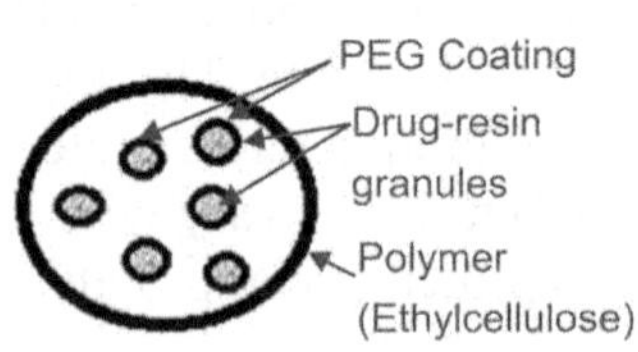

Fig.1.11 Polymer coated drug resin dispersion.

For oral controlled release of acidic or basic drugs at a rate independent of the pH in the GI tract, the granules can be prepared (Fig.1.11). The granules are prepared by mixing the drug with one or more buffering agents and required excipients and finally coated with a suitable film-forming polymer. The polymer used should permeate gastrointestinal fluid.

6. Osmotically controlled release

Osmotic pressure acts as the driving force in this type of drug delivery system and provides constant drug release. Around a core of an osmotically active drug or a core of an osmotically inactive drug combined with osmotically active salt, a semipermeable membrane is applied, and the granules are prepared. In each system, a delivery orifice is drilled by laser or by a high-speed mechanical drill. The optimum size of the orifice can be calculated by using the following equation:

$$A_S = (LV/t)(8\pi)(\eta/P)^{1/2} \quad .....(1.20)$$

Where, A_S is the cross-sectional area of the orifice,

L is the diameter of the orifice,

V/t is the volume released per unit time,

π is 3.14

η is the viscosity of the solution moving from the inside to the outside of the device, and

P is the hydrostatic pressure difference.

A_S is the total cross-sectional area of the orifices, if the osmotic device contains more than one orifice. When an osmotic system meets water or with a body-fluid, because of osmotic pressure difference, water or body fluid will flow into the core through the coating membrane as shown in Fig.1.12. The volume of liquid flown into the core per unit time, dV/dt, can be expressed as:

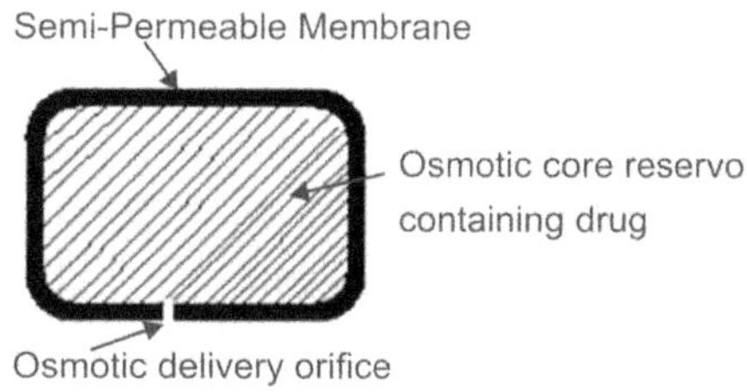

Fig.1.12 Oral osmotic pumps.

$$dV/dt = (Ak/h)(\Delta\pi - \Delta P) \quad .....(1.21)$$

Where, A is the area,

k is the permeability of the membrane,

h is the thickness of the membrane,

$\Delta\pi$ is the osmotic pressure difference, and

ΔP is the hydrostatic pressure difference.

The hydrostatic pressure difference would be small compared to the osmotic pressure difference, if the orifice, is quite large. Under this circumstance, the equation 12 can be reduced to

$$dV/dt = (Ak/h)\Delta\pi \qquad .....(1.22)$$

Through the orifice of the system, drug will be pumped out at a controlled rate, dM/dt. The dM/dt would be equal to the volume of water flew into the core multiplied by the concentration of drug, C_S in unit time, dV/dt. Thus, this could be expressed as;

$$dM/dt = (dV/dt)C_S \qquad .....(1.23)$$

This system is supposed to deliver the drug continuously at a zero order till the concentration of the osmotically active drug reaches below its saturation solubility. For example, preparation of indomethacin has been found to release the drug up to 70% at a zero-order rate.

Design wise the coating membrane is rigid and non-swelling. It is can maintain the structural integrity of the system during the release of drug. The coat is impermeable to the drug particles, permeable to gastrointestinal fluid. Polymers used as semi-permeable membranes have been presented in Table 1.7.

Table 1.7 Water-vapour transmission rate of some polymeric membranes.

Polymer	Rate of water vapor transmission ($g/100mm^2$/day/mm of thickness)
Polyvinyl alcohol	100
Ethylcellulose	75
Methylcellulose	70
Polyurethane	30 – 150
Cellulose acetate	40 – 75
Cellulose acetate butyrate	50
Polyvinyl chloride, cast	10 – 20
Polycarbonate	8
Polyvinyl chloride, excluded	6 – 15
Polyvinyl fluoride	3
Polyesters	2
Ethylene vinyl acetate	1 – 3
Cellophane, polyethylene coated	1.2
Polyvinylidene fluoride	1.0
Ethylene propylene copolymer	0.8
Polypropylene	0.7
Polyvinyl chloride, rigid	0.7
Polyethylene	0.5 – 1.2

The permeability of the rate controlling membrane depends on;

- The diffusion coefficient
- Solubility of water in the polymeric membrane,
- Structure of the polymer,
- Relative pressure difference across the membrane,
- Thickness of the membrane, and
- Temperature.

The flux of water through a semipermeable membrane can be determined and be expressed as water vapor transmission rate.

A layer of bioerodable polymer should be applied to the external surface of semi permeable membrane, to control the bioavailability of gastrointestinal fluid for permeation through the semipermeable membrane. There are various methods developed to modify the osmotic pressure-controlled drug delivery system[66]; one of such development is to separate two compartments by a movable partition as shown in Fig.1.13. The osmotically active compartment downs the GI fluid and develops an osmotic pressure on the partition. The partition moves to reduce the volume of the drug reservoir compartment and releases the drug through the delivery orifice.

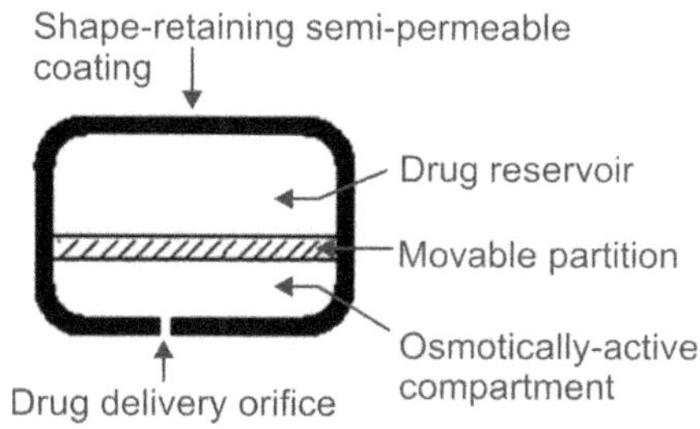

Fig.1.13 Osmotic pressure-controlled drug delivery system with movable partition.

Another modified system does not contain any delivery orifice. In such system, as the GI fluid is downed, hydraulic pressure is built up inside the system until the wall ruptures and the content of the system is released into the surrounding GI fluid. To control the drug release by varying the thickness and the area of the semi-permeable membrane, this type of bursting system can be used.

Thus, osmotically controlled release devices require only an effective osmotic pressure and do not depend on the pH and mixing in the digestive system, these can effectively sustain the release of the drug in GI tract.

7. Altered density formulations

In most of the human beings the GI transit time varies from one to another; in most cases it is less than 24 hr, but in some cases, it can vary from 8 to 62 hr also. There are various factors that influence the GI transit time, among all these the most important are:

- ➢ Physical properties of the delivery system,
- ➢ Presence of food

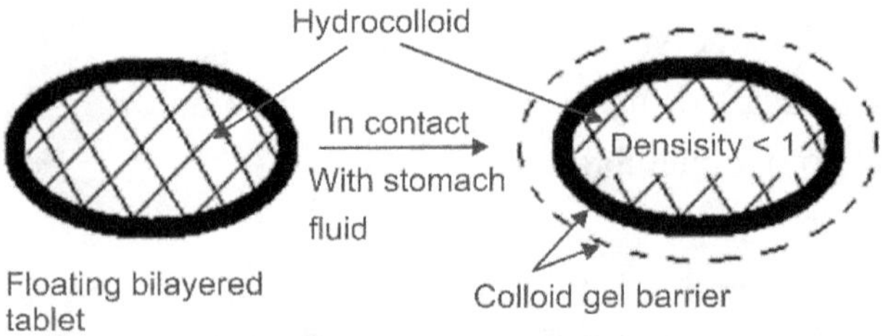

Fig.1.14 Bilayered sustained release tablet containing hydrocolloids.

This has been recently reported that the presence of food can affect the multiple-unit dosage forms to lesser extent than the single-unit dosage forms. Because the subunits of a multiple-unit dosage form are distributed throughout the GI tract. However, the GI transit time is more influenced by specific density of these subunits than the diameter of these subunits. This has been observed that by increasing the density from 1.0 to 1.6, the average GI transit time can be increased from 7 to 25 hr[67]. Although further investigation suggests that the increase in density of the delivery system from 1 to 3 has minimal effect on GI transit time in non-colostomy patients.

It is desired that a delivery system should remain at the nearest to the site of absorption until the drug is almost completely released. Various methods have been developed to prolong the gastric retention time of drug delivery systems. For example,

- ➢ Providing a bio-adhesive drug delivery system that can adhere to the mucin/epithelial surface of the GI tract.
- ➢ The density of the pellets is made heavier than that of the gastric contents, to about 1.4. In such dosage form, the drug is coated on a heavier core or mixed with heavy inert materials such as barium sulphate, titanium dioxide, iron powder, zinc oxide, etc.
- ➢ The apparent density of globular shells is less than that of gastric fluid. These low-density globular shells can be used as carrier of drug for sustained release of drugs. For example, polysterol, poprice, and even popcorn, are used as carriers. This is done by undercoating the surface of these empty shells with sugar or with a polymeric material such as methacrylic polymer and cellulose acetate phthalate. Then the undercoated shell is coated by a mixture of drug with polymers such as ethyl cellulose and hydroxypropyl cellulose. The product obtained by this process floats on the gastric fluid for a prolonged period which slowly release the drug.

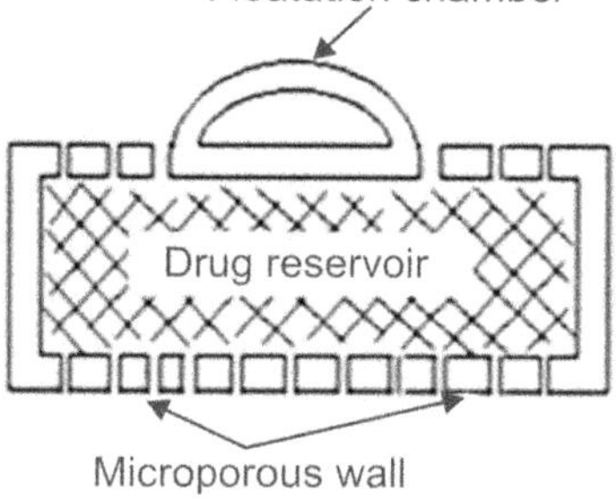

Fig.1.15 Drug delivery system with floatation chamber.

Floating tablets can be prepared by granulating a mixture of drug, excipients, and 20–75% of hydrocolloids. The hydrocolloids generally used are hydroxyethyl cellulose, hydroxy- propyl cellulose, and Hydroxy- propyl methylcellulose. The granules so prepared are compressed to tablets with required hardness. Such tablet after meeting gastric fluid remains floating and forms a water-impermeable colloid-gel barrier aroundthe surface. The bulk density of this is less than one; as a result, it floats. However, such low-density tablet requires presence of water in the stomach to remain floating. For this, frequent water intake which is inconvenient to a patient. This can be solved by making bilayered tablet which contains one layer for immediate release and the other layer for sustained release.

To use the principle of buoyancy another method is to include a gas-filled floatation chamber into the microporous compartment which contains a microporous drug reservoir, as shown in Fig.1.15. The apertures are present at its top and bottom walls. The gastric fluid enters through these pores and dissolves the drug. The side walls are sealed and prevent the entry of stomach fluid[68].

REFERENCES

1. Dixit N, Sheo DM, Bhanu PS. Sustained release drug delivery system. Indian J Res Pharm Biotechnol. 2013;1(3):305.
2. Wai-Yip Lee T, Joseph, Robinson R. The science and practice of pharmacy. 20th ed. Vol. 1; 2002. p. 903.
3. Sahilhusen IJ, Mukesh RP. Pharmaceutical controlled release drug delivery systems: A patent overview. Aperito J Drug Designing Pharmacol. 2014;1(2):1-22.
4. Scientific and regulatory issues. East Brunswick, NJ. Fifth International Symposium on Drug Development; May 1997. p. 15-7.
5. Aulton ME. The science of dosage form design. Philadelphia: Churchill Livingstone; 2002.
6. Marroum PJ, Bioavailability/Bioequivalence for oral controlled release products; Fifth International Symposium on Drug Development, East Brunswick, NJ, May 15-17, 1997.
7. Gohel MS, Barwell JR, Taylor M, Chant T, Foy C, Earnshaw JJ, & others. Long term results of compression therapy alone versus compression plus surgery in chronic venous ulceration (ESCHAR): randomized controlled trial. BMJ. 2007;335(7610):83. doi: 10.1136/bmj.39216.542442.BE, PMID 17545185.

8. Lee M, Chatterjee S, Struhl K. Genetic analysis of the role of Pol II holoenzyme components in repression by the Cyc8-Tup 1 corepressor in yeast. Genetics. 2000; 155(4):1535-42. doi: 10.1093/genetics/155.4.1535, PMID 10924455.
9. Kumar V, Prajapati SK, Soni GC, Singh M, Kumar N. Sustained release matrix type drug delivery system, A review. World J Pharm Pharm Sci. 2012; 1(3):952-4.
10. Banker GS, Rhodes CT. Sustained and controlled drug delivery system. Modern pharmaceutics. 4th ed. New York: Marcel Dekker; 2002.
11. Shargel L, Pong SW, Yu AB. Modified release drug products. Applied Biopharmaceutics & Pharmacokinetics. 5th ed. New York: McGrawHill Medical; 2004.
12. Chugh I, Seth N, Rana AC, Gupta S. Oral sustained release drug delivery system: an overview. Int Res J Pharm. 2012;3(5):57-62.
13. Chauhan MJ, Patel SA. A concise review on Sustained drug delivery system and Its Opportunities. Am J Pharm Tech Res. 2012; 2(2):227-38.
14. Sampath Kumar KP, Biswas D, Shweta S, Shravan P, Dutta AS. Sustained release drug delivery system potential. J Pharm Innov. 2012; 1(2):46-56.
15. Anuj PN, Nagarjuna T, Thulasiramaraju TV. Sustained release drug delivery system: a modern formulation approach. Int J Res Pharm Nanosci. 2013; 2(5):586-601.
16. Bankar AU, Bankar VH, Gaikwad PD. A Review on Sustained release drug delivery system, An. Int J Pharm Sci. 2012; 3:2049-63.
17. Wani MS, Controlled release system-A. Rev 2008;6.
18. Bechgaard H, Nielson GH.; Controlled release multiple units and single unit dosage. Drug Dev Ind Pharm.; 1978; 4(1):53-67.
19. Bhowmik D, Kumar KP, Dutta A, Paswan S. Trends in scope andopportunities of control release oral drug delivery systems. Crit Rev. Pharm Sci. 2012; 1:20-33.
20. Patel H, Panchal DR, Patel U, Brahmbhatt T. Matrix type drug deliverysystem: a review. J PharmSci Bio-Sci Res. 2011;1(3):143-51..
21. Dixit N, Maurya SD, Bhanu PS. Sustained release drug delivery system. Indian J Res Pharm Biotechnol. 2013; 1:305-10.
22. Kola R, Kumar BP.; A detailed description of synthetic and naturalpolymers which are used in the formulation of sustained release drugdelivery system: A review. J Chem Pharm Sci 2013; 6:161-9.
23. Ratnaparkhi, MP, Gupta, JP.; Sustained release oral drug delivery system– An overview. Int J Pharm Res Rev 2013;2:11-21.
24. Pundir, S., Badola, A., Sharma, D.; Sustained release matrix technologyand recent advance in matrix drug delivery system: A review. Int J DrugRes Tech 2013;3:12-20.
25. Chein, YW.; Novel Drug Delivery System. Revised and Expanded.2nd ed. New York: Marcel Dekker; 2005.

26. Ratilal, DA, Gaikwad, PD., Bankar, VH., Pawar, SP. A review on: Sustainedrelease technology. Int J Res Ayurveda Pharm 2011; 2:1701-8.
27. Bansal, BK., Shakya, V., Rewar, S.; A New Trend in Oral SustainedRelease Technology; As J Pharm Res Dev 2014;2:91-5.
28. Vyas, SP., Khar, RK.; Controlled Drug Delivery: Concepts and Advance.New Delhi: Vallabh Prakashan; 2002. p. 155-95.
29. Khalane, L., Alkunte, A., Birajdar, A.; Sustained release drug deliverysystem: A concise review. Available from: http://www.pharmatutor.org/articles/sustained-release-drug-delivery-system-concisereview.
30. Ankit, B., Rathore, RP., Tanwar, YS., Gupta, S., Bhaduka, G.; Oral sustainedrelease dosage form: An opportunity to prolong the release of drug. IntJ Adv Res Pharm Biosci 2013;3(1):7-14
31. Bharagava A., Rathore RPS., Tanwar YS., Gupta S., Oral sustained release dosage form: An opportunity to prolong the release of drug, International Journal of Applied Pharmaceutics and Biomedical Sciences 2013; 3:7-14.
32. Bhowmik D., Matrix Drug Delivery System, Recent trends in Sustained release matrix drug delivery system-An Overview, Journal of Pharmaceutics 2009; 20-28.
33. Levine, RJ. And Sjoerdsma, A.; Estimation of monoamine oxidase activity in man: techniques and applications.; Ann. NY Acad. Sci.; 107, 966,1963
34. Falliers, CJ., Chai, H., Molk, L., Bane, H. and Cardoso, RR de A.; Pulmonary and adrenal effects of alternate-day corticosteroid therapy.; J. Allergy Clin. Immunol.; 49, 156, 1972
35. Wagner, JG., Carpenter, OW., and Collins, EJ.; Sustained action oral medication. I:A quantitative study of prednisolone in man, in the dog, and in vitro.; J. Pharmacol. Exp. Ther.; 129, 101, 1960
36. Robinson JR, Lee VH; Controlled Drug Delivery Fundamentals andApplications. Revised and expanded. 2nd ed. New York: Marcel Dekker;1987
37. Janos B, Klara P, Odon P, Geza RJ, Rok D,Stane S, Istvan E. Film coating as a method
to enhance the preparation of tablets fromdimenhydrinate crystals. Int. J. Pharm. 2004;
269:393-401.
38. Morrison, ME., Yagi, MJ., and Cohen, G.; In vitro studies of 2,4-dihydroxyphenylalanine, a prodrug targeted against malignant melanoma cells.; Proc. Natl. Acad. Sci., USA; 82, 6020, 1985
39. Davis, SS., Hardy, JG., Taylor, MJ., Whaley, DR. and Wilson, CJ.; The effect of food on the gastrointestinal transit of pellets and osmotic device (Osmet); Int. J. Pharm.; 21, 331, 1984
40. Lachman L., Lieberman HA.; Pharmaceutical DosageForms: Tablets. In: The Theory and Practice of IndustrialPharmacy. Lea and Febiger, U.S.A, 1991; 3rd edition: 293-345.

41. The United States Pharmacopoeia, 20th rev.; Mack Publishing Co., Eaton, PA,; 1980, p.959
42. Shah, AC., Poet, CB., and Ochs, JF.; Design and evaluation of a rotating filter-stationary basket in vitro dissolution test apparatus I: Fixed fluid volume system.; J. Pharm. Sci.; 62, 671, 1973
43. Lachman L, Lieberman HA.; Compression coatedand layer tablets. In: Pharmaceutical Dosage Forms: Tablets.Marcel Dekker, Inc., New York,2002; vol 1; 2nd edition: 247-84
44. Takeda, Y., Nambu, N. and Nagai, T.; Microencapsulation and bioavailability in beagle dogs of indomethacin.; Chem. Pharm. Bull.; 29, 264, 1981
45. Benita, S. and Donbrow, M.; Coacervation of ethylcellulose, the role of polyisobutylene and the effect of its concentration.; J. Colloid Interface Sci.; 77, 102, 1980
46. Benita, S. and Donbrow, M.; Dissolution rate control of the release kinetics of water-soluble compounds from ethylcellulose film-type microcapsules.; Int. J. Pharm.; 12, 251, 1982
47. Benita, S.; Microcapsules: New applications and characterization.; Labo-Pharma-Propl. Tech.; 32, 694, 1984
48. Oyaalpar, M. and Walters, V.; The Prolongation of the in-vitro dissolution of a soluble drug (phenethicillin potassium) by microencapsulation with ethylcellulose.; J. Pharm. Pharmacol.; 33, 419, 1981
49. Heller, J. and Trescony, PV.; Controlled drug release by polymer dissolution II; Enzyme-mediated delivery device.; J. Pharm. Sci.; 68, 919. 1979
50. Mellinger, TJ.; Serum concentration of thioridazine after different orl medication forms, Am. J. Psychiatry; 121,1119, 1965
51. Hollister, LE.; Studies of prolonged-action medication. II. Two phenothiazine tranquillizers (thoridazine and chlorpromazine) administered as coated tablets and prolonged action preparations.; Curr. Ther. Res.; 4, 471, 1962
52. Mellinger, TJ., Mellinger, EM. and Smith, WT.; Thioridazine blood levels in patients receiving different oral forms; Clin. Pharmacol. Ther.; 6, 486, 1965
53. Vestre, ND. And Schiele, BC.; An evaluation of slow-release and regular thioridazine and two medication schedules.; Curr. Ther. Res.; 8, 585, 1966
54. Magee, KR. And Westerberg, MR.; Treatment of myasthenia gravis with prolonged-action Mestinon, Neurology 9, 348, 1959
55. Cass, LJ. And Frederik, WS.; Clinical comparison of a sustained- and a regular-release aspirin.; Curr. Ther. Res.; 7, 673, 1965
56. Thies, C.; Microencapsulation; In McGraw-Hill Yearbook of Science and Technology; McGraw-Hill, New York, 1979, p-12
57. Thies, C.; Physicochemical aspects of microencapsulation, Polymer Plast. Technol. Engg.; 5,1,1975.

58. Watanabe, A. and Hayashi, T.; Microencapsulation techniques of Fuji Photo Film Co Ltd., and their applications. In Microencapsulation (J. R. Nixon, Ed.), Marcel Dekker, New York, 1976
59. Harris, MS., Preparation and release characteristics of potassium chloride microcapsules; J. Pharm. Sci.; 70, 391, 1981
60. Kondo, T.; Microcapsules; Their preparation and properties; In, Surface and Colloid Science, vol 10; Plenum Press, New York; chap 1; 1978
61. Bakan, JA.; Microcapsule drug delivery systems. In, Polymer in Medicine and Surgery, Plenum, New York, 1975, p.213
62. Saggers, VH., Chasseaud, IF., and Copper, AJ.; Plasma concentration, duration of analgesia, and bioavailability of micro capsulated aspirin (Levius); Clin. Trials J.; 9, 36, 1972
63. Draper, EB. And Becker, CH.; Some wax formulations of a Sulphaethylthiadiazole produced by aqueous dispersion for prolonged release medication.; J. Pharm. Sci.; 55, 376, 1966
64. Banse, C., Bentz, JJ., Brossard, C., Cognyl, G., Crubezy, JC., Herbemont, F., Thankh Thuy, L., and Sarfati, R.; Microencapsulation, Sci. Technol. Pharm.; 7, 73, 1978
65. Kawashima, Y., Ohno, H. and Takenaka, H.; Preparation of spherical matrices of prolonged-release drugs from liquid suspension.; J. Pharm. Sci.; 70, 913, 1981
66. Siegel, RA. And Langer, R.; Controlled release of polypeptides and other macromolecules.; Pharm. Res.; 1, 2, 1984
67. Lim, F. and Moss, RD.; Microencapsulation of living cells and tissues.; J. Pharm. Sci.; 70, 351, 1981
68. Ishizaka, T., Endo, K. and Koishi, M.; Preparation of egg albumin microcapsules and microspheres; J. Pharm. Sci.; 70, 358, 1981.

EXCERCISE

MULTIPLE CHOICE QUESTIONS

1. The permeability of the rate controlling membrane depends upon
   a. Absorption
   b. Diffusion coefficient
   c. Drug release from dosage form
   d. None
2. The drugs having high solubility and low permeability are classified as-
   a. Class IV
   b. Class III
   c. Class II
   d. Class I
3. What are the characteristics of diffusion-controlled release systems?
   a. Release the drug along the entire length of GIT
   b. Diffusion of the dissolved drug
   c. Release only at a specific drug
   d. Employ waxes to control the rate of dissolution

4. For drug selection, the absolute bioavailability should be-
   a. 70% or less
   b. 75% or more
   c. 75% or less
   d. 70% or more
5. The physicochemical properties of drug include-
   a. Aqueous solubility
   b. Partition coefficient
   c. Drug stability
   d. All of the above
6. What is the characteristic of matrix dissolution-controlled release systems?
   a. Release the drug along the entire length of GIT
   b. Prolonged their residence in the GIT and release
   c. Release only at a specific drug
   d. Employ waxes to control the rate of dissolution
7. The drugs are well absorbed in-
   a. Ionized form
   b. Unionized form
   c. Both of the above
   d. None of the above
8. Which of the following is NOT the technique for the preparation of a Controlled Release Tablets?
   a. Direct compression technique
   b. Wet granulation technique
   c. Dry granulation technique
   d. Sintering technique
9. What are the characteristics of ion exchange resin drug complexes?
   a. Release the drug along the entire length of GIT
   b. Drug disperse in an insoluble matrix of rigid hydrophobic materials
   c. Hollow systems containing drug surrounded by a polymer membrane
   d. Formation of complexes between the drug and anion/cation exchange resins
10. The advantage of microencapsulation is-
   a. Sustained release of prolonged action medication
   b. Taste masked chewable tablet, powders and suspensions
   c. Single layer tablet for chemically incompatible ingredients
   d. All of the above

11. What is the characteristic of pH-independent formulations?
    a. Buffering agents that adjust pH to the desired value
    b. Drug disperse in the insoluble matrix of rigid hydrophobic materials
    c. Hollow systems containing drug surrounded by a polymer membrane
    d. Formation of complexes between the drug and anion/cation exchange resins
12. It is the fraction of drug in an oil phase to that of an aqueous phase
    a. pKa
    b. Permeation
    c. Dissolution
    d. Partition coefficient
13. Floating drug delivery systems include-
    a. Non- effervescent FDDS
    b. Effervescent FDDS
    c. Only a
    d. Both a & b
14. Ion-activated DDS is which type of activated system?
    a. Physical
    b. Biological
    c. Biochemical
    d. Chemical
15. Which of the following are the characteristics of diffusion- controlled release system?
    a. Release the drug along the entire length of GIT,
    b. Diffusion of the dissolved drug
    c. Release only at a specific drug
    d. Employ waxes to control the rate of dissolution,
16. Following is Biochemical type of activated modulated,
    a. Osmotic pressure activated,
    b. Enzyme activated DDS,
    c. Hydrolysis activated DDS,
    d. Vapour pressure activated.
17. Bio-erosion system is which type of delivery system.
    a. Activated modulated drug delivery system,
    b. Feedback regulated drug delivery system,
    c. Both of the above
    d. Vapour pressure activated.
18. The following characteristics are the good candidates for controlled release dosage form
    a. Polar, ionized
    b. Polar, Unionized
    c. Non- polar, ionized
    d. Non-polar, unionized

19. A good candidate for controlled drug delivery should have half life of-
    a. Less than 1 hour
    b. 8-10 hours
    c. More than 4 hours
    d. 2-4 hours
20. The key differences between controlled release and sustained release include:
    a. Sustained release is a slow release of medication over a period of time, whereas control release releases medication over time in correlation with concentration.
    b. Sustained release is a fast release of medication over a period of time, whereas control release releases medication over time in correlation with concentration.
    c. Sustained release is a slow release of medication over a period of time, whereas control release releases medication over time in correlation with viscosity.
    d. Sustained release is a fast release of medication over a period of time, whereas control release releases medication over time in correlation with viscosity.

SHORT ANSWER QUESTIONS

1. What are the objectives of oral sustained release dosage forms?
2. Briefly explain the Biopharmaceutical Classification System of drugs.
3. Write the classification of sustained release products.
4. Write a classification of modified release oral dosage forms.
5. Explain the significance of drug stability for the design of sustained and controlled release dosage forms.
6. What is the role of the partition coefficient of the drug in designing sustained and controlled release dosage form?
7. Briefly explain osmotically controlled release system.
8. Write significance of ion- exchange resins in sustained and controlled release systems.
9. Write a brief note on floating tablets.
10. Write the advantages of sustained release formulations over conventional formulations.

LONG ANSWER QUESTIONS

1. Write the mechanism of drug release from sustained release and controlled release formulations.
2. Explain the complete process of microencapsulation.

3. Write different methods for the preparation of controlled release tablets.
4. Explain the different physicochemical properties of the drug for the design of sustained release and controlled release formulations.
5. Discuss about the various approaches used in the design of oral sustained release or controlled release drug delivery system.
6. Explain the different biological properties of the drug for the design of sustained release and controlled release formulations.
7. Explain the basic concept of drug release from controlled release formulations.
8. Explain Diffusion and Dissolution Controlled system.
9. Explain diffusion-controlled products.
10. Explain the various requirements of drug candidate to be selected for formulation into controlled drug delivery system.

MCQ ANSWERS

1. (b)	2. (b)	3. (b)	4. (b)
5. (d)	6. (d)	7. (b)	8. (a)
9. (d)	10. (d)	11. (a)	12. (d)
13. (d)	14. (d)	15. (b)	16. (b)
17. (b)	18. (d)	19. (d)	20. (a)

CHAPTER - 2

Polymers

Dr. DK Tripathi, Dr. Amber Vyas, Dr. Bina Gidwani, Dr. Vishal Jain, Dr. Shiv Shankar Shukla, and Dr. Ravindra Pandey

Introduction, Polymers, Identification, Definition, Classification, Properties, Applications

INTRODUCTION

The term 'polymer' is derived from the Greek word *poly* means many and *mer* meaning the part or segment of a substance or material consisting of large molecules called macromolecules, composed of many repeating subunits. In 1833, Jones Jacob Berzelius coined this term and defined as per IUPAC system[1]. The modern concept of polymers as covalently bonded macromolecular structures was proposed in 1920 by Hermann Staudinger[2]. During the next decade he investigated to find out the experimental evidence for this hypothesis[3]. They have many more atoms than a water molecule--from 10,000 to 100,000 atoms per molecule. Molecules are compounds that are made of more than one type of atom. For example, carbon monoxide has two molecules– carbon and oxygen. Polymers are very large molecules compared to carbon monoxide. Many of the same units (or 'mers') are connected to form a long chain or polymer. For this reason, polymers are said to be the macromolecules.

To demonstrate the size scale difference, consider one polymer chain as a piece of cooked spaghetti, and one water molecule as one single crystal of salt. This demonstrates the great size difference between one molecule of a substance such as water (molecular weight of 18 gms/mole) and a polymer macromolecule (molecular weight ranging from 2000 to millions in gms/mole.

Polymers have interesting behaviour and special properties, partly because of their size. The large molecules become entangled with each other; much like a single strand of cooked spaghetti gets tangled up with other spaghetti strands in a bowl of pasta. The long polymer chains intermingle with one another and become entangled.

POLYMERS

Daily life of ours would have not been easier and colorful without the discovery and various applications of polymers. The use of polymers in the manufacture of plastic buckets, cups and saucers, children's toys, packaging bags, synthetic clothing materials, automobile tyres, gears and seals, electrical insulating materials and electrical parts has completely revolutionized the daily life as well as the industrial scenario. The polymers are the backbone of four major industries such as plastics, elastomers, fibers, paints, and varnishes. The term polymer is defined as very large molecules having high molecular mass ($10^3 - 10^7$u).

These are also referred to as macromolecules, which are formed by joining of repeating structural units on a large scale. The repeating structural units are derived from some simple and reactive molecules known as monomers and are linked to each other by covalent bonds. The process of formation of polymers from respective monomers is called polymerization. There are several ways of classification of polymers based on some special considerations. One of the common classifications of polymers is based on source from which polymer is derived *monomer* is a small molecule that combines with other molecules of the same or different types to form a polymer. Drawing a complete structure of a polymer is almost impossible, the structure of a polymer can be shown by showing the repeating unit of the monomer and 'n' number that shows how many monomers have participated in the reaction[4-6].

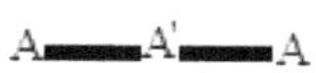

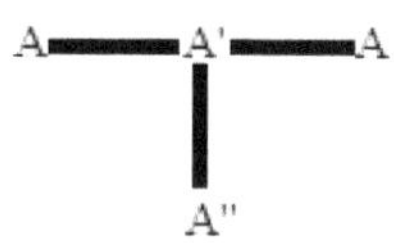

Fig.2.1 Linear polymer. **Fig.2.2** Branched polymer. **Fig.2.3** Cross-linked polymer.

If 2, 3, 4, or 5 monomers are attached to each other, the product is known as dimer, trimer, tetramer, or pentamer, respectively. An *oligomer* is formed when 30 to 100 monomers attach together. Polymers are called to a product that contains more than 200 monomers. Due to high molecular weight, thermodynamically, a polymer cannot remain in the gaseous state; it only remains in solid or liquid state[7-8].

The monomers can be linked together in various ways to produce linear polymers. The Fig.2.1 shows the linear polymer and Fig.2.2 shows the branched polymer and Fig.2.3 shows the crosslinked polymer.

In these representations, A' is the monomer. A" and A are the terminal groups. X represents the number of monomers attached to the terminal group (degree of polymerization). The degree of polymerization is commonly expressed as DP. Linear and branched polymers are known as thermoplastic polymers. This type of material flows when heated; thus, it can be fabricated by applying heat and pressure. Thermoplastic polymers are soluble in certain solvent.

Crosslinked polymers are known as thermosetting polymer. These materials are different from thermoplastic polymers in that they do not flow when heated and thus, cannot be fabricated by application of heat and pressure. All polymer chains are interconnected by covalent crosslinks. These cannot dissolve, can only be swelled polymer depending on the crosslinking density. When these materials are produced, these are either polymerised directly in a suitable mold or a linear prepolymer is first fabricated by conventional techniques used for thermoplastic materials and the fabricated material is then crosslinked by radian or chemical means.

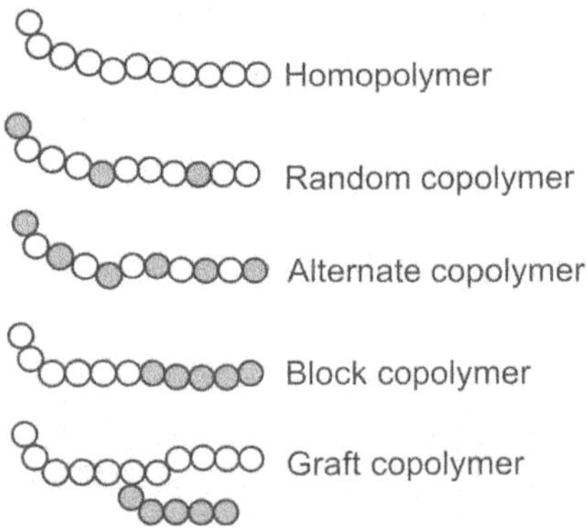

Fig.2.4 Polymers made of two or more monomer units.

Although there are several polymers which are pharmaceutically important. Commonly, the polymers used even in conventional preparations are cellulose-based, hydrocolloids, etc. Polysaccharides and their derivatives can be used as a rate controlling polymer in sustained release formulations due to their gelling property[9]. Chitosan is only soluble in acidic pH, but its carboxymethyl derivative is soluble at a wide pH range. These are biodegradable and their chemical composition varies greatly[10-12]. Iron stabilized into polysaccharide structure can be used in separation of cells and proteins utilising magnetic fields due to its magnetic properties[13,14]. Islets of Langerhans embedded into alginate encapsulates can be transplanted without the risk of protein contamination and suppression of immune system[15]. Carrageenan has been shown to increase the permeation of sodium fluorescein through porcine skin because it changes the rheological properties of the drug-solution[16]. Different enantiomers of racemic compounds such as propranolol and pindolol have been separated using carageenan[17, 18]. Chitosan can be used as a drug carrier, a tablet excipient, delivery platform for parenteral formulations, disintegrant and tablet coating[19,20]. Chitosan can also be mixed with non-ionic surfactants such as sorbitan esters to make emulsion like solutions or creams[21]. However, a sustained release dosage form of salbutamol sulphate bead can be prepared using chitosan in phosphate buffer[22]. Schizophyllan is secreted by fungus; it has been evaluated as an immunostimulant (to suppress tumour growth), antitumor, antihepatitis, anti-HIV, and antiviral agent[23, 24]. Sustained release formulations based on guaran[25], in situ gel-forming ability of xyloglucan[26], and borax-guar gum complexes for colon-specific drug delivery have also been studied[27].

IDENTIFICATION

In our daily lives, we use or see many polymeric materials in the form of disposable container; some are cleaned and used to pack other household materials.

By appearance, identification of polymers may be difficult, however, there are a few types those are readily identifiable. Clear, colourless containers that are used for filling of soft drinks are mostly polyethylene terephthalate (PETE). While opaque, translucent, sometimes white in colour, plastics used for containers such as milk cartons are usually high-density polyethylene (HDPE). Containers used for filling shampoos or cleaning materials are commonly made of polyvinyl chloride (V or PVC). Plastic bags and some plastic wrap are usually made from low-density polyethylene (LDPE).

However, the following tests are performed to identify the polymer/ type of plastic.

- **Water test**

  Approximately 5 ml of water is to be placed in a test tube. The test is started with one of the six plastic resin pellets. Two of the pellets of the resin in the test tube containing water are put. Each of the pellets is to be poked with a stirring rod to remove air bubbles, if any. Tried to make the pellets sink. Whether the pellets sink, or float is to be noted. If both the pellets do not behave the same way, the pellets are removed, dried, and saved for use in later.

  The water test is to be repeated with each of the remaining resin samples and with small pieces of the unknown samples. Save the samples that sank in the water for the copper wire test. The sample is used that floated the isopropyl alcohol test.

- **Isopropyl alcohol test**

  About 5 ml of isopropyl alcohol solution is placed in a test tube. One of the resins that floated in the water is to be used; two pellets are added to the test tube. Each pellet is poked with a stirring rod to remove air bubble, if any, tried to sink it. Whether the pellets sink, or float should be noted. If both pellets do not behave in the same manner, a third pellet of the same type should be tested. The results of two that behaved similarly should be used. The pellets are to be removed, dried, and saved for use later. The test with isopropyl alcohol is to be repeated with each of the remaining resin samples.

- **Oil test**

  About 5 ml of Mazola corn oil is placed in a test tube. Similarly, one of the resins that floated in the isopropyl alcohol solution is taken; two pellets are added to the test tube containing the corn oil. The pellets are poked with a stirring rod to remove air bubble, if any, adhered to the surface of the resin pellets, and they are tried to be sunk. Whether the pellets sink or float, should be noted. If the two pellets do not behave in the same manner, a third pellet of the same type is to be tested, and the results of two are to be used. The pellets are removed, dried, and saved them for use later. The test with oil should be repeated with the remaining resin samples.

- **Copper wire test**

  This test uses the plastic samples that sank in the test with water (samples are denser than water). A piece of copper wire about 5 cm long. One end of the wire is pushed into a small cork. The cork is used as a handle so that the hot wire is not touched during the test. One pellet or plastic sample is placed near a Bunsen burner. This is the sample that will be tested. The free end of the copper wire is held in the burner flame until it is red hot, and the flame no longer has a green colour. The wire is to be removed from the flame and the hot wire is to be touched to the plastic pellet or sample under the test. A small amount of plastic should melt onto the wire. If the wire sticks to the plastic sample, a pair of tongs is used to remove it. The end of the wire is to be placed with a small amount of plastic on it, into the flame. A slight flash of a luminous flame (a yellow-orange color). If the flame turns green in colour, the sample contains chlorine. This test should be repeated for each of the remaining plastic samples that sank in the water.

- **Acetone test**

  Under the hood, there should be a beaker containing acetone. If not, about 10 ml of acetone is to be placed in a 50 ml beaker. To minimize the vapours in the room, the work should be done under a fume hood. For this test, the samples of plastics should be used that did not give a green-colored flame. With the help of tongs, a pellet of the plastic is to be placed in the acetone for 20 seconds. The pellet is removed and firmly pressed between two fingers. If the polymer sample becomes soft and sticky, positive reaction has occurred. The sample is scraped with a fingernail if the outer layer is softened. If the sample shows a positive reaction, it should be discarded. This test may be repeated for each of the remaining plastic samples that did not show green coloured flame.

- **Heat test**

  Take about 100 ml of water in a 250 ml of beaker and heat to boiling. The samples which did not show the positive in the acetone test are to be used. With the help of tongs, a pellet of the plastic is to be placed in the boiling water for 30 seconds. The pellet is then removed, and it is to be pressed to see whether it has been softened. A positive reaction would have occurred if the polymer sample got softened. If a positive reaction has taken place, it must be thrown or discarded, and the conclusion of the test is to be recorded. The test is to be repeated with remaining samples that did not show any positive acetone test.

The summary of the tests performed are given below along with the chemical structure of the polymers.

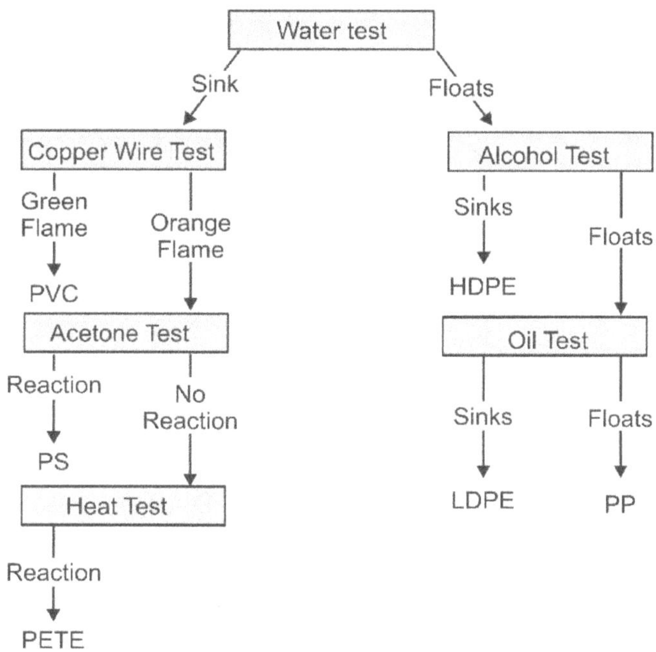

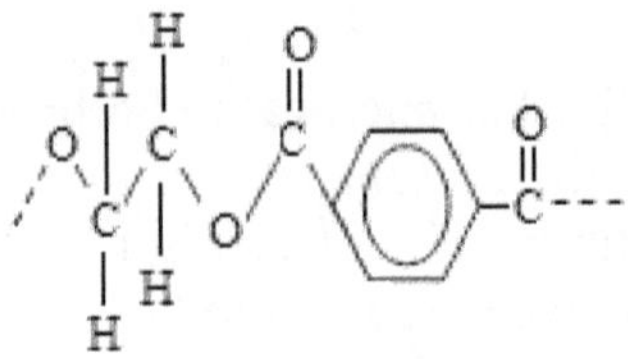

Polyethylene Terephthalate (PETE)

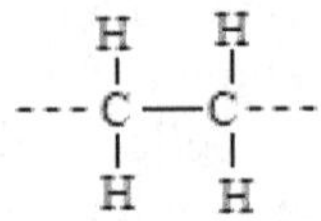

High Density Polyethylene (HDPE)

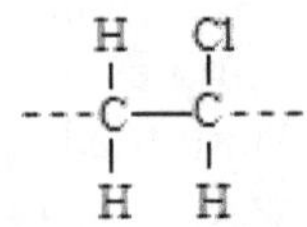

Polyvinyl Chloride (PVC)

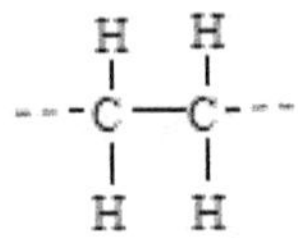

Low Density Polyethylene (LDPE)

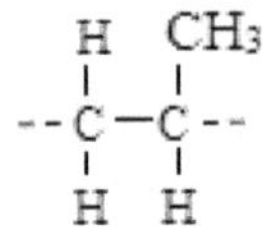

Polypropylene (PP)

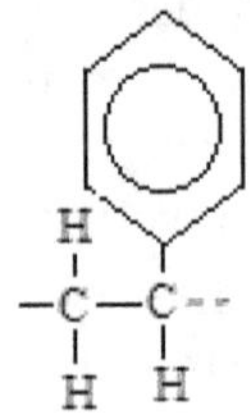

Polystyrene (PS)

The densities of the polymers are given below considering the density of water 1.0 g/ml.

Substance	Density (gs/ml)
Water	1.0
PETE	1.38 – 1.39
HDPE	0.95 – 0.97
PVC	1.16 – 1.35
LDPE	0.92 – 0.94
PP	0.90 – 0.91
PS	1.05 – 1.07

DEFINITION

The word polymers have been derived from Greek prefix– 'poly' meaning *many* and suffix 'mer' meaning *parts*. Thus, the term polymer can be defined as

- Polymers are the materials made of long, repeating chains (units) of molecules.
- A polymer is a large molecule made up of chains or rings of linked repeating subunits which are called monomers.
- The material has unique properties, depending on the type of molecules being bonded and how they are bonded.
- Some polymers bend and stretch, like rubber and polyester. Others are hard and tough, like epoxies and glass.

CLASSIFICATION

Polymers can be classified in different ways based on some special consideration. One of the common classifications of polymers is based on source from which polymer is derived. Under this type of classification, polymers can be categorized into three classes:

1. **Natural polymers**

   These polymers are found in plants and animals. Examples are proteins, cellulose, starch, some resins, and rubber.

2. **Semi-synthetic polymers**

   Cellulose derivatives as cellulose acetate (rayon) and cellulose nitrate, etc. are the usual examples of this subcategory.

3. **Synthetic polymers**

   A variety of synthetic polymers as plastic (polythene), synthetic fibers (nylon 6, 6) and synthetic rubbers (Buna - S) are the examples of man-made polymers extensively used in daily life as well as in industry. Polymers can also be classified based on their structure, molecular forces, or modes of polymerization.

Polymers can be classified as:

- Addition polymers,

  This type of polymers is produced by free addition reaction of free radical from unsaturated monomers containing C = C double bonds. The addition polymers are polyethylene and poly (methacrylate).

- Condensation polymers

  While condensation polymers are produced by reacting two monomers from which a small molecule is eliminated, which is commonly water. Polyamides and polyesters are formed by this reaction. Some condensation polymers may be hydrolyzed in the body and undergo degradation.

Polymerization reactions occur in a distribution of chain lengths and therefore a distribution of molar mass (MW). Biological polymers are the exception, in which the MW is firmly controlled. It is thought that distribution of MW can be broken down into the number of chains in the mixture that each has a defined length.

The number average molecular mass is determined by the methods that count the molecules. It is given by:

$$M_n = \sum \frac{N_i M_i}{N}$$

Where, N_i is the number of molecules of mass i

N is the total number of molecules

M_i is the mass of molecular length i

The weight average molar mass is given by

$$M_w = \Sigma(w_i M_i)$$

Where, w_i is the mass fraction

$$w_i = \frac{N_i M_i}{\Sigma(N_i M_i)}$$

The degree of polymerization indicates the average number of 'mers' per chain and can be defined in terms of either number average or weight average:

$$N = {M_w}/{M_{mer}} \quad \text{or} \quad {M_n}/{M_{mer}}$$

Where, M_{mer} is the molecular weight of the 'mer' unit.

The polydispersity is given by

$$PD = \frac{M_w}{M_n}$$

Generally, thermoplastic polymers consist of 10,000 mers, this gives rise to long chains of high molecular weight.

From solubility point of view, polymers can be classified into two groups:

1) Water-soluble such as cellulose ethers with methyl and hydroxypropyl substitutions. Hydrocolloid gums and synthetic water-soluble polymers such as polyethylene glycol, polyethylene glycol vinyl alcohol polymers, polyethylene oxide, polyvinyl pyrrolidone, polyacrylate or polymethacrylate esters containing anionic and cationic groups.
2) Water-insoluble such as ethyl cellulose and a group of cellulose esters (cellulose acetate butyrate or phthalate). These polymers are soluble in organic solvent.

Based on the applications and solubility characteristics, polymers can be classified into:

1) Cellulose-based polymers
2) Biodegradable polymers,
3) Ion-Exchange resin,

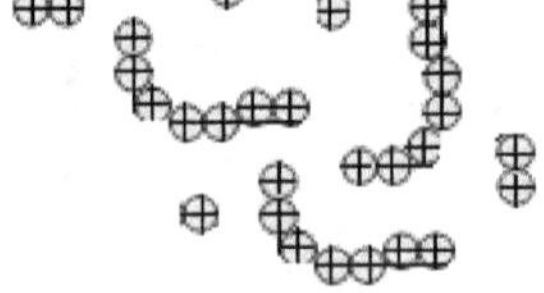

Fig.2.5 Addition polymers.

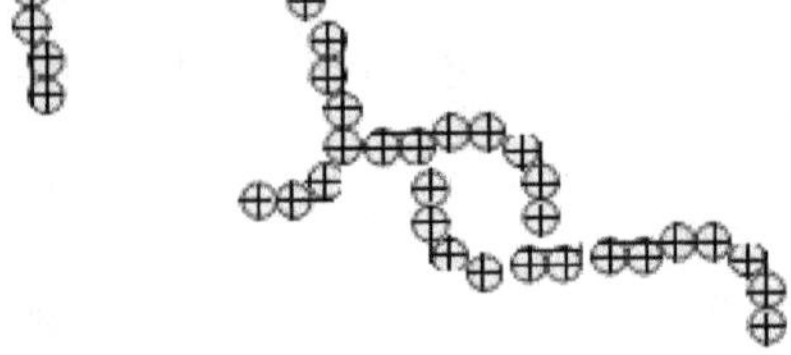

Fig.2.6 Condensation polymers.

PROPERTIES

The properties of thermoplastic polymers depend directly on the molar mass. Polymers are highly entangled in the melt and solid state. Many of the physical properties of polymers can be explained using a mathematical model. The model shown in Fig 1 show that the polymer chain is trapped in a tube of entanglements formed by neighboring chains. The entanglement restricts the movement of the polymer. The movement occurs by 'wiggling' of the chain along the tube or reptation. A scaling law for self-diffusion (D), interdiffusion, dissolution (Ds), and viscosity (η) as a function of chain length has been predicted as:

$$D \infty MW^{-2}$$

$$Ds \infty MW^{-2}$$

$$\eta \infty MW^{3}$$

Subsequently, a reptation chain pull-out model for fracture in thermoplastics as shown in Fig 2 was developed. The model shows how the fracture occurs by disentanglement process involving drawing and stretching of polymer chains across the fracture plane.

Energy is spent in pulling chains out of their tubes. According to the Prentice's model, the toughness (Gc) is proportional to the molecular weight squared. A slope of 2.45 is obtained, rather than a predicted value of 2.0.

- **Molecular weight and Distribution of Molecular weight**

  Polymerization is a random process. Molecules within a given polymer mass will have different weights, and for this reason, molecular weights of polymers are described in terms of average molecular weights. Molecular weights of polymer can be defined in different ways, and the most common molecular weights are the number average molecular weight, Mn, the weight average molecular weight, Mw, and the viscosity average molecular weight, Mv. These averages are defined as follows:

$$Mn = \frac{w}{\sum N_i} = \frac{\sum N_i M_i}{\sum N_i}$$

Where,

$$w = \sum N_i M_i$$

$$Mw = \frac{\sum N_i M_i}{w} = \frac{\sum N_i M_i^2}{\sum N_i M_i}$$

$$Mv = \left[\frac{\sum N_i M_i^{1+a}}{\sum N_i M_i}\right]^{1/a}$$

when n = 1, Mv = Mw

The ratio of $^{M_v}/_{M_n}$, also known ad the polydispersity index, indicates broadness of the molecular weight distribution, and for $^{M_v}/_{M_n} = 1$ the polymer is said to be monodispersed; that is, all polymer molecules within a polymer mass will have the same molecular weight.

The broadness of molecular weight distribution or polydispersity depends on the preparative method used to synthesize the polymer. Anionic living polymer techniques can produce polymers with a polydispersity index closed to one, whereas other chain polymerizations can have a polydispersity index as high as 20. Step-growth polymerizations have a polydispersity index of about two, known as the 'most probable' molecular weight distribution.

The knowledge of molecular weight and distribution of molecular weight of polymers is important since there is a definite relationship between polymer molecular weight and polymer properties. Thus, at very low molecular weights, the polymer has essentially no useful mechanical property of interest also rises.

The relationship between property and Mn can commonly be represented as

$$\text{Property} = a + \frac{b}{M_n}$$

Where, a and b are the constants. This relationship is analogous to one that relates molecular weight and glass transition temperature and, in fact the relationship between property molecular weight can be partially attributed to changes in the free volume of the polymer with changing molecular weight. However, molecular entanglement is also important and appreciable tensile strengths cannot be achieved until the molecular weight is high enough for a significant entanglement network to form.

- **Hydrophobicity of polymer**

  When a polymer is placed in an aqueous environment, it will gradually absorb water. The amount of absorbed water can be determined by the polymer structure. Because use of a polymeric controlled-release device exposes the polymer to an aqueous environment, its interaction with water of considerable importance.

  According to the nature of polymer-water interactions polymers can be broadly classified into – (1) hydrophobic polymers, (2) hydrophilic polymers, (3) water-soluble polymers, and (4) hydrogels.

(1) *Hydrophobic polymers*

These polymers are primarily water impermeable and, when placed in an aqueous environment, will absorb very little water. Clearly, there is no fixed amount for absorbed water below which a polymer is hydrophobic and above which it is hydrophilic. Just for the sake of classification the amount of absorbed water should be less than 5%w/w.

Structural parameters that contribute to polymer hydrophobicity are stiffness of the chain, high degree of crystallinity, and presence of highly hydrophobic groups where C – H bonds have been replaced by C – F bonds.

(2) *Hydrophilic polymers*

These are polymers that can absorb water more than 5%w/w. In fact, there can be a considerable variation between polymers in their ability to absorb water, and structural parameters that contribute to polymer hydrophilicity are flexibility of chain, absence of crystallinity, and presence of certain group such as amino, carboxyl, and hydroxyl, etc.

A useful method for varying the hydrophilicity of a polymer involves the copolymerization of two monomers, one is hydrophilic or even water-soluble polymer and the other one is a hydrophobic polymer. Example of such a method is the copolymerization of hydroxyethyl methacrylate and methyl methacrylate.

(3) *Water-soluble polymers*

Some polymers are freely soluble in water, even though they are of very high molecular weight. Such polymers are poly (vinyl alcohol), poly (acrylic acid), poly(N-vinyl pyrrolidone), polyacrylamide, and poly(ethylene oxide).

(4) *Hydrogels*

These are highly hydrophilic or water-soluble polymers. These polymers have been crosslinked by means of covalent crosslinks, water uptakes far in excess of those achievable with hydrophilic linear polymers can be obtained.

- **Crystallinity and barrier properties**

Polymers show different thermal, physical, and mechanical properties depending on their structure, molecular weight, linearity, intra- and intermolecular interactions. If a polymer is linearly structured, it can be packed together in regular arrays. For example, polypropylene chains can fit together in a way that inter-molecular attractions can stabilize the chains into a regular lattice or crystalline state. When the temperature increases, the crystal cells (crystallites) start melting and whole polymer mass suddenly melts at a certain temperature. Above the melting temperature, the molecules of polymer remain in continuous motion and the molecules can slip past one another.

In many cases, the structure of a polymer is so irregular that crystal formation is thermodynamically infeasible. Such polymers can form glass in place of crystal structures. A glass is solid material existing in a non-crystalline (amorphous) state. Amorphous structure is formed due to either rapid cooling of a polymer-melt in which crystallization is prevented by quenching or due to lack of structural regularity in the structure of the polymer. Rotation around single bonds of the polymer chains becomes very difficult at low temperatures during rapid cooling; therefore, the polymer molecules are forced to adapt a disordered state and form an amorphous structure. Amorphous or glassy polymers do not generally show a sharp melting point; instead, they soften over a wide range of temperature[x/8]. For example, polystyrene and poly (vinyl acetate) are amorphous having melting range of 35°C to 85°C and of 70°C to 115°C, respectively. While, poly (butylene terephthalate) and poly (ethylene terephthalate) are crystalline polymers having sharp melting range of 220°C to 260°C and 250°C to 260°C respectively.

Strength and stiffness of polymer increase with crystallinity because of increased intermolecular interaction. With an increase in crystallinity, the optical properties of a polymer are changed from transparent (crystalline) to opaque (semicrystalline). This is due to the difference in the refractive indices of the amorphous and crystalline structures which result in different levels of light scattering. According to the pharmaceutical necessity good barrier properties are required when polymers are used to prepare the packaging material or for coating. Crystallinity increases the barrier properties of the polymer. Small molecules of drugs or solvent cannot penetrate or diffuse through crystalline structure. Therefore, greater barrier properties and durability are with the crystalline polymers in presence of attacking molecules. Diffusion and solubility of a polymer are related to the degree of its crystallinity. On the other hand, a less crystalline or amorphous polymer is preferred when the release of drug or active material is desired. Crystallinity in each polymer depends on its

- Topology and isomerism (linear vs. branched, isotactic vs. atactic),
- Molecular weight
- Intermolecular forces
- Pendant groups (bulky vs. Small)
- Rate of cooling, and
- Stretching mode (uniaxial vs. biaxial)

Another unique property of a crystalline polymer or polymer-containing crystalline domains is anisotropy. A crystal cell shows different properties along longitudinal and transverse directions. For this reason, a polymer behaves like an anisotropic material.

- **Thermal Transitions**

  Thermal transitions in polymers can occur in various orders. In other words, the volume of a polymer can change with temperature as a first- or second-order transition. When crystal melts, the polymer volume increases significantly as the solid converts into a liquid. The melting temperature ™ represents a first-order thermal transition in polymers. On the other hand, the volume of an amorphous polymer gradually changes over a wide temperature range or so-called glass transition temperature. This behavior represents a second-order thermal transition in polymers.

- **Glass Transition Temperature**

  At very low temperatures, all amorphous polymers exist in a glassy state. T_g denotes the molecular motion, which depends on various factors. Therefore, T_g cannot be an absolute property of a polymer, it is influenced by the factors affecting the movement of polymer chains. At temperatures well below the T_g, amorphous polymers are hard, stiff, and glassy; however, they may not be brittle. On the other hand, at temperatures well above the T_g, polymers become rubbery and might flow. For linear organic polymers the T_g values range from about – 100°C to above 300°C. Even though some organic polymers are expected to have $T_g$values above 300°C, they decompose at temperatures below their transition temperatures. From pharmaceutical point of view, T_g is an important factor for solid dosage forms. For example, a chewable tablet needs to be soft and flexible at mouth temperature around 37°C. this means that the polymer used as a chewable matrix should be softened at this temperature. Pharmaceutically acceptable polymers with their $T_g$values near to 37°C should be the best polymers of choice.

- **$T_g$and length of the polymer chain**

  Long polymer chains provide smaller free volume than their shorter counter parts. Since more free volume corresponds to lower T_g values, polymers containing short chains or having lower molecular weight possess lower $T_g$values.

- **T_g and side group of the polymer chain**

  The side group of a polymer may be bulky or polar. Due to its steric hindrance, higher temperature is required to induce segmental motion in polymer containing bulky groups. For example, polystyrene and polypropylene are only different in terms of their side groups, phenyl vs. methyl, respectively. The larger size of the phenyl group results in a much higher T_g value of polystyrene, 100°C as opposed to –20°C for polypropylene. On the other hand, the polar side groups provide stronger intermolecular interactions that significantly affect the segmental motion of the polymer chains. Poly (vinyl chloride) is likepolyethylene except hydrogen is replaced by the chlorine atom. Since chlorine is more polar than hydrogen, the PVC polymer displays a much higher $T_g$of 100°C compared to – 120°Cfor polyethylene.

- **T_g and flexibility of the polymer chain**

  Flexible polymer chains show higher entropy (desire to move) than rigid chains. Flexible and rigid chains behave like liquid and solid, respectively. Groups such as phenyl, amide, sulphone, and carbonyl either inside the backbone or as a side group hanging on the backbone affect the overall polymer flexibility. For example, poly (ethylene adipate) and poly (ethylene terephthalate) are structurally very similar except for the phenylethylene residuein phthalate vs. the butylene residue in adipate. This results in almost a 100°C difference in $T_g$values of the two polymers (– 70°C vs. 69°C, respectively).

- **T_g and branching of the polymer chain**

  Linear polymer chains possess smaller free volume as opposed to their branched counterparts. Therefore, higher T_g values are expected for linear polymers. On the hand, branches in branched polymers impose hindrance or restriction to segmental motion, for which higher $T_g$values are expected. Therefore, branching has no obvious effect on the $T_g$unless the whole structure of the polymer is known.

- **T_g and cross-linking of the polymer chain**

  Compared to crosslinked chains, linear chains have a higher entropy and the desire to move; hence, they show low $T_g$values. Adding cross-links to linear polymer chains limits chain movement resulting in less entropy at a given temperature and hence a higher $T_g$value. For very highly cross-linked polymers, T_g values are expected to be very high to the extent that the polymer starts to decompose before it shows any segmental motion.

- **T_g and processing rate of the polymer chain**

  To prepare polymer products, the polymer needs to be processed at different temperatures and pressures that can significantly affect the molecular motion in polymers. Therefore, the rate of processes such as heating, cooling, loading, and so on might be considered when evaluating the $T_g$value of a given polymer. Kinetically speaking, if the rate of the process is high (fast cooling, fast loading), the polymer chains cannot move to the extent that they are expected to. They virtually behave like rigid chains which with lower tendency to move, which results in reading high T_g values. The heating rate is to be very realistic and should be consistent with the conditions in which the polymer is expected to work.

- **T_g and plasticizer**

  Plasticizer molecules can increase the entropy and mobility of the polymer chains. This is translated to lower T_g values for plasticized polymers compared with their nonplasticized counterparts.

- **Mechanical properties**

Depending on the structure, molecular weight, and inter-molecular forces, polymers can resist differently when they are stressed. The polymers can resist against stretching, compression (compressive strength), bending (flexural strength), sudden stress (impact strength), and dynamic loading (fatigue). With increasing molecular weight, the level of intermolecular forces, polymer shows superior properties under an applied stress. As regards the structure is concerned, a flexible polymer can perform better under stretching while a rigid polymer is better under compression. Generally, the elastic materials show high stress and very low elongation (deformation, strain) at their breaking point.

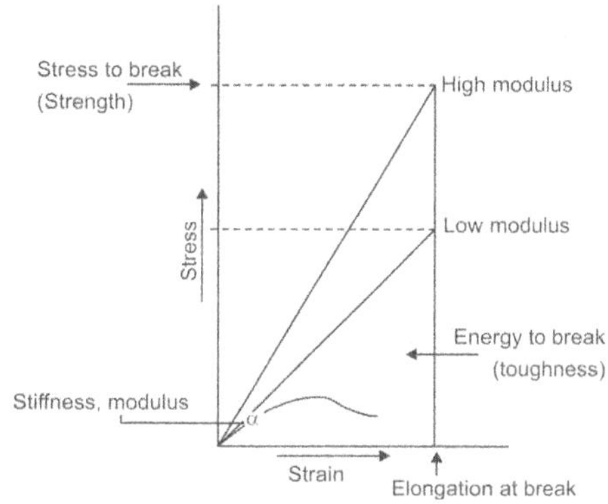

Fig.2.7 Mechanical properties of polymer.

Polymeric materials such as fibers and highly cross-linked polymers show elastic behavior. In other words, a linear stress/strain correlation is seen up to their breaking point. With an increase in intermolecular forces within a fibrous product or cross-link density of a cross-linked polymer, the slope of the stress/strain line becomes steeper. When the slope is sharper, modulus becomes high. Modulus and stiffness are two interchangeable terms that can demonstrate the strength of a polymer. Some polymeric materials do not show a sharp or abrupt breaking point. Instead, they yield at certain stresses and continue to deform under lower stresses before they finally break apart. Tough plastics show this typical behavior. On the other hand, rubber and elastomers show completely different behavior. This depends on the slevel of cross-linking or curing. Generally, under very small stresses, they deform to a large extent to more than 10 to 15 times their original lengths. Highly cross-linked rubbers show very low deformation at their breaking point. In fact, cross-linking is the process by which properties of a rubber can be improved to a very tough plastic or even a fiber. Regardless of the type of polymer (fiber, tough plastic, or rubber), certain amounts of energy are required to break the polymer apart and the area under the stress/strain curve measures it. If the area is larger, the polymer becomes tougher.

- **Viscoelastic properties**

Mechanical properties of a particular polymer are commonly measured at a fixed rate of loading at certain temperature, relative humidity, etc.

Polymers are neither pure elastic nor a pure fluid material. They can store energy displaying elastic behavior and to dissipate it by showing viscous behavior. For this reason, most polymers are viscoelastic materials. For example, poly (vinyl chloride) has a glass transition temperature of about 100°C [28].

APPLICATIONS

Most polymers encountered in our daily life, can be classified in six polymers listed below. Many of these polymers are being used in the form of disposable containers used for many household products. For easy recycling of these polymers, the manufacturers of plastics have adopted codes shown. Clear, colourless, containers used filling soft drinks are commonly the polyethylene terephthalate (PETE). As milk cartons generally, the high density polyethylene (HDPE) polymer is used. This polymer is opaque, translucent, and often white in colour. For shampoos or cleaning materials bottles are prepared using polyvinyl chloride (V or PVC). Similarly, plastic bags and some plastic wrap is often made from low-density polyethylene (LDPE).

Thus, the applications of these polymers are systematically presented below:

- Polyethylene Terephthalate (PETE): Soft drink bottles, mouthwash bottles, peanut butter and salad dressing containers.
- High Density Polyethylene (HDPE): Milk, water and juice containers, grocery bags, toys, liquid detergent bottles.
- Polyvinyl Chloride (PVC): Clear food packaging, shampoo bottles.
- Bread bags, frozen food bags, grocery bags.
- Ketchup bottles, yogurt containers, margarine tubs, and medicine bottles.
- Polystyrene (PS): Cases of video cassette, compact disc jackets, coffee cups, tableware such as knives, spoons and forks, cafeteria trays, grocery store meat trays, and fast-food sandwich containers are generally prepared from this polymer.

Besides these common applications, there are typical pharmaceutical applications. In traditional pharmaceutical manufacturing, polymers are used as binders in making tablets. For protection of drug, masking of taste, release of drug from a controlled release dosage form, targeted delivery of drug, to improve bioavailability of a drug, and so on appropriate polymers are being used. Apart from solid dosage form, polymers are being used liquid dosage form for increasing viscosity of suspensions to suspend the dispersed solid drugs.

Currently the polymers are extensively used to prepare controlled release formulations. In biomedical field, polymers are used for making implants which are performing for long. These polymers have unique properties different from others used for general purposes.

Generally, the properties of polymers expected from pharmaceutically applied polymers are: (1) ability to form film (coating), (2) thickening (rheology modification), (3) ability to form gels (controlled release), (4) ability to adhere (binding), (5) solubilizing at definite pH (controlled release), (6) can solubilize in organic solvent (taste masking), and (7) ability to render barrier properties (protection and packaging).

Type of polymers	Applications
Water-Soluble Synthetic Polymers	
Poly (acrylic acid)	Cosmetics, pharmaceuticals, immobilization of cationic drugs, base for Carbopol polymers
Poly (ethylene oxide)	Coagulant, flocculent, very high molecular-weight up to a few millions, swelling agent
Poly (ethylene glycol)	M_w < 10,000, liquid (M_w < 1000) and wax (M_w>1000) , plasticizer, base for suppositories
Poly (vinyl pyrrolidone)	Used to make betadine (iodine complex of PVP) with less toxicity than iodine, plasma replacement, tablet granulation
Poly (vinyl alcohol)	Water-soluble packaging, tablet binder, tablet coating
Polyacrylamide	Gel electrophoresis to separate proteins based on their molecular weights, coagulant, absorbent
Poly (isopropyl acrylamide) and poly (cyclopropyl methacrylamide)	Thermogelling acrylamide derivatives, its balance of hydrogen bonding, and hydrophobic association changes with temperature
Cellulose-Based Polymers	
Ethyl cellulose	Insoluble but dispersible in water, aqueous coating system for sustained release applications
Carboxymethyl cellulose	Super disintegrant, emulsion stabilizer
Hydroxyethyl and hydroxypropyl celluloses	Soluble in water and in alcohol, tablet coating
Hydroxypropyl methyl cellulose	Binder for tablet matrix and tablet coating, gelatine alternative as capsule material
Cellulose acetate phthalate	Enteric coating
Hydrocolloids	
Alginic acid	Oral and topical pharmaceutical products; thickening and suspending agent in a variety of pastes, creams, and gels, and stabilizing agent for oil-in-water emulsions; binder and disintegrant

Table *contd…*

Carrageenan	Modified release, viscosifier
Chitosan	Cosmetics and controlled release drug delivery applications, mucoadhesive dosage forms, rapid release dosage forms
Hyaluronic acid	Reduction in scar tissues, cosmetics
Pecttinic acid	Drug delivery
Water-Insoluble Biodegradable Polymers	
(Lactide-co-glycolide) Polymers	Microparticle-nanoparticle for protein delivery
Starch-Based Polymers	
Starch	Glidant, a diluent in tablets and capsules, a disintegrant in tablets and capsules, a tablet binder
Sodium starch glycolate	Super disintegrant for tablets and capsules in oral drug delivery
Plastics and Rubbers	
Polyurethane	Transdermal patch backing (soft, comfortable, moderate moisture transmission), blood pump, artificial heart, and vascular grafts, foam in biomedical and industrial products
Silicones	Pacifier, therapeutic devices, implants, medical grade adhesive for transdermal delivery
Polycarbonate	Case for biomedical and pharmaceutical products
Polychloroprene	Septum for injection, plungers for syringes, and valve components
Polyisobutylene	Pressure sensitive adhesives for transdermal delivery
Polycyanoacrylate	Biodegradable tissue adhesives in surgery, a drug carrier in nano- and microparticles
Poly (vinyl acetate)	Binder for chewing gum
Polystyrene	Petri dishes and containers for cell culture
Polypropylene	Tight packaging, heat shrinkable films, containers
Poly (vinyl chloride)	Blood bag, hoses, and tubing
Polyethylene	Transdermal patch backing for drug in adhesive design, wrap, packaging, containers
Poly (methyl methacrylate)	Hard contact lenses
Poly (hydroxyethyl methacrylate)	Soft contact lenses
Acrylic acid and butyl acrylate copolymer	High T_g pressure-sensitive adhesive for transdermal patches

Table *contd...*

2-Ethylhexyl acrylate and butyl acrylate copolymer	Low T_g pressure-sensitive adhesive for transdermal patches
Vinyl acetate and methyl acrylate copolymer	High cohesive strength pressure-sensitive adhesive for transdermal patches
Ethylene vinyl acetate and polyethylene terephthalate	Transdermal patch backing (occlusive, heat sealable, translucent)
Ethylene vinyl acetate and polyethylene	Transdermal patch backing (heat. Sealable, occlusive, translucent)
Polyethylene and polyethylene terephthalate	Transdermal patch backing (when ethylene vinyl acetate copolymer is incompatible with the drug.

REFERENCES

1. Jensen WB. The Origin of the polymer concept. J Chem Educ. 2008; 85(5):624-5. doi: 10.1021/ed085p624.
2. Staudinger H. UberPolymerization. Ber Dtsch Chem Ges (in German). 1920; 53(6):1073-85.
3. Allcock HR, Lampe FW, Mark JE. Contemporary polymer chemistry. 3rd ed. Pearson Education; 2003. p. 21.
4. Rodriguez F. Principles of polymer systems. Tailor & Francis, Filadelphia. PA, 1996.
5. Odian G. Principles of polymerization. 3rd ed. New York: Wiley; 1991.
6. Flory PJ. Principles of polymer chemistry. Ithaca, NY: Cornell University; 1953.
7. Billmeyer FW. Textbook of polymer science. 3rd ed. New York: Wiley; 1984.
8. Sperling LH. Introduction to Physical polymer Science. New York: Wiley; 1992.
9. Jong SC, Birmingham JM, Pai SH, Di E-R. Immunologia Immunofarmacologia, editor. Vol. 11(3); 1991. p. 115-22.
10. Hovgaard L, Brondsted H, Cri. Rev Ther Drug Carrier Syst. 1996; 13:3-4, 185-223.
11. Nishinari K, Takahashi R. Curr Opin Colloid Interface Sci. 2003;8:4-5, 396-400.
12. Basit AW. Advances in Colonic Drug Delivery. Drugs. 2005;65(14):1991-2007. doi: 10.2165/00003495-200565140-00006.
13. Vandamme TF. The use of polysaccharides to target drugs to the colon. Carbohydr Polym. 2002;48(3):219-31. doi: 10.1016/S0144-8617(01)00263-6.
14. Shingle, K. I. and Marchessault, R. H., in Robert H. Marchessault, Francois Ravenelle, Xiao Xia Zhu (Eds.); Polysaccharides for Drug Delivery and Pharmaceutical Applications; ACS Symposium Series 934, American Chemical Society, 2006.

15. Dusseault J, Tam SK, Ménard M, Polizu S, Jourdan G, Yahia L et al.. Evaluation of alginate purification methods: effect on polyphenol, endotoxin, and protein contamination. J Biomed Mater Res A. 2006;76(2):243-51. doi: 10.1002/jbm.a.30541, PMID 16265647.

16. Valenta C, Schultz K. Influence of carrageenan on the rheology and skin permeation of microemulsion formulations. J Control Release. 2004;95(2):257-65. doi: 10.1016/j.jconrel.2003.11.020, PMID 14980774.

17. Beck GM, Neau SH. Chilarity. 1996;8(7):503-10.

18. Beck GM, Neau SH. Chilarity. 2000;12(8):614-20.

19. Felt O, Buri P, Gurny R. Chitosan: a unique polysaccharide for drug delivery. Drug Dev Ind Pharm. 1998; 24(11):979-93. doi: 10.3109/03639049809089942, PMID 9876553.

20. Singla AK, Chawla M. Chitosan: some pharmaceutical and biological aspects–an update. J Pharm Pharmacol. 2001;53(8):1047-67. doi: 10.1211/0022357011776441, PMID 11518015.

21. Chae SY, Jang MK, Nah JW. Influence of molecular weight on oral absorption of water soluble chitosans. J Control Release. 2005;102(2):383-94. doi: 10.1016/j.jconrel.2004.10.012, PMID 15653159.

22. Grant J, Cho J, Allen C. Self-assembly and physicochemical and rheological properties of a polysaccharide-surfactant system formed from the cationic biopolymer chitosan and nonionic sorbitan esters. Langmuir. 2006;22(9):4327-35. doi: 10.1021/la060017g, PMID 16618183.

23. el Fattah EAE, Grant DJW, Gabr KE, Meshali MM. Physical characteristics and release behavior of salbutamol sulfate beads prepared with different ionic polysaccharides. Drug Dev Ind Pharm. 1998;24(6):541-7. doi: 10.3109/03639049809085655, PMID 9876620.

24. Fuchs T, Richtering W, Burchard W. Thermoreversible gelation of a polysaccharide with immunological activity: rheology and dynamic light scattering. Macromol Symp. 1995;99(1):227-38. doi: 10.1002/masy.19950990124.

25. Munzberg J, Rau U, Wagner F, Caarbohydr. Polym. 1995;27(4):271-6.

26. Nagori BP, Mathur NK. Ind J Chem Technol. 1996;3(5):279-81.

27. Kawasaki N, Ohkura R, Miyazaki S, Uno Y, Sugimoto S, Attwood D. Thermally reversible xyloglucan gels as vehicles for oral drug delivery. Int J Pharm. 1999;181(2):227-34. doi: 10.1016/s0378-5173(99)00026-5, PMID 10370218.

28. Rubinstein A, Glikokabir I [STP]. Pharm Sci. Vol. 5(1, 41) – 46; 1995.

EXCERCISE

MULTIPLE CHOICE QUESTIONS

1. What is not true about polymers?
   a. Polymers do not carry any charge
   b. Polymers have high viscosity
   c. Polymers scatter light
   d. Polymers have low molecular weight
2. Which of the following polymer type is not classified on the basis of its application and properties?
   a. Rubbers b. Plastics
   c. Fibres d. Synthetic
3. Which of the following is fully fluorinated polymer?
   a. Neoprene b. PVC
   c. Teflon d. Thiokol
4. Which of the following is a thermosetting polymer?
   a. Polystyrene b. Polyolefins
   c. Nylons d. Phenolic resins
5. Cellulose is a polymer of :
   a. Fructose b. Ribose
   c. Glucose d. Sucrose
6. What is the range of tensile strength, exhibited by fibres?
   a. 300-3,000 b. 4,000-15,000
   c. 20,000-150,000 d. 5,000-10,000
7. Which of the following kind of polymers are known for their high crystallinity?
   a. Isotactic b. Syndiotactic
   c. Atactic d. None of the above
8. Which is a naturally occurring polymer?
   a. Polythene b. PVC
   c. Acetic acid d. Protein
9. Polyethylene is
   a. Random copolymer b. Homopolymer
   c. Alternate copolymer d. Crosslinked copolymer

10. Natural rubber is which type of polymer
    a. Condensation polymer
    b. Addition polymer
    c. Co-ordination polymer
    d. None of these
11. Which of the following polymer has ester linkage?
    a. Nylon-66 b. PVC
    b. Terylene d. SBR
12. Monomers are converted to polymers by-
    a. Hydrolysis of monomers
    b. Condensation reaction between monomers
    c. Protonation of monomers
    d. None of these
13. Which of the following polymer is an example of fibre?
    a. Silk b. Dacron
    c. Nylon–66 d. All of these
14. Which of the following is not a copolymer?
    a. Cellulose b. Buna-S
    c. Protein d. Nucleic acid
15. The starting material for the preparation of styrene is
    a. Ethane b. Ethyne
    c. Ethene d. Vinyl chloride
16. An example of a synthetic polymer is:
    a. Nucleic acid b. Starch
    c. Bakelite d. Protein
17. Monomers used in the production of nylon-66 are
    a. Hexamethylene diamine and ethylene glycol
    b. Adipic acid and ethylene glycol
    c. Adipic acid and hexamethylene diamine
    d. Dimethyl terephthalate and ethylene glycol
18. PVC is used for ___
    a. Manufacture of cosmetics

b. Manufacture of tyres

c. Manufacture of nonstick pans

d. Manufacture of plastic pipes

19. Which of the following is an example of a thermoplastic?

a. PVC b. Bakelite

c. Perspex d. PVA

20. Which of the following is a biodegradable polymer?

a. Cellulose b. Polythene

c. Polyvinyl chloride d. Nylon-6

SHORT ANSWER QUESTIONS

1. What are monomers and polymers? Give suitable examples.
2. What do you mean by copolymer and give two examples?
3. Define the term polymerization.
4. How polymers are are classified on the basis of their structure?
5. Explainthe addition polymerization method.
6. Explain condensation polymerization.
7. Write down the characteristic property of a good plasticizer. Give examples of good plasticizers.
8. What is a biodegradable polymer? Give examples.
9. What are thermosetting and thermoplastic polymers? Give examples for each.
10. What is the significance of molecular weight in the property of polymer?

LONG ANSWER QUESTIONS

1. Write different applications of polymers in drug delivery.
2. Explain Synthetic polymers with their classification.
3. Briefly explain Hydrogels.
4. Explain polymers as rheology modifiers.
5. Write a note on a variety of polymers.
6. Write pharmaceutical applications of polymer.
7. Write biomedical applications of polymer.
8. Explain the viscoelastic properties of the polymer.

9. Write a note on glass transition temperature.
10. Explain different methods of polymerization.

MCQ ANSWERS

1.	(d)	2.	(d)	3.	(c)	4.	(d)
5.	(c)	6.	(c)	7.	(a)	8.	(d)
9.	(b)	10.	(b)	11.	(c)	12.	(b)
13.	(d)	14.	(a)	15.	(b)	16.	(c)
17.	(c)	18.	(d)	19.	(b)	20.	(a)

CHAPTER - 3

Dosage Forms for Personalized Medicine

Dr. Deependra Singh, Dr. Manju Rawat Singh, and Dr. D.K. Tripathi

Introduction, Definition, Classification, Pharmacogenetics, Categories of Patients for Personalised Medicines, Customized Drug Delivery Systems, Bioelectronic Medicines, 3D Printing of Pharmaceuticals, Tele Pharmacy

INTRODUCTION

Many of us wonder why some people develop cancer while others do not and why a medication might work well for one person but be less effective or cause serious side effects in another. Although these differences are due to a number of important factors such as age, weight and lifestyle, our genetic make-up also plays a part. Using information about genetic predisposition to disease is a key part of personalized medicine. Personalized medicine is definitely one of the most exciting topics in medicine today. Personalized medicine (PM) has the potential to tailor therapy for the best response with the highest safety margin to ensure better patient care. By enabling each patient to receive earlier diagnoses, risk assessments, and optimal treatments, PM holds promise for improving health care while also lowering costs.

DEFINITION

Personalized medicine is *the tailoring of medical treatment to the individual characteristics- basically genomic information of each patient.* Personalized medicine is also known as *precision medicine* or individualized medicine.

It does not literally mean the creation of drugs or medical devices that are unique to a patient, but rather the ability to classify individuals into sub populations that differ in their susceptibility to a particular disease or their response to a specific treatment. Preventive or therapeutic interventions can then be concentrated on those who will benefit, sparing expense and side effects for those who will not[1].

The ability to offer-

- ✓ The right drug
- ✓ To the right patient
- ✓ For the right disease

✓ At the right time

✓ With the right dosage form

The goal for personalized medicine must be to move as swiftly as possible toward the identification of individual risk factors, be they environmental or genetic, which play a direct role in disease risk[2].

The new science of personalized medicine is embodied in an approach dubbed P4 medicine by Institute for Systems Biolo and Dr. Hood, because of its four attributes:

- **Personalized:** It is based on an understanding of how genetic variation drives individual treatment.
- **Predictive:** It can identify what conditions a person might contract in the future and how the person will respond to a given treatment, enabling the development of a tailored health strategy.
- **Preventive:** It facilitates a proactive approach to health and medicine, which shifts the focus from illness to wellness.
- **Participatory:** It empowers patients to make informed choices and take responsibility for their own health.

This last attributes of P4 medicine patient empowerment is part of a broader trend toward consumer-focused healthcare, enabled by easy access to health information that was once available only to medical professionals[3].

The paradigm of personalized medicine can be illustrated as follows: This arrow reflects the current and anticipated flow of healthcare services, and changing points of intervention, as medicine becomes more personalized. Early detection testing will continue based on large population risk (e.g., mammograms), while new forms of risk assessment will be incorporated (e.g., determining which women carry the genetic variation that increases their risk for developing cancer). Though true prevention must occur before disease symptoms are present, better risk assessment enables more targeted monitoring (e.g., women with the genetic variation should have more frequent mammograms); followed by symptom-driven diagnosis, in which molecular monitoring could possibly identify disease subtypes that cannot be clinically determined. Such diagnosis may or may not lead to targeted therapy but in either event we may also benefit from improvements in monitoring a patient's response to a particular therapy[4].

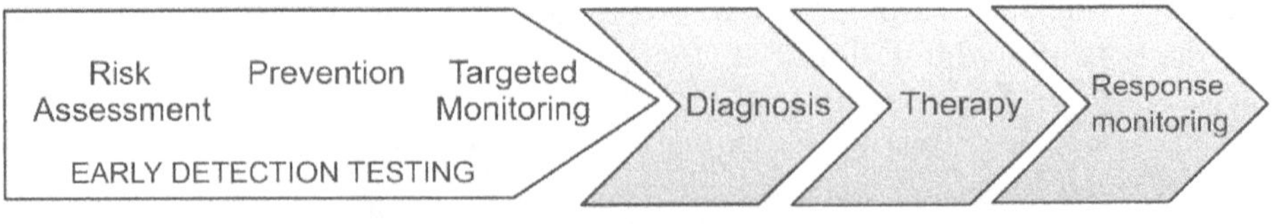

Fig.3.1 Paradigm of personalized medicine.

Benefits of Personalized Medicine

- Detect disease at an earlier stage, when it is easier to treat effectively.
- Enable the selection of optimal therapy and reduce trial-and-error prescribing.
- Reduce adverse drug reactions.
- Increase patient compliance with therapy.
- Improve the selection of targets for drug discovery.
- Reduce the time, cost, and failure rate of clinical trials.
- Revive drugs that failed clinical trials or were withdrawn from the market.
- Avoid withdrawal of marketed drugs.
- Shift the emphasis in medicine from reaction to prevention.
- Reduce the overall cost of healthcare.
- Predict susceptibility to disease, improve disease detection, and preempt disease progression.
- Customize disease prevention strategies.

Personalized Medicine: A Legal and Regulatory Perspective[5, 6]

Following regulatory policies and guidance documents are issued by Food and Drug Administration

Personalised Medicine and Its Challenges

There are various challenges in the field of personalized medicines[7]. Some are as follows:

Insufficient Understanding of Internal Biology of Disease:

This field is not known to all, people are not much aware about the concept of personalized medicine. People thought that Conventional medicines are sufficient for the treatment; another reason is insufficient knowledge about the genetic makeup of person and the biomarkers responsible for the disease.

Limited Infrastructure:

It is main aspect that should be consider during the preparation of personalized medicine, the requirement of accessories or computerized during the gene detection or manipulation need more time as well as money also. Because of this reason also there is lack of information about the gene sequencing or setup of gene. For establishing an infrastructure of any work fund is a most important requiremen

CLASSIFICATION

2005	:	Guidance on PG Data Submissions Concept Paper on Drug-Diagnostic Co-Development.
2007	:	Guidance on Pharmacogenomic Tests and Genetic Tests for Heritable Markers.
2008	:	E15 Definitions for Genomic Biomarkers, Pharmacogenomics, Pharmacogenetics, Genomic Data and Sample Coding Categories
2010	:	Guidance on Qualification Process for Drug Developmen Tools
2011	:	E16 Guidance on Biomarkers Related to Drug or Biotechnology Product Development: Context, Structure and Format of Qualification Submissions.
		Guidance on in vitro Companion Diagnostic Devices.
2012	:	Guidance on Clinical PG: Premarketing Evaluation in Early Phase Clinical Studies.
		Guidance on Clinical Trial Designs Employing Enrichment Designs.
2013	:	Guidance on Clinical Pharmacogenomics: Premarket Evaluation in Early-Phase. Clinical Studies and Recommendations for Labeling.
In Process	:	Guidance on Drug-Diagnostic Co-development.

It acknowledges that the classification system is too outdated and diseases mostly all the diseases comes under same class and based on their sign and symptoms they are classified. Accommodation of emerging information of any disease is not easy in this system therefore, subtype of any disease with different molecular factors is considered as same disease. This outdated classification of disease systems became the barrier for the entry of personalized medicine. National Academy of science called for a new creation called new taxonomy of all disease which will enhance and update the understanding of pathogenesis of disease and also improve the human health. This will also give information about the intrinsic biology as well as the sign and symptoms of any disease.

Accessibility of Personalized Medicine to the Patients:

It is a newer approach towards the diagnosis and treatment of disease and most of the people get benefit when they get diagnosed based on their genetic makeup and also they get treated but still most of the population is unaware about this. Because of this problem all people are not get diagnosed or treated so, the initiative should be reach to all people and increase the awareness about the precision medicine.

Implementation of Newer Diagnostics

Clinically it is difficult for the people as well as physicians to apply new technique when older therapies are already present. It is difficult for them to interpret, identify and order and the overloading of information is also a problem, it makes the adoption difficult during new testing without any decision[7]

PHARMACOGENETICS

Pharmacogenetics describes the science that explores how genetic differences can lead to differences in the way certain medicines interact with the human body. These interactions can affect both the effectiveness of the medication and any side effects[8].

The term **pharmacogenomics**, which often is used interchangeably with pharmacogenetics, refers to the application of genomic technologies to the study of pharmacogenetics.

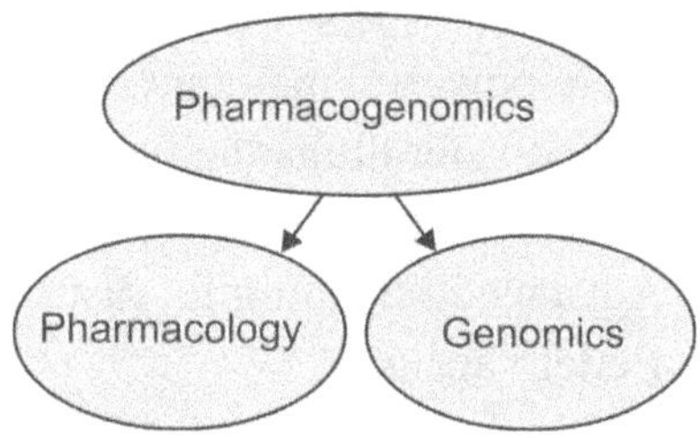

Fig.3.2 Pharmacogenomics.

A patient's response to a drug is often linked to common genetic variations present in their genes. One type of genetic variation is the single nucleotide polymorphisms (SNPs). Knowing the types of SNPs/ genetic variations present in a patient can help predict the associated drug response. This can not only help physicians individualize drug therapy, it will also help improve effectiveness of the drug, decrease the chance of negative side effects and save healthcare costs[8].

Accurate prediction about drug response is crucial for individualized treatment. This is best made by combining an individual's genetic data with clinical findings and classifying individuals into subpopulations that differ in their response to a specific drug[9]. Using this approach, health care providers may be better equipped to move beyond the "one-size-fits-all" treatment strategy that defined much of patient care in the past, to care that is appropriate for unique patient subgroups.

Applying pharmacogenetics ensures patients are prescribed the most effective drug or optimal dosage from the beginning of treatment. Pharmacogenetics can be used to minimise the likelihood of an adverse reaction to a medicine[9]. For example, the drug Abacavir is approved in Australia for the treatment of patients with HIV. However, approximately 5% of patients suffer a potentially fatal hypersensitive reaction to this medication. Research has found that with a particular variation of a gene people with a gene called HLA-B are more likely to develop a reaction to Abacavir. Clinicians are advised to consider testing patients for the presence of this gene variant before they prescribe Abacavir[10].

Pharmacogenetics eventually can lead to an overall decrease in the cost of health care because of decreases in:

1) The number of adverse drug reactions;

2) The number of failed drug trials;
3) The time it takes to get a drug approved;
4) The length of time patients is on medication;
5) The number of medications patients must take to find an effective therapy;
6) The effects of a disease on the body (through early detection).

Benefits of Pharmacogenetics

Pharmacogenetics combines traditional pharmaceutical sciences such as biochemistry with annotated knowledge of genes, proteins, and single nucleotide polymorphisms. Following are the benefits

1) More powerful medicines
2) Better, safer drugs the first time
3) More accurate methods of determining appropriate drug dosages.
4) Advanced screening for disease
5) Better vaccines
6) Improvements in the drug discovery and approval process
7) Decrease in the overall cost of health care.

Pharmacogenetics in future

New developments in this field will impact on drug design at three main levels:

- The interaction of the drug with its receptor binding site
- The absorption and distribution of the drug
- The elimination of the drug from the body

Barriers to progress of Pharmacogenetics

Pharmacogenetics is a developing research field that is still in its infancy. Several of the following barriers will have to be overcome before many pharmacogenomics benefits can be realized. They are the followings.

- Complexity of finding gene variations that affect drug response.
- Limited drug alternatives
- Disincentives for drug companies to make multiple pharmacogenomic products.

Impact on Pharmacy Profession

Presently doctors diagnose and prescribe a drug on the trial and error basis and pharmacist advices about side effects and drug-drug interaction. But a day will come when you will take a gene report instead of blood reports. Thus after the diagnosis, pharmacist would interpret the panels of genetic results and advice you which drug would be best for your particular gene so that you have fast recovery[11].

CATEGORIES OF PATIENTS FOR PERSONALISED MEDICINES

This is acknowledged that the classification system is very old and the diseases mostly all the diseases comes under the same class and based on their sign and symptoms they are classified. Accommodation of emerging information of any disease is not easy in this system therefore, subtype of any disease with different molecular factors is considered as same disease. This outdated classification of disease systems became the barrier for the entry of personalized medicine. National Academy of science called for a new creation called new taxonomy of all disease which will enhance and update the understanding of pathogenesis of disease and also improve the human health. This will also give information about the intrinsic biology as well as the sign and symptoms of any disease[12].

Accessibility of Personalized Medicine to the Patients

It is a newer approach towards the diagnosis and treatment of disease and most of the people get benefit when they get diagnosed based on their genetic makeup and also they get treated but still most of the population is unaware about this. Because of this problem all people are not get diagnosed or treated so, the initiative should be reach to all people and increase the awareness about the precision medicine. The patients can be categorized based on the categories of diseases.

Table 3.1 Categories of diseases.

Name of the disease	Name of the disease	Name of the disease
Non-small cell lung cancer	Melanoma	Gaucher disease type I
Ovarian cancer	Schizophrenia	Hepatitis C
Mucopolysaccharidosis	Colorectal cancer	Acute lymphoblastic lymphoma
T- cell lymphoma	Hypercholesterolemia	Asthma
Cystic fibrosis	Breast cancer	Renal Carcinoma
Rheumatoid Arthritis		

Personalized medicine for lung cancer

The systemic treatment for lung cancer is very limited, the targeted treatment of the disease is common today and cancer, rheumatoid arthritis, many more drugs and synthesis as well as approved like monoclonal antibody (mAbs) and tyrosine kinase inhibitors (TKIs). These are active against epidermal growth factor receptor (EGRF) and got response more than 70%[13]. According to the studies, it has been observed that targeted drugs worsen the condition more than the cytotoxic drugs and these drugs are more costly than conventional drugs[14]. Non-small cell lung cancer (NSCLS) causes more number of cancers and these cells are having the properties of developing uncontrolled cell growth. An approach towards personalized medicine for cancer management is positron emission tomography (PET) and radioactive labeled drugs. Concentration of metabolite and pharmacokinetics was determined by regular determination of blood sample urine etc[15]. The PET is a type of imaging technique used as a personalized medicine by utilizing gamma rays which produces 3 dimensional (3D) images[16]. The PET is having an advantage of targeting the diseased site by using radio labeled drugs. These drugs will further help in developing targeted drugs for the treatment as a personalized medicine. The pharmacokinetics (PK) of targeted drugs was studied and new medicine can be made and also binding of radio labeled drug with tumour can also be predicted. Immuno-PET is a type imaging system that is mostly used as an antigen therapy. The mAbs had been investigated as an agent in Immuno-PET and mAbs are labelled with radio-nucleoids for example ^{89}Zr[17]. Because of slow PK, dynamic scanning was not possible in case of radio labelled mAbs. Static image utilizes the tumor-to-blood, standardized uptake value (SUV) and tumour-to- reference tissue ratios. After the binding of mAbs, target cell internalize the mAbs.

Personalized medicine for renal carcinoma

There are two types of renal carcinoma one is renal pelvis carcinoma and other is renal cell carcinoma. Thousands of people are diagnosed with malignant tumour every year and the most common is nephroblastoma. This is also called Wilm's tumour (WT). The common symptoms are abdomen pain and swelling and it mostly occurs in children. Children oncology group (COG) identified the biomarker that is responsible for nephroblastoma. Doxorubicin (DOX) with Vincristine (VCR) and Actinomycin-D (ACT-D) was given to the stage I, and II patients but there was no significant effect[18]. In preclinical testing this has been observed that after targeting the Insulin growth factor (IGF) pathway by IMC-A12 (monoclonal antibody), the cell cycle was arrested as well as the size of tumour was reduced. It showed good antitumor activity and it has been found effective for rhabdomysarcoma patient also[18]. For early detection of tumour a combine therapy (drug and antibody) was used. An example of this combination system is lorvotuzumabmertansine, conjugation of cytotoxic and mAbs to CD-56 which shows good antitumor activity against WT xenografts[19]. There is 50-70% patients suffering from clear cell renal cell carcinoma (ccRCC). The pathophysiology of treatment is to target the Von hipplelindau (VHL) and inactivation of components present in signalling pathway. The VHL is a biomarker that is responsible for renal carcinoma and other markers are carbonic anhydrase and VEGF. The recently developed personalized medicines are bevacizumab for bevicizumab, axitinib, sorafinib, and temsirolimus[20, 21]. Now some people became resistant to these medicines and sunitinib is the commonly used first line drug for treatment. So, for overcoming to this problem and also for enhancing the efficacy of RCC therapy drugs should be combined with antiangiogenic agent[22].

Personalized Medicine for rheumatoid arthritis

The main aim of this study was to identify the biomarkers which can predict the outcomes of therapy in rheumatoid arthritis patient who get treated by TNF-α blocker that is, etanercept. The 19 RA (Rheumatoid arthritis) patients were selected and out of those, 7 patients are non-responders and 12 patients were responders and changes in pre-existing genes were monitored. The Affymetrix microarray generated a result, which was compared with post treatment analysed data. After 72 hours of treatment, gene expression got changed and showed good (DAS) disease activity score – about 28 >1.2. Some patients developed Interferon (IFN), which showed worse response to the treatment. Therefore, it had been concluded that early prediction of RA response is possible when TNF-α blocker is administered based on their gene expression and better medication can be given according to their gene setup[23].

The effect of combination of drug methotrexate and infliximab has been studied and the response was observed after three months. 13 patients and gene profiling were done, by using mononuclear cells of peripheral blood. Out of those selected patients, 7 patients are non-responder, and 6 patients are responder to the treatment. There is a hybridization of baseline RNAs and transcription of mRNA. Difference in transcription level was compared with response and down regulation was observed in non-responders. There are 279 genes which are expressed differently in case of respondents and non-respondents[24].

CUSTOMIZED DRUG DELIVERY SYSTEMS

The medical practitioners or physicians note the genetic history of the patient or individual as per the rules of the personalized medicine (PM) or precision medicine. Along with the genetic history the physicians note living environment, and lifestyle of the patients which are considered when prescribing medicines. As a result, the individual patient suffering from various diseases to different extents can be prescribed appropriate medicines and duration of release of respective or suitable drug. In fact, once a patient is diagnosed with certain conditions, a specific method of treatment is chosen. This can be can be done by fabricating a personalised tablet for the patient. Personalization means a customized dosage and duration of drug release that can be served as per the need of the patient. Moreover, there are many patients who require multiple different tablets together and at different times in a day to meet specific requirements. This is a task that can appear as challenging to some patients such as elderly or disabled. Conceptually, the medical practitioner is allowed to prescribe personalized medicine in the form of a single medication that may consist multiple drugs depending on the patient's requirement with a suitable dosage and release profile. In this way, the combination of drugs in a single tablet needs to be taken only once, instead of taking multiple pills together and at different times in a day[25]. For effective method of personalized medicine, the tablet should be easily fabricated, customizable, and highly affordable – these characteristics would encourage widespread usage of the customized tablets and allow the drug to be fabricated in the form of tablet on the spot after diagnosis. Customization of materials such as via small-scale fabrication is challenging, tedious, and may be costly. On the other hand, 3D printing technology can be a potential method for overcoming the challenges of small-scale fabrication – it allows the tablets to be fabricated easily and quickly at a lower cost[26-29]. In this way, the dosage form and duration of release of drug from the tablet can be customized for each individual patient. This allows incorporation of multiple drugs of different doses in a single tablet, this property may be desired for patients who face multiple distinct medical conditions and require taking multiple pills in a day. Previously studies have reported that different 3D printing methods for fabrication of drug tablets have been used. With these methods usually, a variety of problems are faced. 3D printing of drug tablets are frequently designed to make use of different structures that are responsible for the drug release profile, dosage form, combination of drugs, and shape of tablet, for example, for allowing the tablets to be easily swallowed. However, the fabrication of these structures is generally complex, intricate, imprecise, delicate, and/or nonintuitive[29-36] and tablets with weak mechanical properties are produced[37]. Moreover, 3D printing of the tablets is usually challenging. Most probably, the most important and common problem is the fabrication of very viscous formulation of tablets. Therefore, it is extremely difficult to print the tablets with the help of small nozzles of the printers. These small nozzles tend to clog and inconsistences in printing result, this may affect the shape, drug dosage and release profile of the tablet. Moreover, there may be other disadvantages of using the printer having clogging problems such as limited numbers of materials can be selected for printing[38] and some 3D printing technologies require heating that may degrade the drug[39]. Thus, optimization of the printing process must be done on a case-by-case basis for each combination of drug and excipient, the process of optimization is generally time-consuming. The problems associated with 3D printing of tablets can be solved by a novel method that allows fabrication of fully customizable tablets via 3D printed templates in place of printing the tablets directly using the 3D printers[40, 41]. Thus, the tablet prepared by this method becomes customized in terms of dosage form, duration of release, release profiles, and combination of multiple drugs in a single tablet. The method depends on simple structures, both interior and exterior of the drug. The physically simple structure of the tablets facilitates the precise fabrication of the tablets with precise customization. The method is safe and inexpensive.

Previous studies indicate that only preliminary results for illustrating the proof of concept of the technology. They did not establish the technology for specifically important release profiles and commonly used excipients in pharmaceutical science. FDA approved the tablet prepared with commonly used excipients and ready-made functional polymers such as Eudragit[42]. Eudragit is also available as aqueous dispersion, granules, organic solutions, or ready-to-use powders[43]. Depending on the usage, Eudragit polymers is available as extremely insoluble powder to serve as the insoluble polymer matrix that can be used for erosion of bulk[44] or for surface erosion[45]. Eudragit polymers are highly useful and can be used to control the active site, solubility, and release profile[46]. The constant release profile allows the therapeutic effect of the drug to be the most effective while not causing any side effects[47].

BIOELECTRONIC MEDICINES

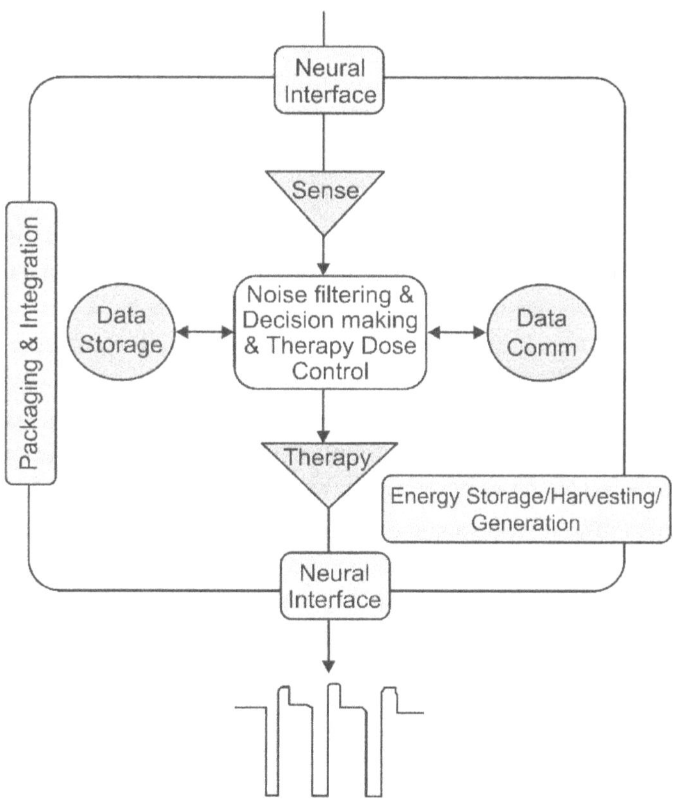

Fig.3.3 Schematic diagram of implantable neuromodulation device.

Bioelectronic medicines (BEM) are defined as a new class of treatment. This depends on the precision, detection, and modulation of electrical signalling patterns in the nervous system. The functions controlled by peripheral nervous system are extensive during chronic diseases, more targeted modulation is achieved. Small implantable devices are linked to the nerves of an individual in the viscera of peripheral nervous system. These are able to decode and regulate neutral signalling patterns and accomplishing therapeutic effects targeted at specific organs[48]. To upgrade the precision these devices, record neural electrical activity, physiological parameters and analyse the results in real time and modulated neural signal accordingly. With the developing research from laboratory, industry and government have explored bioelectronic medicines. For emergency the development of BEM technology roadmap serves as a planning tool which collects the meaningful information related to neurotechnology based diagnosis and treatment of disease at a quickened rate along with the gaps that needs greater consideration. This roadmap is proposed to give best evaluation of current abilities, projections of innovation requirements, research priorities to support industries and institutes on important coordinated effort to accomplish the expected advantages.

Goals of Bioelectronic Medicines: Following are the goals which are required to be achieved in bioelectronic medicine therapy:

1) Identification of targeted diseases is considered as good candidate for Bioelectronic medicine.
2) For better understanding of mechanism, there is requirement of investigative devices which would integrate to realize the remaining gaps in the therapy.
3) There is a requirement for coordinated efforts between biologic/medical//computing disciplines.
4) Relative to normal state, there must be such biological, chemical, electrical and mechanical modelswhich could help in realizing the proper and complete system of the body's behavior when it is in diseased state[50].
5) Bioelectronic medicinesare the devices which are implanted anywhere in the viscera and record the neural activity. This information is then decoded and analysed. However, there are three principal areas of research.
6) Making of a natural nerve chart is essential because this emphases on mapping the innervation of visceral organs such as lungs, heart, liver, kidney, bladder, gastrointestinal tract, and lymphoid and reproductive organs with the objective of achieving resolution at the level of nerve fibers and action potentials.

7) Neural interfacing technology helps in mapping neural signals which includes methods such as ultrasonic and tomography techniques for recording and modulation.
8) Characterizing the signaling pattern and focusing the drift on confirmation of rule. This implies describing the neural circuit that uses impact on the disease in representative animal model[50, 51].

After that the experimental phase is sought after including the development of the correlation of neural signals and biomarkers patterns. This also investigates the effect of blocking and stimulates neural activity during established disease. Finally, this new research describes the aims for developing community and the whole system of a closed loop BEM microsystem has been shown in the figure:

The device processes the bio signals which are obtained from the implantable electrode through neural interface that either stimulates or blocks the nerve activity. After processing the data is stored in the device. While designing the device five areas which are required to be considered are:

1. ***Sensitivity***: to sense and decode the signals from neurons
2. ***Selectivity***: able to target the main nucleic by avoiding off target neurons.
3. ***Responsiveness***: capable of detecting biomarkers.
4. ***Acceptance***: must be accepted by patients with minimum invasive implantation.
5. ***Closing the loop***: should form a closed loop system to achieve the targeted function.

BEM platform can be characterized as a blend of electronic equipment, segments and calculations combined in a manner that explains the system's basic operational attributes.

BEM microsystem is composed of:

1) Energy
2) Analog blocks
3) Communication unit
4) Logic unit
5) Non-volatile memory
6) Packaging enclosure/ encapsulation

1) ***Energy source***: One of the major problems is to keep the implants powered to sustain a long stimulation time. To meet the energy requirement caseless micro batteries have been suggested as a solution which consisted of two electrodes immersed in fluids like blood, serum etc. With regards to BEM system, energy harvesting alludes to gathering of energy from external

source and converting it into power. So, these external sources can be in the form of radiation (light, RF), mechanical energy, (ultrasound, vibrations) or thermal energy. Some other hidden sources of energy present in the body. This considers some research areas:

- Fuel cells
- Temperature gradients
- Electric potential in inner ear from cochlea
- Muscle/organ movement

2) ***Logic/Analog Mixed signal circuits***: The system intelligence is usually determined by its capability to validate the decisions regarding actuation using combination of mixed signals, logic and memory elements which should be maximized to reduce the latency.

3) ***Non-volatile Memory***: The most important attributes of a BEM memory unit are reliability and its long lifetime. At present Ferro electric random-access memory technology has huge potential for applications in implantable therapeutic gadgets as it empowers rapid, low power and virtually unlimited. Some other technologies are:

   i) Magnetic (MRAM),
   ii) Phase changing (PCRAM), and
   iii) Resistive (RRAM) memory technologies

4) ***Communication***: An important function of BEM is continuous communication with external monitoring, so mostly ultrasound is operated as RF communication becomes inefficient in small systems. Ultrasound communication in comparison to RF communication undergoes small propagation losses, that is, it is being used for battery-less communication.

5) ***Electronic packaging***: Generally small, packaged device is preferred as it will cause less difficulty during implantation[52-55].

3D PRINTING OF PHARMACEUTICALS

Three-dimensional (3D) printing technologieshave been gaining immense interest both in academic and industrial sector. Areas such as aerospace, engineering, FMCG, architecture, military, fashion industry, chemical industry, and medical field are almost untouched by this technology[56]. 3D printing has a wide range of applications such as tissue design, printing of organ, diagnostics, manufacture of biomedical devices, and design of the drug and delivery systems in the medical field[57]. From the data generated by various techniques like computed tomography (CT) scan and magnetic resonance imaging (MRI), complex anatomical and medical structures according to the need of patient can be fabricated[58].

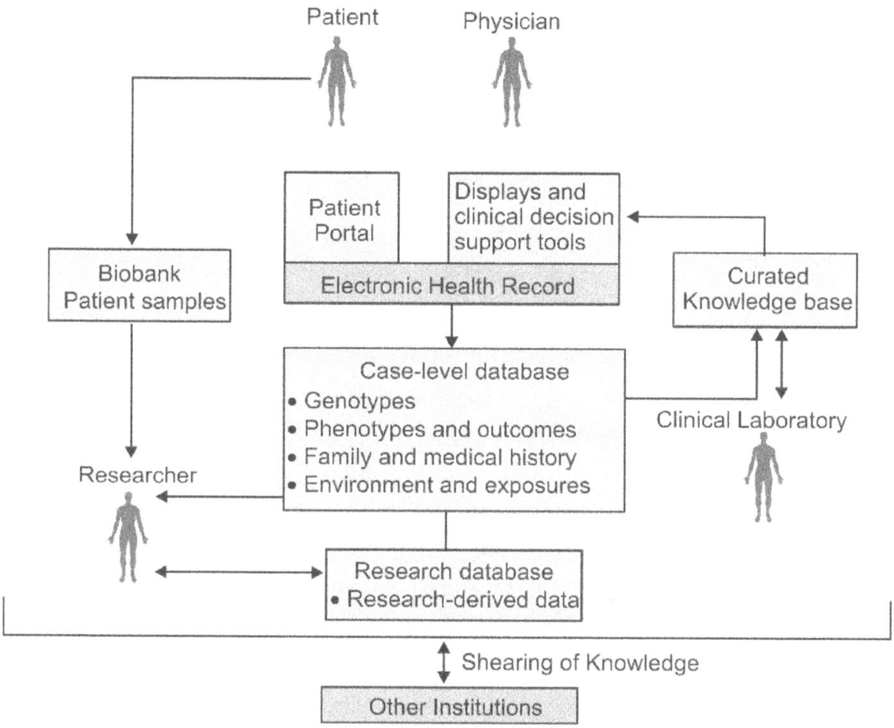

Fig.3.4 Schematic diagram of development of bioelectronic medicine.

Some additional uses of this technology are replacing and repairing the defective organs such as kidney, heart etc. or all together creating a new organ those canperform the same functions as that of original [59]. This technology is so common and widely used that its applications include the things that are very necessary for human life like clothing, eyeglasses, jewellery, parts of cars, and drugs that can be printed in almost any geometry and shape as per the requirement of the user[60]. In this technology a concept is transformed into its copy by taking help of 3D computer-aided design (CAD) files. Hence, digitally controlled and customized product can be produced[61]. This technology uses a bottom-up approach in which the layers of materials like living cells, wood, alloy, thermoplastic, metals etc. are placed on top of each other to make the required 3D object[62]. Therefore, 3D printing is also known by other terminologies such as layered manufacturing, additive manufacturing, computer automated manufacturing, rapid prototyping, or solid freeform technology (SFF)[63]. In subtractive methodology or conventional methodology, the product is designed from the bulk substance. The non-advanced tools used are non-standard geometries and objects made from many materials cannot be made with high quality[64]. In contrast to the conventional method, 3DP technology is more automated, rapid and easy to use, customized and sophisticated and cost-effective[65].

3D printing procedure

The following procedure is followed for 3D printing unless otherwise is mentioned there in.

- Using digital design software like on shape, Solid works, Creo parametric, AutoCAD, Autodesk etc. a virtual 3D design of an object is created [66].
- Then this digital model is to be converted to (.STL) digital file format which stands for standard tessallation language or stereolithography [66].
- Triangulated facets give information regarding the surface of the 3D model that remains present in the (.STL) file[66].
- The (.STL) file is converted into G file by slicing the design into a series of 2D horizontal cross-sections by the help of specialized slicer software, which is installed in the 3D print.
- The print head is moved in the x-y axis to create the base of the 3D object.
- The print head is then allowed to move in the z-axis, thereby depositing the layers sequentially of the desired material, hence creating a complete 3D object [66].

Maximum numbers of 3D printing technologies are compatible with (.STL) file format. Some errors might occur during the conversion of the 3D model to. STL digital file; however, software like Magics (Materialise) can be used to correct the errors during conversion. File formats other than. STL like additive manufacturing file format (AMF) and 3D manufacturing format (3MF) when used as. STL does not have information regarding the type of material, its colour, texture, properties, and other features[67].

Types of 3D printing technology

➢ **Fused deposition modeling (FDM)**

The process involves the selection of the desired polymer, which is melted and forced through a movable heated nozzle. Along the entire 3 axis (i.e., x-y-z), the polymer is laid down as layer-by- layer, which on solidification gives the exact shape as was designed by computer aided design models. Multiple dosage forms like implants, zero-order release tablets etc. that include polymer as a part of their formulation can be made by this method 68.

Table 3.2 Major Developments in 3D printing Technology.

Year	Major development
1980	Dr. Hideo Kodama filed first patent for RP technology
1984	Stereo lithography apparatus (SLA) was invented by Charles Hull
1986	Carl Deckard invented apparatus for producing parts by selective sintering
1989	Patent was granted to Carl Deckard for SLA
1990	Fused deposition modelling (FDM)
1992	First SLA machine was produced using 3D system
1993	3D printing patent was granted to E.M Sachs
1996	Clinical application of biomaterials for tissue regeneration
1999	Luke Massella received first 3D printed bladder which was an amalgamation of 3D printed biomaterials and his own cells
2000	MCP technologies introduced the SLM technology
2002	Miniature functional kidney was fabricated
2003	Term organ printing was coined
2004	Dr. Bowyer conceived the RepRap concept of an open-source, self-replicating 3D printer
2005	First color 3D printer was introduced by Z Corp
2007	Selective layer customization and on-demand manufacturing of industrial parts
2009	Organovo, Inc., announced the release of data on the first fully bioprinted blood vessels
2011	3D printing was applied in gold and silver World's first 3D printed car, robotic air-carft was introduced
2012	Extrusion-based bioprinting for an artificial liver 3D printed prosthetic jaw was implanted
2013	Solid Concepts produced a 3D printed metal gun
2014	Implementation of multi-arm bioprinter to integrate tissue fabrication with printed vasculature
2015	First 3D printed pill was approved by US FDA Organovo announced the release of data on the first fully bioprinted kidney

Table 3.2 ***contd...***

➢ Thermal inkjet (TIJ) printing

It involves the heating of fluidinkwith the help of micro-resistor, thereby creating a bubble of vapor that concentrates near the nozzle and due tothe forces of expansion the ink comes out of the nozzle drop by drop. Dispensing of extemporaneous preparation/solution of drug onto 3D scaffolds is an area where this technique can be used[68].

➢ **Inkjet printing**

It is a powder-based 3D printing method utilizing the powder as a substrate on which layer by layer different combinations of active ingredients and ink of varying droplet size is sprayed which is eventually solidifies into solid dosage form [68].

➢ **Direct-wise**

It surrounds a pattern that is generated by the device and moves according to the guidance of computer-controlled translational stage so that these are put on layers after layers to create a 3D microstructure [68].

➢ **Zip dose**

This technology gives a personalized dose in addition to the delivery of a high drug-load with high disintegration and dissolution levels by manufacturing highly porous material [68].

➢ **Vat photopolymerization**

It is a light-induced polymerization process where materials such as photopolymers, radiation curable resins, and liquid are collected in vats. Whichare then put onfor successivecuring into layers. One layer is deposited at a time by irradiating with a light source, thereby providing a 2D patterned layer. This involves techniques such as stereolithography (SLA), digital light processing (DLP), and continuous direct light processing (CDLP).

Depending on the orientation of light source and the surface where polymerization of the photoactive resin occurs, Smooth Love Potion Price (SLA) can be divided into two different configurations:

1. Bath configuration (free surface approach)
2. Bat configuration (constrained surface approach) [68].

Advantages of 3D printing in the pharmaceutical field[69, 70]:

1. **Enhanced productivity:** In contrast to traditional methods\3D printing works more quickly especially when it comes for fabrication of items like prosthetics and implants with an additional benefit of better resolution, repeatability, more accuracy, and reliability.
2. **Customization and personalization:** One of the pioneer benefits of this technology is the liberty of fabrication of customized medical equipment and products. Customized implants, prosthetics, surgical tools, fixtures can be a great boon to patients as well as physicians.

3. **Increased cost efficiency:** Products produced by 3D printing are of low cost. It is an advantage for small-scale production units or for companies that produce highly complex products or parts because almost all ingredients are inexpensive. By eradicating the use of unnecessary resources, manufacturing cost can also be reduced. For example, 20-mg tablets could be potentially formulated as 1-mg tablets as per the need.
4. 3D printing allows controlled size of droplets, complex drug release profiles, strength of dosage form and multi-dosing.

Disadvantages of 3D Printing[69, 70]:

1. In inkjet printing, proper flow of ink can only be achieved with ink that has precise viscosity.
2. Ink formulation material should have the property of self-binding but should not bind to other printer elements.
3. In some formulations when the ink does not possess adequate self-binding property, or it binds with other elements of printer then the resultant formulation does not have required hardness.
4. Rate of drug release may get affected due to binding of ink with other printer materials.

TELE PHARMACY

The U.S.and Australia has the largest experience in reducing the shortage in health services. Pharmacies have utmost importance in the health care system and offer various health services. Pharmacists have important role in the patient counselling and also in the pharmacovigilance services. Telepharmacy can be described as *providing pharmaceutical care to the patients by pharmacist via telecommunication wherever pharmacist may not have direct contact with patients.*

In telepharmacy services pharmacist may not physically present at the location of patient or at the pharmacy. Telepharmacy services supply the medicines and clinical services to the patients at a remote area without any pharmacist physically present at that location. The telepharmacy is very crucial in reducing the possibility of adverse drug events, reducing medication cost and risk of treatment failure. Telepharmacy initially established at a hospital level by virtue of pharmaceutical care provision through telephone. In 2001, telepharmacy was 1st officially evaluated in the United States, when North Dakota had become the 1st state to evaluate its use by conducting a study having 81 pharmacies, carried out at North Dakota State University. Telepharmacy services are available in United States (U.S.), Canada, Italy, Germany, Scotland, France, Denmark, Spain and Egypt. Nowadays, there is scarcity of health professionals. Information and Communication Technologies (ICTs) applied to the health sector to face the problem of shortage of health professionals. Telepharmacy plays a vital role in addressing this issue. Many patients from the remote and rural area have difficulties in accessing pharmacy services. Small pharmacies in rural areas, nursing homes, hospitals, medical offices, prisons, military bases, ships, etc. are the areas where telepharmacy services are mainly applicable. Endorser of the practice of telepharmacy believe that it is the most favourable way to provide patient care to rural and other medically underserved areas across the country. Telepharmacy is a new opportunity for pharmacists to sprout and ally with technology to benefit patients. It endorses pharmacists to expand their role and access more people than ever[71].

Types of Telepharmacy

1. **Inpatient / remote order-entry review**

   In the inpatient telepharmacy, a pharmacist presents at a remote location and performs remote order-entry services for an inpatient pharmacy at a hospital. Pharmacist at remote location reviews medication orders prior to the hospital staff gives medication to the patient. Inpatient telepharmacy is beneficial for the hospitals, clinics, and health systems as it enables real-time mediation order examination and monitoring. In this inpatient telepharmacy pharmacist can provide 24/7 service.

2. **Remote dispensing (retail/ outpatient/ discharge)**

   It is also called as retail community telepharmacy. It is licensed, physical retailer pharmacy having certified pharmacy technician. A pharmacist advises and monitors the technician, analyses prescription and carries out his or her responsibilities from a remote location through video conferencing or telecommunication. Many rural patients have difficulties in accessing pharmacy services due to geographic location. This remote dispensing telepharmacy gives convenient accessibility to these patients. These remote dispensing provides an opportunity to healthcare organizations to start retail telepharmacy sites in the areas where traditional pharmacy may not be possible. It also helps in improving the economic performance and patient adherence.

3. **IV admixture**

   IV admixture is outlined by The Joint Commission on Accreditation of Healthcare Organizations (JCAHO) as, "the preparation of pharmaceutical product which needs the measured addition of a drug to a 50ml or larger bag or bottle of intravenous fluid." By implementing the telepharmacy in IV admixture cleanroom, hospital pharmacies may consume less time and can also save money. If the IV admixture is reviewed by a pharmacist remotely, they can save the time required to kit up and to get inside the cleanroom for reviewing the solution. By saving the pharmacist's time make them able to concentrate on clinical activities and other earning tasks.

4. **Remote counselling**

   Pharmacist furnishes counselling to the patients through secure, live and interactive video calls or / through telecommunications. Remote patient counselling gives potential for discharge counselling, speciality counselling, etc[72].

Telepharmacy system and services

Telepharmacy systems are based on

1) The appointment of pharmacists in the centre from where the whole system is handled, and
2) The engagement of pharmacy technicians.

Pharmacists are the member of health care team with the most adequate knowledge of drug therapy. Telepharmacy may not be operated without a pharmacy technician onduty. Technician play an important role to drive both inpatient and outpatient services. Technician must have proper qualification and sufficient practice to perform the activity. It is necessary to be up-to-date with the prevalent communication devices by which the connection is recognized with the centre for system management where the pharmacist is situated. The main role of pharmacist in a central location is to provide consulting services for all medicines which are dispensed at remote location.

To facilitate telepharmacy services suitable telecommunication equipment are necessary. This equipment includes:

1. Computer, i.e., PC with specialized software
2. Video equipment
3. Some transmission systems (e.g. Digital Subscriber Line (DSL), Modem, Leased E1 links, Internet connection, Mobile connections.)
4. Spare telepharmacy equipment.

Telepharmacy services include drug review and monitoring, compounding verification, dispensing, medication therapy management, counselling, patient assessment, drug information and clinical consultation[73].

Working of Telepharmacy

Usually, a smaller hospital, clinic or pharmacy is linked to a ordinary service model in larger urban centre which have better availability to pharmacist staff (usually 24 hours). This connection is achieved by automated dispensing machine. The rural site is generally furnished with nurses or pharmacy technicians, depending on the site. They may exchange the prescriptions (e.g.

fax) from patients to the central site, which is handled by a qualified pharmacist. The pharmacist reviews all the medication orders under the telepharmacy model for the hospital's inpatient population. When a physician writes a medication orders, then the older is scanned and saved in .pdf format on the hospital's secure network via Internet, using an impregnable Virtual Private Network (VPN) connection, to analyse the order and collate it with the computerized patient profile. The pharmacist attempts all appropriate insinuation with respect to the orders, including defining unclear or illegal orders, making suggestions for compliance with the hospital formulary, checking for the drug interactions, providing medication warningsfor nurses, suggesting automatic therapeutic interchanges and ensuring that no restricted abbreviations are used. The pharmacist then introduces each order into the pharmacy's computer system and the medication labels are printed automatically in the hospital's pharmacy department. Then the central pharmacist delivers the appropriate items at the rural site and label[74]. The pharmacy technician or nurse present at remote or rural area scans the barcode to check whether the prescription matches with its label or not, then assigns the label and delivers it to the patient. The central pharmacist can observe the technician's work to make sure that the correct medications have been filled and dispensed correctly. Then at the end, the central pharmacist comes up with a two-way video discussion for the patient to make sure that they properly understand the intended medication use and administration[75].

Advantages:

1. Access to healthcare system
2. Patient satisfaction
3. Minimal Shortage of Pharmacists
4. Economic benefits
5. Effective patient counselling

Disadvantages:

1. Practical challenges
2. Pharmacy regulation laws
3. Security
4. Plenty of time,
5. Effort and money
6. Inability to use technology.

REFERENCES

1. President's Council of Advisors on Science and Technology, Subcommittee on Personalized Medicine, Priorities for Personalized Medicine: Report [Internet]. Report; 2008 Sept [cited 2014 Dec 26]. Available from: http://www.whitehouse.gov/files/documents/ostp/PCAST/pcast_report_v2.pdf

2. Francis C. The language of life. Vol. 163.
3. Leroy H, Mauricio F. A personal view on systems medicine and the emergence of proactive P4 medicine: predictive, preventive, personalized and participatory. Elsevier; 2012. p. 1-12.
4. Personalized Medicine 101: the story [internet]; 2015. Personalized Medicine Coalition [cited Dec. 22, 2014]. Available from: http://personalizedmedicinecoalition.org/Resources/Personalized_Medicine_101_The_Story.
5. The case for personalized medicine; November 2006.
6. Genetics and your health: the Jackson Laboratory, personalized medicine and you: benefits of personalized medicine [internet]. The Jackson Laboratory; 2014 [cited Dec 22 2014]. Available from: http://genetichealth.jax.org/personalized-medicine/what-is/benefits.html.
7. Available form: http://www.fda.gov/downloads/ScienceResearch/SpecialTopics/PersonalizedMedicine/UCM372421.
8. Meyer UA. Pharmacogenetics - Five decades of therapeutic lessons from genetic diversity. Nat Rev Genet. 2004;5(9):669-76. doi: 10.1038/nrg1428, PMID 15372089.
9. Ma Q, Lu AY. Pharmacogenetics, pharmaco-genomics, and individualized medicine. Pharmacol Rev. 2011;63(2):437-59. doi: 10.1124/pr.110.003533, PMID 21436344.
10. Mallal S, Phillips E, Carosi G, Molina JM, Workman C, Tomazic J et al. HLA-b*5701 screening for hypersensitivity to abacavir. N Engl J Med. 2008;358(6):568-79. doi: 10.1056/NEJMoa0706135, PMID 18256392.
11. Magdum CS, Velingkar VS, Gupta MK. Pharmacogenomics: the search for the Individualized Therapy. Indian J Pharm Educ Res. April-June 2006, page no:84-91;40(2).
12. Torre LA, Siegel RL, Ward EM, Jemal A. Global cancer incidence and mortality rates and trends—an update. Cancer Epidemiol Biomarkers Prev. 2016;25(1):16-27. doi: 10.1158/1055-9965.EPI-15-0578, PMID 26667886.
13. Gazdar AF. Personalized medicine and inhibition of EGFR signaling in lung cancer. N Engl J Med. 2009;361(10):1018-20. doi: 10.1056/NEJMe0905763, PMID 19692681.
14. Rocco G., Morabito A., Leone A., Muto P., Fiore F., Budillon A. Management of non-small cell lung cancer in the era of personalized medicine. Int J Biochem Cell Biol. 2016;78:173–179.
15. Roberts PJ, Stinchcombe TE, Der CJ, Socinski MA. Personalized medicine in non–small-cell lung cancer: is KRAS a useful marker in selecting patients for epidermal growth factor receptor–targeted therapy? J Clin Oncol. 2010;28(31):4769-77. doi: 10.1200/JCO.2009.27.4365, PMID 20921461.

epidermal growth factor receptor–targeted therapy? J Clin Oncol. 2010;28(31):4769-77. doi: 10.1200/JCO.2009.27.4365, PMID 20921461.

16. Zegers CM, van Elmpt W, Szardenings K, Kolb H, Waxman A, Subramaniam RM, et al. Repeatability of hypoxia PET imaging using [(1) (8)F]HX4 in lung and head and neck cancer patients: a prospective multicenter trial. Eur J Nucl Med Mol Imaging. 2015;42(12):1840-9. doi: 10.1007/s00259-015-3100-z, PMID 26136164.
17. Mitsudomi T, Morita S, Yatabe Y, Negoro S, Okamoto I, Tsurutani J, et al. Gefitinib versus cisplatin plus docetaxel in patients with non-small-cell lung cancer harbouring mutations of the epidermal growth factor receptor (WJTOG3405): an open label, randomised phase 3 trial. Lancet Oncol. 2010;11(2):121-8. doi: 10.1016/S1470-2045(09)70364-X, PMID 20022809.
18. Hsieh JJ, Purdue MP, Signoretti S, Swanton C, Albiges L, Schmidinger M, et al. Renal cell carcinoma. Nat Rev Dis Primers. 2017;3:17009. doi: 10.1038/nrdp.2017.9, PMID 28276433.
19. McDermott DF, Cheng SC, Signoretti S, Margolin KA, Clark JI, Sosman JA, et al. The high-dose aldesleukin "select" trial: a trial to prospectively validate predictive models of response to treatment in patients with metastatic renal cell carcinoma. Clin Cancer Res. 2015;21(3):561-8. doi: 10.1158/1078-0432.CCR-14-1520, PMID 25424850.
20. Motzer RJ, Escudier B, Tomczak P, Hutson TE, Michaelson MD, Negrier S, et al. Axitinib versus sorafenib as second-line treatment for advanced renal cell carcinoma: overall survival analysis and updated results from a randomised phase 3 trial. Lancet Oncol. 2013; 14(6):552-62. doi: 10.1016/S1470-2045(13)70093-7, PMID 23598172.
21. Rini BI, Halabi S, Rosenberg JE, Stadler WM, Vaena DA, Archer L, et al. Phase III trial of bevacizumab plus interferon alfa versus interferon alfa monotherapy in patients with metastatic renal cell carcinoma: final results of CALGB 90206. J Clin Oncol. 2010; 28(13):2137-43. doi: 10.1200/JCO.2009.26.5561, PMID 20368558.
22. Motzer RJ, Rini BI, Bukowski RM, Curti BD, George DJ, Hudes GR, et al. Sunitinib in patients with metastatic renal cell carcinoma. JAMA. 2006;295(21):2516-24. doi: 10.1001/jama.295.21.2516, PMID 16757724.
23. Berkun Y, Levartovsky D, Rubinow A, Orbach H, Aamar S, Grenader T, et al. Methotrexate-related adverse effects in patients with rheumatoid arthritis are associated with the A1298C polymorphism of the MTHFR gene. Ann Rheum Dis. 2004;63(10):1227-31. doi: 10.1136/ard.2003.016337, PMID 15361376.
24. Bridges SL, Jr. Personalized medicine in rheumatoid arthritis: hopes and challenges. Bull NYU Hosp Jt Dis. 2007; 65(3):174-7. PMID 17922665.
25. Katakam P, Dey B, Assaleh FH, Hwisa NT, Adiki SK, Chandu BR, et al. Top-down and bottom-up approaches in 3D printing technologies for drug delivery challenges. Crit Rev Ther Drug Carrier Syst. 2015;32(1):61-87. doi: 10.1615/critrevtherdrugcarriersyst.2014011157, PMID 25746205.

26. Goyanes A, Buanz AB, Hatton GB, Gaisford S, Basit AW. 3D printing of modified-release aminosalicylate (4-ASA and 5-ASA) tablets. Eur J Pharm Biopharm. 2015;89:157-62. doi: 10.1016/j.ejpb.2014.12.003, PMID 25497178.
27. Masood SH. Application of fused deposition modelling in controlled drug delivery devices. Assembly Autom. 2007 Aug 7;27(3):215-21. doi: 10.1108/01445150710763231.
28. Buanz AB, Saunders MH, Basit AW, Gaisford S. Preparation of personalized-dose salbutamol sulphate oral films with thermal ink-jet printing. Pharm Res. 2011;28(10):2386-92. doi: 10.1007/s11095-011-0450-5, PMID 21544688.
29. Meléndez PA, Kane KM, Ashvar CS, Albrecht M, Smith PA. Thermal inkjet application in the preparation of oral dosage forms: dispensing of prednisolone solutions and polymorphic characterization by solid-state spectroscopic techniques. J Pharm Sci. 2008;97(7):2619-36. doi: 10.1002/jps.21189, PMID 17876767.
30. Sachs E, Cima M, Cornie J. Three dimensional printing: rapid tooling and prototypes directly from a CAD model. J Manuf Sci Eng. 1992;114:481-8.
31. Khaled SA, Burley JC, Alexander MR, Roberts CJ. Desktop 3D printing of controlled release pharmaceutical bilayer tablets. Int J Pharm. 2014;461(1-2):105-11. doi: 10.1016/j.ijpharm.2013.11.021, PMID 24280018.
32. Gu Y, Chen X, Lee JH, Monteiro DA, Wang H, Lee WY. Inkjet printed antibiotic- and calcium-eluting bioresorbable nanocomposite micropatterns for orthopedic implants. Acta Biomater. 2012;8(1):424-31. doi: 10.1016/j.actbio.2011.08.006, PMID 21864730.
33. Sandler N, Määttänen A, Ihalainen P, Kronberg L, Meierjohann A, Viitala T, et al. Inkjet printing of drug substances and use of porous substratestowards individualized dosing. J Pharm Sci. 2011;100(8):3386-95. doi: 10.1002/jps.22526, PMID 21360709.
34. Lewis JA, Gratson GM. Direct writing in three dimensions. Mater Today. 2004;7(7-8):32-9. doi: 10.1016/S1369-7021(04)00344-X.
35. Pharmaceuticals A. FDA approves the first 3D printed drug product. Aprecia introduces its first product using the ZipDose® formulation platform for the treatment of epilepsy; 2015.
36. Khaled SA, Burley JC, Alexander MR, Yang J, Roberts CJ. 3D printing of tablets containing multiple drugs with defined release profiles. Int J Pharm. 2015;494(2):643-50. doi: 10.1016/j.ijpharm.2015.07.067, PMID 26235921.
37. Martinez PR, Goyanes A, Basit AW, Gaisford S. Fabrication of drug-loaded hydrogels with stereolithographic 3D printing. Int J Pharm. 2017;532(1):313-7. doi: 10.1016/j.ijpharm.2017.09.003, PMID 28888978.
38. Goyanes A, Det-Amornrat U, Wang J, Basit AW, Gaisford S. 3D scanning and 3D printing as innovative technologies for fabricating personalized topical drug delivery systems. J Control Release. 2016;234:41-8. doi: 10.1016/j.jconrel.2016.05.034, PMID 27189134.

39. Fina F, Goyanes A, Gaisford S, Basit AW. Selective laser sintering (SLS) 3D printing of medicines. Int J Pharm. 2017;529(1-2):285-93. doi: 10.1016/j.ijpharm.2017.06.082, PMID 28668582.
40. Salmoria GV, Klauss P, Zepon KM, Kanis LA. The effects of laser energy density and particle size in the selective laser sintering of polycaprolactone/progesterone specimens: morphology and drug release. Int J Adv Manuf Technol. 2013;66(5-8):1113-8. doi: 10.1007/s00170-012-4393-8.
41. Goyanes A, Kobayashi M, Martínez-Pacheco R, Gaisford S, Basit AW. Fused-filament 3D printing of drug products: microstructure analysis and drug release characteristics of PVA-based caplets. Int J Pharm. 2016; 514(1):290-5. doi: 10.1016/j.ijpharm.2016.06.021, PMID 27863674.
42. Gioumouxouzis CI, Katsamenis OL, Bouropoulos N, Fatouros DG. 3D printed oral solid dosage forms containing hydrochlorothiazide for controlled drug delivery. J Drug Deliv Sci Technol. 2017;40:164-71. doi: 10.1016/j.jddst.2017.06.008.
43. Jamróz W, Kurek M, Łyszczarz E, Szafraniec J, Knapik-Kowalczuk J, Syrek K, et al. 3D printed orodispersible films with aripiprazole. Int J Pharm. 2017;533(2):413-20. doi: 10.1016/j.ijpharm.2017.05.052, PMID 28552800.
44. Wu BM, Borland SW, Giordano RA, Cima LG, Sachs EM, Cima MJ. Solid free-form fabrication of drug delivery devices. J Control Release. 1996;40(1-2):77-87. doi: 10.1016/0168-3659(95)00173-5.
45. Wang J, Goyanes A, Gaisford S, Basit AW. Stereolithographic (SLA) 3D printing of oral modified-release dosage forms. Int J Pharm. 2016;503(1-2):207-12. doi: 10.1016/j.ijpharm.2016.03.016, PMID 26976500.
46. Katstra WE, Palazzolo RD, Rowe CW, Giritlioglu B, Teung P, Cima MJ. Oral dosage forms fabricated by three dimensional printing™. J Control Release. 2000;66(1):1-9. doi: 10.1016/s0168-3659(99)00225-4, PMID 10708873.
47. Jacob J et al. Aprecia pharmaceuticals LLC. Rapid disperse dosage form containing levetiracetam. US9339489B2.
48. Giagka V, Serdijn WA. Realizing flexible bioelectronic medicines for accessing the peripheral nerves – technology considerations. Bioelectron Med. 2018;4:8. doi: 10.1186/s42234-018-0010-y, PMID 32232084.
49. Birmingham K. Bioelectronic medicines: a research roadmap. Nat Rev Drug Discov. 2013;13:399-400.
50. Fattahi P, Yang G, Kim G, Abidian MR. A review of organic and inorganic biomaterials for neural interfaces. Adv Mater. 2014;26(12):1846-85. doi: 10.1002/adma.201304496, PMID 24677434.
51. Park S, Guo Y, Jia X, Choe HK, Grena B, Kang J et al. One-step optogenetics with multifunctional flexible polymer fibers. Nat Neurosci. 2017;20(4):612-19. doi: 10.1038/nn.4510, PMID 28218915.
52. Hageman KN, Kalayjian ZK, Tejada F, Chiang B, Rahman MA, Fridman GY et al. A CMOS Neural Interface for a multichannel vestibular prosthesis. IEEE Trans Biomed Circuits Syst. 2018;10:269-79.

53. Yue L, Weiland JD, Roska B, Humayun MS. Retinal stimulation strategies to restore vision: fundamentals and systems. Prog Retin Eye Res. 2016;53:21-47. doi: 10.1016/j.preteyeres.2016.05.002, PMID 27238218.

54. Löffler S, Melican K, Nilsson KPR, Richter-Dahlfors A. Organic bioelectronics in medicine. J Intern Med. 2017;282(1):24-36. doi: 10.1111/joim.12595, PMID 28181720.

55. Bouton C. Cracking the neural code, treating paralysis and the future of bioelectronic medicine. J Intern Med. 2017;282(1):37-45. doi: 10.1111/joim.12610, PMID 28419590.

56. Florence AT, Lee VHL. Personalised medicines: more tailored drugs, more tailored delivery. Int J Pharm. 2011;415(1-2):29-33. doi: 10.1016/j.ijpharm.2011.04.047, PMID 21565262.

57. Wilsdon T, Edwards G, Lawlor R. The benefits of personalised medicine to patients, society and healthcare systems. EBE biopharma; 2018 [cited May 2021]. Available from: https://www.ebe-biopharma.eu/wp-content/uploads/2018/07/CRA-EBE-EFPIA-Benefits-of-PM-Final-Report-6-July-2018-STC.pdf.

58. Awad A, Trenfield SJ, Gaisford S, Basit AW. 3D printed medicines: A new branch of digital healthcare. Int J Pharm. 2018;548(1):586-96. doi: 10.1016/j.ijpharm.2018.07.024, PMID 30033380.

59. Awad A, Trenfield SJ, Goyanes A, Gaisford S, Basit AW. Reshaping drug development using 3D printing. Drug Discov Today. 2018;23(8):1547-55. doi: 10.1016/j.drudis.2018.05.025, PMID 29803932.

60. Goyanes A, Scarpa M, Kamlow M, Gaisford S, Basit AW, Orlu M. Patient acceptability of 3D printed medicines. Int J Pharm. 2017;530(1-2):71-8. doi: 10.1016/j.ijpharm.2017.07.064, PMID 28750894.

61. Lee JS, Hong JM, Jung JW, Shim JH, Oh JH, Cho DW. 3D printing of composite tissue with complex shape applied to ear regeneration. Biofabrication. 2014;6(2):024103. doi: 10.1088/1758-5082/6/2/024103. [PubMed] [CrossRef] [Google Scholar]

62. He Y, Xue G, Fu J. Fabrication of low cost soft tissue prostheses with the desktop 3D printer. Sci Rep. 2014;4:6973. doi: 10.1038/srep06973. [PMC free article] [PubMed] [CrossRef] [Google Scholar]

63. Unkovskiy A, Spintzyk S, Brom J, Huettig F, Keutel C. Direct 3D printing of silicone facial prostheses: A preliminary experience in digital workflow. J Prosthet Dent. 2018; 10.1016/j.prosdent.2017.11.007. [PubMed]

64. del Junco M, Okhunov Z, Yoon R, Khanipour R, Juncal S, Abedi G, Lusch A, Landman J. Development and initial porcine and cadaver experience with three-dimensional printing of endoscopic and laparoscopic equipment. J Endourol 2015;29(1):58–62. [PMC free article] [PubMed]

65. Zopf DA, Hollister SJ, Nelson ME, Ohye RG, Green GE. Bioresorbable airway splint created with a three-dimensional printer. N Engl J Med. 2013;368(21):2043–2045. doi: 10.1056/NEJMc1206319.

66. Park K. 3D printing of 5-drug polypill. J Control Release. 2015;217:352. doi: 10.1016/j.jconrel.2015.10.014. [PubMed] [CrossRef] [Google Scholar]

67. Yang Y, Wang H, Li H, Ou Z, Yang G. 3D printed tablets with internal scaffold structure using ethyl cellulose to achieve sustained ibuprofen release. Eur J Pharm Sci. 2018;115(December 2017):11–18. [PubMed] [Google Scholar]

68. Luzuriaga MA, Berry DR, Reagan JC, Smaldone, Ronald A., Gassensmith JJ. Biodegradable 3D printed polymer microneedles for transdermal drug delivery. Lab Chip 2018. 10.1039/C8LC00098K [PubMed]

69. McAllister DV, Wang PM, Davis SP, Park J-H, Canatella PJ, Allen MG, Prausnitz MR. Microfabricated needles for transdermal delivery of macromolecules and nanoparticles: fabrication methods and transport studies. Proc Natl Acad Sci. 2003;100(24):13755–13760. doi: 10.1073/pnas.2331316100. [PMC free article] [PubMed] [CrossRef] [Google Scholar]

70. Kaae S, Lind JLM, Genina N, Sporrong SK. Unintended consequences for patients of future personalized pharmacoprinting. Int J Clin Pharm. 2018;(123456789):1–4. [PubMed]

71. Kimber MB, Peterson GM. Telepharmacy – enabling technology to provide quality pharmacy services in rural and remote communities. J Pharm Pract Res. 2006; 36(2):128-33. doi: 10.1002/j.2055-2335.2006.tb00588.x.

72. Zundel KM. Telemedicine: history, applications, and impact on librarianship. Bull Med Libr Assoc. 1996; 84(1):71-9. PMID 8938332.

73. Angaran DM. Telemedicine and telepharmacy: current status and future implications. Am J Health Syst Pharm. 1999; 56(14):1405-26. doi: 10.1093/ajhp/56.14.1405, PMID 10428449.

74. Peterson CD, Rathke A, Skwiera J, Anderson HC. Hospital telepharmacy network: delivering pharmacy services to rural hospitals. J Pharm Technol. 2007; 23(3):158-65. doi: 10.1177/875512250702300305.

75. Casey M, Elias W, Knudson A, Gregg W. Implementation of telepharmacy in rural hospitals: potential for improving medication safety. Upper Midwest Rural Health Research Center; 2011 [cited Jul 18, 2016]. Available from: http://rhrc.umn.edu/wp-content/files_mf/telepharmacy.pdf.

EXCERCISE

MULTIPLE CHOICE QUESTIONS

1. Personalized medicine also known as-
   a. Precision medicine b. Stratified medicine
   c. P4 medicine d. All the above

2. The precision medicine approach to disease treatment and prevention takes into account patient's individual variability in which factors?
   a. Age, sex, and body mass index
   b. Education, literacy and health knowledge
   c. Genes, environment and lifestyle
   d. Social status, quality of relationships and access to health services.
3. Benefits of precision medicine is/are-
   a. Improve disease detection
   b. Prescribe more effective
   c. Both
   d. None of the above
4. The "4P" include in personalized health care-
   a. Prevention, Prediction, Personalization, Participation
   b. Prevention, Prediction, Personalization, Pathological
   c. Prevention, Prediction, Prescriptions, Participation
   d. Prevention, Prescriptions, Personalization, Participation
5. ________________refers to a pharmacist at a remote location performing remote order-entry services for an inpatient pharmacy at a hospital.
   a. Inpatient telepharmacy
   b. remote-dispensing site
   c. Remote-patient counselling
   d. None of the above
6. ________________allows pharmacists to consult and provide a variety of pharmacy-care services to patients via secure, live-video calls.
   a. Inpatient telepharmacy
   b. remote-dispensing site
   c. Remote-patient counselling
   d. None of the above
7. ______________means a place where drugs are dispensed or sold by retail to the public under the supervision of a pharmacist who is not physically present.
   a. Remote order- entry
   b. Remote-dispensing site
   c. Remote-patient counselling
   d. None of the above
8. What is an STL?
   a. The initial pre-sliced file.
   b. The final sliced file.
   c. A type of filament
   d. The coding program
9. What are the basic characteristics of 3D Printing
   a. 3D objects are made in layers, it is an additive process

b. 3D objects are created using a subtractive process
c. 3D objects print from the computer
d. 3D objects are downloaded and printed from the internet

10. What is a G-Code?
    a. The initial pre-sliced file
    b. The final sliced file that the printer reads
    c. A type of filament
    d. The coding program
11. What does layer resolution mean?
    a. A kind of filament
    b. The shape of the object
    c. How detailed the object prints
    d. A file types
12. Pharmacogenomics is the combination of what two fields of study.
    a. Genetic testing and pharmaceuticals
    b. Pharmacology and genetics
    c. Genomics and pharmacology
    d. Kinetics and dynamics
13. Personalized medicine allows doctors and healthcare providers to
    a. Use genetic information to diagnose more patients.
    b. Create specific treatments for patients with fewer side effects.
    c. Prescribe the right medications in the right dose without having to use "trial and error" in trying to determine whether the medicine will help.
    d. All the above.
14. Which of these statements is true?
    a. Targeted therapies are not currently being studied.
    b. Targeted therapies usually have more side effects than traditional chemotherapy.
    c. A scientist continues to investigate new cancer therapies.
    d. None of the above
15. In______ year, the first 3D printed pill was approved by US FDA organovo announced the release of data on the first full bioprinted kidney.
    a. 2000 b. 2003
    c. 2009 d. 2015

16. Stereo lithography apparatus (SLA) awas invented by_________
    a. Dr. Hideo Kodama
    b. Charles Hull
    c. Dr. Bowyer
    d. Carl Deckard
17. Bioelectronic machines depends on________
    a. Precision
    b. Detection
    c. Modulation of electrical signalling patterns in the Nervous System
    d. All the above
18. _________ is also called as "mask less or tool less" approach.
    a. Inkjet printing
    b. Thermal inkjet printing
    c. Zip Dose
    d. None of the above
19. __________ Technology gives a personalized dose in order to the delivery of a high drug-load with high disintegration and dissolution levels.
    a. Zip dose
    b. Direct wise
    c. Vat Photopolymerization
    d. Thermal Inkjet Printing
20. ________ is the study of how genes affect a person's response to drugs.
    a. Biotechnology
    b. Genetics
    c. Genomics
    d. Pharmacogenomics

SHORT ANSWER QUESTIONS

1. How might people with cancer benefit from personalized medicine?
2. What are some of the challenges to making personalized medicine available to all patients?
3. What is personalised medicine? What dosage forms is used in the treatment.
4. 19. What are the benefits of telepharmacy compared to traditional pharmacy?
5. What are the bioelectric medicines?
6. Explain the role of pharmacogenetics in pharmaceutical industry.
7. Give two examples of bioelectric devices.
8. Write a note on customized drug delivery system.

9. How Will Personalized Medicine Affect the Costs of Medical Care?
10. How you would be Implementing Personalized Medicine into Medical Practice.

LONG ANSWER QUESTIONS

1. What is bioelectric medicine? Discuss in detail with examples
2. Explain Pharmacogenetics in detail.
3. Discuss customised drug delivery system
4. Discuss about 3D printing technology and its major development in pharmaceuticals
5. Explain 3D Printing Procedure and its advantage in pharmaceutical.
6. Explain various types of 3D printing
7. What do you mean by telepharmacy and discuss its types.
8. Discuss about the working of telepharmacy
9. Describe about the personalized medicine and its importance in Pharmaceutical.

MCQ ANSWERS

1. (a)	2. (c)	3. (c)	4. (a)
5. (a)	6. (c)	7. (b)	8. (a)
9. (a)	10. (b)	11. (c)	12. (c)
13. (d)	14. (c)	15. (d)	16. (b)
17. (d)	18. (d)	19. (a)	20. (d)

CHAPTER - 4

Rate Controlled Drug Delivery Systems

Dr. Bina Gidwani, Dr. Vishal Jain, Dr. Shiv Shankar Shukla, and Dr. Ravindra Pandey

Principles, Fundamentals, Types[6-9], Activation Modulated Drug Delivery Systems, Mechanically Activated, pH Activated, Enzyme Activated Drug Delivery System, Osmotic Pressure, Activated Drug Delivery Systems, Feedback Regulated Drug Delivery Systems

PRINCIPLES

The publication of books and review articles have focused on the development of controlled or sustained drug delivery systems. The basic reason for controlled drug delivery is to alter pharmacokinetic and pharmacodynamic characteristics of a pharmacologically active moity with the help of novel drug delivery systems or by altering or modifying the molecular structure and/or physiological parameters inherent in a selected route of administration. Sustained release, sustained action, controlled release, extended action, timed release dosage forms are the terms used to identify drug delivery systems, designed to achieve a prolonged therapeutic effect by continuous releasing the drug throughout an extended period of time after administration of a single dose[1].

The term-controlled release has become associated with those systems from which therapeutic agents may be automatically delivered at pre-determined rates, at predetermined sites over a long period of time. There is some confusion in terminology between controlled release and sustained release.

The term sustained release has been constantly used to describe a pharmaceutical dosage form formulated to retard the release of therapeutic agent such that its appearance in the systemic circulation is delayed and/or prolonged and its plasma profile is sustained in duration. On the other hand, this term has a meaning that goes beyond the scope of sustained drug action. It also implies a predictability and reproducibility in the drug release kinetics, this means that the release of drug ingredient from a controlled delivery system proceeds at a rate profile that is not only kinetically predictable, but also reproducible from one unit to another[2].

FUNDAMENTALS

Treatment of an acute disease or a chronic illness has been mostly performed by delivering a drug to the patient through one of the various conventional pharmaceutical dosage forms, such as tablets, capsules, ointment, liquids, aerosols or injectables, which are used as drug carriers for many years. A number of advancements have been made for development of new technologies for optimizing drug delivery. These technologies are capable of regulating the rate of drug delivery, sustaining the duration of therapeutic action, and/or targeting the drug delivery to a specific tisuue[3].

The pharmaceutical industries provide various dosage forms and dosage levels of particular drugs, this enable the physicians to control the onset and duration of drug therapy by altering the dose and/or mode of administration. In some cases, control of drug therapy can be achieved by taking advantage of beneficial drug interactions. This affect drug disposition and elimination, such as the action of probenecid inhibits the excretion of penicillin, as a result the blood level of penicillin is prolonged. Mixtures of drugs might be utilized to potentiate, synergize, or antagonize drug actions. Alternately, drug mixtures can be formulated in such a way that the rate and/or extent of drug absorption is modified. Thus, sustained release dosage form is designed either to modify the absorption or excretion characteristics of the drug.

However, all drugs are not suitable for formulating sustained release products. To design a process for making sustained release formulation, it is necessary to evaluate the properties of drug blood-time profile characteristics of multiple dosing therapy of the drug of conventional (immediate) release forms[4].

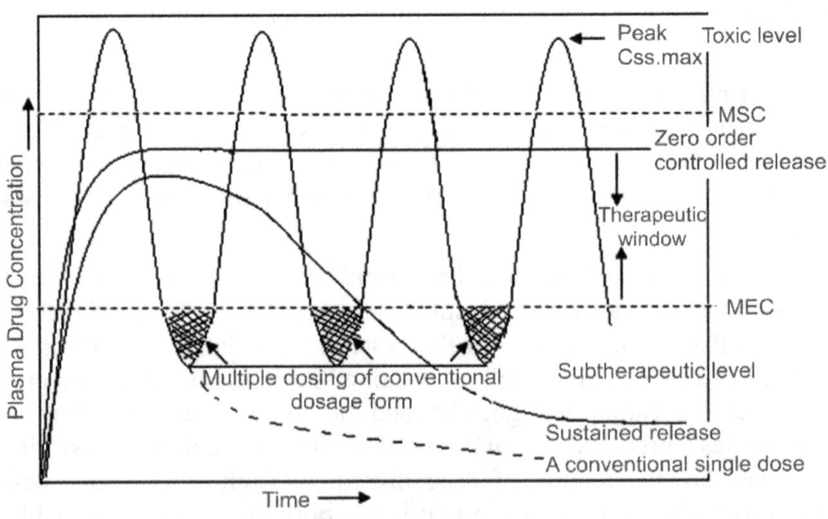

Fig.4.1 Plasma drug concentration of conventional, sustained release, and zero order controlled release dosage forms.

The Fig.4.1 shows typical release profiles observed from conventional, sustained release, and zero-order controlled release dosage form. The graph also indicates the minimum effective concentration (MEC) and maximum safe concentration (MSC), therapeutic window, and toxic level. With reduction of dosage interval, the number of doses required to maintain a steady-state drug level increases, the amplitude of oscillation of drug level reduces with the increased steady state average blood level[5].

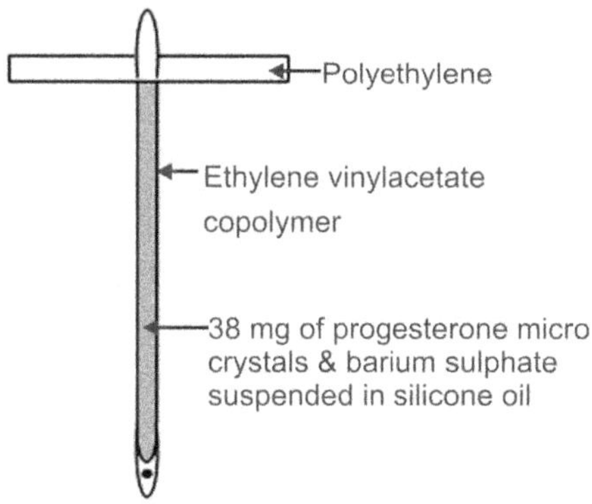

Fig.4.2 Schematic diagram of progestasert.

TYPES[6-9]

There are four types of rate-controlled drug delivery systems

1) Rate pre-programmed drug delivery system.
2) Activation modulated drug delivery system.
3) Feedback regulated drug delivery system.
4) Site targeting drug delivery system.

1) Rate pre-programmed drug delivery system[10]

In this, the release of drug molecule from thedelivery system is pre-planned with flowrate profile of medicine. The system controls the molecular diffusion of drugmolecules in or across the barrier medium within or surrounding the delivery system.

Types:

i. Polymer membrane permeation-controlled system
ii. Polymer matrix diffusion-controlled system
iii. Micro reservoir partition-controlled system
iv. Polymer membrane permeation-controlled system

In this system, the drug is completely or partially encapsulated in a drug reservoir cubicle whose drug releasing surface is covered by flow rate controlling polymeric membrane. In drug reservoir, the drug can be solid or dispersion ofsolid drug particle or concentrated drug solution in aliquid or in a solid type of dispersion medium. The polymeric membrane may be made-up of the fabricated form of homogeneous or heterogeneous nonporous or partial microporous or semipermeable membrane[11-13].

The rate of drug release is defined by-

$$\frac{Q}{t} = \frac{K_{m/r} K_{a/m} D_d D_m}{K_{m/r} D_m h_d + K_{a/m} D_d h_m} \times C_R$$

Where,

$K_{m/r}$ and $K_{a/m}$ are the partition coefficient of the drug molecule from reservoir to rate controlling membrane and from membrane to aqueous layer respectively.

D_d and D_m are thediffusion coefficient of rate controlling membrane and aqueous diffusion layer respectively.

h_m and h_d are the thickness of rate controlling membrane & aqueous diffusion layer respectively.

C_R is the drug conc. in reservoir compartment.

Thus, the release of drug molecules is controlled by:

- Partition coefficient of the drug molecule.
- Diffusivity of the drug molecule.
- The thickness of the rate controlling membrane.

For example,

➢ **Progestasert**

It is a T shaped intrauterine device (IUD) made of ethylene and vinyl acetate copolymer containing titanium dioxide. The vertical stem contains a reservoir of 38 mg progesterone together with barium sulphate dispersed in silicone fluid. The progesterone is released at the rate of 65 μg per day to achieve contraception for 1 year[14].

➢ **Transdermal drug delivery systems**

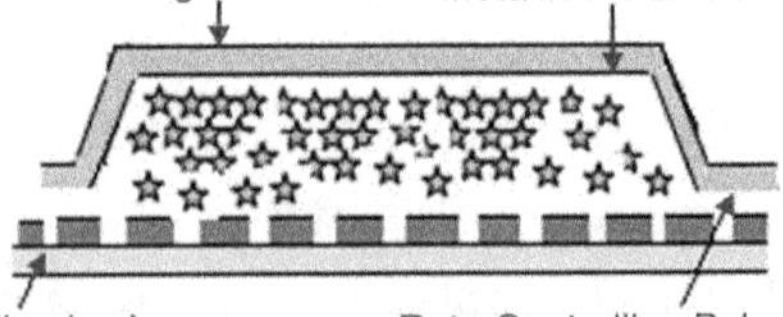

Fig.4.3 Schematic diagram of transdermal drug delivery system.

Nitroglycerin-releasing Transdermal system (Transdermal-Nitro/ciba, USA) for once-a-day medication in angina pectoris. Scopolamine-releasing Transdermal system (Transdermal-Scop/Ciba, USA) for 72 hrs prophylaxis of motion sickness. Clonidine-releasing Transdermal system (Catapres/ Boehriger Ingelheim, USE) for 7-day therapy of hypertension. Estradiol Estradiol-releasing releasing Transdermal system (Estraderm/Ciba, (Estraderm/Ciba, USA) for treatment of menopausal syndrome for 3-4 days[13].

➢ Polymer matrix diffusion-controlled system

In this drug, the reservoir is prepared by the homogeneously dispersing drug particles in the rate controlling hydrophilicor lipophilic polymer matrix. The resultant medicated polymer matrix provides them educated disk with defined surface area and controlled thickness. The drug dispersion in the polymer matrix is accomplished by either, blending therapeutic dose of drug with polymer or highly viscous base polymer, followed by cross linking of polymer chains mixing drug solid with rubbery polymer at elevated temp[11,12].

The rate of the drug release from this system,

$$\frac{Q}{t^{1/2}} =. (2AC_R D_p)^{1/2}$$

Where,

$Q/t^{1/2}$ is the rate of release of drug

A is the initial drug loading dose in the polymer matrix

C_R is the drug solubility in polymer, and

$D_p$is the diffusivity of drug in polymer matrix

Thus, release of drug molecule is controlled by

- Loading dose
- Polymer solubility of drug
- Drug diffusivity in polymer matrix.

➢ Compudose

This is a subdermal implant formulated based on dispersing of estradiol crystals in a viscous silicone elastomer and coating the dispersion over a silicone rod by extrusion technique to form a cylindrically-shape implant. Compudose is subcutaneously implanted for a duration of 200 to 400 days for the delivery of estradiol.

➢ Micro reservoir partition-controlled system

The drug reservoirs are a suspension of solid particle in the aqueous solution of the water-miscible polymer.

Micro-dispersion partition-controlled system is prepared by the applying high dispersion techniques.

In short reservoir and matrix dispersion forms micro-reservoir. Depending upon the physicochemical properties of drugs and desired rate of drug release, the device can be further coated with a layer of biocompatible polymer to modify the mechanism and the rate of drug release.

The rate of drug release is defined by:

$$\frac{dQ}{dt} = \frac{D_p D_d m K_p}{D_p h_d + m K_p D_d h_p}\left(nS_p - \frac{D_l S_l}{h_l}(1-n)\left[\frac{1}{K_l} + \frac{1}{K_m}\right]\right)$$

Where,

n = The ratio of drug conc at the inner edge of the interfacial barrier over the drug solubility in the polymer matrix.

$m = \frac{a}{b}$, a is the ratio of drug conc in the bulk of elution solution over drug solubility in the same medium. B is the ratio of drug conc at the outer edge of the polymer coating membrane over drug solubility in the same polymer.

K_l, K_m &K_p = Partition coefficient for the interfacial partitioning of the drug from the liquid compartment to the polymer matrix, from the polymer matrix to the polymer-coating membrane & from the polymer coating membrane to the elution solution respectively.

D_l, D_p and D_d = Diffusivities of the drug in the lipid layer surrounding the drug particle, the polymer coating membrane enveloping the polymer matrix, & the hydrodynamic diffusion layer surrounding the polymer coating membrane with the thickness h_l, h_p and h_d.

S_l and S_p = Solubilities of the drug in the liquid compartments & in the polymer matrix, respectively.

Release of drug molecules from this type of system can follow either a dissolution or a matrix diffusion-controlled process depending upon the relative magnitude of S_l and S_p.

Release of drug molecule is controlled by,

- Partition coefficient
- Diffusivity of drug
- Solubility of drug

➢ **Syncromate – C**

It is fabricated by dispersing the drug reservoir, which is a suspension of norgestomet in an aqueous solution of PEG 400, in a viscous mixture of silicone elastomer.

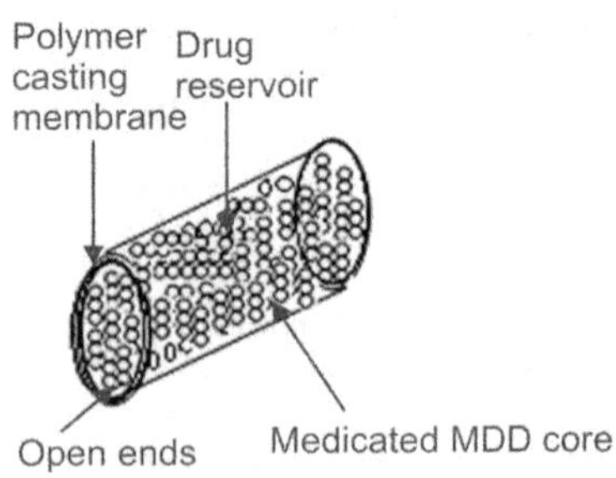

Fig.4.4 Schematic diagram of syncromate - C.

After adding the catalyst, the suspension will be delivered into the silicone medical grade tubing, which serves as mold as well as the coating membrane & then polymerized *in situ*.

The polymerized drug polymer composition is then cut into a cylindrical drug delivery device with the open ends. It is designed to be inserted into the subcutaneous tissue of the livestock's ear flap and to release norgestomet for up to 20 days for control of estrus & ovulation as well as for up to 160 days for growth promotion[15].

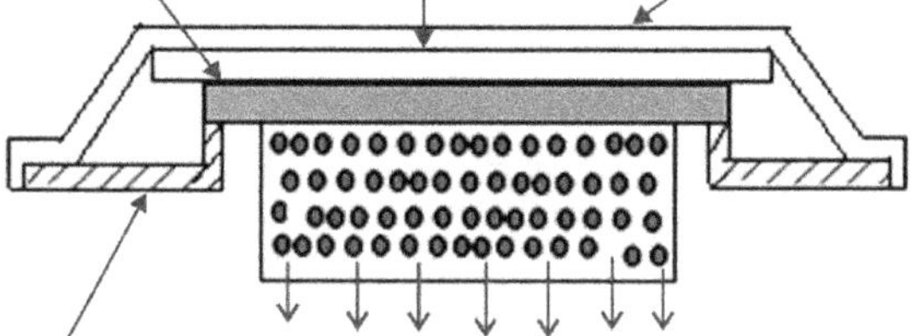

Fig.4.5 Schematic diagram of nitro dur.

➢ Nitro Dur

Nitro-Dur is a transdermal system contains nitroglycerin in acrylic-based polymer adhesives with a resinous cross-linking agent to provide a continuous source of active ingredient. It is designed for application on to intact skin for 24 hrs to provide a continuous transdermal infusion of nitroglycerin at dosage rate of 0.5mg/cm^2 /day for the treatment of angina pectoris.

Positioning the medicated disc at the center and surrounding it with an adhesive produce a Transdermal therapeutic system. For example: Nitroglycerin releasing Transdermal therapeutic system (Nitrodisc, Searle, USA) for once-a-day therapy of angina pectoris[12].

ACTIVATION MODULATED DRUG DELIVERY SYSTEMS

It is necessary that most drugs are and should be delivered at zero-order. However, there are many other circumstances where zero-order drug delivery is not possible in the optimum drug action. While treating certain diseasesthe daily rhythm is known as *circadian*. Many physiological functions exhibit prominent rhythmic changes, and the onset of some diseases is known to depend strongly on circadian temporal rhythm. For example, gastric acid secretion rate is high in the evening hours and low in the morning hours[16]. Myocardial infarction, sudden cardiac death, thrombotic stroke, and arterial embolism show a strong circadian rhythm with a morning peak and an evening trough[17]. Modulated drug delivery system/ self-regulated drug delivery system/ signal-responsive/ signal-receptive/ signal-sensitive/ signal-triggered/ on-demand drug-delivery systems can be defined as *the drug delivery systems that deliver required amount oof drugs on demand, that isas per the biological requirement and stop until required again at a later period.* In addition to the requirement of non-traditional delivery modes, many new peptide and protein drugs require unique delivery systems[18]. The recombinant protein drugs have been approved by FDA or under development. The advances in biotechnology resulted in getting new drugs, especially peptide and protein drugs, onto the market, getting them into patients is proven to be quite challenging. One factor that adds to the difficulty in the delivery for protein drugs is that proteins, in general, are usually not very stable and have a tendency to adsorb to solid surfaces. In treating certain diseases, following the daily rhythm, known as circadian, is proven to be quite important[19]. Many physiological functions exhibit prominent rhythmic changes, and the onset of some diseases is known to depend strongly on circadian temporal rhythm. This suggests that the chronobiological aspects of the pathophysiology of the disease can be applied better management of patients. The recombinant protein drugs approved by FDA or under development are given below in the form of Table 4.1[20]. The advances in biotechnology resulted in getting new drugs, especially peptide and protein drugs, onto the market, actually getting them into patients is proven to be quite challenging. As mentioned before, the delivery of peptide and protein drugs cannot be achieved using the techno-logies used for the low molecular weight drugs. Of the many drugs requiring modulated drug-delivery systems, insulin presents the most difficult challenges. The timing of insulin delivery and the amount of delivered insulin must be precise[21]. The amount of delivered insulin is determined by the glucose level in the blood, and this requires use of a glucose sensor. The insulin release must stop once the glucose level is reduced[22]. Thus, the modulated insulin delivery system needs to have the abilities to measure the glucose level, to control the amount of insulin, to release insulin within several minutes of glucose level increase, and to shut off insulin release. One factor that adds to the difficulty in the delivery for protein drugs is that proteins, in general, are usually not very stable and have a tendency to adsorb to solid surfaces[18].

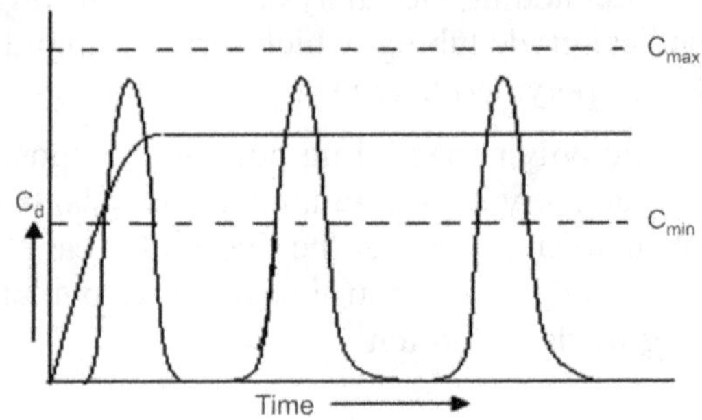

Fig.4.6 Two different profiles of the drug concentration in blood (C_d) obtained from zero-order release (dotted line) and modulated release (solid line) from the dosage forms.

Table 4.1 Recombinant Protein Drugs Approved by FDA or under Development.

Protein Drug	Indication	Protein Drug	Indication
Tissue plasminogen activator	Acute myocardial infarction	Erythropoietin	Renal failure anaemia
Interferon-α	Hepatitis C	Interferon-$\alpha 2a$	Hairy cell leukaemia and AIDS- related Kaposi's sarcoma
Interferon-$\alpha 2b$	Hairy cell leukaemia and AIDS- related Kaposi's sarcoma, and genital warts	Hepatitis B virus vaccine	Prophylaxis against hepatitis B
Insulin	Diabetes	Haemophilus B conjugate Vaccine type B	Prophylaxis against haemophilus influenza
Granulocyte-macrophage factor	Regeneration of immune colony-stimulating system in AIDS, cancer	Superoxide dismutase	Acute myocardial infarction, organ transplantation
Epidermal growth factor	Corneal repair	Atrial peptide	Congestive heart failure
Monoclonal antibodies	gram negative sepsis, treatment of graft vs host disease	CD4 protein	AIDS, AIDS-related complex

The adsorption may result in conformational changes causing the loss of bioactivity. Furthermore, the surface adsorption may begin an aggregation process of the protein drugs. Release of drug from the delivery systems is activated by some physical, chemical, or biochemical processes and facilitated by the energy supplied externally. The rate of drug release is then controlled by regulating the process applied or energy input[19, 20].

Based on the nature of the process applied or the type of energy used, this activation modulated DDS can be classified into:

- Physical means
- Chemical means
- Biochemical means

Types of activation modulated drug delivery systems

1) Physical means
   a) Osmotic pressure-activated DDS
   b) Hydrodynamic pressure-activated DDS
   c) Vapour pressure-activated DDS
   d) Mechanically activated DDS
   e) Magnetically activated DDS
   f)Sonophoresis-activated DDS
   g) Iontophoresis-activated DDS
   h) Hydration-activated DDS
2) Chemical means
   a) P^H activated DDS
   b) Ion activated DDS
   c) Hydrolysis activated DDS
3) Biochemical means
   a) Enzyme activated DDS
   b) Biochemical activated DDS

MECHANICALLY ACTIVATED DRUG DELIVERY

Drug delivery systems (DDS) are of great importance to improve the treatment efficacy of medications[23]. Sustained drug delivery systems have developed during last three decades. Although, there are many clinical situations which require more than a zero-ordered, continuous drug release profile, but an on-demand control of therapeutics. Dosage-, spatial-, and temporal-controllable drug release, which can target diseased tissue, improve uptake efficiency, prolong action time, and improve bioavailability of drugs, has been heavily pursued in recent years. Such DDS can respond to either endogenous environmental conditions, such as pH, redox, hypoxia, ATP, glucose, and enzymes, or exogenous signals such as temperature, light, magnetic field, and electric current. Mechanical force can further be classified into compressive, tensile, and shear forces. These forces are achieved in the body or easily applied externally[24]. In vascular systems, and external acoustic and magnetic force remotely are remotely applied through the skin. Sources of force can be generated from internal/intrinsic compression/stretching through joint movements to internal shear force[26]. Easy access of mechanical stimuli facilitates treatment in various conditions with convenient commands. In case of emergence such as heart attack and hypoglycaemia, the mechanical force-mediated trigger can prompt delivery of therapeutics by patients in a self-administered manner. Moreover, compared to chemical or biological triggers, application of mechanical force provides a relatively predictable control in direction and an adjustable magnitude management toward precision release of therapeutics. In addition, patient-controlled drug delivery may potentially increase patient satisfaction compared with intermittent administration, since the patients themselves can conveniently regulate the release of drug from the dosage form administered and timing of the drug[27].

Collectively, mechanical force is a promising candidate to realize controlled drug release. To be specific, the compressive and tensile forces can be readily obtained by using hands or from simple daily motions, such as tension in muscles, tendons, bone joints, and compression in cartilage and bones. Therefore, DDS integrated with mechano responsive modality provides self-administration therapy without requiring additional instruments, while the shear force generated by bloodflow in vascular systems promises for non-invasive cardiovascular drug delivery. The features of the formulation design or devices based on the two directly interacting triggers commonly involve physical deformation or mechano-chemical changes of drug carriers. On the other hand, ultrasound, a highly efficient and non-invasive trigger, has been extensively used in drug development. The force applied longitudinally by ultrasound can induce hyperthermia, cavitation, and radiation, resulting in destruction of drug carriers and drug release by either thermal or non-thermal functions. Moreover, magnetic force induced by a magnetic field can activate the magneto-responsive components. Integrated with thermos-sensitive materials or flexible matrices, the activated magneto-responsive particles can achieve a controlled release of cargoes by dissociation or morphology variation[28].

Compressive or tensile force triggered drug delivery

Commonly, compressive or tensile force-responsive DDSs are based on stretchable materials, such as hydrogels and elastomers. Many formulations and devices, including nanoparticles and microgel depots, have been exploited to be hybridized into a flexible substrate to achieve the release on-demand in response to mechanical stimuli. Typically the mechanisms of releasing the entrapped ingredients from the system are based on either physical deformation of carriers or chemical changes of materials, such as breakage of chemical bonds.

Deformation

For spatiotemporal-controlled drug delivery, thermo sensitive hydrogels have been extensively used. To activate the release, the heat source is required externally. The dissipative properties of hydrogel is used as an internal heat source. The

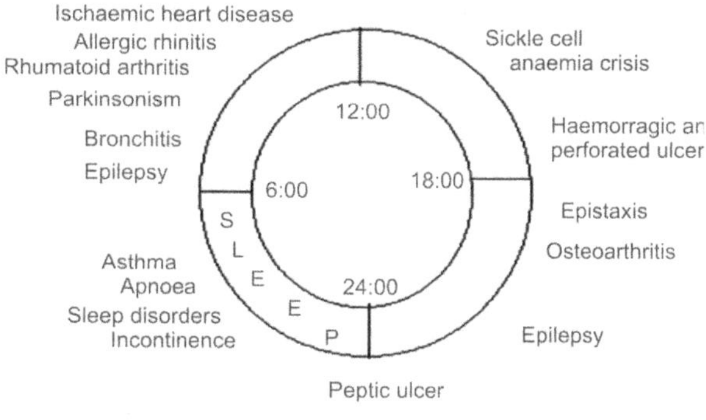

Fig.4.7 Diseases known to display circadian rhythm.

hydrogel matrix can be formed with thermoresponsive nanoparticles, which produce self-heat after a cyclic mechanical loading for 5 min. This increases the temperature from 36 – 37°C. The increase in temperature results in shrinkage of the nanoparticles, followed by release of contents after 5 – 8 min. This hybrid hydrogel with high dissipation holds promise in the delivery of growth factors by mechanical activation. A controlled delivery system based on synthetic extracellular matrices (ECMs). The natural ECMs of tissues, in form of the depots of growth factors, are responsible to many physiological signals and can correspondingly release factors to surrounding cells. To mimic the behaviour of natural ECMs, a hydrogel has been designed with reversible binding to drugs. The reversible chemical binding was done to overcome the limited sensing period, because physically loaded hydrogel commonly fail to respond to compression after several release cycles due to rapid depletion of drug from the hydrogel. Under this circumstances, unbound vascular endothelial growth factor (VEGF) was released on compression. However, with re-equilibration of bound VEGF turning into unbound VEGF, the hydrogel could continuously control the release of VEGF through compressive force.

Chemically cross-linked hydrogels integrated with mechano-sensitive block copolymer micelles (BCMs) are reported to have the capability to modulate drug release by mechanical force. Drug-loaded BCMs were applied with reactive handles as the microscopic cross-linkers, in place of traditional molecular cross-linkers for poly (acrylamide) (PAAm)-based networks. The restricted BCMs provided the mechano-responsive elements for BCM-PAAm gels, and the force-induced deformation of BCMs led to drug release upon strain application. The BCMs presented a more elongated appearance at a strain of 200% with an average dimension ratio of 1.53$\pm$ 0.23. The BCMs returned to their original morphology after removal of the external force due to reversible structural deformation. Strain-dependent shape alternation could effectively control the drug release rate from the BCM-cross-linked gel. The same group also prepared hyaluronic acid (HA) gels covalently embedded with dexamethasone (DEX)-loaded BCMs to control inflammation within mechanically stressed tissues. The HA gels markedly reduced the initial burst release and allowed sustained release in a stress-dependent manner, which offers an alternative strategy to take advantage of mechanical stress to promote tissue repair during the wound-healing process.

A strain-controlled system has been developed that released molecules from an array of stretchable micro-capsules based on a poly (dimethyl siloxane) (PDMS) elastomer substrate using a hydrogel pattern fabrication technique. The mechanical strain applied on the substrate led to deformation of the polystyrene (PS) microcapsule, followed by pumped-out preload molecules. A strain of 2.5% on the substrate reduced the microcapsules volume by 17%, while a higher strain of 7.5% decreased the volume by 98%. The dosage form of released molecules was highly dependent on the degree of strain. The deformed PS capsules could return to their initial shape and volume upon release from stretching, which favoured repeatable drug diffusion from the patch.

On the other hand, pulsating release can be achieved through intentional administration. This allows patients to control the release timing and dose of the drug on their own. When combined with microneedle arrays, this device could be utilized to regulate blood glucose levels (BGLs) by on-demand transcutaneous insulin delivery for type 1 diabetic mice. After several cycles of stretching and releasing, the BGLs of mice quickly reduced to a normoglycemic level within half an hour. Meanwhile, pulsating regulation of BGLs was observed when strain was applied at 4 h intervals. With this technology, diabetic patients can easily maintain BGLs through simple joint movement instead of traditional, painful insulin injection.

Apart from the change in volume, crack propagation generated by an applied strain can also be used to trigger drug release. On the basis of this concept, a superhydrophobic polymer composite for a stretch-triggered DDS. In this device, the drug-loaded hydrophilic mesh core was encased by two super-hydrophobic coating with different mechanical properties. This mismatch led to mechanical failure of the coatings under applied tension, and the resulting crack propagation allowed the cargo to diffuse from the mesh core. The localized *ex-vivo* study of this stretch-responsive device incorporated with a metal oesophageal stent indicated that the model drug could be released to the oesophageal epithelial mucosa layer from the expanded system.

A multilayer film was developed with a mechanotransductive surface for two reversible biocatalysis activation. The multilayer film, made by a layer-by-layer (LbL) method, consisted of a poly(L-lysine)/ hyaluronic acid (PLL/ HA) film as a reservoir. This film was loaded with alkaline phosphatase (ALP) enzymes and capped with a poly (diallyl dimethyl ammonium)/ poly (styrene sulphonate) (PDAD-MA/ PSS) film as a barrier. ALP, a hydrolase enzyme, can dephosphorylate fluorescein diphosphate (FDP). On stretching, the loaded ALP was exposed through the barrier; then the biocatalysis was started and the progress was shown in confocal fluorescent images. Besides triggering of biocatalysis through stretching, biocatalytic activity can also be controlled by the thickness of the barrier film[29]. With relatively thicker barrier layers, fewer enzymes could be brought to the substrates, resulting in a lower jump of fluorescence. Reversible stretch-triggered biocatalytic activation can be achieved in this LbL system. The same group further applies similar biodegradable polyelectrolyte multilayers as a mechanoresponsive drug delivery platform. Paclitaxel has been embedded in the PLL/HA reservoir, capped with a poly (allylamine hydrochloride)/ poly (styrene sulphonate) (PAH/PSS) film as the barrier. On immersion in trypsin solution, PLL inside the reservoir was cleaved by trypsin once the PAH/PS barrier was opened by mechanical stretch. Thus, the entrapped paclitaxel was released from films due to biodegradation of PLL/HA film in a stretch-controlled manner[30].

pH ACTIVATED DRUG DELIVERY SYSTEM

The logic behind pH activation modulated DDS is that, different organs have different biological environments (physical, chemical, electrical, and biochemical). For example, different organs/body parts have different pH, such as blood (pH 7.4), tumour tissues (pH 6.5–7.2), lysosomes (pH 4.5–5.0), and gastrointestinal tract (pH 6.2–7.9)[31].

This makes it possible to formulate the pH-responsive DDS to release the drug only in the region where it is aimed at. Several pH-responsive DDS have been successfully formulated to release the drug in tumour tissues, simply because the tumour tissues have a different pH than healthy tissues. Thus, pH becomes an internal stimulus for the targeted delivery of the therapeutic agents[32].

pH sensitive drug delivery systems (PSDDS) are gaining popularity because these systems deliver the drug at specific time as per the pathophysiological requirement of the disease. As a result, improved therapeutic efficacy of the drug and better patient are observed. Diseases wherein PSDDS is found most effective are

- Asthma,
- Peptic ulcer
- Cardiovascular diseases
- Cancer and
- Hypertension

The specific time at which the patients take their medicines is very important because it has a significant effect on the success of treatment. In other words, on this the recovery of the patient/ curing rate of the disease depends. Optimal clinical outcome cannot be achieved if the concentration of drug in plasma is found constant. If the symptoms of a disease show circadian variation, over the time drug release may also vary. Pharmacokinetics of the drug can also be pH sensitive. Therefore, variation both in plasma-drug concentration and in a disease state should be considered while developing drug delivery systems intended for the treatment of a disease with an adequate dose. In PSDDS where the release of drug is controlled primarily by the delivery system; sometimes stimuli is induced by the PSDDS where the release of the drug is controlled by the stimuli. For example, pH of the gastrointestinal fluid[33].

Many polyanionic materials, such as poly (acrylic acid), are pH sensitive and the degree of swelling of such polymers can be modulated by changing the pH. An application of such technology has been in the development of biomimetic secretory granules for drug delivery applications.

Within certain cells secretory granules consist of a polyanionic polymer network encapsulated within a lipid membrane. The polymer network contains biological mediators such as histamine. This remains present in a collapsed state as a consequence of the internal pH and ionic content which is maintained by the lipid surrounding the granules. From such granules release of histamine is initiated through the fusion of the granules with the cell membrane exposing the polyanionic internal matrix to the extracellular environment. The change in pH and ionic strength cause the ion exchange and swelling of the polyanionic network which in turn causes release of the endogenous mediators[34].

The charge density of the polymers depends on pH and the ionic composition of the outer solution. Altering the pH of the solution will cause swelling or deswelling of the polymer. These polymers causing drug release from the devices will show release rates that are pH sensitive[35]. At low pH, polyacidic polymers will remain unswollen, because the acidic groups will remain protonated; thus will remain unionized. When pH increases the polyacidic polymers start swelling. In opposite situation polybasic polymers swell, because the basic groups will ionize at increased rate when the pH of the solution will decrease[36]. It has been found that the swelling property of the polybasic gels are influenced by buffer. These gels may not be reliable to mediate pH sensitive swelling controlled release in oral formulations, since the levels of buffer acids in the stomach cannot be controlled. The most commonly used pH- sensitive polymers are derivatives of acrylic acid and cellulose. By combining the knowledge of polymer and their solubility at different pH, the delivery systems can be designed to deliver drugs at different target sites[37,38].

Advantages:

Advantages of drugs available directly at the target site are:

- Decreased dose to be administered.
- Decreased side effects.
- Improved drug utilization
- Improved patient compliance

- Lowers the daily cost of medication to the patient due to fewer dosage units required by the patient during treatment.
- Adapts the drug to suit circadian rhythms of the diseases.
- Drug can target the specific site such as colon.
- Provides protection of mucosa from irritating drugs
- Loss of drug can be prevented by extensive first pass metabolism[39].

Diseases targeting pH sensitive drug delivery

The design of drug delivery systems has been controlled by the homeostatic theory. This theory is based on the biological functions such as heart rate, blood pressure, body temperature, plasma concentration of different hormones, gastric pH and renal functions. The rhythmic processes are indispensable for the treatment of human diseases. The physiological functions ary over time, pathological states of disease having circadian rhythms[40].

It is necessary to have a thorough understanding of the disease physiology before designing the pH-sensitive drug delivery systems.

- **Anti-ulcer therapy**

It is well known that patients suffering from peptic ulcer often experience the greatest degree of pain near to sleeping time at night, because at night the stomach secrete the maximum acid. Therefore, the time at which ulcer medication has a significant effect on the therapeutic efficacy of the drugs taken[41].

- **Anti-inflammatory therapy**

In case of individual patient suffering from rheumatoid arthritis and related painful joint disorders, the non-steroidal anti-inflammatory drug such as ibuprofen has been found more effective for relieving pain. The drug should be administered at least 4 – 6h before the pain the takes its peak value. It would be helpful for the anti-inflammatory patient to take the NSAIDs well before going to bed if they have experienced discomfort in the morning[42].

- **Anti-asthma therapy**

This has been observed that the symptoms of asthma occur 50 – 100 times more often at night than at daytime[43]. Many circadian-sensitive factors contribute to worsen the nocturnal asthmatic symptoms. For example, the levels of cortisol, an anti-inflammatory substance, are highest at the time of awakening and lowest at the time of mid-night and histamine, a mediator of broncho constriction, concentrations peaked at a level that coincided with the greatest degree of broncho constriction at 4:00 am. Absorption of theophylline is slow at night[44].

- **Cardiovascular therapy**

The differences in patterns of illness between day and night for cardiovascular disorders such as angina, hypertension, heart attack, sudden cardiac death and stroke have been recorded. Drugs have been formulated and dosing schedules have been determined to provide appropriate concentration of a drug in the target area of the body when the drug is most needed. For example, the blood pressure of hypertensive patients increases in the early morning hours after awakening, it gradually decreases and become the lowest when the patients go to bed at night. The risk heart attack has been found to be greatest during early morning hours after awakening[45].

- **Chemotherapy**

Antineoplastic drugs cause cytotoxic effects on healthy and diseased tissues. The biological rhythms of both healthy and tumor cells may influence the susceptibility of normal and malignant cells to these agents. It has been shown that susceptibility rhythms to drugs may differ between healthy tissue and cancerous tissue. Therefore, the correct timing of treatment with drug may reduce host toxicity, increase drug tolerance, and ultimately result in better tumor management. The pharmacologic and pharmacokinetic properties of the drug, rhythmic changes in DNA and RNA synthesis, RNA translational activity and mitotic may influence tumor cell susceptibility. Hence, timing of drug administration in the treatment of cancer can have a significant impact on the success of treatment[46].

- **Colonic drug therapy**

The colon can be seen as the preferred absorption site for oral administration of protein and peptide drugs due to relatively low proteolytic enzyme activities in the colon. Moreover, to provide effective therapy of diseases related to colon such as irritable bowel syndrome, Inflammatory Bowel Disease (IBD) including Crohn's disease and ulcerative colitis, colon specific delivery can meetthe important unmet therapeutic needs including oral delivery of macromolecular drugs. Therefore, targeted drug delivery with an appropriate release pattern could be important therapy for the chronic disease[47].

Methods used to prepare pH sensitive drug delivery systems

- **pH-sensitive hydrogels**

All the pH-sensitive polymers contain acidic groups such as carboxylic and sulphonic acids or basic groups such as ammonium salts. These groups either accept or donate protons to the environment according to the pH of the medium. The polymers with a large number of ionizable groups are called polyelectrolytes – anionic or cationic. Poly (acrylic acid) (PAA) becomes ionized at high pH, and poly (N, N-diethylamino ethyl methacrylate)

(PDEAEM) becomes ionized at low pH. The cationic polyelectrolytes dissolve more, or swell more if cross linked, at low pH due to ionization. Similarly, polyanions dissolve more at high pH[48].

- **Other applications**

pH-sensitive hydrogels have been used hydrogels in making biosensors and permeation switches. For these applications, the pH-sensitive hydrogels are usually loaded with enzymes. These enzymes change the pH of the local microenvironment inside the hydrogels. Glucose oxidase, an enzyme is commonly used to prepare pH-sensitive hydrogel. Glucose oxidase transforms glucose to gluconic acid. The formation of gluconic acid reduces the pH of the local environment; as a result the swelling of pH-sensitive hydrogels is affected[49].

- **Enteric-coated systems**

To modify the release of active substances the enteric coated formulations are suitable vehicle. These formulations can release the drug at specific target areas of gastrointestinal tract, although effectiveness of these formulations has long been a point of discussion. The intended use includes masking of taste (9.6%) and odor (1%), stabilization of drug (31%), protection against local irritation (38%) and release focused on defined segments of GI tract (51%). Traditionally enteric coatings have been used to prevent the release of a drug in the stomach. The enteric-coated formulations of drugs such as enzymes, and proteins are sensitive or unstable at acidic pH[50]. These macromolecules are rapidly hydrolyzed and inactivated in acidic medium. Macrolide antibiotics such as erythromycin, are also rapidly degraded by gastric juices. Other drugs such as diclofenac, valproic acid, or salicylic acid (NSAIDs) should be enteric coated to prevent local irritation of the stomach mucosa. Enteric-coated dosage form may be tablets, capsules, orgranules[51].

- **Liposomes**

The idea of pH-sensitive liposomes appeared from the observation that certain enveloped viruses infect cells afteracidification of the endosomal lumen finally to infect the cells. The knowledge about some pathological tissues such as tumors, inflamed and infected tissues, have a more acidic environment compared to normal tissues. However, pH-sensitive liposomes are stable at physiological pH, the liposomes can destabilize under acidic conditions, this results in release of their aqueous contents. Moreover, the liposomes seem to destabilize or fuse with the membranes of macromolecular liposome contents to enter the cytoplasm[52].

Several conditions facilitate the formation of liposomes containing mostly phosphatidyl ethanolamine (PE):

1) PE can be mixed with other phospholipids, including the zwitterionic phosphatidylcholine (PC) and the net negatively charged phosphatidylglycerol or phosphatidylserine (PS). These lipids decrease the intermolecular interactions between the polar headgroups of PE and increase the hydration layer of the membrane.
2) High pH, about 9.0 confers a net negative charge on PE molecules, due to deprotonation of the amino groups, reduces the intermolecular interactions between the polar headgroups and increases the hydration layer[53].
3) Amphiphilic molecules containing a protonatable acidic group that is negatively charged at physiological pH can be incorporated alongside PE in the liposome membrane. These molecules not only cause electrostatic repulsion between bilayers, but also disrupt the strong interactions between PE headgroups, thereby allowing the formation of bilayer structures and liposomes at physiological pH and temperature. By using this approach, stable liposomes are formed at physiological pH, while at mildly acidic pH the carboxyl groups of the amphiphiles are protonated and their stabilizing effect on PE bilayers is reduced[54].

- **Microspheres**

Recently studies conducted with the help of sensitive and reliable equipment have indicated that the pH values in the stomach range from 1.2 – 5.0, while the pH values in the duodenum, jejunum, ileumand colon are 6.6 ± 0.5, 7.4 ± 0.4, 7.5 ± 0.4 and 7.0 ± 0.7, respectively[55]. The gastric emptying of multiple units is in the range from 1 to 3 h in a fasted state and in a fed state 2 – 4h. The small intestinal transit is almost constant at 3 – 4 h and is found to be insensitive of the type of dosage form and whether the person is in fasted or fed state. Thus, a dosage form can take from 4 h to 8 h to arrive at the colon after oral administration. Many pH-sensitive polymers such as Eudragit E, Eudragit L, Eudragit S, HP -55 and CAP, etc., can dissolve at different pH values; have been widely used in designing dosage forms[56].

Based on the above, a pH-sensitive drug delivery system containing nitrendipine has been mixed with three types of pH dependent microspheres made up of acrylic resins Eudragit E-100, Hydroxy-propyl methylcellulose phthalate and Hydroxy propyl methyl cellulose acetate succinate[57]. An attempt has been made to deliver theophylline into colonby taking the advantage of the fact that colon has a lower pH value (6.8) than that of the small intestine (7.0 – 7.8). Hence, a mixture of polymers such as Eudragit L and Eudragit S in an appropriate proportion, pH-sensitive release in the colon can be achieved[58].

Table 4.2 pH-sensitive polymers with their threshold pH.

Polymer	Threshold pH	Polymer	Threshold pH
Eudragit L 100	6.0	Eudragit L 30D	5.6
Eudragit S 100	7.0	Eudragit FS 30D	6.8
Eudragit L 100 – 55	5.5	Polyvinyl acetate phthalate	5.0
Hydroxy propyl methyl cellulose phthalate	4.5 – 4.8	Hydroxy propyl methyl cellulose phthalate - 50	5.2
HPMC 55	5.4	Cellulose acetate trimelliate	4.8
Cellulose acetate phthalate	5.0		

- **Nanoparticles**

It has been reported that particles in the size range of 40 – 120 nm can translocate both transcellularly and paracellularly[59]. These particles have the potential for enhancing bioavailability of drug through particle uptake mechanisms; particulate oral delivery systems can protect labile macromolecules from stomach acid and from the first-pass metabolism in the gastrointestinal tract. The particulate formulations also can increase the local concentration gradient across absorptive cells[60]. Natural polysaccharide pullulan for doxorubicin (DOX) release has been prepared and found that pullulan has been functionalized by successive carboxymethylization and amidation to introduce hydrazide groups. DOX was grafted onto pullulan backbone through the pH-sensitive hydrazone bond to form a pullulan/DOX conjugate.

For preparing polymeric nanoparticles the methods such as ionic gelation, coacervation, solvent evaporation, spontaneous emulsification/solvent diffusion, salting out/ emulsification-diffusion, supercritical fluid technology and polymerization have been tried[61].

ENZYME ACTIVATED DRUG DELIVERY

Every day, thousands of chemical reactions occur in our body and essential metabolic processes occur. Enzymes are proteins in nature that act upon the substrate molecules and decrease the energy of activation required for a chemical reaction to occur by stabilizing the transition state. This stabilization increases the rates of reaction and makes them to occur at physiological conditions with significant rates. Enzymes bind the substrate at key locations in their structure called *active sites*. Hence, the enzymes are highly specific and bind only specific substrates for specific reactions. Without enzymes, most metabolic reactions would have taken much longer time and would not be fast enough to sustain life[62].

Therefore, enzymes are bio-molecules present in the body performing a variety of functions. There are six types of enzymes such as oxidoreductases, transferases, hydrolases, lyases, isomerases, and ligases. Each of the six types catalyses particular type of reaction. Some enzymes, called *apoenzymes*, remain inactive until they are bound to a *cofactor*, which activates the enzyme. A cofactor can either be metal ions such as Zn or organic compounds that attach the enzyme, either by covalent bond or noncovalent bond. The cofactor and apoenzyme complex is called a *holoenzyme*. Hence, these cofactors are non-protein compounds. Enzymes are proteins comprising amino acids which are linked together in one or more polypeptide chains. The sequence of amino acids in a polypeptide chain is called the primary structure which determines the three-dimensional structure of the enzyme, including the shape of the active site. The secondary structure of a protein describes the localised polypeptide chain structures such as α-helices or β-sheets. The complete three-dimensional fold of a polypeptide chain into a protein subunit is called tertiary structure. A protein can contain a *monomer* or more subunits called *dimer*. Enzymes are typically specific because the conformation of amino acids in the active site stabilizes the specific binding of the substrate. The active site generally takes up a relatively small part of the entire enzyme and is normally filled with free water when it is not binding a substrate[63].

Some of the enzymes are specific to particular organs, such as renin in kidney, pepsin and chymotrypsin are in gut, ptyalin in mouth oral cavity, etc.

There are two different models of substrate binding to active site of an enzyme. (1) Lock and key model, which proposes that the shape and chemistry of the substrate are complementary to the shape and chemistry of the active site on the enzyme. This means that the substrate enters the active site, it fits perfectly, and the two binds together, forming the enzyme-substrate complex. (2) The induced fit model, it hypothesises that the enzyme and substrate do not initially have the precise complementary shape/ chemistry or alignment, but rather, this alignment becomes induced at the active site by substrate binding. Generally, the local molecular interactions with amino acid residues on the polypeptide chain stabilizes the substrate binding to an enzyme. There are commonly four mechanisms by which most of these interactions are formed and alter the active site to create the enzyme-substrate complex:

(1) Covalent catalysis,
(2) General acid-base catalysis,
(3) Catalysis by approximation, and
(4) Metal-ion catalysis.

The enzyme activated drug delivery system (EADDS) is a bio-chemical activated type of rate-controlled system. This type of drug delivery is utilized for the treatment of various diseases such as cancer. Traditional system of cancer treatment called chemotherapy has been in practice, it shows rapid toxicity to other types of cells because of its non-specificity. In EADDS, the discharge of drugs from the system is activated by the enzymatic process[62]. The drug is initially dissolved in a suitable medium to form the drug reservoir and can be enclosed physically as microsphereor by chemical means which includes the use of biopolymers such as albumins or polypeptides to which the drug is bounded to their polymer chains. The main procedure involved in the hydrolysis of biopolymers by the distinguishing type of enzyme present in the target site, such as albumin microspheres of 5-fluoorouracil can be targeted to the cancer cells based on the enzyme called protease present in the cancer cells, that act specifically on the proteins such as albumin. In this system, the degradation of albumin microspheres occurs by the action of the protease enzyme[64].

The EADDS can be developed by activation of the drug delivery system by the physiological enzymes present at respective sites to which the drug is planned to be delivered. Commonly in certain disease conditions such as cancer, intracellular enzymes become overexpressed to uphold the rapid cell proliferation and obtaining more nutrients for cellular growth. This altered cellular enzymatic expression can be made as the target for drug delivery by which the system gets activated at the respective site or organ. Abnormal functioning of enzymes causes severe diseases[65].

Delivery carriers

These substances are used to deliver the drug. The drug molecules are entrapped/ linked to its polymer chains. Nanotubes of carbon molecules are the effective carriers of the drug because they are easily internalized by mammalian cells and acts as the room for drugs till they reach the target cell. They are less preferrable owing to its toxic effects[66].

Strategies

- **Polymer type nanoparticles**

One of the methods for preparing the NP is by using the polymers of concerned physicochemical properties. The extensively used polymers as nanocarriers are polyethylene glycol (PEG), dextran, hydroxypropyl methyl acrylamide (HPMA). Various types of polymers can be used for preparing the NP that offers a targeted drug delivery especially in the case of cancer. They are prepared for site targeting and also provides an enhanced and retention type of effect. During designing, there is a necessity of incorporation of molecule that can be identified and acted by the respective enzyme to satisfy the enzyme-based drug release. Moreover, the polymer should have required properties, and be non-toxic. There is no influence on drug action and a chemical modification. This method of combining healing and diagnostic drugs within a single nanoscale 'theragnostic' offers significant potential for personalized nanomedicine to cancer patients. Theragnostic type of NP employed in various conditions including cancer treatment, diabetes, neural disorders, cardiovascular, inflammatory, or autoimmune disease and pulmonary afflictions[67].

Several types of NP have been established for imaging and treating cancer, based on organic and inorganic materials such as quantum dots, carbon nanotubes, gold, silica, iron oxide, and polymers.

- **Microbubbles**

Microbubbles are gas-filled spheres dispersed in aqueous medium with an average size between 1 and 8 μm. these have been widely used in ultrasound imaging as ultrasound contrast agents. The bubbles involve oscillations under a high frequency ultrasound (HFUS) field when driven by a frequency near resonance and even can end up with a rupture. By decreasing the threshold for cavitation, the collapse of drug-encapsulating microbubbles can also be used in ultrasound-activated drug delivery. It has been observed that microbubbles can serve as cavitation nuclei and can enhance ultrasound energy deposition in the cells and tissues. Thus, can facilitate intra-cellular drug transport by disruption of their membranes.

Recently, numerous studies have been reported on the application of microbubbles for drug or gene delivery, particularly in brain tumour *in situ*/targeted treatment and cardiovascular therapy. Effective drug delivery to brain is limited due to the blood–brain barrier (BBB) and the blood–tumour barrier (BTB). Focused ultrasound has shown to be capable of transiently opening the BBB in the presence of microbubbles. To date, a large number of therapeutic agents have overcome the barrier and have been delivered into the brain or a brain tumour. Yeh and co- workers designed super paramagnetic iron oxide nanoparticles conjugating with doxorubicin-loaded microbubbles (DOX- SPIO-MBs) for imaging-guided drug delivery to brain tumours. It was found that the superparamagnetic/acoustic properties of DOX-SPIO-MBs were suitable for imaging. Ultrasound concurrently induced BBB opening and promoted drug delivery, which enhanced the brain tumour treatment effect. They further modified targeting ligands on microbubbles to facilitate directing chemotherapeutic agents to regions of tumour vasculature. Kovacs et al., also demonstrated that micro- bubbles might serve as an effective method for glioblastoma multiforme (GBM) treatment after investigating ultrasonic microbubble therapy in two GBM mouse models[68].

- **Liposomes**

The relatively large size of microbubbles results in a shorter retention time compared to nanocarriers. The expected retention in the lungs also limits the use of microbubbles in cardiovascular targets and tumor endothelia. Hence, acoustically activated liposomes, sometimes called nanobubbles, have become more noticeable in ultrasonic drug delivery. This kind of ultrasound-responsive liposomes (echogenic liposomes) are typically formed with a gas core covered with a lipid monolayer. These were initially studied for ultrasound imaging as contrast agents. It has beenfound that low frequency ultrasound (LFUS) could control the release of the consignment from drug-encapsulating echogenic liposomes with nonthermal effects. Under the appropriate ultrasound frequency, echogenic liposomes rapidly grew, oscillated, collapsed, and spewed consignment by cavitation. Several factors like wave frequency, membrane constituents, encapsulated gas, drug, presented media, and size and shell thickness of liposomes can affect the stability of liposomes and liposomal drug release[69].

Liposomes containing monolayer lipid-covered bubbles are known as bubble liposomes (BLs). These liposomes have been used along with ultrasound exposure to directly deliver plasmid DNA (pDNA) to skeletal muscles by local injection for peripheral artery disease treatment. PEG-modified BLs with perfluoro propane gas were easily fabricated through a reverse-phase evaporation method. It was found that high gene transfection efficiency was achieved in the muscle administrated with BLs and ultrasound in a hind-limb ischemia mice model, as well as an increase in capillary density and blood flow.

- **Microspheres**

A series of hollow biodegradable polymeric microcapsules have been prepared and the mechanical effects of PFO–PLLA [perfluorooctanol–poly (lactic acid)] capsules were studied at different ratios of shell thickness to diameter under different acoustic pressures. Thus, drug release from the PFO–PLLA capsules could be triggered independently in a stepwise or selective fashion by control of mechanical index. In another work, alginate microcapsules were utilized as drug carriers and incorporated with pulsating ultrasound to deliver diclofenac for anti-inflammatory purposes. These capsules produce a release rate 30% higher *in vivo*. When polyelectrolyte microcapsules were fabricated with ZnO nanoparticles embedded in the shell, resulted in considerably higher ultrasound sensitivity. It was demonstrated that the shell thickness and roughness is dependent on the number of ZnO nanoparticle layers. Their different mechanical properties affected sensitivity to ultrasonic treatment. This ZnO nanocomposite showed its potential as a drug carrier with the possibility of opening with the application of ultrasound.

Moreover, lasers can also generate focused ultrasound for spatiotemporal control of drug delivery. A laser-generated focused ultrasound (LGFU)-triggered drug delivery device was also developed. Compared to the traditional HIFU, LGFU can focus on a tight spot with a higher resolution and reduce the heating effect on tissue. Different types of drugs, such as DOX for anticancer treatment and ciprofloxacin for antibacterial treatment, were encapsulated in PLGA nano-particles. Then the PLGA nanoparticles were further loaded into alginate microgels. Upon applying LGFU onto microgels, a significant drug release was observed at the focal point due to the cavitation effect. This has been demonstrated that spatiotemporally remote control of drug release could be achieved in *in vitro* antitumor and antibacterial studies via application of LGFU[70].

- **Prodrug**

Albert used the word " prodrug & quot; in 1958 to refer to compounds that undergo biotransformation before manifesting their pharmacological effects. A prodrug is a drug substance that needs to undergo metabolic or physicochemical transformation in order to become a pharmacologically active agent. Prodrugs are converted from inactive precursors to active metabolites[71]. The main objective of developing a prodrug is to change a drug & chemical make-up in order to add desired physicochemical and/or pharmacokinetic features. Prodrugs are therapeutic agent precursors that, although potentially being mostly inert on their own, are converted by the host into one or more active metabolites that are therapeutically effective *in vivo*[72]. Prodrugs are typically used to improve lipophilicity in order to increase drug penetration or solubility in water. This process often entails a chemical modification of the prodrug, typically including the chemical elimination of a particular prodrug component, to produce the active drug form. This could be an enzymatic reaction or just a regular hydrolytic process. Antibody-directed enzyme prodrug treatment (ADEPT) can be used to increase prodrug activity at the site of action with minimum systemic effects. With gene-directed enzyme prodrug treatment, an enzyme that has been given to the tumour can activate an inert prodrug to release a cytotoxic drug to express oneself. Thymidine kinase, nitro reductase, cytosine deaminase, and cytochrome P450 are some of the specific enzymes used. Prodrugs can be created via carrier-linked or bio-based synthetic techniques[73].

When the carrier-linked method is applied, a transient covalent bond is used to bind the API to a carrier moiety. Following cleavage of a carrier prodrug, a molecule with improved biological activity and at least one side product is produced. The bio precursors lack a carrier group (BPs). Instead, an enzymatic biotransformation of a functional group activates them. The API typically undergoes a molecular change. This produces a new substance that can serve as a substrate for the enzymes that produce metabolites (API)[74]. Prodrugs can be grouped according to chemical classes or mechanism that activates. Chemical classes include things like carrier-linked prodrugs, macromolecular prodrugs, labile esters, phosphorylated prodrugs, and antibody-drug conjugates. The prodrug needs to have appropriate lipophilicity, water solubility, safety, and decent *in vivo* conversion to the parent drug[75]. Targeted prodrug methods are novel developments in the treatment of cancer because they improve the therapeutic index and lessen toxicity problems associated with cytotoxic chemotherapy. There are numerous instances of ophthalmic prodrugs that have been successfully marketed, including dipivalyl ester of epinephrine (dipivephrine). Additionally, ester prodrugs of PGF2 analogues as latanoprost, travoprost, and bimatoprost are quite powerful. Prodrug-based nanosystems are also of great interest because they can offer important advantages like improved longer drug release times, minimal toxicity before degradation, and chemical stability in vivo In the future, more novel, commercially viable prodrugs should be produced as a result of extensive study in this area and rising drug delivery understanding [76].

- **Co-drug**

Covalent chemical bonds that connect two or more medicinal substances together are referred to as; codrugs; or mutual prodrugs. Despite being comparable to the prodrug, it is different in that it replaces the inactive group with an active group that is connected either directly or indirectly (by a cleavable spacer)[77]. The approach & requirement for linking just certain functional categories is a significant drawback. When two medications are taken at the same time, it is possible that neither will be carried to the site of action or absorbed, but the codrug has a higher absorption rate and is more easily transported. It must be gastrointestinally stable before being hydrolyzed to produce two (or more) distinct medicines[78]. Occasionally, the mutual prodrug technique can be used to an advantage if the mutual prodrug is well absorbed and both components are released concurrently and quantitatively after absorption without altering the therapeutic affinity and efficacy. Sulfasalazine (Salazopyrin), a mesalazine derivative, was the first clinically utilized medication for the treatment of rheumatoid arthritis. The distribution and elimination of the two components are identical, and the combined impact of the two drug molecules occurs at a 1:1 ratio. Hybrid drugs (conjugated pharmacophores), a double drug method like codrug in which the two active medications are permanently coupled with no cleavable bond, have also been effectively used[79]. The optimal qualities of a medicine can include being biologically active, keeping action until the release of an active medicine, having a sufficient loading capacity, having no accumulation in the body, being chemically stable, non- antigenic, nonimmunogenic, nontoxic, and none of the above[80].

OSMOTIC PRESSURE ACTIVATED DRUG DELIVERY SYSTEMS

In this type, the drug reservoir can either be a solution or a solid formulation contained within semi-livery a constant rate through a special delivery orifice[81]. The rate of drug release is modulated by controlling the gradient of osmotic pressure. The drug release is activated by osmotic pressure and controlled at a rate determined by the water permeability and the effective surface area of the semi-permeable housing as well as the osmotic pressure gradient[82]. For the drug delivery system containing a solution formulation, the intrinsic rate of drug release is defined by,

$$\frac{Q}{t} = \frac{P_w A_m}{h_m}(\Pi_s - \Pi_e)$$

For the drug delivery system containing a solid formulation, the intrinsic rate of drug release is defined by,

$$\frac{Q}{t} = \frac{P_w A_m}{h_m}(\Pi_s - \Pi_e)S_d$$

Where,

Q/t is the rate of drug release

P_w is the permeability of semipermeable housing

A_m is the effective S.A. of semipermeable housing

h_m is the thickness of semipermeable housing

$(\Pi_s - \Pi_e)$ is the differential osmotic pressure between the drug delivery system with osmotic pressure Π_s and the environment with osmotic pressure Π_e.

S_d is the aqueous solubility of the drug contained in the solid formulation

Rate controlling factors are:

- Water permeability of the semi permeable membrane.
- Effective surface area of the semi permeable membrane.
- Osmotic pressure difference across the semi permeable membrane

In this type, drug reservoir can be either solution or solid formulation contained within semi-permeable housing with controlled water permeability[83]. The drug is activated to release in solution form at a constant rate through a special delivery orifice[84]. The rate of drug release is modulated by controlling the gradient of osmotic pressure[85]. The drug release is activated by osmotic pressure and controlled at a rate determined by the water permeability and the effective surface area of the semi-permeable housing as well as the osmotic pressure gradient[86-88]

FEEDBACK REGULATED DRUG DELIVERY SYSTEMS

Principle

The release of drug from delivery system is acitivated by a triggering agent, such as a biochemical substance, in the body and also regulated by its concentration via some feedback mechanism. Rate of drug release is controlled by the concentration of triggering agent detected by a sensor in the feedback regulated mechanisms[89].

Fundamentals

These different approaches to delivering a drug can have different routes of administration. Some of the most preferred routes are oral, pulmonary inhalation, transdermal, transmucosal, and implantable systems. The rate of drug release is controlled by the concentration of the triggering agent[90-93].

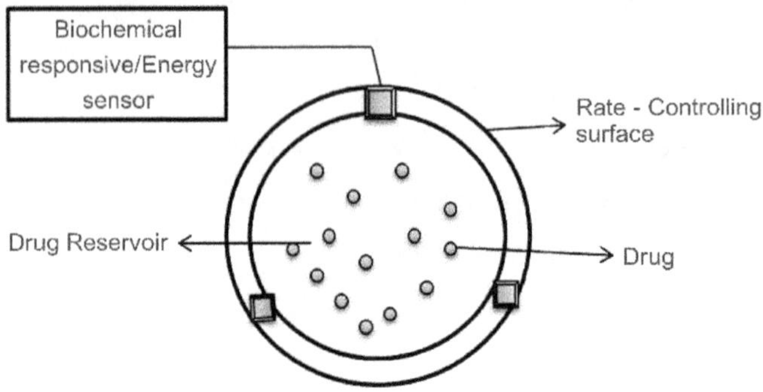

Fig.4.8 Feedback regulated drug delivery.

This can be classified into two classes: modulated and triggered device.

- A modulated device involves the ability to monitor the chemical environment and changes the drug delivery rate continuously in response to the specific external marker
- In a triggered device no drug release takes place until it is triggered by a marker.

They are further classified based on mechanism of action as

1. Bioerosion-regulated drug delivery system
2. Bioresponsive drug delivery system
3. Self-regulating drug delivery system

Bioerosion-regulated drug delivery system

The system consisted of drug dispersed bioerodible matrix fabricated from poly (vinyl methyl ether) ester which is coated with the layer of immobilized urease. In a solution with near-neutral pH, the polymer only erodes very slowly. In presence of urea, urease metabolizes urea to form ammonia. This causes an increase in pH & rapid degradation of polymer matrix as well as release of drug molecules.

Bioresponsive drug delivery system

The drug reservoir is contained in a device enclosed by bioresponsive polymeric membrane whose drug permeability is controlled by the concentration of biochemical agent

Example: glucose-triggered insulin drug delivery system. In this system, the insulin reservoir is encapsulated within hydrogel membrane having –NR2 group. In alkaline solution, the –NR2 are neutral & the membrane is unswollen & impermeable to insulin. Glucose penetrates into the membrane, it oxidizes enzymatically by the glucose oxidase entrapped in the membrane to form gluconic acid. The –NR2 group is protonated to form –NR2H+ & the hydro gel membrane then becomes swollen & permeable to insulin molecules.

Self-regulating drug delivery system

This type of system depends on a reversible & competitive binding mechanism to activate and to regulate the release of a drug. Drug reservoir is a drug complex encapsulated within a semipermeable polymeric membrane. The release of drugs from the delivery system is activated by the membrane permeation of a biochemical agent from the tissue in which the system is located. For Example- In the complex of glycosylated insulin concanavalin A, which is encapsulated inside a polymer membrane, Glucose penetrates the system & it activates the release of glycosylated insulin from the complex for controlled delivery out of the system[94, 95]

REFERENCES

1. Dixit N, Sheo DM, Bhanu PS. Sustained release drug delivery system. Indian J Res Pharm Biotechnol. 2013;1(3):305.
2. Wai-Yip Lee T, Joseph, Robinson R. The science and practice of pharmacy. 20th ed. Vol. 1; 2002. p. 903.
3. Sahilhusen IJ, Mukesh RP. Pharmaceutical controlled release drug delivery systems: A patent overview. Aperito J Drug Designing Pharmacol. 2014;1(2):1-22
4. Wani MS, Controlled release system-A. Rev 2008;6.
5. Bechgaard H, Nielson GH.; Controlled release multiple units and single unit dosage. Drug Dev Ind Pharm.; 1978; 4(1):53-67.
6. Bhowmik D, Kumar KP, Dutta A, Paswan S. Trends in scope andopportunities of control release oral drug delivery systems. Crit Rev. Pharm Sci. 2012; 1:20-33.
7. Chein, YW.; Novel Drug Delivery System. Revised and Expanded.2nd ed. New York: Marcel Dekker; 2005.
8. Ratilal, DA, Gaikwad, PD., Bankar, VH., Pawar, SP. A review on: Sustainedrelease technology. Int J Res Ayurveda Pharm 2011; 2:1701-8.
9. Bansal, BK., Shakya, V., Rewar, S.; A New Trend in Oral SustainedRelease Technology; As J Pharm Res Dev 2014;2:91-5.
10. Vyas, SP., Khar, RK.; Controlled Drug Delivery: Concepts and Advance.New Delhi: Vallabh Prakashan; 2002. p. 155-95.

11. Pharriss BB, Erickson R, Bashaw J, Hoff S, Place VA, Zaffaroni A. Progestasert: a uterine therapeutic system for long-term contraception: I. Philosophy and clinical efficacy. Fertil Steril. 1974 Nov;25(11):915-21. doi: 10.1016/s0015-0282(16)40748-x. PMID: 4426403.
12. Ayres JW, Lindstrom FT. Diffusion model for drug release from suspensions: theoretical considerations. J Pharm Sci. 1977;66(5):654-62. doi: 10.1002/jps.2600660513, PMID 874746.
13. Berner B. Pharmacokinetics of transdermal drug delivery. J Pharm Sci. 1985;74(7):718-21. doi: 10.1002/jps.2600740704, PMID 3928870.
14. Pharriss BB, Erickson R, Bashaw J, Hoff S, Place VA, Zaffaroni A. Progestasert: a uterine therapeutic system for long-term contraception: I. Philosophy and clinical efficacy. Fertil Steril. 1974 Nov;25(11):915-21. doi: 10.1016/s0015-0282(16)40748-x. PMID: 4426403
15. Rentfrow LR, Randel RD, Neuendorff DA. Effect of estrus synchronization with Syncro-Mate-B((R)) on serum luteinizing hormone, progesterone and conception rate in Brahman heifers. Theriogenology. 1987 Sep;28(3):355-62. doi: 10.1016/0093-691x(87)90023-9. PMID: 16726318.
16. Baker RW. Controlled release of biologically active agents. New York: John Wiley & Sons; 1987. p. 1-83.
17. Baker RW, Lonsdale HK. Controlled release: mechanisms and rates. In: Tanquary AC, Lacey RE, editors. Controlled release of biologically active agents. New York: Plenum Press; 1974. p. 15-71. doi: 10.1007/978-1-4684-7239-4_2.
18. Balazs AC, Calef DF, Deutch JM, Siegel RA, Langer R. The role of polymer matrix structure and interparticle interactions in diffusion-limited drug release. In: Gebelein CG, Carraher CE, Jr., editors. Polymeric materials in medication. New York: Plenum Press; 1985. p. 87-102.
19. Mitragotri S, Lahann J. Materials for drug delivery: innovative solutions to address complex biological hurdles. Adv Mater. 2012;24(28):3717-23. doi: 10.1002/adma.201202080, PMID 22807037.
20. Chow EK-H, Ho D. Cancer nanomedicine: from drug delivery to imaging. Sci Transl Med. 2013;5(216):216rv4. doi: 10.1126/scitranslmed.3005872, PMID 24353161.
21. Wilhelm S, Tavares AJ, Dai Q, Ohta S, Audet J, Dvorak HF et al. Analysis of nanoparticle delivery to tumours. Nat Rev Mater. 2016;1(5):16014. doi: 10.1038/natrevmats.2016.14.
22. Tibbitt MW, Dahlman JE, Langer R. Emerging frontiers in drug delivery. J Am Chem Soc. 2016;138(3):704-17. doi: 10.1021/jacs.5b09974, PMID 26741786.
23. Allen TM, Cullis PR. Drug delivery systems: entering the mainstream. Science. 2004;303(5665):1818-22. doi: 10.1126/science.1095833, PMID 15031496.
24. Fleige E, Quadir MA, Haag R. Stimuli-responsive polymeric nanocarriers for the controlled transport of active compounds: concepts and applications. Adv Drug Deliv Rev. 2012;64(9):866-84. doi: 10.1016/j.addr.2012.01.020, PMID 22349241.

25. Qiu Y, Park K. Environment-sensitive hydrogels for drug delivery. Adv Drug Deliv Rev. 2012;64:49-60.

26. Mura S, Nicolas J, Couvreur P. Stimuli-responsive nanocarriers for drug delivery. Nat Mater. 2013;12(11):991-1003. doi: 10.1038/nmat3776, PMID 24150417.(17) Lu Y, Sun W, Gu Z. Stimuli-responsive nanomaterials for therapeutic protein delivery. J Control Release. 2014;194:1-19. doi: 10.1016/j.jconrel.2014.08.015, PMID 25151983.

27. Brudno Y, Mooney DJ, Drug O-D. On-demand drug Delivery from local depots. J Control Release. 2015;219:8-17. doi: 10.1016/j.jconrel.2015.09.011.

28. Torchilin VP. Multifunctional, stimuli-sensitive nanoparticulate systems for drug delivery. Nat Rev Drug Discov. 2014;13(11):813-27. doi: 10.1038/nrd4333, PMID 25287120.

29. Karimi M, Ghasemi A, Sahandi Zangabad P, Rahighi R, Moosavi Basri SM, Mirshekari H et al. Smart micro/nanoparticles in stimulus-responsive drug/ gene delivery systems. Chem Soc Rev. 2016;45(5):1457-501. doi: 10.1039/c5cs00798d, PMID 26776487.

30. Caldorera-Moore M, Peppas NA. Micro- and nanotechnologies for intelligent and responsive biomaterial-based Medical Systems. Adv Drug Deliv Rev. 2009;61(15):1391-401. doi: 10.1016/j.addr.2009.09.002, PMID 19758574.

31. Park K. Controlled drug delivery systems: past forward and future back. J Control Release. 2014;190:3-8. doi: 10.1016/j.jconrel.2014.03.054, PMID 24794901.

32. Felber AE, Dufresne MH, Leroux JC. pH-sensitive vesicles, polymeric micelles, and nanospheres prepared with polycarboxylates. Adv Drug Deliv Rev. 2012;64(11):979-92. doi: 10.1016/j.addr.2011.09.006, PMID 21996056.

33. Gao W, Chan JM, Farokhzad OC. pH-responsive nanoparticles for drug delivery. Mol Pharm. 2010;7(6):1913-20. doi: 10.1021/mp100253e, PMID 20836539.

34. Liu J, Huang Y, Kumar A, Tan A, Jin S, Mozhi A et al. pH-sensitive nano-systems for drug delivery in cancer therapy. Biotechnol Adv. 2014;32(4):693-710. doi: 10.1016/j.biotechadv.2013.11.009, PMID 24309541.

35. Pillai PP, Huda S, Kowalczyk B, Grzybowski BA. Controlled pH stability and adjustable cellular uptake of mixed-charge nanoparticles. J Am Chem Soc. 2013;135(17):6392-5. doi: 10.1021/ja4001272, PMID 23527630.

36. Zhang S, Bellinger AM, Glettig DL, Barman R, Lee Y-AL, Zhu J; et al. A pH-responsive supramolecular polymer gel as an enteric elastomer.for Use in Gastric Devices. Nat. Mater. 2015, 14 (10), 1065−1071.

37. Kono K, Tabata F, Takagishi T. pH-responsive permeability of poly(acrylic acid)-poly(ethylenimine) complex capsule membrane. J Membr Sci. 1993;76(2-3):233-43. doi: 10.1016/0376-7388(93)85220-Q

38. Hariharan D, Peppas NA. Modelling of water transport and solute release in physiologically sensitive gels. J Control Rel. 1993;23(2):123-35. doi: 10.1016/0168-3659(93)90038-7

39. Siegel RA, Firestone BA. PH-dependent equilibrium swelling properties of hydrophobic polyelectrolyte copolymer gels. Macromolecules. 1988;21(11):3254-9. doi: 10.1021/ma00189a021

40. Allcock HR, Ambrosio AM. Synthesis and characterization of pH-sensitive poly(organophosphazene) hydrogels. Biomaterials. 1996;17(23):2295-302. doi: 10.1016/0142-9612(96)00073-7, PMID 8968526

41. Bell CL, Peppas NA. Water, solute and protein diffusion in physiologically responsive hydrogels of poly(methacrylic acid-g-ethylene glycol). Biomaterials. 1996;17(12):1203-18. doi: 10.1016/0142-9612(96)84941-6, PMID 8799505.

42. Järvinen K, Akerman S, Svarfvar B, Tarvainen T, Viinikka P, Paronen P. Drug release from pH and ionic strength responsive poly(acrylic acid) grafted poly(vinylidenefluoride) membrane bags in vitro. Pharm Res. 1998;15(5):802-5. doi: 10.1023/a:1011995725320 . PMID 9619794.

43. Siegel RA, Johannes I, Hunt CA, Firestone BA. Buffer effects on swelling kinetics in polybasic gels. Pharm Res. 1992;9(1):76-81. doi: 10.1023/a:1018983828027, PMID 1589413 .

44. Giannos SA, Dinh SM, Berner B. Temporally controlled drug delivery systems: coupling of pH oscillators with membrane diffusion. J Pharm Sci. 1995;84(5):539-43. doi: 10.1002/jps.2600840505, PMID 7658341 .

45. Heller J, Trescony PV. Controlled drug release by polymer dissolution II: Enzyme-mediated delivery device. J Pharm Sci. 1979;68(7):919-21. doi: 10.1002/jps.2600680740, PMID 37327.

46. Ghandehari H, Kopecková P, Kopecek J. In vitro degradation of pH-sensitive hydrogels containing aromatic azo bonds. Biomaterials. 1997;18(12):861-72. doi: 10.1016/s0142-9612(97)00007-0, PMID 9184750 .

47. Petka WA, Harden JL, McGrath KP, Wirtz D, Tirrell DA. Reversible hydrogels from self-assembling artificial proteins. Science. 1998;281(5375):389-92. doi: 10.1126/science.281.5375.389, PMID 9665877 .

48. Li JJ. Circadian variation in myocardial ischemia: the possible mechanisms involving in this phenomenon. Med Hypotheses. 2003;61(2):240-3. doi: 10.1016/s0306-9877(03)00154-3, PMID 12888312 .

49. Smolensky MH, Labreque G. Chronotherapeutics. Pharm News. 1997;2:10-6.

50. Washington N, Wilson CG. Can oral controlled drug delivery meet the challenges posed by chronotherapeutics?; 2009. Available from: http://www.egalet.com/multimedia/Chronotherapy_May_061.pdf.

51. Ura J, Shirachi D, Ferrill M. The chronotherapeutic approach to pharmaceutical treatment. Calif Pharm. 1992;23:46-53.

52. Lamberg L. Chronotherapeutics: implications for drug therapy. Am Pharm. 1991;31(11):20-3. doi: 10.1016/S0160-3450(15)31301-5, PMID PubMed.

53. Firestone BA, Siegel RA. Kinetics and mechanisms of water sorption in hydrophobic, ionizable copolymer gels. J Appl Polym Sci. 1991;43(5):901-14. doi: 10.1002/app.1991.070430507 .

54. Falamarzian M, Varshosaz J. The effect of structural changes on swelling kinetics of polybasic/hydrophobic pH-sensitive hydrogels. Drug Dev Ind Pharm. 1998;24(7):667-9. doi: 10.3109/03639049809082369, PMID 9876512 .

55. Kou JH, Amidon GL, Lee PI. PH-dependent swelling and solute diffusion characteristics of poly(hydroxyethyl methacrylate-co-methacrylic acid) hydrogels. Pharm Res. 1988;5(9):592-7. doi: 10.1023/a:1015998131160, PMID 3247322 .

56. Brannon-Peppas L, Peppas NA. Dynamic and equilibrium swelling behaviour of pH-sensitive hydrogels containing 2-transhydroxyethyl methacrylate. Biomaterials. 1990;11(9):635-44. doi: 10.1016/0142-9612(90)90021-h, PMID 2090297.

57. Khare AR, Peppas NA. Release behavior of bioactive agents from pH-sensitive hydrogels. J Biomater Sci Polym Ed. 1993;4(3):275-89. doi: 10.1163/156856293x00564 . PMID 8476795.

58. Peppas NA, Klier J. Controlled release by using poly(methacrylic acid-g-ethylene glycol) hydrogels. J Control Release. 1991;16(1-2):203-14. doi: 10.1016/0168-3659(91)90044-E .

59. Siegel RA, Falamarzian M, Firestone BA, Moxley BC. pH-controlled release from hydrophobic/polyelectrolyte copolymer hydrogels. J Control Release. 1988;8(2):179-82. doi: 10.1016/0168-3659(88)90044-2 .

60. Patel VR, Amiji MM. Preparation and characterization of freeze-dried chitosan-poly(ethylene oxide) hydrogels for site-specific antibiotic delivery in the stomach. Pharm Res. 1996;13(4):588-93. doi: 10.1023/a:1016054306763, PMID 8710751 .

61. Akala EO, Kopecková P, Kopecek J. Novel pH-sensitive hydrogels with adjustable swelling kinetics. Biomaterials. 1998;19(11-12):1037-47. doi: 10.1016/s0142-9612(98)00023-4, PMID 9692802 .

62. Gutowska A, Bark JS, Kwon IC, Bae YH, Kim SW, Wan Kim S. Squeezing hydrogels for controlled oral drug delivery. J Control Release. 1997;48(2-3):141-8. doi: 10.1016/S0168-3659(97)00041-2 .

63. Bilia A, Carelli V, Di Colo G, Nannipieri E. In vitro evaluation of a pH-sensitive hydrogel for control of GI drug delivery from silicone-based matrices. Int J Pharm. 1996;130(1):83-92. doi: 10.1016/0378-5173(95)04297-0.

64. Carelli V, Coltelli S, Di Colo G, Nannipieri E, Serafini MF. Silicone microspheres for pH-controlled gastrointestinal drug delivery. Int J Pharm. 1999;179(1):73-83. doi: 10.1016/s0378-5173(98)00387-1, PMID 10053204.

65. Aikawa K, Matsumoto K, Uda H, Tanaka S, Shimamura H, Aramaki Y et al.. Hydrogel formation of the pH response polymer polyvinylacetal diethylaminoacetate (AEA). International Journal of Pharmaceutics. 1998;167(1-2):97-104. doi: 10.1016/S0378-5173(98)00057-X.

66. Aikawa K, Mitsutake N, Uda H, Tanaka S, Shimamura H, Aramaki Y et al.. Drug release from pH-response polyvinylacetal diethylaminoacetate hydrogel,

and application to nasal delivery. International Journal of Pharmaceutics. 1998;168(2):181-8. doi: 10.1016/S0378-5173(98)00096-9.

67. Dong LC, Hoffman AS. Controlled enteric release of macromolecules from pH sensitive macroporous heterogels. Control Release Bioact Mater. 1990; 17:325-6.

68. Dong LC, Hoffman AS. Synthesis and application of thermally reversible heterogels for drug delivery. J Control Release. 1990;13(1):21-31. doi: 10.1016/0168-3659(90)90071-Z

69. Dong LC, Hoffman AS. A novel approach for preparation of pH-sensitive hydrogels for enteric drug delivery. J Control Release. 1991;15(2):141-52. doi: 10.1016/0168-3659(91)90072-L .

70. Vakkalanka SK, Brazel CS, Peppas NA. Temperature- and pH-sensitive terpolymers for modulated delivery of streptokinase. J Biomater Sci Polym Ed. 1996;8(2):119-29. doi: 10.1163/156856296x00192, PMID 8957708.

71. Li X, Jasti BR. Design of controlled release of drug delivery systems. McGraw-Hill; 2006. Osmotic controlled drug delivery systems. p. 203-29.

72. Markovic M, Ben-Shabat S, Dahan A. Prodrugs for improved drug delivery: Lessons learned from recently developed and marketed products. Pharmaceutics 2020;12:1–12. https://doi.org/10.3390/pharmaceutics12111031.

73. Edition RT, Ates-alagoz Z, Adejare A. Chapter 9 - Prodrugs 2021:2021–2.

74. Healy AT, Vogelbaum MA. Delivery of Therapy to Brain Tumors : Problems 117 and

75. Potentials. Youmans Winn Neurol Surgery, 4-Volume Set 2017:849–55.e3.

76. Duan N, Li J, Song S, Wang F, Yang Y, Nie D, et al. Enzyme-Activated Prodrug-Based Smart Liposomes Specifically Enhance Tumor Hemoperfusion with Efficient Drug Delivery to Pancreatic Cancer Cells and Stellate Cells. Adv Funct Mater 2021;31:1–14. https://doi.org/10.1002/adfm.202100605.

77. De Montellano PRO. Cytochrome P450-activated prodrugs. Future Med Chem 2013;5:213–28. https://doi.org/10.4155/fmc.12.197.

78. Sun IC, Yoon HY, Lim DK, Kim K. Recent Trends in in Situ Enzyme-Activatable Prodrugs for Targeted Cancer Therapy. Bioconjug Chem 2020;31:1012–24. https://doi.org/10.1021/acs.bioconjchem.0c00082.

79. Aljuffali IA, Lin CF, Chen CH, Fang JY. The codrug approach for facilitating drug delivery and bioactivity. Expert Opin Drug Deliv 2016;13:1311–25. https://doi.org/10.1080/17425247.2016.1187598.

80. Mahkam M, Zeynabad FB, Alizadeh E, Rahimi M, Rahimi F, Salehi R. Novel methotrexate-ciprofloxacin loaded alginate-clay based nanocomposite as anticancer and antibacterial co-drug delivery system. Adv Pharm Bull 2021;11:477–89. https://doi.org/10.34172/apb.2021.055.

81. Das N, Dhanawat M, Dash B, Nagarwal RC, Shrivastava SK. Codrug: An efficient approach for drug optimization. Eur J Pharm Sci 2010;41:571–88. https://doi.org/10.1016/j.ejps.2010.09.014.

82. Pastor A, Machelart A, Li X, Willand N, Baulard A, Brodin P, et al. A novel codrug made of the combination of ethionamide and its potentiating booster: Synthesis, self-assembly into nanoparticles and antimycobacterial evaluation. Org Biomol Chem 2019;17:5129–37. https://doi.org/10.1039/c9ob00680j.

83. Rose S, Nelson JF. A continuous long-term injector. Aust J Exp Biol Med Sci. 1955;33(4):415-9. doi: 10.1038/icb.1955.44, PMID 13269346.

84. Higuchi T. Osmotic dispenser with collapsible supply container. US Patent No. 3. 1973;760:805.

85. Fara JW. Osmotic delivery systems for research. Methods Enzymol. 1985;112:470-84. doi: 10.1016/s0076-6879(85)12037-9, PMID 2413336, .

86. Theeuwes F. Elementary osmotic pump. J Pharm Sci. 1975;64(12):1987-91. doi: 10.1002/jps.2600641218, PMID 1510 .

87. Cortese R, Theeuwes F. Osmotic device with hydrogel driving member. US Patent No. 4. 1982;327:725.

88. Zentner GM, McClelland GA, Sutton SC. Controlled porosity solubility- and resin-modulated osmotic drug delivery systems for release of diltiazem hydrochloride. J Control Release. 1991;16(1-2):237-43. doi: 10.1016/0168-3659(91)90047-H .

89. Parmar NS, Vyas SK. Advances in controlled and novel drug delivery. CBS; 2008. .

90. McClelland GA, Sutton SC, Engle K, Zentner GM. The solubility-modulated osmotic pump: in vitro/in vivo release of diltiazem hydrochloride. Pharm Res. 1991;8(1):88-92. doi: 10.1023/a:1015890525495, PMID 2014214 .

91. Jerzewski RL, Chien YW. Osmotic drug delivery. In: Kydonieus A, editor. Treatise on controlled drug delivery: fundamentals, optimization, application. New York: Marcel Dekker; 1992. p. 225-53. .

92. Guo JH. Effects of plasticizers on water permeation and mechanical properties of cellulose acetate: antiplasticization in slightly plasticized polymer Film. Drug Dev Ind Pharm. 1993;19(13):1541-55. doi: 10.3109/03639049309069325, .

93. Kelbert M, Béchard SR. Evaluation of cellulose acetate (CA) latex as coating material for controlled release products. Drug Dev Ind Pharm. 1992;18(5):519-38. doi: 10.3109/03639049209043709.

94. Chen C, Lee D, Xie J. Controlled release formulation for water insoluble drugs in which a passageway is formed in situ. US patent No. 5736159; 1998.

95. Liu L, Ku J, Khang G, Lee B, Rhee JM, Lee HB. Development of new trend of pulsatile drug delivery. J Control Release. 2000;68(2):145-56. doi: 10.1016/s0168-3659(00)00243-1, PMID 10925123.

EXCERCISE

MULTIPLE CHOICE QUESTIONS

1. Rate determining step for controlled release delivery system is:
   a. Absorption
   b. Drug release from dosage form
   c. Both
   d. None
2. By controlled release drug delivery systems bioavailability is
   a. Improved
   b. Decreases
   c. Both
   d. None
3. Products designed to release their medication in a controlled manner at a predetermined rate, duration and locatio achleve and maintain therapeutic blood levels of drug.
   a. Immediate Release
   b. Extended Release
   c. Targeted Release
   d. None of the above
4. Drug having molecular weight ———— is good candidate for controlled release dosage form:
   a. More than 2000 dalton
   b. Less than 600 dalton
   c. Over and above 1000 dalton
   d. None of the above
5. The drugs that cannot be administered transdermally are:
   a. Drugs with very short half-lives
   b. Drugs with narrow therapeutic indices
   c. Easy removal and termination
   d. Drugs against peptic ulcer
6. Mechanism of controlled drug delivery include.
   a. Osmosis controlled.
   b. Bio responsive controlled release
   c. Dissolution controlled.
7. All the above Select the type of drug that can be incorporated in liposomes.
   a. Lipophilic
   b. Hydrophilic
   c. Both
   d. None Both

8. Advantage of controlled release dosage form
   a. Patient Compliance
   b. Reduction in the frequency of designing
   c. Improved efficacy in treatment.
9. All of the above Ion activated DDS is ——— type of activated systems.
   a. Physical
   b. Chemical
   c. Biochemical
   d. All the above
10. What is the characteristic of pH-independent formulations?
    a. Buffering agents that adjust pH to the desired value
    b. Drug disperse in the insoluble matrix of rigid hydrophobic materials
    c. Hollow systems containing drug surrounded by a polymer membrane
    d. Formation of complexes between the drug and anion/cation exchange resins
11. What are the characteristics of osmotic pressure-controlled systems?
    a. Buffering agents that adjust pH to the desired value.
    b. Releases the drug at a zero-order kinetics.
    c. Hollow systems containing drug surrounded by a polymer membrane.
    d. Formation of complexes between the drug and anion/cation exchange resins
12. The driving force in Osmotically controlled release formulation is-
    a. Osmotic pressure
    b. Hydraulic pressure
    c. Atmospheric pressure
    d. Absolute pressure
13. The drug release from osmotic release pump follows:
    a. First order
    b. Zero order
    c. Both a and b
    d. Pseudo first
14. In ________ drug delivery system, the release of drug molecule from the delivery is pre-planed with flow rate profile of medicine.
    a. Rate Pre-programmed
    b. Activation modulated.
    c. Feedback regulated.
    d. Site Targeting
15. Rate pre-programmed drug delivery system follows-
    a. Noyes whitney equation
    b. Fick's law diffusion
    c. Henry's Law
    d. None of the above

16. Rate controlling Step for osmotic pressure-controlled system is-
    a. Orifice Diameter
    b. Membrane area
    c. Osmotic properties of drug
    d. All the above
17. Progestasert (progesterone releasing intrauterine device) made up of.
    a. Polyethylene
    b. Polyvinyl chloride
    b. Polyvinyl co-polymer
    d. All the above
18. Enzyme activated drug delivery is a-
    a. Biochemically acitivated system
    b. Chemically activated system.
    c. Both a and b
    d. None
19. pH activated drug delivery system is a –
    a. Biochemically acitivated system
    b. Chemically activated system.
    c. Both a and b
    d. None
20. Which one of the following is a mechanically activated DDS
    a. Compudose
    b. Progestasert
    b. Nebulizers
    d. None of the above

SHORT ANSWER QUESTIONS

1. What are the principles of rate-controlled drug delivery system
2. What are the types of rate-controlled drug delivery system pH activated drug delivery systems.
3. What do you mean by the progestasert and syncromate-C?
4. Write a note on activation modulated DDS.
5. Write about the types of activation modulated DDS.
6. Define microsphere and microcapsules.
7. Write a note on matrix diffusion system.
8. Explain the osmotically regulated implants as a new drug delivery system.
9. What is feedback regulated drug delivery system?
10. Describe formulations of mechanically activated.

LONG ANSWER QUESTIONS

1. Explain in detail about various types of osmotic pumps.
2. Describe formulations of mechanically activated DDS.
3. Explain the concepts and design of rate-controlled drug delivery systems.
4. Explain about feedback regulated drug delivery system.
5. Disscus about the principles and fundamental of rate-controlled drug delivery system
6. Discuss in detail about the various strategies of Enzyme activated DDS.
7. Explain in brief about the methods involved in preparing pH sensitive DDS.
8. Explain any two types of rate-controlled drug delivery system.
9. Describe formulations of mechanically activated, and pH activated rate-controlled Drug Delivery system.
10. Desecribe about activation modulated DDS and its various types.

MCQ ANSWERS

1. (b)	2. (a)	3. (b)	4. (b)
5. (d)	6. (d)	7. (c)	8. (d)
9. (b)	10. (a)	11. (b)	12. (a)
13. (b)	14. (a)	15. (b)	16. (d)
17. (a)	18. (a)	19. (b)	20. (c)

CHAPTER - 5

Gasto-Retentive Drug Delivery Systems

Dr. Kapil Agrawal, Dr. Deependra Singh, Dr. Manju Rawat Singh, and Dr. Amber Vyas

Principle, Factors Controlling Gastric Retention of Dosage Forms, Advantages, Disadvantages, Physiology of Stomach, Approaches to Extend GI Transit Time.

PRINCIPLE

GRDDS is an approach to prolong the gastric residence time, thereby aiming site-specific drug release in the upper GIT for local or systemic effects. Gastro retentive dosage forms can remain in the gastric region for long periods and hence significantly prolong the gastric retention time (GRT) of drugs. Prolonged GRT enables the controlled delivery of drugs in stomach which can evade the repeated administration of dosage form of the drugs with short half-life. Literature suggests that GRDDS has gained huge popularity in the field of oral drug delivery recently, as it can release the drug slowly that can combat many shortcomings allied with conventional oral delivery, including poor bioavailability. Studies demonstrate that the drugs which have to be in the upper part of the GIT have been prepared as gastro retentive dosage forms using various approaches. Such formulation improves the therapeutic efficacy of the drug and enhances the patient compliance [1,2].

GRDFs have been researched for many ant diabetic drugs and studies revealed that the gastro retentive form of drug has led to better management of the disease status. Although, a lot of work has been done, but still there is tremendous scope to develop such dosage form of ant diabetic drugs. Moreover, there are certain ant diabetic drugs which have a strong rationale for developing GRDDS, but no research has been reported to be performed on them [3].

The development of oral controlled release systems has been a challenge to formulation scientists due to their inability to restrain and localize the system at targeted areas of the gastrointestinal (GI) tract. Controlled drug delivery systems aim to maintain plasma concentration of drugs within the therapeutic window for a longer period of time, thereby to ensure sustained therapeutic action and for that reason an increasing interest in their development exist. Moreover, many of new therapeutics under development are large molecules such as peptides, proteins, oligonucleotides, and vaccines [4].

Gastro retentive drug delivery systems are designed to prolong the gastric retention time of the drugs which are:

- Locally active in the stomach
- Unstable in the intestinal environment
- Have narrow absorption window in the GIT
- Have low solubility at the high pH regions [5]

Advantages of gastro/intestinal retentive delivery systems

- Improvement of bioavailability and therapeutic efficacy of the drugs and possible reduction of dose.
- Maintenance of constant therapeutic levels over a prolonged period and thus reduction in fluctuation in therapeutic levels.
- Retention of drug delivery systems in the stomach prolongs overall Gastrointestinal transit time there by increasing bioavailability of sustained release delivery systems intended for once-a-day administration.
- For drugs that have low bioavailability in acidic pH, and are well absorbed in intestinal pH, Intestinal retentive delivery system is advantageous.

Limitations of the techniques of gastro/intestinal retention

- Not suitable for drugs that may cause gastric lesions e.g. Non-steroidal anti-inflammatory drugs.
- More predictable and reproducible floating properties should be achieved in all the extreme gastric conditions.
- For Intestinal retention, dosage form has to cross gastric conditions intact, which is not easily achievable.
- Not suitable for drugs that are unstable in the strong acidic or basic environment.
- These systems do not offer significant advantages over the conventional dosage forms for drugs that are absorbed throughout the gastro intestinal tract.[6]

Other limitations associated with specific types of GRDDS are given the table below[7-9].

High density system	Very difficult to incorporate large amount of drugs. No such systems are available in the market till date
Floating system	Floating highly depends on the fed state of the stomach and higher level of fluid is required in gastric region
Expandable system	Chocking problem; storage problem due to hydrolysable and biodegradable polymers; difficult to manufacture and not economical
Mucoadhesive system	Can be detached from gastric mucosa due to rapid turnover of mucus and peristaltic wave of stomach. It may also attach to the mucus of oesophagus
Magnetic system	Problem with patient compliance

FACTORS CONTROLLING GASTRIC RETENTION OF DOSAGE FORMS

The stomach anatomy and physiology contain parameters to be considered in the development of gastroretentive dosage forms. To pass through the pyloric valve in to the small intestine the particle size should be in the range of 1 to 2 mm[10]. The most important parameters controlling the gastric retention time (GRT) of oral dosage forms include : density, size and shape of the dosage form, food intake and its nature, caloric content and frequency of intake, posture, gender, age, sex, sleep, body mass index, physical activity and diseased states of the individual (e.g. chronic disease, diabetes etc.) and administration of drugs with impact on gastrointestinal transit time for example drugs acting as anticholinergic agents (e.g. atropine, propantheline), Opiates (e.g. codeine) and prokinetic agents (e.g. metclopramide, cisapride.)[11]. The molecular weight and lipophilicity of the drug depending on its ionization state are also important parameters[12].

- **Density of dosage forms:**

The density of a dosage form also affects the gastric emptying rate and determines the location of the system in the stomach. Dosage forms having a density lower than the gastric contents can float to the surface, while high density systems sink to bottom of the stomach[13]. Both positions may isolate the dosage system from the pylorus. A density of < 1.0 gm/ cm3 is required to exhibit floating property[14].

- **Shape and size of the dosage form:**

Shape and size of the dosage forms are important in designing indigestible single unit solid dosage forms. The mean gastric residence times of nonfloating dosage forms are highly variable and greatly dependent on their size, which may be large, medium, and small units. In most cases, the larger the dosage form the greater will be the gastric retention time (GRT) due to the larger size of the dosage form would not allow this to quickly pass through the pyloric antrum into the intestine[15]. Dosage forms having a diameter of more than 7.5 mm show a better gastric residence time compared with one having 9.9 mm[14]. Ring-shaped and tetrahedron-shaped devices have a better gastric residence time as compared with other shapes[16].

- **Food intake and its nature:**

Food intake, viscosity and volume of food, caloric value and frequency of feeding have a profound effect on the gastric retention of dosage forms. The presence or absence of food in the gastrointestinal tract (GIT) influences the gastric retention time (GRT) of the dosage form. Usually, the presence of food in the gastrointestinal tract (GIT) improves the gastric retention time (GRT) of the dosage form and thus, the drugs absorption increases by allowing its stay at the absorption site for a longer period. Again, increase in acidity and caloric value shows down gastric emptying time (GET), which can improve the gastric retention of dosage forms[17].

- **Effect of gender, posture, and age:**

Generally, females have slower gastric emptying rates than male. The effect of posture does not have any significant difference in the mean gastric retention time (GRT) for individuals in upright, ambulatory, and supine state. In case of elderly persons, gastric emptying is slowed down.

Potential drug candidates for gastroretentive drug delivery systems

1) Drugs those are locally active in the stomach e.g. misroprostol, antacids etc.
2) Drugs that have narrow absorption window in gastrointestinal tract (GIT) e.g. L-DOPA, para aminobenzoic acid, furosemide, riboflavin etc.
3) Drugs those are unstable in the intestinal or colonic environment e.g. captopril, ranitidine HCl, metronidazole.
4) Drugs that disturb normal colonic microbes e.g. gastric emptying is slowed down[18]. antibiotics against Helicobacter pylori.
5) Drugs that exhibit low solubility at high pH values e.g. diazepam, chlordiazepoxide, verapamil HCl.

Drugs those are unsuitable for gastroretentive drug delivery systems

1) Drugs that have very limited acid solubility e.g. phenytoin etc.
2) Drugs that suffer instability in the gastric environment e.g. erythromycin etc.
3) Drugs intended for selective release in the colon e.g. 5- amino salicylic acid and corticosteroids etc.

ADVANTAGES

1. The bioavailability of therapeutic agents can be significantly enhanced especially for those which get metabolized in the upper GIT by this gastroretentive drug delivery approach in comparison to the administration of nongastroretentive drug delivery. There are several different factors related to absorption and transit of the drug in the gastrointestinal tract (GIT) that act concomitantly to influence the magnitude of drug absorption[18].
2. For drugs with relatively short half-life, sustained release may result in a flip- flop pharmacokinetics and also enable reduced frequency of dosing with improved patient compliance.
3. They also have an advantage over their conventional system as it can be used to overcome the adversities of the gastric retention time (GRT) as well as the gastric emptying time (GET). As these systems are expected to remain buoyant on the gastric fluid without affecting the intrinsic rate of employing because their bulk density is lower than that of the gastric fluids.
4. Gastroretentive drug delivery can produce prolong and sustain release of drugs from dosage forms which avail local therapy in the stomach and small intestine. Hence they are useful in the treatment of disorders related to stomach and small intestine.
5. The controlled, slow delivery of drug form gastroretentive dosage form provides sufficient local action at the diseased site, thus minimizing or eliminating systemic exposure of drugs. This site-specific drug delivery reduces undesirable effects of side effects.
6. Gastroretentive dosage forms minimize the fluctuation of drug concentrations and effects. Therefore, concentration dependent adverse effects that are associated with peak concentrations can be presented. This feature is of special importance for drug with a narrow therapeutic index [9].
7. Gastroretentive drug delivery can minimize the counter activity of the body leading to higher drug efficiency.
8. Reduction of fluctuation in drug concentration makes it possible to obtain improved selectivity in receptor activation.
9. The sustained mode of drug release from Gastroretentive doses form enables extension of the time over a critical concentration and thus enhances the pharmacological effects and improves the chemical outcomes.

DISADVANTAGES

1. Unsuitable for drugs with limited acid solubility, e.g. Phenytoin.
2. Unsuitable for drugs that are unstable in acidic environment, e.g. Erythromycin.

3. Drugs that irritate or causes gastric lesions on slow release, e.g. Aspirin and NSAIDs.
4. Drugs that absorb selectively in colon, e.g. Corticosteroid.
5. Drugs that absorb equally well through GIT, e.g., Isosorbide dinitrate, Nifedipine.
6. Floating drug delivery systems require high fluid level in stomach to float and work effectively.

PHYSIOLOGY OF STOMACH

Anatomically the stomach is divided into three regions: Fundus, body and antrum (pylorus). The proximal part made of fundus and body act as reservoir for undigested materials where as the antrum is the main site for mixing motions and act as pump from gastric emptying by propelling the actions. Gastric emptying occurs during fasting as well as feed state. The patent of motility is however distinct in 2 states. During fasting state an inter digestive series of electrical events takes place, which cycle both through stomach and intestine every 2 to 3 hours[19]. This is called the interdigestive myoelectric cycle or migrating myloelectric cycle (MMC), which is further divided into following 4 phases as described by Wilson and Washington[10]

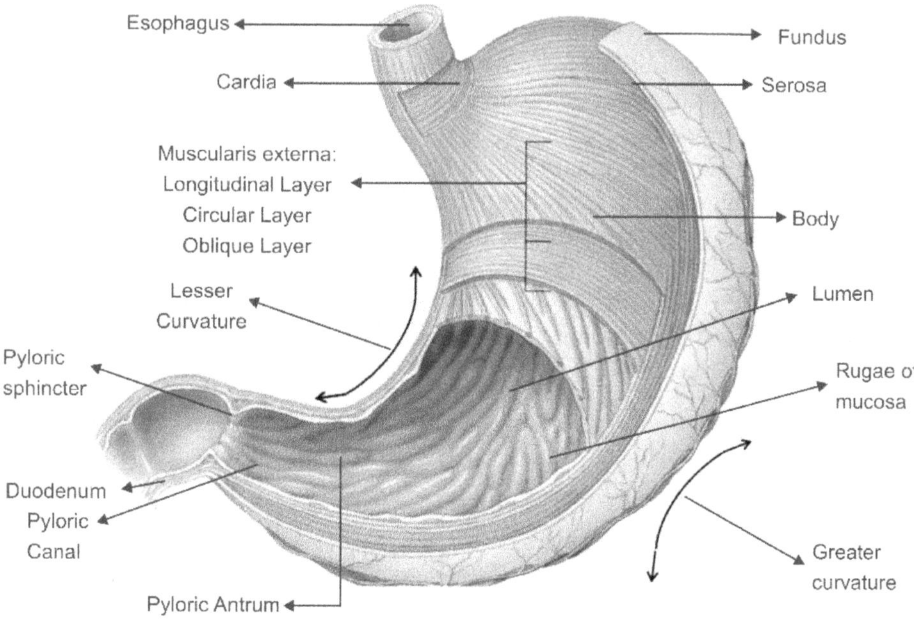

Fig.5.1 Anatomy of stomach.

1. Phase 1- (Basic phase) last from 30-60 minutes with rare contractions.
2. Phase II- (Preburst phase) last for 20-40 minutes with intermittent action potential and contractions.
3. Phase III- (Burst phase) last for 10-20 minutes which includes intense and regular contractions for short period.
4. Phase IV-last for 0-5 minutes and occurs between phase 2 and 1 of 2 consecutive cycles.

After the ingestion of a mixed meal, the pattern of contractions changes from fasted to that of fed state. This is also known as digestive motility pattern and comprises continuous contractions as in phase II of fasted state. These contractions results in reducing the size of food particles (to less than 1mm) which are propelled toward the pylorus in a suspension form. During the fed state onset of MMC is delayed resulting in slowdown of gastric emptying rate. Scintigraphic studies determining gastric emptying rates revealed that orally administered controlled release dosage form are subjected to basically two complications that of short gastric residence time and unpredictable gastric emptying rate[20].

APPROACHES TO EXTEND GI TRANSIT TIME

Floating Drug Delivery Systems

Floating drug delivery systems is one of the important approaches to achieve gastric retention to obtain sufficient drug bioavailability[21]. This delivery system is desirable for drugs with an absorption window in the stomach or in the upper small intestine[22]. These systems have a bulk density lower than that of gastric fluids and thus remain buoyant in the stomach without affecting the gastric emptying rate for a prolonged period of time. While the system is floating in the gastric contents, the drug is released slowly at a desired rate from the system. After the release of the drug, the residual system is emptied from the stomach. This results in an increase in the gastric retention time and a better control of fluctuations in plasma drug concentration[23]. The major requirements for floating drug delivery system are

- It must maintain specific gravity lower than gastric contents (1.004 gm/cm3).
- It must form a cohesive gel barrier.
- It should release contents slowly to serve as a reservoir[24,25].

The inherent low density can be provided by the entrapment of air (e.g. hollow chambers) or by the incorporation of low density materials (e.g. fatty materials or oils, or foam powder)[21, 22]. These following approaches have been used for the design of floating dosage forms of single and multiple-unit systems. Recently a single-unit floating system was proposed consisting of polypropylene foam powder, matrix forming polymers, drug and filler[22]. The good floating behavior of these systems could be successfully combined with accurate control of the resulting drug release patterns. Single-unit dosage forms are associated with problems such as sticking together or being obstructed in the gastrointestinal tract (GIT) which may produce irritation. On the other hand multiple-unit floating systems may be an attractive alternative since they have been shown to reduce the inter- and intra- subject availabilities in drug absorption as well as to lower the possibility of dose dumping[26]. Various multiple-unit floating system like air compartment multiple-unit system[2], hollow microspheres (microballoons) prepared by the emulsion solvent diffusion method[27], microparticles based on low density foam powder[22], beads prepared by emulsion gelatin method[28] etc. can be distributed widely throughout the GIT, providing the possibility of achieving a longer lasting and more reliable release of drugs. Based on the mechanism of buoyancy two distinctly different technologies, i.e. non-effervescent and effervescent systems have been utilized in the development of floating drug delivery system.

Non-effervescent Systems

Non-effervescent floating drug delivery systems are normally prepared from gel-forming or highly swellable cellulose type hydrocolloids, polysaccharides or matrix forming polymers like polyacrylate, polycarbonate, polystyrene and polymethacrylate. In one approach, intimate mixing of drug with a gel forming hydrocolloid which results in contact with gastric fluid after oral administration and maintain a relative integrity of shape and a bulk density less than unity within the gastric environment[29]. The air trapped by the swollen polymer confers buoyancy to these dosage forms. Excipients used most commonly in these systems include hydroxypropyl methylcellulose (HPMC) polyacrylates, polyvinyl acetate, carbopol, agar, sodium alginate, calcium chloride, polyethylene oxide and polycarbonates[3]. This system can be further divided into the sub-types:

Hydrodynamically Balanced Systems

Sheth and Tossounian[30] first designated these 'hydrodynamically balanced systems'. These systems contains drug with gel-forming hydrocolloids meant to remain buoyant on the stomach content. These are single-unit dosage form, containing one or more gel-forming hydrophilic polymers. Hydroxypropyl methylcellulose (HPMC), hydroxethyl cellulose (HEC), hydroxypropyl cellulose (HPC), sodium carboxymethyl cellulose (NaCMC), polycarbophil, polyacrylate, polystyrene, agar, carrageenans or alginic acid are commonly used excipients to develop these systems[31,32]. The polymer is mixed with drugs and usually administered in hydrodynamically balanced system capsule. The capsule shell dissolves in contact with water and mixture swells to form a gelatinous barrier, which imparts buoyancy to dosage form in gastric juice for a long period. Because, continuous erosion of the surface allows water penetration to the inner layers maintaining surface hydration and buoyancy to dosage form[32]. Incorporation of fatty excipients gives low-density formulations reducing the erosion. Madopar LP®, based on the system was marketed during the 1980's[33]. Effective drug deliveries depend on the balance of drug loading and the effect of polymer on its release profile.

Several strategies have been tried and investigated to improve efficiencies of the floating hydrodynamically balanced systems[32, 33].

Microballoons / Hollow Microspheres

Microballoons / hollow microspheres loaded withdrugs in their other polymer shelf were prepared by simple solvent evaporation or solvent diffusion / evaporation methods[34] (Figure 1) to prolong the gastric retention time (GRT) of the dosage form. Commonly used polymers to develop these systems are polycarbonate, cellulose acetate, calcium alginate, Eudragit S, agar and low methoxylated pectin etc. Buoyancy and drug release from dosage form are dependent on quantity of polymers, the plasticizer polymer ratio and the solvent used for formulation. The microballoons floated continuously over the surface of an acidic dissolution media containing surfactant for >12 hours[3]. At present hollow microspheres are considered to be one of the most promising buoyant systems because they combine the advantages of multiple-unit system and good floating.

Alginate Beads

Talukdar and Fassihi[24] recently developed a multiple-unit floating system based on cross-linked beads. They were made by using Ca2+ and low methoxylated pectin (anionic polysaccharide) or Ca2+ low methoxylated pectin and sodium alginate. In this approach, generally sodium alginate solution is dropped into aqueous solution of calcium chloride and causes the precipitation of calcium alginate. These beads are then separated and dried by air convection and freeze drying, leading to the formulation of a porous system, which can maintain a floating force for over 12 hrs. These beads improve gastric retention time (GRT) more than 5.5 hrs [3, 35].

Microporous compartment system: This approachis based on the principle of the encapsulation of a drug reservoir inside a microporous compartment with pores along its top and bottom walls [36]. The peripheral walls of the device were completely sealed to present any direct contact of the gastric surface with the undissolved drug. In the stomach the floatation chamber containing entrapped air causes the delivery system to float in the gastric fluid[22]. Gastric fluid enters through the aperture, dissolves the drug and causes the dissolved drug for continuous transport across the intestine for drug absorption.

Effervescent (gas generating) systems

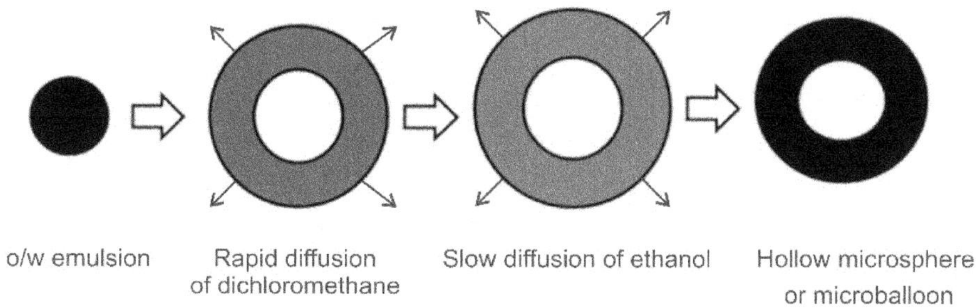

Fig.5.2 Formulation of floating hollow microsphere/microballoon.

Floatability can be achieved by generation of gas bubbles. These buoyant systems utilize matrices prepared with swellable polymers such as polysaccharides (e.g. chitosan), effervescent components (e.g. sodium bicarbonate, citric acid or tartaric acid)[36]. The optimal stoicheometric ratio of citric acid and sodium bicarbonate for gas generation is reported to be 0.76: 1[19]. In this system carbon dioxide is released and causes the formulation to float in the stomach. Other approaches and materials that have been reported are a mixture of sodium alginate and sodium bicarbonate, multiple unit floating dosage forms that generate gas (carbon dioxide) when ingested, floating mini capsules with a core of sodium bicarbonate, lactose and polyvinyl pyrrolidone (PVP) coated with hydroxypropyl methylcellulose (HPMC), and floating system based on ion exchange resin technology etc[3]. Bilayer or multilayer system has also been designed[37, 38]. Drugs and excipients can be formulated independently and the gas generating material can be incorporated in to any of the layers. Further modifications involve coating of the matrix with a polymer which is permeable to water, but not to carbon dioxide. The main difficulty of these formulations is finding a good compromise between elasticity, plasticity and permeability of the polymers.

Bioadhesive or Mucoadhesive Drug Delivery Systems

Bioadhesive drug delivery systems are used as adelivery device within the human to enhance drug absorption in a site-specific manner. In this approach, bio adhesive polymers are used and they can adhere to the epithelial surface in the stomach[39]. Thus, they improve the prolongation of gastric retention. The basis of adhesion in that a dosage form can stick to the mucosal surface by different mechanism. These mechanisms[40, 41] are:

1. The wetting theory, which is based on the ability of bioadhesive polymers to spread and develop intimate contact with the mucous layers.

2. The diffusion theory, which proposes physical entanglement of mucin strands the flexible polymer chains, or an interpenetration of mucin strands into the porous structure of the polymer substrate.
3. The absorption theory suggests that bioadhesion is due to secondary forces such as Vander Waal forces and hydrogen bonding.
4. The electron theory, which proposes attractive electrostatic forces between the glycoprotein mucin net work and the bio adhesive material.

Materials commonly used for bioadhesion are poly acrylic acid, chitosan, cholestyramine, sodium alginate, hydroxypropyl methylcellulose (HPMC), sucralfate, tragacanth, dextrin, polyethylene glycol (PEG) and polylactic acids etc. Even though some of these polymers are effective at producing bioadhesive, it is very difficult to maintain it effectively because of the rapid turnover of mucus in the gastrointestinal tract (GIT).

Raft forming systems Raft forming systems have received much attention for the drug delivery for gastrointestinal infections and disorders. Floating Rafts have been used in the treatment of Gastric esophageal reflux disease (GERD). The mechanism involved in the raft formation includes the formation of viscous cohesive gel in contact with gastric fluids, where in each portion of the liquid swells forming a continuous layer called a raft. This raft floats on gastric fluids because of low bulk density created by the formation of CO_2. Usually, the system ingredients includes a gel forming agent and alkaline bicarbonates or carbonates responsible for the formation of CO_2 to make the system less dense and float on the gastric fluids. Jorgen et al described an antacid raft forming floating system. The system contains a gel forming agent (e.g. sodium alginate), sodium bicarbonate and acid neutralizer, which forms a foaming sodium alginate gel (raft), which when comes in contact with gastric fluids, the raft floats on the gastric fluids and prevents the reflux of the gastric contents (i.e. gastric acid) into the esophagus by acting as a barrier between the stomach and esophagus[30, 31].

Low Density Systems

Gas-generating systems suffer from a lag time before floating on the stomach contents, during which the dosage form may undergopremature evacuation through the pyloric sphincter. Low density systems (Hollow microspheres loaded with drug in their outer polymer shelf were prepared by a novel emulsion solvent diffusion method. The ethanol/dichloromethane solution of the drug and an enteric acrylic polymer was poured into an agitated solution of Poly Vinyl Alcohol (PVA) that was thermally controlled at 40ºC. The gas phase is generated in the dispersed polymer droplet by the evaporation of dichloromethane formed and internal cavity in the microsphere of the polymer with drug. The microballoon floated continuously over the surface of an acidic dissolution media containing surfactant for more than 12 h [40].

Expandable, Unfoldable and Swellable Systems

A dosage form in the stomach will withstand gastric transit if it bigger than pyloric sphincter. However, the dosage form must be small enough to be swallowed, and must not cause gastric obstruction either singly or by accumulation. Thus, their configurations[42, 43] are required to develop an expandable system to prolong gastric retention time

(GRT):

1) A small configuration for oral intake,
2) An expanded gastroretentive form, and
3) A final small form enabling evacuation following drug release from the device.

Thus, gastroretentivity is improved by the combination of substantial dimension with high rigidity of dosage form to withstand peristalsis and mechanical contractility of the stomach. Unfoldable and swellable systems have been investigated and recently tried to develop an effective gastroretentive drug delivery. Unfoldable systems are made of biodegradable polymers. They are available in different geometric forms like tetrahedron, ring or planner membrane (4 - label disc or 4 - limbed cross form) of bioerodible polymer compressed within a capsule which extends in the stomach[44, 45]. Swellable systems are also retained in the gastro intestinal tract (GIT) due to their mechanical properties. The swelling is usually results from osmotic absorption of water and the dosage form is small enough to be swallowed by the gastric fluid. Expandable systems have some drawbacks like problematical storage of much easily hydrolysable, biodegradable polymers relatively short-lived mechanical shape memory for the unfolding system most difficult to industrialize and not cost effective. Again, permanent retention of rigid, large single-unit expandable drug delivery dosage forms may cause brief obstruction, intestinal adhesion and gastropathy[19].

Super Porous Hydrogel Systems

These swellable systems differ sufficiently from the conventional types to warrant separate classification. In this approach to improve gastric retention time (GRT) super porous hydrogels of average pore size >100 micro miter, swell to equilibrium size within a minute due to rapid water uptake by capillary wetting through numerous interconnected open pores [44, 45]. They swell to a large size (swelling ratio: 100 or more) and are intended to have sufficient mechanical strength to withstand pressure by gastric contraction. This is advised by co-formulation of hydrophilic particulate material [44, 45].

Magnetic Systems

This approach to enhance the gastric retention time (GRT) is based on the simple principle that the dosage form contains a small internal magnet, and a magnet placed on the abdomen over the position of the stomach. Although magnetic system seems to wok, the external magnet must be positioned with a degree of precision that might compromise patient compliance [41].

REFERENCES

1. Ali J, Arora S, Khar RK. Floating drug delivery system: a review. AAPS Pharm Scitech. 2001;06(03):E372-90.
2. Amit KN, Ruma M, Biswarup D. Gastro retentive drug delivery system; a review. Asian J Pharm Clin Res. 2010;3(1):2-10.
3. Bardonnet PL, Faivre V, Pugh WJ, Piffaretti JC, Falson F. Gastro retentive dosage forms; overview and special case of helicobacter pyroli. J Control Release. 2006;111(1-2):1-18. doi: 10.1016/j.jconrel.2005.10.031, PMID 16403588.
4. Lee TW, Robinson JR. Remington's the science and practice of Pharmacy, Lippincott Williams & Wilkings; Philadelphia. Vol. 20; 2000.
5. Chen YC, Ho HO, Lee TY, Sheu MT. Physical characterizations and sustained release profiling of gastroretentive drug delivery system with improved floating and swelling capabilities. Int J Pharm. 2013;441(1-2):162-9. doi: 10.1016/j.ijpharm.2012.12.002, PMID 23237874.
6. Oth M, Franz M, Timmermans J, Möes A. The bilayer floating capsule: a stomach directed drug delivery system for misoprostol. Pharm Res. 1992;9(3):298-302. doi: 10.1023/a:1015870314340, PMID 1614959.
7. Pawar VK, Kansal S, Asthana S, Chourasia MK. Industrial Perspective of Gastro retentive Drug Delivery System: physiochemical, Biopharmaceutical, Technological and regulatory considerations. Expert Opin Drug Deliv. 2012;9(5):551-65. doi: 10.1517/17425247.2012.677431, PMID 22512596.
8. Singh BN, Kim KH. Floating drug delivery systems: an approach to oral controlled drug delivery via gastric retention. J Control Release. 2000;63(3):235-59. doi: 10.1016/s0168-3659(99)00204-7, PMID 10601721.
9. Vyas SP, Khar RK. Controlled drug delivery: concept and advances. Vallabh prakashan. Delhi; 2002.
10. Wilson CG, Washington N. The stomach: its role in oral drug delivery. In: Rubinstein MH, editor. Physiological Pharmaceutical: biological barriers to drug absorption. Chichester, U.K.: Ellis Horwood; 1989. p. 47-70.
11. Streubel A, Siepmann J, Bodmeier R. Drug delivery to the upper small intestine window using Gastroretentive technologies. Curr Opin Pharmacol. 2006;6(5):501-8. doi: 10.1016/j.coph.2006.04.007, PMID 16890020.

12. Larhed AW, Artursson P, Gråsjö J, Björk E. Diffusion of drugs in native and purified gastrointestinal mucus. J Pharm Sci. 1997;86(6):660-65. doi: 10.1021/js960503w, PMID 9188047.

13. Dubernet C. Syste`mes a` liberation gastrique prolonge`e. In: Falson-Rieg F, Faivre V, Pirot F, editors. Novelles formes me`dicamenteuses. Editions Me`dicales Internationales. Editions. TEC and Cachan: DOC; 2004. p. 119-33.

14. Arrora S, Ali J, Khar RK, Baboota S. Floating drug delivery systems: a review. AAPS PharmSciTech. 2005;6(3):372-90.

15. El-Kamel AH, Sokar MS, Al Gamal SS, Naggar VF. Preparation and evaluation of ketoprofen floating oral delivery system. Int J Pharm. 2001;220(1-2):13-21. doi: 10.1016/s0378-5173(01)00574-9, PMID 11376963.

16. Garg S, Sharma S. Gastroretentive drug delivery systems. Bus Briefing Pharmtechn. 2003;20:160-66.

17. Khosla R. Feely LC, Davis SS. Gastrointestinal transit of non-disintegrating tablets in fed subjects. Int J Pharm. 1989;53:107-17.

18. Mojaverian P, Vlasses PH, Kellner PE, Rocci Jr ML. Effects of gender, posture and age on gastric residence time of an indigestible solid: pharmaceutical considerations. Pharm Res. 1988;5(10):639-44. doi: 10.1023/a:1015922903843, PMID 3244616.

19. Benchgaard H, Ladefoged K. Distribution of pellets in gastrointestinal tract: the influence on transit time exerted by the density or diameter of pellets. J Pharm Pharmacol. 1978:30:690Y692.

20. Vantrappen GR, Petters TL, Janssens J. The secretory component of inter digestive migratory motor complex in man. Scand J Gastroenterol. 1979;14663:Y667.

21. Streubel A, Siepmann J, Bodmeier R. Floating microparticles based on low density foam powder. Int J Pharm. 2002;241(2):279-92. doi: 10.1016/s0378-5173(02)00241-7, PMID 12100855.

22. Streubel A, Siepmann J, Bodmeier R. Floating matrix tablets based on low density foam powder: effects of formulation and processing parameters on drug release. Eur J Pharm Sci. 2003;18(1):37-45. doi: 10.1016/s0928-0987(02)00223-3, PMID 12554071.

23. Sato Y, Kawashima Y, Takeuchi H, Yamamoto H. Physicochemical properties to determine the buoyancy of hollow microspheres (microballoons) prepared by the emulsion solvent diffusion method. Eur J Pharm Biopharm. 2003;55(3):297-304. doi: 10.1016/s0939-6411(03)00003-1, PMID 12754004.

24. Talukder R, Fassihi R. Gastroretentive delivery systems: hollow beads. Drug Dev Ind Pharm. 2004;30(4):405-12. doi: 10.1081/ddc-120030935, PMID 15132183.

25. Hilton AK, Deasy PB. In vitro and in vivo evaluation of an oral sustained release floating dosage form of amoxicillin trihydrate. Int J Pharm. 1992;86(1):79-88. doi: 10.1016/0378-5173(92)90033-X.

26. Sheth PR, Tossounian J. The hydrodynamically balanced system, a novel drug delivery system for oral use. Drug Dev Ind Pharm. 1984;10(2):313-39. doi: 10.3109/03639048409064653.

27. Hwang SJ, Park H, Park K. Gastroretentive delivery systems. Crit Rev Ther Drug Carrier Syst. 1998;15(3):243-84. PMID 9699081.

28. Reddy LH, Murthy RS. Floating dosage system in drug delivery. Crit Rev Ther Drug Carrier Syst. 2002;19(6):553-85. doi: 10.1615/critrevtherdrugcarriersyst.v19.i6.20, PMID 12822735.

29. Bardonnet PL, Faivre V, Pugh WJ, Piffaretti JC, Falson F. Gastroretentive dosage forms: overview and special case of Helicibacter pylori. J Control Release. 2006;111(1-2):1-18. doi: 10.1016/j.jconrel.2005.10.031, PMID 16403588.

30. Kawashima Y, Niwa T, Takeuchi H, Hino T, Itoh Y. Hollow microspheres for use as a floating controlled drug delivery system in the stomach. J Pharm Sci. 1992;81(2):135-40. doi: 10.1002/jps.2600810207, PMID 1372046.

31. Whiteland L, Fell JT, Collett JH. Development of gastroretentive dosage form. Eur J Pharm Sci. 1996;4;Suppl:S182.

32. Harrigan RM. Drug delivery device for preventing contact of undissolved drug with the stomach lining. US Patent 405 5178; October 25, 1977.

33. Ingani HM, Timmermans J, Moes A. Conception and in vivo investigation of per oral sustained release floating dosage forms with enhanced gastrointestinal transit. Int J Pharm. 1987;35(12):157-64.

34. Krögel I, Bodmeier R. Floating or pulsatile drug delivery system based on coated effervescent cores. Int J Pharm. 1999;187(2):175-84. doi: 10.1016/s0378-5173(99)00189-1, PMID 10502623.

35. Moës AJ. Gastroretentive dosage forms. Crit Rev Ther Drug Carrier Syst. 1993;10(2):143-95. PMID 8370085.

36. Faivre V. Aspects theoriques de la bioadhesion. In: FalsonRieg V, Faivre V, Pirot F, editors. Nonvelles formes medicamenteuses, Editions Medicales Internationales, Editions TEC and DOC, Cachan; 2004. p. 1-24.

37. Huang Y, Leobandung W, Foss A, Peppas NA. Molecular aspects of muco- and bioadhesion: tethered structures and site-specific surfaces. J Control Release. 2000;65(1-2):63-71. doi: 10.1016/s0168-3659(99)00233-3, PMID 10699271.

38. Klausner EA, Lavy E, Friedman M, Hoffman A. Expandable gasrtroretentive dosage forms. J Control Release. 2003;90(2):143-62. doi: 10.1016/s0168-3659(03)00203-7, PMID 12810298.

39. Klausner EA, Lavy E, Stepensky D, Friedman M, Hoffman A. Novel gasrtroretentive dosage form: evaluation of gastroretentivity and its effect on riboflavin absorption in dogs. Pharm Res. 2002;19(10):1516-23. doi: 10.1023/a:1020412817716, PMID 12425470.

40. Caldwell LJ, Gardner CR, Cargill RC. Drug delivery device which can be retained in the stomach for controlled period of time. US Patent 473 5804; April 5, 1988.

41. Caldwell LJ, Gardner CR, Cargill RC, Higuchi T. Drug delivery device which can be retained in the stomach for a controlled period of time. US Patent 475 8436; July 19, 1988.

42. Klausner EA, Lavy E, Barta M, Cserepes E, Friedman M, Hoffman A. Novel gasrtroretentive dosage form: evaluation of gastroretentivity and its effect on levodopa absorption in humans. Pharm Res. 2003;20(9):1466-73. doi: 10.1023/a:1025770530084, PMID 14567643.

43. Chen J, Blevins WE, Park H, Park K. Gastric retention of superporous hydrogel composites. J Control Release. 2000;64(1-3):39-51. doi: 10.1016/s0168-3659(99)00139-x, PMID 10640644.

44. Chen J, Park K. Synthesis and characterization of superporous hydrogel composites. J Control Release. 2000;65(1-2):73-82. doi: 10.1016/s0168-3659(99)00238-2, PMID 10699272.

45. Goole J, Vanderbist F, Amighi K. Development and evaluation of new multiple-unit levodopa sustained-release floating dosage forms. Int J Pharm. 2007;334(1-2):35-41. doi: 10.1016/j.ijpharm.2006.10.018, PMID 17097841.

EXCERCISE

MULTIPLE CHOICE QUESTIONS

1. The main role of the stomach is to……
   a. Store the food temporarily
   b. Grinding of food
   c. Slowly release food into the duodenum
   d. All of the above
2. Which statement is true for gastro retentive drug delivery system?
   a. High risk of toxicity.
   b. Less patient compliance.
   c. Suitable for delivery of drugs with narrow absorption window in small intestinal region.
   d. No risk of dose dumping

3. In which system of GRDDS, the retention of device in the stomach is due to external Magnet
   a. Swelling system
   b. Floating system
   c. Mucoadhsion system
   d. Magnetic system
4. Which is not the approach of GRDDS?
   a. Floating
   b. High density sytem
   c. Osmotic pump
   d. Swelling system
5. Microballoon is the types of GRDDS
   a. Floating system
   b. High Density system
   c. Mucoadhesive sytem
   d. None of the above
6. In GRDDS, the retention of device in the stomach is due to..........
   a. Swelling
   b. Floating
   c. Adhesion
   d. All the above
7. Gastroretentive drug delivery is
   a. An approach to prolong gastric residence time
   b. targeting site specific drug release
   c. Release the medication in the upper GIT or systematic effect
   d. All the above
8. Drawback of Gastroretentive Drug Delivery system is
   a. Improved drug absorption
   b. Fluctuation in drug concentration is reduced
   c. Unsuitable for drugs those are unstable in acidic environment
   d. Targetting site-specific drug release
9. In which drug delivery sytem formulation is retained in the stomach
   a. Site specific DDS
   b. Gastroretentive DDS
   c. Oral DDS
   d. Controlled release

10. Density of gastric content is g/cm ^{3}

    a. 2.005 b. 1.004

    c. 1.05 d. 0.80

11. In which GRDDS approach, heavy dosage form is developed?

    a. Low density system b. High density system

    c. Floating system d. Expandable system

12. Which of the following system is known as plug type system?

    a. Floating b. Magnetic

    c. Swelling and Expandable d. Low density

13. Which of the following is not includes in region of stomach?

    a. Cardia b. Pylorus

    c. Fundus d. None of the above

14. ____________ present in the gastric glands that produce hydrochloric acid and instrinsic factor

    a. Mucous neck cells b. Chief cell

    c. Parietal cells d. All of the above

15. ________ prepared by dropping sodium alginate solution into aqueous solution of calcium chloride

    a. Alginate beads b. Microballoons

    c. High density d. None of the above

16. ____________ is effervescent agent used to formulate low density system of GRDDS.

    a. Dicalcium phosphate b. Lactose

    c. Citric acid d. Mannitol

17. The time taken by the dosage form to float on the top of the dissolution medium, after it is placed in the medium is termed as:

    a. Buoyancy log time b. Floating time

    c. Transit time d. None of the above

18. GRDDS is evaluated by-

    a. X-ray /Gamma scintigraphy b. Swelling study

    c. Surface characterization d. All of the above

19. The basis of adhesion in that a dosage form can stick to the mucosal surface by-
    a. Wetting theory
    b. Diffusion theory
    c. Absorption theory
    d. All of the above
20. is the most noticeable disadvantages gastroretentive floating Drug Delivery
    a. System Requirement of high level of fluid
    b. Delay release
    c. Absorption of of acid soluble drug
    d. Vigorous intestinal movement

SHORT ANSWER QUESTIONS

1. What are the different mechanism involved on the basis of adhesion that a dosage form can stick to the mucosal surface.
2. Explain about microballoons as gastroadhesive drug delivery system
3. What are the factors affecting gastric retention in gastro retentive drug delivery
4. What you understand by the interdigestive myoelectric cycle.
5. What are the limitations of GRDD
6. Write short note on Effervescent (gas generating) systems
7. Write short note on Raft forming systems
8. Name the different approaches to extend GI transit time
9. Describe about 4 phases given by Wilson and Washington
10. What are three different region of stomach

LONG ANSWER QUESTIONS

1. Explain the various approaches to formulate gastro retentive drug delivery systems.
2. Explain about approaches to extend gi transit time.
3. Describe in detail the principle involved and formulation of gastro retentive drug delivery system.
4. What are floating drug delivery systems and explain its different types?
5. Explain about the factors involved in controlling gastric retention of dosage forms
6. Describe the noneffervescent gastroadhesive drug delivery system

7. What are gastrorententive drug delivery systems? Explain various approaches of gastrorententive drug delivery system.
8. Discuss in detailed about gastrorententive floating drug delivery systems.
9. Discuss in detailed about the Hydrodynamically balanced systems
10. Write short note on
    a. Low density system
    b. Swelling and Expandable system
    c. Mucoadhesive system

MCQ ANSWERS

1. (a)	2. (d)	3. (c)	4. (d)
5. (c)	6. (a)	7. (d)	8. (d)
9. (c)	10. (d)	11. (b)	12. (b)
13. (c)	14. (d)	15. (c)	16. (a)
17. (c)	18. (a)	19. (d)	20. (d)

CHAPTER - 6

Buccal Drug Delivery Systems

Dr. Kapil Agrawal, Dr. Bina Gidwani, Dr. Vishal Jain, Dr. Shiv Shankar Shukla, Dr. Ravindra Pandey, and Dr. Amber Vyas

INTRODUCTION

The preferred and most popular method of medicine delivery is oral ingestion. It has a number of benefits, including as being more patient-friendly, painless, easy to self-medicate and enabling variable and controlled dose schedules than the majority of other drug delivery methods[1]. Although the oral route is preferable for drug delivery, it also has significant drawbacks, including first-pass effect, gastrointestinal enzymatic breakdown, and a delay between administration and absorption, which is harmful for medications that need to take effect quickly. These challenges have prompted researchers to consider different drug delivery methods, including pulmonary, ocular, nasal, rectal, buccal, sublingual, vaginal, and transdermal. Transmucosal drug delivery methods, which offer significant chances and possible advantages over peroral administration for systemic drug delivery because it is made up of the mucosal linings of the nasal, rectal, vaginal, ocular, and oral cavities[2]. Depending on the specific medicine, these benefits may include a better enzymatic flora for drug absorption, the potential bypass of the first pass effect, and prevention of pre-systemic clearance inside the GI tract[3]. Drug delivery can be roughly divided into two groups in the oral mucosa: Medication administration through the mucosal membranes lining the floor of the mouth is known as sublingual delivery, and drug administration through the mucosal membranes lining the cheeks is known as buccal delivery[4]. Due to the simplicity of drug distribution, the buccal portion of the mouth cavity is a popular location[5]. Drug delivery in the oral mucosal cavity can be broadly divided into two types: (a) sublingual delivery, which involves systemic drug delivery through the mucosal membranes lining the mouth's floor, and (b) buccal delivery, which involves drug administration through the mucosal membranes lining the cheeks. The buccal region of the oral cavity is a desirable site for drug delivery due to its ease of administration[6].

Drug delivery via this route is effective for both mucosal (local effect) and transmucosal (systemic effect) effects. As opposed to the second scenario, which involves drug absorption via the mucosal barrier to reach the systemic circulation, the first scenario aims to achieve a site-specific release of the medication on the mucosa[7]. Because the medication content in buccal formulations may be significantly smaller than that in tablets and capsules, there may be a significant reduction in toxicity or undesirable side effects[8].

Anatomy of the buccal mucosa

factors to take into account while creating mucoadhesive buccal drug delivery systems (MBDDS) The buccal mucosa's main function, similar to the skin's, is to shield underlying structures from foreign objects. The buccal mucosa's surface is made up of a stratified squamous epithelium that is separated from the submucosa and lamina propria beneath by an undulating basement membrane[9]. The keratinocytes that make up this stratified squamous epithelium differ in size, shape, and composition as they move from the basal region to the superficial region, where the cells are shed[10].

Based on different areas of the oral cavity, light microscopy reveals a number of diverse patterns of maturation in the epithelium of the human oral mucosa[11]. The soft palate, the ventral surface of the tongue, the floor of the mouth, the alveolar mucosa, the vestibule, the lips, and the cheeks all have non-keratinized surfaces, while the hard palate and non-flexible areas of the oral cavity have keratinized surfaces[12]. The epithelium serves as a protective layer for the tissues beneath. The basal cells give rise to the epithelial cells, which develop, change shape, and enlarge as they move towards the surface. The connective tissues and the epithelium are separated by the basement membrane, which creates a discrete layer[13].

It serves as a mechanical support for the epithelium and provides the necessary adhesion between the epithelium and the underlying connective tissues. The oral mucosa's mechanical characteristics are largely provided by the underlying connective tissues. Mucus The mucous tissue layer is in charge of creating the sticky interface[14]. Mucus is a translucent, viscous fluid that adheres to the mucosal epithelial surface in the form of a thin, continuous gel blanket. In humans, this layer's average thickness ranges from roughly 50 to 450 m. The balance between the rates of secretion and breakdown and shedding determines the mucous blanket's thickness, which is site-specific. This matrix may actually contribute to cell-cell adhesion by lubricating cell movement in relation to one another. Similar to how it does in bioadhesion of mucoadhesive drug delivery systems, mucus normally plays a crucial role. Minor salivary glands can contribute up to 70% of the total mucin in saliva. Mucus can create a very cohesive gel structure at physiological pH that will adhere to the surface of epithelial cells as a gelatinous layer. Mucins and inorganic salts floating in water make up the bulk of mucus. About 95% of mucins are made up of water, 0.5-5% is lipids and glycoproteins, 1% is mineral salts, and up to 1% is free proteins[15].

High molecular weight proteins called mucous glycoproteins have oligosaccharide units connected to them. The epithelium surface's mucous layer, which it covers, serves a number of purposes. The oral mucosa is strong and recovers quickly from trauma or stress. Saliva continuously washes the mucosal surface (0.5-2 litres per day), which aids in drug absorption. In the event of a negative drug reaction, this approach also makes the system accessible and simple to remove. Therapeutic serum concentrations of some medications can be reached more quickly because the drug is not exposed to the stomach's harmful acidic environment. Additionally, the medication reaches the bloodstream without first passing through the liver for metabolism[16].

The oral mucosa's abundant blood supply (20.3 mL/min/100 g tissue) provides great permeability to a variety of medicinal treatments (e.g. nitroglycerine). Other useful characteristics of the buccal mucosa include its relatively high surface area (50.2 cm2) and thin membrane, with a thickness of about 500–600 m, which may increase the rate of medication absorption. The aforementioned elements work together to increase bioavailability. Therefore, the oromucosal cavity is supported by these criteria as a highly viable and sensible site for systemic drug delivery[17].

Mechanism of buccal absorption

Buccal drug absorption occurs via passive diffusion of non-ionized species through the epithelial intercellular spaces, which is primarily governed by a concentration gradient. The primary transport mechanism is the passive transport of non-ionic species across the lipid membrane of the buccal cavity[18]. The buccal mucosa, like many other mucosal membranes, has been described as a lipoidal barrier to drug passage, and the more lipophillic the drug molecule, the more readily it is absorbed. A first order rate process could adequately describe the dynamics of drug absorption in the buccal cavity[19]. Several potential barriers to buccal drug absorption have been identified. According to Dearden and Tomlison (1971), salivary secretion alters the buccal absorption kinetics from drug solution by changing the concentration of drug in the mouth.

Drug absorption across buccal route

The physicochemical properties of the drug govern its transport across the buccal mucosa. The drug dissolves first, and then it is ready to be portioned across the buccal mucosal layer. Passive drug transport across the buccal mucosa occurs via two pathways: transcellular and paracellular. Depending on the physicochemical properties of the drug molecules, drug partitioning occurs, which may follow one or both of the previous mentioned pathways[20]. Transcellular pathways are intracellular pathways (drugs must cross the cell membrane to enter the cell) through which drugs move via passive transport, active transport, endocytosis, and transcytosis. Transcellular transport is dominated by lipophilic and small hydrophobic molecules[21]. Hydrophilic drugs will have difficulty permeating the cell membrane due to the cell membrane's lipophilic nature and low partition coefficient.

1. The transcellular path,
2. The paracellular path,
3. Epithelial cells, and
4. Blood vessels

The intercellular pathway is the intracellular pathway (drug passes in between the epithelial cells). The drug can travel via two routes: the hydrophobic route (via the lipid bilayer) and the hydrophilic route (narrow aqueous regions adjacent to the polar head groups of the lipid bilayer). Drugs with a balanced partition co-efficient can pass through both paracellular and transcellular barriers[22].

Mechanism of bioadhesion[23]

The bioadhesion mainly depends upon nature of bioadhesive polymer-

- First stage involves an intimate contact between a bioadhesive & a membrane
- Second stage involves penetration of the bioadhesive into tissue
- Drug released.
- Bypasses first pass metabolism
- Enters systemic circulation.

Theories of bioadhesion and mucoadhesion

The bond created when a pressure-sensitive adhesive makes contact with a surface is known as adhesion. Depending on the setting in which the process takes place, adhesion can be categorised under several different terminological subsets. Adhesion that takes place in a biological environment is frequently referred to as "bioadhesion," and if it does so on mucosal membranes, it is referred to as "mucoadhesion." The state of two materials, at least one of which is biological in nature, being held together for a long time by interfacial forces is known as bioadhesion[24]. The term "bioadhesion" for drug delivery indicates attachment of a drug carrier system to a particular biological site. The use of bioadhesive hydrophilic polymers in pharmaceutical formulations combined with the active pharmaceutical ingredient has been widely promoted as a means of obtaining targeted drug delivery to an active site of choice (API)[25]. The idea is that by "holding" the formulation on or near the biological surface, the API will release close to the absorptive membrane and increase bioavailability. Adsorption theory, wetting theory, diffusion theory, electrical theory, and fracture theory are just a few of the many hypotheses that have been put out to explain mucoadhesion. According to the "adsorption theory," when mucous and the mucoadhesive polymer first come into contact, primary and secondary chemical bonds of both the covalent and non-covalent types are created[26].

- The "wetting hypothesis" simply measures how easily a drug delivery system can spread across a biological substrate and is most commonly relevant to liquid or low viscosity mucoadhesive systems.
- Chain entanglement between mucosal glycoproteins and the mucoadhesive polymer, which results in the formation of a semi-permanent adhesive connection, is the foundation of the "diffusion hypothesis."
- According to the "electronic theory," adhesion happens when electrons are transferred from the mucous to the mucoadhesive system as a result of variations in their electronic structures[27].

Perhaps the most prevalent notion in research on the mechanical assessment of mucoadhesion is the "fracture theory." It examines the amount of pressure needed to separate two surfaces once adhesion has been achieved[28].

MUCOADHESIVE DOSAGE FORMS

Although the buccal mucosa is currently the subject of extensive research as a novel medication delivery channel, humans have long been aware of its potential. In order to develop new drug delivery methods, modern researchers are investigating the numerous pathways accessible for drug delivery, particularly through the oral mucosa. Tablets have a diameter of about 5-8 mm and are tiny, flat, and oval in shape. Mucoadhesive tablets, in contrast to traditional tablets, enable for speaking and drinking without any significant discomfort. These are applied directly to the mucosal surface to administer drugs locally or systemically[29]. These become softer, stick to the mucosa, and remain there until the disintegration or release is complete.

Although mucoadhesive tablet features coupled with a tablet have added benefits, mucoadhesive tablets generally have the ability to be employed for controlled release drug delivery. For instance, it promotes a considerably more intimate contact with the mucosal layer and provides effective absorption and higher bioavailability of the medications due to a high surface-to-volume ratio[30]. Tablets that are mucoadhesive can be made to stick to stomach mucosa as well as other mucosal tissues, opening the door to localised and systemic controlled drug release. Tablets, like other non-wetting solid MDDS, cause a portion of the mucosa to become dehydrated, which leads to mucoadhesion.

Slow dissolving and maintenance of a therapeutic concentration of the active ingredient are two characteristics of commercially marketed tablets component in the patient's blood for a long time: 1-2 hours (Buccastem®) to 8 hours or longer (Striant®)[31].

Although mucoadhesive buccal tablets have been shown to be effective when applied locally, such as in the treatment of oral candidiasis, the main barrier to their widespread usage is their size and shape because the drug delivery system needs to make close contact with the mucosal surface. Films/Patches Because they are more flexible and comfortable, mucoadhesive films may be preferable to adhesive tablets. Additionally, they can get around the mucosa's very brief length of residence for oral gels, which is readily washed away and eliminated by saliva. Additionally, when oral diseases are treated locally, the films help preserve the wound surface, which lessens pain and helps the condition be treated more successfully[32].

The perfect film should be soft, pliable, elastic, and sturdy enough to resist breaking under the strain of mouth movements. To stay in the mouth for the necessary amount of time and have the desired effect, it must also have strong mucoadhesive strength. Buccal patches are described as laminates made of an impermeable backing layer, a reservoir layer containing the medicine that releases it gradually, and a surface that is mucoadhesive for mucosal attachment. Drugs can be directly administered to a mucosal membrane using patches. These resemble the ones employed in the transdermal medication delivery system. Due to their physical flexibility and minimally uncomfortable nature for the patient, they have higher patient compliance than tablets. Additionally, they have benefits over lotions and ointments[33].

Gels and creams Gels and ointments are examples of semisolid dose forms that have the benefit of being simple to spread over the mouth mucosa. As opposed to tablets, patches, or films, semisolid dosage forms may not provide the most precise drug dosage. The use of mucoadhesive formulations has improved the gels' poor retention at the application site. Hyaluronic acid, carbopol, sodium carboxymethylcellulose, and xanthan gum are a few mucoadhesive polymers that go through a phase change from liquid to semisolid. This alteration increases viscosity, which causes medications to release slowly and under control. Another interesting dosage type for buccal medication administration is hydrogel[34].

Advantages

The primary benefit of the buccal drug delivery route is the internal jugular vein's direct access to the systemic circulation, which avoids the hepatic first-pass metabolism of medicines like propranolol hydrochloride and nifedipine. High bioavailability, low enzymatic activity, and appropriateness for medications or excipients that irritate or moderately harm the mucosa are the effects of this. The ability to include a permeability enhancer, enzyme inhibitor, or pH modifier in the formulation and the flexibility to build multidirectional or unidirectional release systems for local or systemic activities are further benefits[35]. Furthermore, because the membrane locations are so easily accessible, the drug delivery system can be administered, placed, and removed with ease. Additionally, there is a strong chance for delivery through the mucosal cavity is extended. The prolonged contact time that bioadhesive polymers have with tissues allows them to considerably[36].

1. Prevents first-pass metabolism
2. Prevents enzyme/acid metabolism
3. In comparison to Skin & TDDS, permeation is faster (4 4000)
4. Greater surface area compared to the sublingual mucosa
5. Good adherence to parental instructions by the patient
6. Simple administration and extraction in the event of toxicity
7. For patients who are comatose or unconscious

Disadvantages

For systemic medication distribution, the environment of the mouth cavity poses several formidable obstacles. In order to reach the delivery site (such as the buccal or sublingual area) and cross the mucosal layers, the medication needs to be released from the formulation. The pH, fluid volume, enzyme activity, and permeability of the oral mucosa are just a few physiological factors that have a big impact on the process. Performance is also influenced by the shape and turnover of the mucosal surface for drug delivery systems intended for prolonged release in the oral cavity (such as mucoadhesive systems). It compares the physiological traits of the buccal mucosa and the mucosa of the gastrointestinal tract[37].

The secretion of saliva shapes the oral cavity's primary physiological environment in terms of pH, fluid volume, and content. Three primary salivary glands—the parotid, submaxillary, and sublingual glands—as well as smaller salivary or buccal glands located in or just beneath the mucosa secrete saliva. In contrast to the sublingual glands, which mostly generate viscous saliva with minimal enzyme activity, the parotid and submaxillary glands secrete watery secretions. Saliva's primary purposes are to lubricate the mouth, make swallowing easier, and keep teeth from demineralizing[38]. Also permitted is carbohydrate by preserving the pH and enzyme activity of the mouth, alcohol digestion controls the microbial flora in the mouth. The volume of saliva secreted everyday is in the range of 0.5 to 2.0 L. However, compared to the GIT, the amount of fluid accessible for medication release from delivery systems is relatively modest due to the constant presence of 1.1 ml of saliva in the mouth. If the oral cavity provides a somewhat stable and hospitable physiological environment for drug administration, which is maintained by the continual flow of saliva, this challenge can be addressed. Saliva is a very mobile fluid with little mucus, minimal enzymatic activity, and almost no proteases as compared to GIT secretions. Saliva's pH ranges from 5.5 to 7.0, making it a poor buffer. Due to the higher percentage of salt and bicarbonate, this may somewhat rise based on the high flow rate. This obstacle can be surmounted by the limited enzymatic activity of the saliva[39].

1. Drugs that have a foul smell, a bitter taste, or both
2. Not for kids
3. Eating and drinking challenges
4. Salivary erosion and the possibility that it will enter the digestive tract and suffocate the esophagus
5. Fewer surfaces than the skin
6. At Buccal pH, drugs are unstable (6.5 to 7)

Evaluation of buccal drug delivery system[40]

1. **Thickness:** With the use of a digital micrometer, the thickness of buccal tablets was measured. The average of the data was calculated using ten individual tablets from each batch.
2. **Weight variation:** 20 tablets from each batch were subjected to weight variation using an electronic scale, and average values were determined.
3. **Hardness:** Monsanto's hardness tester was used to assess the hardness of 3 tablets from each batch, and average values were computed.
4. **Assay:** Ten tablets were measured and crushed into a fine powder using a mortar and pestle. One tablet's worth of powder was dissolved in methanol using a sonicator for 30 minutes before being filtered through paper. A UV spectrophotometer was used to perform a spectrophotometric analysis of the drug content at 274 nm.
5. **Disintegration test:** For buccal tablets without backing, a test is conducted. From each batch, six tablets were chosen at random and placed in the USP disintegration apparatus (baskets type). After 4 hours of operation, the apparatus was stopped, and the fluid-filled basket was removed to check if all of the tablets had broken down.
6. **Tissue isolation studies:** Porcine buccal tissue from domestic pigs were purchased from a nearby butcher and used within three hours of the animal's demise. Pigs The pigs were 6.5 0.5 months old when they passed away[41]. Or the animals were electrocuted and then exsanguinated to death. After collection, the tissue was kept in a pH 6.6 phosphate buffer at 4 degrees Celsius. Excess connective and adipose tissue (epithelium) were removed to create 0.8 mm thick slides, which were then given an hour to equilibrate in receptor buffer (acidic buffer) at room temperature

to regain lost elasticity. A Franz diffusion cell was then used to conduct an *ex vivo* drug permeation study on the tissue.

7. **Infrared spectroscopy using a Fourier transform:** To investigate the possibility of any chemical interactions between the drug and the polymers used in the preparation, the samples were crushed with KBr to make pellets under hydraulic pressure of 10 tonnes.
8. **Differential scanning calorimetric analysis:** The samples were heated using a microcalorimeter from 0 to 300 degrees at a rate of 10 degrees per meter under an argon atmosphere, and thermograms were then taken.
9. **Stability of buccal tablets:** Studies on the stability of buccal tablets were carried out for improved synthesis in typical human saliva. Human saliva was gathered from individuals and run through filter paper. In separate Petri dishes with 5 mL of human saliva, buccal tablets were placed. The Petri dishes were then placed in a temperature-controlled oven for 8 hours at 37°C 0.2°C. The buccal tablets were administered at predetermined intervals (0, 2, 4, 6, and 8 hours). inspected for color, surface, and integrity changes.
10. **Surface pH analysis:** Buccal tablets were put in glass tubes and left to swell when they came into contact with pH 7.4 phosphate buffers (12ml). After that, the pH of the surface of the swollen tablets was measured using pH paper. Three readings were taken, and the mean was noted.
11. **Study of palatability:** After bitterness and physical appearance, it is judged based on taste. According to the criteria, each batch is given an A, B, or C grade. The formulation is regarded as average if it receives at least one A grade. Obtaining two A-grades is considered good, and obtaining three A-grades is regarded as a successful buccal formulation[42].

Evaluation Parameter of Buccal Patch

1. **Film thickness:** At various locations on the film, the thickness is measured using a screw gauge with a minimum count of 0.01 mm. The film's thickness was measured three times, with the average thickness being calculated.

2. **Surface pH:** Three films of each formulation are permitted in contact with 1ml of distilled water to measure the surface pH. By placing a combined glass electrode or pH paper close to the surface of the films and allowing them to equilibrate for one minute, the surface pH was measured. A three-reading average is recorded.

3. **Folding endurance:** By repeatedly folding one film at the same location until it breaks, which is considered sufficient to reveal good film properties, the folding endurance of the film is determined. The value of folding endurance was determined by how many times films could be

folded in the same location without breaking. Three randomly chosen films from each formulation were used in this test[43].

4. **Drug content uniformity:** A drug-containing film with a diameter of 1 cm was dissolved in 50 ml of simulated salivary fluid while being occasionally shaken to determine this parameter. After filtering out insoluble material, 1 ml of the filtrate was diluted to 10 ml with artificial salivary fluid (pH 6.8). A UV spectrophotometer was used to measure the absorbance at a specific nm. For all formulations of films, the tests were run in triplicate[44].

5. **In-vitro dissolution studies:** The stimulated salivary fluid (pH 6.8) was used as the dissolution medium in a dissolution study that was conducted in a USP basket-type apparatus at a speed of 50 rotations per minute. At one-minute intervals, 10 ml aliquots were removed, and the same volume of the new dissolution medium was then added. Using a UV spectrophotometer, the aliquots were tested for drug content at a specific wavelength. It was calculated how much medication was released all at once[45].

6. **Moisture absorption:** For three days, relative humidity of 75% was used in the moisture absorption study of films. At 75% relative humidity, low moisture absorption by all formulations were noted. All buccal films have a low moisture absorption rate, which can delay any hydrolytic deterioration and keep the films stable.

7. **Swelling studies:** In phosphate buffer at pH 6.8, swelling severity is assessed. All batches have good swelling characteristics and retain moisture for a longer period. All formulations swelled within 10 min, and those that delayed swelling did so after 2 h, resulting in the buccal patch's weight remains constant. It is emphasized that when assessing film integrity, swelling properties are significant.

8. **Percent elongation at break:** For the determination of percentage Following the following formula, the distance between the tensile grips of the tensile strength testing machine was measured before and after the film's fracture to determine the percentage elongation of the film formulations. The following formula was then used to calculate the films' percentage elongation.

   % Elongation at break =Increase in length Initial weight×100

9. **Dispersion test:** 200 ml of phosphate buffer with a pH of 6.8 were added to a strip containing 5 mg of the drug, and the mixture was stirred for 3 minutes. The final product was run through sieve number 22. Only when there is no trace of the film on the sieve is it considered to have passed the dispersion test[46].

10. **Mucoadhesion and residence times in vitro:** In a well-stirred beaker containing 500 ml of phosphate buffer pH 6.8 at 37 °C, the time it took for the patch to separate from goat buccal mucosa was used to measure the *in vitro* adhesion time of films. Cyanoacrylate glue was used to attach the mucosal membrane to the beaker's side. For 60 seconds, the patch was fastened to the membrane by lightly pressing down with the tip of a finger. The beaker was then magnetically stirred to mimic saliva and buccal motion at a speed of about 150 rpm. The amount of time required for the films to completely erode or separate from the mucosal membrane was used as a measure of the *in vitro* adhesion time[47].
11. **Tensile strength:** A universal strength testing machine was used to determine the buccal films' tensile strength. The device has a one-gram sensitivity. There are two load cell grips in it. According to the figure, the upper one is movable while the lower one is fixed. Between these cell grips, a test patch of a specific size is fixed, and force is gradually applied until the patch breaks. The dial reading was used to determine the patch's tensile strength[48].
12. **Percentages of moisture content:** Accurately weighed buccal patches are stored indesiccators with anhydrous calcium chloride. The patches were removed after three days and weighed. The formula determined the moisture content (%).

    % Moisture content = Initial weight

    – Final weight Initial weight×100
13. **Effect of humidity and temperature:** The optimization formulation was tested for a month at 40°C+2°C, 75% 5% RH, which was maintained in an environmental stability chamber. The patches were placed in the afore mentioned circumstances while being wrapped in aluminum foil. Samples were assessed for parameters such as appearance, surface pH, folding endurance, and drug release (percentage) at 0, 7, 14, 21, and 28 days[49].

FUTURE PROSPECTS AND CHALLENGES

The last few decades have seen a remarkable rise and development in research on buccal medication administration. The buccal mucosa offers a viable and alluring alternative for the non-invasive administration of powerful peptide and protein therapeutic molecules as well as significant potential for the systemic distribution of medications that are ineffective when taken orally. Drug delivery methods that cling to mucosal tissues, such as those in the mouth, gastrointestinal tract, vagina, eyes, etc., offer a novel carrier system for a variety of medications[50]. The innovative buccal adhesive delivery system, which directs medication administration toward the buccal mucosa by safeguarding the local environment, is one of the topics of attention. Despite considerable developments in the field of mucoadhesion, there is no agreement among researchers regarding concerns the processes by which the elements and parts of mucosal tissue interact. There are still a lot of unanswered questions regarding the creation of MBDDS and the effectiveness of their application because there is no standardised method for evaluating mucoadhesive qualities. The absence of defined methods frequently produces outcomes that are inconsistent and ambiguous[51]. To evaluate and compare various materials and formulations in terms of their capacity to increase medication absorption via the buccal route, standard *in vitro* and *ex vivo* biological models must be developed. Future research indicates that vaccine formulations and distribution of tiny proteins/peptides will replace buccal adhesive medication delivery. Because they provide protection to medicinal entities as well as the improved adhesion, microparticulate bioadhesive systems are particularly intriguing. The bioadhesive components extended contact time, which leads to enhanced absorption[52]. The essential importance of mucoadhesion in non-parenteral protein drug delivery methods is obvious[53].

CONCLUSION

Scientists are working to create buccal adhesive systems through a variety of methods to increase the bioavailability of orally ineffective or less effective medications by modifying the formulation tactics. In order to find newer mucoadhesive polymers that also have the additional properties of being biodegradable, biocompatible, non-toxic, mucoadhesive for particular cells or mucosa, and that could also serve as enzyme inhibitors for the effective delivery of proteins and peptides, polymeric science needs to be explored. New biomaterials, such as custom copolymers, show significant potential for mucoadhesive drug delivery; nevertheless, formulations based on them still need to go a long way before they can be used in true clinical settings.

REFERENCES

1. Singh PK, Singh D, Bijauliya RK. A Comprehensive Review on Buccal DrugDelivery System. Int J Res Dev Pharm Life Sci 2017;6:2606–18. https://doi.org/10.21276/ijrdpl.2278-0238.2017.6(3).2606-2618.
2. Jacob S, Nair AB, Boddu SHS, Gorain B, Sreeharsha N, Shah J. An updated overview of the emerging role of patch and film-based buccal delivery systems. Pharmaceutics 2021;13. https://doi.org/10.3390/pharmaceutics13081206.
3. Kumar M, Kaushik D. An Overview on Various Approaches and Recent Patents on Gastroretentive Drug Delivery Systems. Recent Pat Drug Deliv Formul 2018;12:84–92. https://doi.org/10.2174/1872211312666180308150218.

4. Drug M, Systems D. M a Rosa Jim&nez-Castellanos2, Hussein Zial and C. T. Rhodes' Department of Pharmaceutics, University of Rhocle Island, Kingston, RI 02881 1993;19:143–94.
5. Langoth N, Kahlbacher H, Schöffmann G, Schmerold I, Schuh M, Franz S, et al. Thiolated chitosans: Design and In Vivo evaluation of a mucoadhesive buccal peptide drug delivery system. Pharm Res 2006;23:573–9. https://doi.org/10.1007/s11095-005-9533-5.
6. R S, D S, R G. Review on Mucoadhesive Drug Delivery System with Special Emphasis on Buccal Route: An Important Tool in Designing of Novel Controlled Drug Delivery System for the Effective Delivery of Pharmaceuticals. J Dev Drugs 2017;06. https://doi.org/10.4172/2329-6631.1000169.
7. Ramana M, Nagda C, Himaja M. Design and evaluation of mucoadhesive buccal drug delivery systems containing metoprolol tartrate. Indian J Pharm Sci 2007;69:515–8. https://doi.org/10.4103/0250-474X.36936.
8. Feitosa RC, Geraldes DC, Beraldo-De-Araújo VL, Costa JSR, Oliveira-Nascimento L. Pharmacokinetic aspects of nanoparticle-in-matrix drug delivery systems for oral/buccal delivery. Front Pharmacol 2019;10. https://doi.org/10.3389/fphar.2019.01057.
9. Mamatha Y, Selvi A, Prasanth V V, Sipai MAB, Yadav V. Buccal Drug Delivery: a Technical Approach. J Drug Deliv Ther 2012;2. https://doi.org/10.22270/jddt.v2i2.96.
10. Montenegro-Nicolini M, Morales JO. Overview and Future Potential of Buccal Mucoadhesive Films as Drug Delivery Systems for Biologics. AAPS PharmSciTech 2017;18:3–14. https://doi.org/10.1208/s12249-016-0525-z.
11. Fonseca-Santos B, Chorilli M. An overview of polymeric dosage forms in buccal drug delivery: State of art, design of formulations and their in vivo performance evaluation. Mater Sci Eng C 2018;86:129–43. https://doi.org/10.1016/j.msec.2017.12.022.
12. Madhav NVS, Shakya AK, Shakya P, Singh K. Orotransmucosal drug delivery systems: A review. J Control Release 2009;140:2–11. https://doi.org/10.1016/j.jconrel.2009.07.016.
13. Campisi G, Paderni C, Saccone R, Fede O, Wolff A, Giannola L. Human Buccal Mucosa as an Innovative Site of Drug Delivery. Curr Pharm Des 2010;16:641–52. https://doi.org/10.2174/138161210790883778.
14. Bala R, Khanna S, Pawar P, Arora S. Orally dissolving strips: A new approach to oral drug delivery system. Int J Pharm Investig 2013;3:67. https://doi.org/10.4103/2230-973x.114897.
15. Al-Dhubiab BE, Nair AB, Kumria R, Attimarad M, Harsha S. Formulation and evaluation of nano based drug delivery system for the buccal delivery of acyclovir. Colloids Surfaces B Biointerfaces 2015;136:878–84. https://doi.org/10.1016/j.colsurfb.2015.10.045.

16. Rohani Shirvan A, Bashari A, Hemmatinejad N. New insight into the fabrication of smart mucoadhesive buccal patches as a novel controlled-drug delivery system. Eur Polym J 2019;119:541–50. https://doi.org/10.1016/j.eurpolymj.2019.07.010.
17. Puratchikody A, Prasanth V V., Mathew ST, Kumar AB. Buccal drug delivery: Past, present and future - A review. Int J Drug Deliv 2011;1:171–84.
18. Hu S, Pei X, Duan L, Zhu Z, Liu Y, Chen J, et al. A mussel-inspired film for adhesion to wet buccal tissue and efficient buccal drug delivery. Nat Commun 2021;12. https://doi.org/10.1038/s41467-021-21989-5.
19. Khanna R, Agarwal SP, Ahuja A. Mucoadhesive buccal drug delivery: A potential alternative to conventional therapy. Indian J Pharm Sci 1998;60:1–11.
20. Hauptstein S, Hintzen F, Müller C, Ohm M, Bernkop-Schnürch A. Development and in vitro evaluation of a buccal drug delivery system based on preactivated thiolated pectin. Drug Dev Ind Pharm 2014;40:1530–7. https://doi.org/10.3109/03639045.2013.836213.
21. Patel DA, Patel MR, Patel KR, Patel NM. Buccal mucosa as a route for systemic drug delivery: A review. Int J Drug Dev Res 2012;4:99–116.
22. Madhavi B R. Buccal Film Drug Delivery System-An Innovative and Emerging Technology. J Mol Pharm Org Process Res 2013;1:1–6. https://doi.org/10.4172/2329-9053.1000107.
23. Patel VF, Liu F, Brown MB. Modeling the oral cavity: In vitro and in vivo evaluations of buccal drug delivery systems. J Control Release 2012;161:746–56. https://doi.org/10.1016/j.jconrel.2012.05.026.
24. Chinna Reddy P, Chaitanya KSC, Madhusudan Rao Y. A review on bioadhesive buccal drug delivery systems: Current status of formulation and evaluation methods. DARU, J Pharm Sci 2011;19:385–403.
25. Shaikh R, Raj Singh T, Garland M, Woolfson A, Donnelly R. Mucoadhesive drug delivery systems. J Pharm Bioallied Sci 2011;3:89–100. https://doi.org/10.4103/0975-7406.76478.
26. Manohar SD, Sridhar DA, Mallikarjuna SC. Drug delivery from the oral cavity: A focus on mucoadhesive buccal drug delivery systems. PDA J Pharm Sci Technol 2012;66:466–500. https://doi.org/10.5731/pdajpst.2012.00877.
27. Şenel S, Kremer MJ, Kaş S, Wertz PW, Hincal AA, Squier CA. Enhancing effect of chitosan on peptide drug delivery across buccal mucosa. Biomaterials 2000;21:2067–71. https://doi.org/10.1016/S0142-9612(00)00134-4.
28. Ramesh B, Saravanakumar K, Nagaveni P, Mohan Kumar A, Jaya Preethi P, Vivek Kumar P. A review on buccal drug delivery system. Int J Res Pharm Sci 2014;5:200–4. https://doi.org/10.5958/0975-4377.2017.00019.2.
29. Pichayakorn W, Monton C, Sampaopan Y, Panrat K, Suksaeree J. Fabrication and Characterization of Buccal Film Loaded Self-emulsifying Drug Delivery System containing Lysiphyllum strychnifolium Stem Extracts. AAPS PharmSciTech 2022;23. https://doi.org/10.1208/s12249-022-02341-6.

30. Xu J, Strandman S, Zhu JXX, Barralet J, Cerruti M. Genipin-crosslinked catechol-chitosan mucoadhesive hydrogels for buccal drug delivery. Biomaterials 2015;37:395–404. https://doi.org/10.1016/j.biomaterials.2014.10.024.

31. Srivastava N, Aslam S. Recent Advancements and Patents on Buccal Drug Delivery Systems: A Comprehensive Review. Recent Pat Nanotechnol 2021;16:308–25. https://doi.org/10.2174/1872210515666210609145144.

32. Leonard TE, Liko AF, Gustiananda M, Putra ABN, Juanssilfero AB, Hartrianti P. Thiolated pectin-chitosan composites: Potential mucoadhesive drug delivery system with selective cytotoxicity towards colorectal cancer. Int J Biol Macromol 2023;225:1–12. https://doi.org/10.1016/j.ijbiomac.2022.12.012.

33. Buang F, Chatzifragkou A, Cairul M, Mohd I, Khutoryanskiy V V. Synthesis of Methacryloylated Hydroxyethylcellulose and Development of Mucoadhesive Wafers for Buccal 2023.

34. Pather SI, Rathbone MJ, Şenel S. Current status and the future of buccal drug delivery systems. Expert Opin Drug Deliv 2008;5:531–42. https://doi.org/10.1517/17425247.5.5.531.

35. Kaul M. An Overview of Buccal Drug Delivery System. Int J Pharm Res 2021;13:1303–21. https://doi.org/10.31838/ijpr/2021.13.01.556.

36. Puri V, Sharma A, Maman P, Rathore N, Singh I. Overview of mucoadhesive biopolymers for buccal drug delivery systems. Int J Appl Pharm 2019;11:18–29. https://doi.org/10.22159/ijap.2019v11i6.35438.

37. Cite S. Pharmaceutical Science & Technology Today Drug delivery via the buccal mucosa Buccal absorption 1998;1.

38. Junginger HE, Hoogstraate JA, Verhoef JC. Recent advances in buccal drug delivery and absorption - In vitro and in vivo studies. J Control Release 1999;62:149–59. https://doi.org/10.1016/S0168-3659(99)00032-2.

39. Hooda R, Tripathi M, Kapoor K. A Review on Oral Mucosal Drug Delivery System. Pharma Innov 2012;1:14–21.

40. Şenel S, Rathbone MJ, Cansz M, Pather I. Recent developments in buccal and sublingual delivery systems. Expert Opin Drug Deliv 2012;9:615–28. https://doi.org/10.1517/17425247.2012.676040.

41. Kianfar F, Ayensu I, Boateng JS. Development and physico-mechanical characterization of carrageenan and poloxamer-based lyophilized matrix as a potential buccal drug delivery system. Drug Dev Ind Pharm 2014;40:361–9. https://doi.org/10.3109/03639045.2012.762655.

42. Shaikh R, Raghu T, Singh R, Donnelly RF. Mucoadhesive drug delivery systems Bioadhesion and Mucoadhesion Theories of Mucoadhesion Wetting Theory of Mucoadhesion Electrostatic Theory of Mucoadhesion Diffusion Theory of Mucoadhesion 2015:1–17.

43. Macedo AS, Castro PM, Roque L, Thomé NG, Reis CP, Pintado ME, et al. Novel and revisited approaches in nanoparticle systems for buccal drug delivery. J Control Release 2020;320:125–41. https://doi.org/10.1016/j.jconrel.2020.01.006.

44. Gandhi RB, Robinson JR. Oral cavity as a site for bioadhesive drug delivery. Adv Drug Deliv Rev 1994;13:43–74. https://doi.org/10.1016/0169-409X(94)90026-4.
45. Uddin M, Allon A, Roni MA, Kouzi S. Overview and future potential of fast dissolving buccal films as drug delivery system for vaccines. J Pharm Pharm Sci 2019;22:388–406. https://doi.org/10.18433/jpps30528.
46. Pawar RR, Raut DB, Karde VK, Wadikar JC, Jadhav AS, Chintale AG. Mucoadhesive buccal drug delivery system: A review. Res J Pharm Technol 2013;6:506–15. https://doi.org/10.46624/ajptr.2020.v10.i2.020.
47. Gandhi PA. A Review Article on Mucoadhesive Buccal Delivery System. Int J Pharm Res Dev 2011;3:159–73.
48. Sheoran R. Buccal Drug Delivery System: A Review 2021.
49. Bhati R, Nagrajan RK. A detailed review on oral mucosal drug delivery system. Int J Pharm Sci Res 2012;3:659–81.
50. Ayensu I, Mitchell JC, Boateng JS. Development and physico-mechanical characterisation of lyophilised chitosan wafers as potential protein drug delivery systems via the buccal mucosa. Colloids Surfaces B Biointerfaces 2012;91:258–65. https://doi.org/10.1016/j.colsurfb.2011.11.004.
51. Shojaei AH, Chang RK, Guo X, Burnside BA, Couch RA. Systemic drug delivery via the buccal mucosal route. Pharm Technol North Am 2001;25: 70–81.
52. Kianfar F, Antonijevic MD, Chowdhry BZ, Boateng JS. Formulation Development of a Carrageenan Based Delivery System for Buccal Drug Delivery Using Ibuprofen as a Model Drug. J Biomater Nanobiotechnol 2011;02:582–95. https://doi.org/10.4236/jbnb.2011.225070.
53. Birudaraj R, Mahalingam R, Li X, Jasti BR. Advances in buccal drug delivery. Crit Rev Ther Drug Carrier Syst 2005;22:295–330. https://doi.org/10.1615/CritRevTherDrugCarrierSyst.v22.i3.20.

EXCERCISE

MULTIPLE CHOICE QUESTIONS

1. Advantage of buccal drug delivery systems over conventional oral DDS
   a. Bypass first pass metabolism
   b. Release drug slowly
   c. Easy to analyze
   d. Ease of administration
2. Drug permeation through the buccal mucosa is by
   a. Paracellular
   b. Transcellular
   c. Both paracellular and transcellular
   d. Pinocytosis

3. Chitosan is a __________ mucoadhesive polymer
   a. Cationic
   b. anionic
   c. Synthetic
   d. non-ionic
4. Hydrogen bonding capacity is related to which type of factor affecting mucoadhesion.
   a. Physiological
   b. Polymer
   c. Environment
   d. Physicochemical
5. Factors affecting Mucoadhesion are
   a. Flexibility of a polymer chains
   b. Presence of functional group
   c. pH of polymer substrate interface and Mucinturn over
   d. All the above
6. Advantages of of mucosal drug delivery system include
   a. Excellent accessibility
   b. Painless administration
   c. Prolongation of Residence time
   d. All the above
7. The oral cavity has been used as a site________for drug delivery.
   a. Local
   b. Systemic
   c. both
   d. none of the them ans-c
8. Which drugs get mostly absorbed from the mouth?
   a. Acidic drugs and lipophilic drugs
   b. Lipophilic drugs and neutral drugs
   c. Neutral drugs and lipophilic drug
   d. Lipophilic, neutral, Basic drug
9. The pH of the mouth is:
   a. 6.8
   b. 5.8
   c. 5.6
   d. 7.0
10. Which one of the following is the sublingual route?
    a. Drug placed between cheek and gum.
    b. Drug placed between the tongue and upper palate.
    c. Drug placed under the tongue.
    d. Drug crushed and placed under the tongue.

11. Which one of the following is the buccal route?
    a. Drug placed between cheek and gum.
    b. Drug placed between the tongue and upper palate.
    c. Drug placed under the tongue.
    d. Drug crushed and placed under the tongue.

12. Which one of the following is not an advantage of buccal administration?
    a. Rapid absorption and higher blood levels
    b. No first pass hepatic metabolism
    c. No degradation of drugs
    d. Limited surface area

13. The theory which analyses the maximum tensile stress develop during detachment of BDDS from mucosal surface is known as...................
    a. Wetting theory
    b. Electronic theory
    c. Diffusion theory
    d. Fracture theory

14. Which of the following drug delivery system can be easily administered and terminated-
    a. Buccal DDS
    b. Implantable DDS
    c. Oral DDS
    d. Parenteral DDS

15. Which of the following factors affects buccal drug absorption?
    a. Molecular weight of drug
    b. Lipid solubility of drug
    c. pKa of drug
    d. All of the above

16. Maximal duration of buccal delivery is approximately
    a. 2-4 h
    b. 4-6 h
    c. 6-8 h
    d. 8-12 h

17. Buccal films should be evaluated for
    a. Tensile strength
    b. Film endurance
    c. Moisture absorption
    d. All of the above

18. Buccal films and patches are manufactured by-
    a. Solvent casting
    b. Direct milling
    c. Both a and b
    d. Compression

19. Which of the following buccal dosage form suffers from significant drug loss due to swallowing
    - a. Single layer tablet
    - b. Double layer tablet
    - c. Unidirectional coated
    - d. All of the above
20. Which theory explain about the polymer chains and the mucus to a sufficient depth to create a semi-permanent adhesive bond-
    - a. Diffusion theory
    - b. Absorption theory
    - c. Electronic theory
    - d. Wetting theory

SHORT ANSWER QUESTIONS

1. Write the principle of mucoadhesion in buccal drug delivery system.
2. Discuss about the buccal tablets and Buccal strips.
3. Write about the different Theories of bioadhesion
4. What are the evaluation parameters of mucoadhesive drug delivery?
5. What are the Merits and demerits of buccal drug delivery systems
6. Desecribe the mechanism of buccal absorption
7. Explain about different Evaluation Parameter for Buccal Patch
8. What are the basic components of buccal Drug Delivery System?
9. Name some commonly used penetration enhancer in buccal formulation?
10. Name some commonly used bioadhesive in buccal formulation?

LONG ANSWER QUESTIONS

1. What are the factors affecting the buccal absorption?
2. Describe the basic components of buccal drug delivery system?
3. Define bioadhesion & describe mechanism of bioadhesion?
4. What are the different approaches of buccal drug delivery system?
5. Explain different evaluation of buccal patch?
6. Explain structure and composition of mucus membrane?
7. What are the classifications of bioadhesive polymer?
8. Describe various bioadhesive formulations?
9. Explain about the buccal drug delivery system
10. Describe about the various evaluation parameters of buccal tablets

MCQ ANSWERS

1. (a)	2. (c)	3. (a)	4. (b)
5. (b)	6. (d)	7. (c)	8. (a)
9. (a)	10. (c)	11. (a)	12. (d)
13. (d)	14. (a)	15. (d)	16. (b)
17. (d)	18. (c)	19. (a)	20. (c)

CHAPTER - 7

Ocular Drug Delivery Systems

Priya Namdev, Sakshi Tiwari, Dr. Kapil Agrawal and Dr. Amber Vyas

Introduction, Barriers of Drug Permeation, Methods to Overcome

INTRODUCTION

The eye is a unique and very valuable (Fig 7.1) organ which must be protected from exogenous substances and external stress by various barriers. The therapeutic drugs must be transported across various protective barriers of which route of administration is utilized, such as eye-drops, and subconjunctival, sub-tenon's and intravitreal injection and /or implant.

For the treatment of the anterior segment of the eye (cornea, conjunct-tiva, sclera, anterior uvea), usually topical eye-preparations are used. These preparations are classified as traditional and new drug delivery system. Topical application of drugs to the eye is the most common, popular and well-accepted route of administration. The bioavailability of ophthalmic drugs is very poorbecause eye has the most effective protective mechanisms. Blinking, baseline and reflex lachrymation, and drainage remove foreign substances rapidly even drugs from the surface of the eye[1]. An eye-drop, irrespective of the instilled volume, often eliminates rapidly within five – six minutes after administration, leaves only a small amount (1 – 3%) of the instilled volume actually reaches the intraocular tissue[2]. More than 75% of applied ophthalmic solution is lost via nasolachrymal drainage and absorbed systemically via

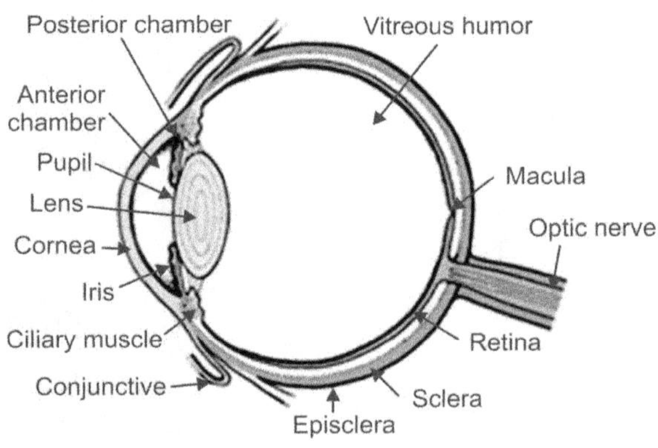

Fig.7.1 Schematic diagram of structure of eye ball.

conjunctiva. As a result, ocular drug availability is very low[3]. Thus, it is difficult to provide and maintain an adequate concentration of drug in the precorneal area. To increase the ocular bioavailability and prolong the retention time on the ocular surface, numerous ophthalmic vehicles such as viscous solutions, suspensions, emulsions, ointments, aqueous gel, and polymeric inserts in form of in-situ gel, nanoparticle, liposome, nanosuspension, microemulsion, iontophoresis, and ocular inserts can be used for topical application to the eye[4-11]. Therefore, drugs topically applied cannot reach the posterior segment of the eye (retina, vitreous, choroid) and hence, for systemic administration, periocular or intraocular injections of drugs are normally required to be done[12, 13].

Ocular pharmacokinetics[14-16]

Pharmacokinetics of the drug from the eye follows the following routes:

1) Transcorneal permeation from lacrimal fluid into the anterior chamber.
2) Non-corneal drug permeation across the conjunctiva and sclera into the anterior uvea.
3) Drug distribution from the blood stream through blood-aqueous barrier into the anterior chamber.
4) Elimination of drug from the anterior chamber by the aqueous humor turnover to the trabecular meshwork and sclemm's canal.
5) Drug elimination from the aqueous into the systemic circulation across the blood-aqueous barrier.
6) Drug distribution from the blood into the posterior eye across the blood-retina barrier.
7) Drug elimination from the vitreous through posterior route across the blood-retina barrier.
8) Intravitreal drug administration.
9) Drug elimination from the vitreous via anterior route to the posterior chamber.

BARRIERS OF DRUG PERMEATION

The flow of lacrimal fluid removes the instilled compounds from the surface of the eye. Though the lacrimal turnover rate is about 1 μL/min, the excess volume of the instilled fluid is flown to the nasolacrimal duct rapidly in few minutes[17]. Another source of non-productive removal of drug is its systemic absorption in place of ocular absorption. Systemic absorption may occur either directly from the conjunctival sac via local blood capillaries or after the solution flow to the nasal cavity[18, 19]. Anyway, most of small molecular weight drug dose is absorbed into systemic circulation rapidly in few minutes. The constant drug release from solid delivery system to the tear fluid may lead only to ocular bioavailability of about 10%, since most of the drug is cleared by the local systemic absorption anyway[20].

The unique anatomy and physiology of the eye and its protective barriers prevent the administration drugs from penetrating into the target tissues. Currently, there is also rapidly growing interest in drug delivery systems (DDSs) to the posterior segment of the eye.

- **Tear**

One of the precorneal barriers is tear film which reduces the effective concentration of the administered drugs due to dilution by the tear turnover (about 1 μL/min), accelerated clearance, and binding of the drug molecule to the tear proteins. Moreover, the dosing volume of the instillation is usually 20 – 50 μL whereas the size of cul-de-sac is only 7 – 10μL. The excess volume may spill out on the cheek or exit through the nasolacrimal duct[21-23].

- **Cornea**

The cornea is made up of three layers: (1) epithelium, (2) stroma, and (3) endothelium, and a mechanical barrier to inhibit transport of exogenous substances into eye[24]. Each layer possesses a different polarity and a rate-limiting structure for drug permeation. The corneal epithelium is of a lipophilic nature, and tight junctions among cells are formed to restrict paracellular drug permeation from the tear film. The stroma is composed of an extracellular matrix of a lamellar arrangement of collagen fibrils. The highly hydrated structure of the stroma acts as a barrier to permeation of lipophilic drug molecules. Corneal endothelium is the innermost monolayer of hexagonal-shaped cells, and acts as a separating barrier between the stroma and aqueous humor. The endothelial junctions are leaky and facilitate the passage of macromolecules between the aqueous humor and stroma[25].

- **Conjunctiva**

Conjunctiva of the eyelids and globe is a thin and transparent membrane, which is involved in the formation and maintenance of the tear film. Moreover, conjunctiva or episcleral has a rich supply of capillaries and lymphatics[26-28]; therefore, drugs administered in the conjunctival or episcleral space may be cleared through blood and lymph. The conjunctival blood vessel do not form a tight junction barrier[29], which means drug molecules can enter into the blood circulation by pinocytosis and/or convective transport through paracellular pores in the vascular endothelial layer.

The conjunctival lymphatic acts as an efflux system for the efficient elimination from the conjunctival space. Recently, it has been reported that at least 10% of a small molecular weight hydrophilic model compound (sodium fluorescein), administered in the subconjunctival space, and is eliminated via the lymphatics within the first hour in rat eyes[30]. Therefore, drugs transported by lymphatics in conjunction with the elimination by blood circulation can contribute to systemic exposure, since the interstitial fluid is returned to the systemic circulation after filtration through lymph nodes.

- **Sclera**

Generally, sclera consists of collagen fibers and proteoglycans embedded in an extracellular matrix[31]. Scleral permeability has been shown to have a strong dependence on the molecular radius; scleral permeability decreases roughly exponentially with molecular radius[32]. Moreover, the posterior sclera is composed of a looser weave of collagen fibers than the anterior sclera[33], and the human sclera is relatively thick near the limbus (0.53±0.14mm), thin at the equator (0.39±0.17mm), and much thicker near the optic nerve (0.9 – 1.0 mm). Thus, the ideal location for transscleral drug delivery is near the equator at 12 – 17 mm posterior to the corneoscleral limbus[34]. Hydrophobicity of drugs affects scleral permeability; increase of lipophilicity shows lower permeability; and hydrophilic drugs may diffuse through the aqueous medium of proteoglycans in the fiber matrix pores more easily than lipophilic drugs[35, 36].

Furthermore, the charge of the drug molecule also affects its permeability across the sclera. Positively charged compounds may show less permeability due to their binding to the negatively charged proteoglycan matrix[37].

- **Choroid/ Bruch's Membrane**

Choroid is one of the most highly vascularized tissues of the body to supply the blood to the retina. Its blood flow per unit tissue weight is ten-fold higher than in the brain. In addition, the choroidal capillary endothelial cells are fenestrated and, in humans, are relatively large in diameter (20 – 40 µm).

An Optical CoherenceTomography (OCT) can measure the thickness of retina and choroid noninvasively[38-41]. Using an OCT, it has been shown that choroidal thickness becomes thinner with age[42, 43]. Previous histological studies have shown choroidal thickness changes from 200 µ m at birth decreasing to about 80µm at about age of 90 years[44]. Moreover, chorioretinal decreases including AMD with pigment epithelial detachment, central serous chorioretinopathy, age-related choroidal atrophy, and high myopia, affect choroidal thickness.

In contrast, Bruch's membrane (BM) causes thickening with age[45]. These changes cause increased calcification of elastic fibers, increased cross-linkage of collagen fibers and increased turnover of glycosaminoglycans. Moreover, advanced glycation end products and lipofuscin accumulate in BM. Thickness-changes of choroid and BM might affect drug permeability from subconjunctiva or episcleral space into the retina and the vitreous.

- **Retina**

The drugs in the vitreous are eliminated by two main routes from anterior and posterior segments. All drugs can eliminate through the anterior route. This means drugs can diffuse across the vitreous to the posterior chamber and then, eliminate through aqueous turnover and uveal blood flow. Elimination through the posterior route takes place by permeation across the retina. One of the barriers that restrict penetration of drug from the vitreous to the retina is the internal limiting membrane (ILM). The ILM separates the retina and the vitreous, and is composed of 10 distinct extracellular matrix proteins[46]. Although a study using primates has suggested that molecules more than 100 kDa cannot cross the retinal layers into the subretinal space, it has been confirmed by immunohistochemical analysis, a full-length, humanized, anti-vascular endothelial growth factor (VEGF) monoclonal antibody, composed of 214 amino acids with a molecular weight of 149 kDa, injected into the vitreous cavity, can penetrate through the sensory retina into retinal pigment epitheliums (RPE), subretinal and choroidal space, in monkey and rabbit[47,48]. Moreover, nanometer-sized particle whose mean diameter is below 200 nm can penetrate across the sensory retina into RPE after intravitreal injection in rabbit[49,50].

In intact retina, theoretically, the drugs in the subretinal fluid could either be absorbed by the sensory retinal blood vessels or transported across the RPE, where it may be absorbed into the choroidal vessels or pass through the sclera. Drug transport across the RPE takes place both by transcellular and paracellular routes. The driving forces of outward transport of molecules from the subretinal spaces are hydrostatic and osmotic, and small molecules might transport through the paracellular inter-RPE cellular clefts and by active transport through the transcellular route.

- **Blood-Retinal Barrier**

Blood-retinal barrier (BRB) restricts drug transport from blood into the retina. BRB is composed of tight junctions of retinal capillary endothelial cells and RPE, called iBRB for the inner and oBRB for the outer BRB, respectively. The function of iBRB is supported by Muller cells and astrocytes.

The retinal capillary endothelial cells are not fenestrated and have a paucity of vesicles. The function of these endothelial vesicles has been described as endocytosis or transcytosis that may be receptor mediated or fluid phase requiring adenosine triphosphate. A close spatial relationship exists. Between Muller cells and retinal capillary vessels to maintain the iBRB in the uptake of nutrients and in the disposal of metabolites under normal conditions. Muller cells are known to support neuronal activity and maintain the proper functioning of the iBRB under normal conditions. They are involved in the control and homeostasis of K^+ and other ions signaling molecules, and in the control of extracellular pH. Dysfunction of Muller cells may contribute to a breakdown of the iBRB in many pathological conditions, such as diabetes. Muller cells increase the secretion of VEGF under hypoxic and inflammatory conditions. *In vitro* study showed that VEGF-induced occluding phosphorrylation and ubiquitination causes trafficking of tight junction and leads to enhanced retinal vascular permeability.

The astrocytes originate from the optic nerve and migrate to the nerve fiber layer during development. They are closely associated with the retinal capillary vessels and help to maintain the capillary integrity. Astrocytes are known to increase the barrier properties of the retinal vascular endothelium by increasing the expression of the tight junction protein ZO-1 and modifying endothelial morphology.

After systemic administration of drugs, drugs can easily enter the choroid since choroid is highly vascularized tissue compared to retina. The choriocapillaris are fenestrated resulting in rapid equilibration of drug molecules present in the bloodstream with the extravascular space of the choroid. Thus, oBRB (RPE) restricts further entry of drugs from the choroid into retina. RPE is a monolayer of highly specialized hexagonal-shaped cells, located between the sensory retina and the choroid. The tight junctions of the RPE efficiently restrict intercellular permeation into the sensory retina.

METHODS TO OVERCOME

Approaches in ophthalmic drug delivery systems

A number of approaches have been used in the early stages for better results. These approaches, categorized into two types, are:

- Bioavailability improvement and
- Controlled release drug delivery

The first type aims to maximize corneal drug absorption and minimize precorneal drug loss using viscosity and penetration enhancers, prodrugs, gels and liposomes.

The second one is for the delivery of active ophthalmic moiety in the form of a sustained delivery system by providing controlled and continuous delivery like implants, inserts, nanoparticles, micro particulates, and colloids. There are a number of traditional approaches, such as viscosity enhancers, gel, penetration enhancer, prodrug and liposomes which enhance the bioavailability, while the newer developments, *i.e.,* ocuserts, nanosuspension, nanoparticles, liposomes, niosomes and implants improve both bioavailability and release of drugs in a controlled manner in the anterior segment of the eye. In the posterior segment of the eye, drug reaches through intravitreal injections, iontophoresis, subconjunctival injection and periocular routes[51,52].

Approaches to improve ocular bioavailability

Use of viscosity enhancers

Viscosity-increasing polymers are highly preferred additive in the ophthalmic formulations due to their properties of enhancing viscosity and thereby imparting benefit to the penetration of the drug into the anterior chamber of the eye by lowering the elimination rate from the preocular area, resulting in increase in precorneal residence time and transcorneal penetration, but having very fewer effects for enhancing bioavailability in human beings. Examples of polymers are polyvinyl alcohol (PVA), polyvinylpyrrolidone (PVP), methylcellulose, hydroxylethylcellulose, hydroxylpropyl methylcellulose (HPMC) and hydroxypropyl cellulose[53]. As per Saettone *et al.* (1984), in their study of tropicamide solution, by using PVA, HPMC, and PVP solution, at concentrations yielding the same viscosity of 20 cst, PVA has been reported to be the most effective among all, probably due to the adhesive property of PVA and its capability to enhance the thickness of the precorneal tear film[53]. Saettone *et al.* (1982) have stated in their study that the retention of drug in the precorneal tear film does not strictly belong to vehicle viscosity, but also with surface spreading properties of the vehicle and to the capability of a polymer to use water as the vehicle spreads over the ocular surface with each eye blinking[54].

Gel formulation

Gels are known to be significantly diluting cross-linked systems, which show rigidity in the steady-state. Gels are generally liquid, but behave like solids due to their three-dimensional cross-linked structure within the liquid[55-57]. On the other side, if the gels have extremely high viscosity, they cannot improve bioavailability; instead, they will control the release, which leads to reduced frequency of dosing to once a day. The highly viscous solution even leads to blurred vision and matted eyelids, which substantially decrease patient's compliance. In aqueous gel, viscosity building agents, such as PVA, polyacrylamide, poloxamer, HPMC, Carbomer, polymethylvinylether, Maleic anhydride, and hydroxylpropyl ethyl cellulose are incorporated, whereas hydrogel or swellable water-insoluble polymers give rise to controlled drug delivery systems[58].

Prodrug formulation

By the development of prodrugs, many properties of the formulation can be improved, which make it suitable for increasing drug permeability through the cornea. It includes modification of the chemical structure that imparts new characteristics to the active moiety *i.e.* site-specificity and selectivity[59]. This can be explained through examples; the formulations which have been developed as prodrugs are epinephrine, phenylephrine, timolol, and Pilocarpine. Other prodrugs are dipiverine, diester of pivalic acid and epinephrine showing seventeen fold more permeability via cornea as compared to that of epinephrine, which is caused by its six hundred folds more lipophilicity at pH 7.2. So a minor dose of the drug solution (dipiverine) spreads over the entire eyeball and has a therapeutic effect exactly the same as of epinephrine. When compared with conventional eye drops consist of 2% epinephrine, eye drops of dipiverine 0.1% show only mild activity by lowering the intraocular pressure with a significant reduction of side effects[60].

Penetration enhancers

Corneal epithelial membrane plays an important role in terms of permeability. So, by increasing its permeability, the transport property around cornea can be enhanced. Agents showing such properties are chelating agents, preservatives (like benzalkonium chloride), surfactants and bile acid salts, but due to local toxicity, they cannot be used in development ophthalmic formulation[61,62.]

Liposomes

Liposomes are defined as microscopic vesicles which consist of one or more concentric lipid bilayers, divided via water or aqueous buffer compartments. Liposomes are widely used in ocular formulations due to their property of having intimate contact with eye surfaces, mainly corneal and conjunctival area, thus drug absorption through ocular route can be increased[63]. Formulation of liposomes can be developed by using phosphatidylcholine, stearylamine and various amounts of cholesterol or lecithin and L-dipalmitoyl-phosphatidylcholine[64-67]. Major advantages of this type of delivery system are due to their properties, *i.e.*, biocompatibility, biodegradability, amphiphilic property, relative toxicity[64, 65, 68]. Delivery of drug on targeted site or sitespecificity and release of drug in a sustained manner, are also its advantages. Liposomes are generally prepared for the drugs which have poor absorption, lower partition coefficient, poor solubility and having molecular weights in the range of medium to high[69]. Surface charge of liposomes is to be considered during the formulation of ocular delivery system; if liposomes are positively charged, they are observed to be preferably captured by negatively charged corneal surface, while the neutral or negatively charged liposomes are not captured by corneal surface. According to the number of researches reported, the active pharmaceutical ingredients being used in liposomal ophthalmic formulations are acyclovir, pilocarpine, acetazolamide, chloramphenicol and ciprofloxacin[66, 67].

Niosomes and discosomes

Niosomes are chemically stable, bi-layered nanocarriers made up of nonionic surfactants and used as carriers for both hydrophilic and hydrophobic drugs. They do not have drawbacks like liposomes that are chemical instable, susceptible to oxidative degradation and made up of phospholipids that are very much unstable as well as expensive[64, 65, 70, 71]. Thus, niosomes have lots of advantages including that they are biodegradable, biocompatible and nonimmunogenic, which make them increase the contact time between drug and cornea, thereby increasing the bioavailability of drugs. A modified form of niosomes is discosomes that also acts as carrier for ophthalmic drugs. The size of discosomes lies between 12 to 16 μm. This gives it a benefit of not allowing it to enter in the general circulation and its disc shape provides better fit into the conjunctival sac [72,73]. The size of discosomes makes it different from niosomes, as the former consists of nonionic surfactants and SolulanC, a derivative of lanolin and a mixture of ethoxylated cholesterol (ether of cholesterol and polyethylene glycol) and ethoxylated fatty alcohols (ether of cetyl alcohol and polyethylene glycol). Use of niosomal carrier as a drug delivery system has been reported for genciclovir[74], cyclo-pentolate, or timolol[65].

Nanoparticles/nanospheres

These are polymeric colloidal particles, size varying from 10 nm to 1 nm, where the drug is being dissolved, entrapped, encapsulated, or adsorbed[75]. It consists of a number of biodegradable substances, like natural or synthetic polymers, lipids, phospholipids and metals. To obtain nanoparticles, the drugs can be formulated in many ways as by integrating with the matrix or by attaching to the surface of biodegradable polymers used for the preparation. Nanoparticles used in delivering drug to ocular tissues are polylactides (PLAs), polycyanoacrylate, poly (D, L-lactides) and natural polymers such as chitosan, gelatine, sodium alginate and albumin. Approximately, since last 10 y, nanoparticles have been used as carriers in delivering drug for ocular disorders and given promising results. A specific type of nanoparticles can be classified as small capsules having a central cavitymsurrounded by a polymeric membrane and solid matrix spheres, known as nanocapsules and nanospheres, respectively. Marchal *et al.* (1993) have reported that the nanocapsules exhibit better effect as compared to that of the nanospheres, because drug (betaxolol, carteolol) present in unionized form in the oily core, diffuses at a higher rate into the cornea. A number of authors have reported that the nanocapsules are more efficient due to the presence of mucoadhesive property in it that shows a rise in the residence time and biological responses. So, these can enhance the bioavailability of drugs at ocular site and also decrease the frequency of dosing. Alonso *et al.* (1995) have reported in their study that the nanoparticles made from poly-e-caprolactone havin cyclosporine exhibit better corneal absorption with respect to the drug's oily solution[76].

Nanosuspension and nanodispersions

Nanosuspensions are generated for poorly water-soluble drugs suspended at nano size range in a suitable dispersion medium. This technology can be utilized in a good way for drug moiety that forms crystals with high energy content, due to which they are insoluble in organic (lipophilic) or hydrophilic media. Polymeric nanoparticles suspensions are being formulated using inert polymeric resins, which can be used as vital drug delivery vehicles, having the capacity to increase drug release as well as improve its bioavailability. The carriers having such type of properties can be used as inert carriers for ophthalmic drugs, because they donot cause any irritation to the cornea, iris or conjunctiva. An example of such carrier is polymeric nanoparticle suspension having flurbiprofen (FLU) as an active ingredient and eudragit RS 1001 and RL 1001 are polymers used. Nanodispersions of alginate chitosan produced for sustained drug delivery and improved transcorneal permeation have been reported by Morsi *et al.* 2015[77,78].

Microemulsion

A stable dispersion of water in oil, facilitated by adding surfactant and co-surfactant in combination in a way to decrease interfacial tension, is termed as a microemulsion. Microemulsion leads to decrease in administration frequency and enhancing ocular drug bioavailability. Major advantages of this dosage form are its high thermodynamic stability, smaller droplet size, *i.e.*, 100 nm (approx.) and clear appearance. Ansari *et al.* (2008) have reported a microemulsion formulation, which is oil in water system consisting of pilocarpine as a drug, lecithin, propylene glycol, PEG 200 as surfactant/co-surfactants and isopropyl myristate forming the oil phase[79].

Dendrimers

Dendrimers are symmetric structures made from repetitive branched molecules surrounding a central core, proposed recently as topical ocular drug delivery systems. Frequently used dendrimers for delivery in ocular system are poly-(amidoamine) (PAMAM), PLL, polypropylenimines (PPI) and phosphorus dendrimers. These are used as carriers to deliver nucleic acid-based drugs, mostly in ocular delivery system, but sometimes used for drugs with low molecular weight that can be hydrophilic (antibiotics) or lipophilic (anti-glaucoma) drugs as well[80, 81].

According to the reported methods, it has been found that the carrier's performance can be increased by making a change on their surface using methods like PEGylation or acetylation, which also help in reducing their toxicity factors. So, the advantages of using dendimers as carrier of drugs for topical applications are enhancement of the drug residence time in the pre-corneal area, increase in bioavailability of drugs and prolonged therapeutic effect[82].

In situ forming gel

Researchers have found the new concept of *in situ* gel in the early1980s. Delivery of drug to ocular system through *in situ* gel is mainly for enhancing viscosity to decrease drug drainage from the cornea. The pourable gels are in liquid form when applied, after which they undergo a phase transition, when reaches to cul-de-sac of eye and converted into a visco-elastic gel giving rise to a response to changes environmentally, thereby increasing the bioavailability of the drug automatically. The major disadvantages of the *in situ* gels are that they get affected by temperature, pH or ions. Bazzaz *et al.* (2018) reported that *in situ* gelling system provides better and prolonged effect of a drug rather than conventional eye drops[83].

Approaches for controlled and continuous ocular drug delivery

The following ocular drug delivery systems have been reported for controlled as well as continuous release of drugs:

Microparticles

Microparticles are isotropic, transparent, translucent, thermodynamically stable system of oil, surfactant and water droplets the size of which ranges between 20 to 200 nm. Microparticles are defined as micron-sized polymeric particles in which drugs in the polymeric matrices are suspended in liquid medium. Drugs are uniformly dispersed in the polymeric matrix or covalently bound to the backbone of the polymer. During topical application in the eye these particles go into the ocular culde- sac and the drug releases from it through a number of processes like diffusion, chemical reaction or polymer degradation. Microparticles increase precorneal residence time, which allow continuous and sustained release of the drug. Ultimately this leads to increased ocular bioavailability of the drug and minimizes frequency of dosing, but microparticulate preparations are generally not administered to the eye as they cause irritation due to their large particle size. Microparticles have properties like biodegradation, bio-adhesion, and biocompatibility, which make it suitable for fabrication with polymers[84, 79].

Ocular inserts

Ophthalmic inserts are solid patches, which, when placed in the conjunctival sac of the eye, slow down the rate of drug release. Ocular inserts also overcome the problem of frequent dosing by maintaining drug concentration in an effective manner and give rise to controlled, sustained and continuous drug delivery. Ocular Inserts also have various advantages like enhanced drug absorption due to increased contact time and minimized dose and application frequency. The major disadvantages of these inserts are patient noncompliance with frequent feeling like the entry of foreign body in the eye, difficulty in self-insertion feels and feeling of loss of the insert from eye.

Ocular inserts are made by various techniques that make them soluble, erodible and in hydrogel form[85].

Implants

The aim of designing an intraocular implant is to prolong the activity of the drug, along with its controlled release by using a polymer or polymer system. An injectable delivery system of drug, like liposomes and nanoparticles, is easy to administer, but having limitation that after insertion, it becomes difficult to retract those particles during any complication, like toxic responses. So, it is beneficial to use implants for balancing the rate and duration of drug release. Removal of ocular implants is easy and can be removed by surgical intervention. Implants can be categorized into two types based on the characteristics of the polymer(s) used:

Nonbiodegradable implants

They do not dissolve to any significant extent and are not even eroded *in vivo*[66].

Biodegradable implants

They mostly dissolve *in vivo* with soluble components by processes such as enzymatic or nonenzymatic degradations[85]. Examples of marketed implants used worldwide have been cited.

Approaches for posterior segment drug delivery

Intravitreal injections

Research reports reveal that intravitreal injections for the posterior segment are gaining worldwide popularity as a drug delivery system, over the past few years. Injections are directly given into the posterior segment via pars plana for delivering drugs to overcome all barriers. A number of studies have been conducted to find out the pharmacokinetic parameters of antiviral agents, like ganciclovir[86], foscarnet and cidofovir, antibiotics: Cefazolin, amikacin, moxifloxacin[87], ceftizoxime, ceftriaxone ceftazidime, clindamycin and gentamicin, steroids: dexamethasone, triamcinolone acetonide and monoclonal antibodies, such as rituximab, bevacizumab[88] following intravitreal injections. If the molecular weight of the drug is very high, vitreal retention times seem to be higher as well. Molecules that are larger, *i.e.*, linear>40 kDa and globular molecules>70 kDa seem to have long retention time due to the presence of tight barriers around the vitreous humor. So, this route is preferable for higher molecular weight drugs (>500 Da) and also having longer half-lives. First-order rate kinetics is mainly responsible for the elimination of residues out of the vitreous humour. Even the drug delivery through intravitreal injections can be gained by increasing concentrations of drugs in neural retina; side effects like retinal detachment due to repeated injections, retinal hemorrhage, endophthalmitis and other toxicities in the retina occurs because of more concentrations upon bolus dose administration that can cause patient's non-compliance. Development in designing of drug delivery system and surgical procedures has led to thedevelopment of intravitreal implants that can be instilled inside the vitreous chamber for a longer duration. The difference between intravitreal injections and intravitreal implants is their administration time. Injections can be taken 2 or 3 times a week and preferably can be changed every month, respectively[89, 90].

Iontophoresis

Ocular iontophoresis is one of the growing fields in research due to its noninvasive nature of delivering drugs to both the anterior and posterior segments of eye. Iontophoresis is defined as a noninvasive procedure for the transfer of ionized drugs via membranes with low electrical current [91]. The drugs can move across the membranes by two ways, migration and electro-osmosis. Ocular iontophoresis, categorized as transcorneal, corneoscleral, or transscleral[91], is considered as one of the most attractive options. OcuPhor™ system has been designed with the help of an applicator, dispersive electrode and a dose controller for Trans sclera iontophoresis[92]. The device works, as it releases the active drug moiety into retina-choroid. Another similar device being made known by name called Visulex™, which allows specific transport of ionized molecules through the sclera. Antibiotics, which are successfully used, are gentamycin, tobramycin, and ciprofloxacin, but not vancomycin, due to its high molecular weight. Fruitful results of delivery have been observed with drugs such as dexamethasone and antisense ODNs [93].

Advantages

- It can overcome the major side effects caused by intraocular injections and implants.
- Disease that might be cured using iontophoresis includes fungal keratitis, uveitis, retinitis, retinoblastoma, proliferative vitreal retinopathy and various retinal degenerations.

Disadvantages

- As there is a chance of burns and pains because of excessive current density; it should be used in such a manner that it takes a short period for delivering the drug.
- Drug should be in ionic form and have sufficient concentration because of high molecular weight, *i.e.*, 8 000–12 000.

Periocular route

Periocular region is the region surrounding the eye. Among all the present routes, the periocular route is least painful and a promising route for delivery of the drug to the posterior segment of the eye. In drug delivery through periocular route, the drug is placed in the nearest position to sclera; as a result, vitreal drug levels can be noticed after 20-30 min. Periocular delivery includes retrobulbar, peribulbar, subtenon and subconjunctival routes.

Retrobulbar injection

Retrobulbar injection consists of drug solution deposition into retrobulbar space within the muscle cone. This route is used when the formulation needs to be in direct contact with the macular region. These injections are mostly given through specific 23 gauge sharp, 1.5-inch needle with a rounded tip and a 10 bend.

Peribulbar injection

Peribulbar injections are used for lowering the risk of injury to intraorbital structures related to retrobulbar administration during cataract surgery. The injection is given in the quadrant between the inferior and the lateral of the orbit using a 26-gauge half-inch disposable needle[94].

Subtenon injection

The Tenon's capsule is a facial sheath of connective tissue sandwiched between the conjunctiva and episcleral plexus. The episcleral or subtenon's space is a void space between the tenon's capsule and sclera[95]. Subtenon injection is used to administer the drug in contact with sclera for prolonged periods because of its vascular nature.

Subconjunctival injection

The conjunctiva is a membrane that covers the sclera. The injection administered as a drug solution below the conjunctiva follows minimally invasive technique for delivering a drug to the posterior segment of the eye. About 500 µl of a drug solution as dosage form is injected into the subconjunctival area (bulbar conjunctiva) using a 25/30 gauge, 30 mm long needle. Subconjunctival injection can be used in critical conditions in which a molecule diffuses directly through sclera[96].

REFERENCES

1. Lee, V.H.L., Robinson, J.R.; Topical Ocular drug delivery: recent developments and future challenges.; J. Ocular Pharmacology; 2, 1986, 67 – 108.
2. Maurice, D.M., Mishima, S.; Ocular pharmacokinetics.; In Handbook of Experimental Pharmacology; Sears, M.L., Edn.; Springer: Berlin-Heidelberg, Germany; 1984.
3. Schoenwald, R.D.; Ocular pharmacokinetics. In Textbook of Ocular Pharmacology; Zimmerman, T.J., Edn.; Lippincott-Raven: Philadelphia, PA, USA, 1997.
4. Lang, J.C.; Ocular drug delivery conventional ocular formulation: Advanced drug delivery review; 16, 1995, 39 – 43.

5. Basavaraj, K., Nanjawade, Manvi, F.V. and Manjappa, A.S.; In situ-forming hydrogels for sustained ophthalmic drug delivery.; J. Control. Release; 122, 2007, 119 – 134.
6. Sahoo, K.S., Fatima, S.A.D., Kumar, K.; Nanotechnology in ocular drug delivery; Drug delivery today; 13, 2008, 144 – 151.
7. Weidener, J.; Mucoadhesive ocular inserts as an improved delivery vehicle for ophthalmic indications.; Drug Discovery Today; 8, 2003, 906 – 907.
8. Lang, J.C., Roehrs, R.T.E. and. Jani, R.; Ophthalmic preparations, Edn. 21, vol-1; Lippincott Williams and Wilkins, 2005.
9. Andrews, G.P., Laverty, T.P. and Jones, D.S.; Mucoadhesive polymeric platforms for controlled drug delivery-Review article.; European J. Pharmaceutics and Biopharmaceutics; 71, 2009, 505 – 518.
10. Alany, R.G.,Rades, T., Nicoll, J., Tucker, I.G. and Davies, N.M.; W/O microemulsions for ocular delivery; Evaluation of ocular irritation and precorneal retention.; J. Control. Release; 111, 2006, 145 – 152.
11. Binstock, E.E. and Domb, A.J.; Iontophoresiss: A non-invasive ocular drug delivery; J. Control. Release; 110, 2006, 479 – 489.
12. Geroski, D.H.; Edelhauser, H.F. Drug delivery for posterior segment eye disease. Invest. Ophthalmol. Vis. Sci.; 41, 2000, 961 – 964.
13. Lee, S.S., Hughes, P.M., Robinson, M.R.; Recent advances in drug delivery systms for treating ocular complications of systemic diseases.; Curr. Opin. Ophthalmol.; 20, 2009, 511 – 519.
14. Nagyova, B. and Tiffany, J.M.; Components responsible for the surface tension of human tears.; Curr. Eye Research; 19, 1999, 4 – 11.
15. Ahmed, L., Gokhale, R.D., Shah, M.V. and Paton, T.F.: Phytochemical determinants of drug diffusion across the conjunctiva, sclera, and cornea.; J. Pharmaceutical Science; 76, 1987, 583 – 587.
16. Urtti, A., Salminen, L.; Minimizing systemic absorption of topically administered ophthalmic drugs.; Surv. Ophthalmol.; 37, 1993, 435 – 457.
17. Urtti, A., Salminen, L., Miinalainen,O.; Systemic absorption of ocular pilocarpine is modified by polymer matrices.; Int. J. Pharm.; 20, 1985, 147 – 161.
18. Urtti, A., Rouhianinen, H., Kaila, T., Saano, V.; Controlled ocular timolol delivery: systemic absorption and intraocular pressure effects in humans.; Pharm. Res.; 11, 1994, 1278 – 1282.
19. Urtti, A., Pipkin, J.D., Rock, G.S., Sendo, T., Finne, U., Repta, A.J.; Controlled drug delivery devices for experimental ocular studies with timolol.; 2. Ocular and systemic absorption in rabbits.; Int. J. Pharm.; 61, 1990, 241 – 249.
20. Maurice, D. M., Mishima,, S.; Ocular pharmacokinetics, in: Sears, M.L.(Ed.); Handbook of experimental pharmacology, vol. 69, Springer Verlag, Berlin-Heidelberg, 1984.

21. Mishima, S.,Gasset, A., Klyce, S.D.; Jr.; Baum, J.L.; Determination of tear volume and tear flow.; Invest. Ophthalmol.; 5, 1966, 264 – 276.
22. Lee, V.H., Robinson, J.R.; Topical ocular drug delivery: Recent development and future challenges.; J. Ocul. Pharm.; 2, 1986, 67 – 108.
23. Schoenwald, R.D.; ocular drug delivery. Pharmacokinetic considerations.; Clin. Pharm.; 18, 1990, 255 – 269.
24. Pederson, J.E.; Fluid physiology of the subretinal space.; In Retina. Fourth edition; Ryan, S.J., Ed.; Elsevier Inc.: Philadelphia, PA, USA, 2006; Volume III, pp. 1909 – 1920.
25. Fischbarg, J.; The corneal endothelium.; In The Biology of Eye, Fischbarg. J., Ed.; Academic Press, New York, NY, USA, 2006.
26. Sugar, H.S., Riazi, A.,Schaffiner, R.; The bulbar conjunctival lymphatics and their clinical significance.; Trans. Am. Acad. Opphthalmol.; Otolaryngol.; 61, 1957, 212 – 223.
27. Gausas, R.E., Gonnering, R.S., Lemke, B.N., Dortzbach, R.K., Sherman, D.D.; Identification of human orbital lymphatics.; Ophthal. Plast. Reconstr. Surg.; 15, 1999, 252 – 259.
28. Singh, D.; Conjunctival lymphatic system.; J. Cataract. Refract. Surg.; 29, 2003, 632 – 633.
29. Raviola, G.; Conjunctival and episcleral blood vessels are permeable to bloodborns horseradish peroxidase.; Invest. Ophthalmol. Vis. Sci.; 24, 1983, 725 – 736.
30. Lee, S.J., He, W., Robinson, S.B., Robinson, M.R., Csaky, K.G., Kim, H.; Evaluation of clearance mecchanisms with trans-scleral drug delivery.; Invest. Ophthalmol. Vis. Sci.; 51, 2010, 5205 – 5212.
31. Oyster, C.w..; The cornea and sclera. In The Human Eye; Oyster, C.W., Ed.; Sinauer Associates, Inc.: Sunderland, UK, 1999.
32. Ambati, J., Canakis, C.S., Miller, J.W., Gragoudas, E.S., Edwards, A., Weissgold, D.J., Kim, I., Delori, F.C., Adamis, A.P.; Diffusion of high molecular weight compounds through sclera.; Invest. Ophthalmol. Vis. Sci.; 41, 2000, 1181 – 1185.
33. Curtin, B.J,; Physiologic aspects of scleral stresss-strain.; Trans. Am. Ophthalmol. Soc.; 67, 1969, 417 – 461.
34. Myles, M.E., Neumann, D.M., Hill, J.M.; Recent progress in ocular drug delivery for posterior segment disease: Emphasis on transscleral iontophoresis.; Adv.Drug Del. Rev.; 57, 2005, 2063 – 2079.
35. Maurice, D.M., Polgar, J.; Diffusion across the sclera.; Exp. Eye Res.; 25, 1977, 577 – 582.
36. Cruysberg, L.P., Nuijts, R.M., Geroski, D.H., Koole, L.H., Hendrikse, F., Edelhauuser, H.F.; *In vitro* human scleral permeability of fluorescein,

dexamethasone-fluorescein and rhodamine 6G and the use of a coated coil as a new drug delivery system.; J. Ocul. Pharmacol. Ther.; 18, 2002, 559 – 569.

37. Dunlevy, J.R., Rada, J.A..; Interaction of lumican with aggrecan in the aging human sclera.; Invest. Ophthalmol. Vis. Sci..; 45, 2004, 3849 – 3856.

38. Huang, D., Swanson, E.A., Lin, C.P., Schuman, J.S., Stinson, W..G., Chang, W., Hee, M.R., Flotte, T., Gregory, K., Puliafito, C.A..; Optical coherence tomography.; Science; 254, 1991, 1178 – 1181.

39. Schuman, J.S., Hee, M.R., Arya, A.V., Pedut-Kloizman, T., Puliafito, C.A., Fujimoto, J.G., Swanson, E.A.; Reproducibility of nerve fiber layer thickness measurements using optical coherence tomography.; Ophthalmology; 103, 1996, 1889 – 1898.

40. Hee, M.R.,Puliafito, C.A., Duker, J.S., Reichel, E., Coker, J.G., Wilkins, J.R., Schuman, J.S., Swanson, E.A., Fujimoto, J.G.; Topography of diabetic macular edema with optical coherence tomography.; Ophthalmology; 105, 1998, 360 – 370.

41. Margolis, R., Spaide, R.F.; A pilot study of enhanced depth imaging optical coherence tomography of the choroid in normal eyes.; Am. J. Ophthalmol.; 147, 2009, 811 – 815.

42. Ikuno, Y., Kawaguchi, K., Nouchi, T., Yasuno, Y.; Choroidal thickness in healthy Japanese subjects.; Invest. Ophthalmol. Vis. Sci.; 51, 2010, 2173 – 2176.

43. Nickla, D.L., Wallman, J.; The multifunctional choroid .; Prog. Retin. Eye Res.; 29, 2010, 144 – 168.

44. Ramrattan, R.S., van der Schaft, T.L., Mooy, C.M., de Bruijin, W.C., Mulder, P.G., de Jong, P.T.; Morphometric analysis of Bruch's membrane, the choriocapillaris, and the choroid in aging.; Invest. Ophthalmol. Vis. Sci.; 35, 1994, 2857 – 2864.

45. Candiello, J., Balasubramani, M., Schreiber, E.M., Cole, G.J., Mayer, U., Halfter, W., Lin, H.; Biomechanical properties of native basement membranes.; FEBS J.; 274, 2007, 2897 – 2908.

46. Heiduschka, P., Fietzz, H., Hofmeister, S., Schultheiss, S., Mack, A.F., Peters, S., Ziemssen, F., Niggemann, B., Julien, S., Bartz-Schmidt, K.U., Schraemeyer, U..; The tubingen Bevacizumab study, G. penetration of Bevacizumab through the retina after intravitreal injection in the monkey.; Invest. Ophthalmol. Vis. Sci.; 48, 2007, 2814 – 2823.

47. Dib,E., Maia, M., Longo-Maugeri, I.M., Martins, M.C., Mussalem, J.S., Squaiella, C.C., Penha, F.M., Magalhaes, O.,Jr., Rodrigues, E.B., Farah, M.E., Subretinal bevacizumab detention after intravitreeous injection in rabbits.; Invest. Ophthalmol. Vis. Sci.; 49, 2008, 1097 – 1100.

48. Sakurai, E., E., Ozeki, H., Kunou, N., Ogura, Y.; Effect of particle size of polymeric nanospheres on intravitreal kinetics.; Ophthalmic Res.; 33, 2001, 31 – 36.

49. Bourges, J.L., Gautier, S.E., Delie, F., Bejjani, R.A., Jeanny, J.CGurny, r., BenEzra, D., Behar-Cohen, F.F.; Ocular drug delivery targeting the retina and

retinal pigment epitheliumusing polylactide nanoparticles.; Invest. Ophthalmol. Vis. Sci.; 44, 2003, 3562 – 3569.

50. CunhaVaz, J.; The blood-ocular barriers. Surv. Ophthalmol.; 23, 1979, 279 – 296.
51. Lambert G, Guilatt RL. Current ocular drug delivery challenges. Drug dev report industry overview deals. 2005; 33:1-2.
52. Lang JC. Ocular drug delivery conventional ocular formulations. Adv Drug Deliv Rev. 1995; 16(1):39-43. doi: 10.1016/0169-409X(95)00012-V.
53. Saettone MF, Giannaccini B, Ravecca S, La Marca F, Tota G. Polymer effects on ocular bioavailability-the influence of different liquid vehicles on the mydriatic response of tropicamide in humans and in rabbits. Int J Pharm. 1984; 20(1-2):187-202. doi: 10.1016/0378-5173(84)90229-1.
54. Saettone MF, Giannaccini B, Ravecca S, LaMarca F, Tota G. Evaluation of viscous ophthalmic vehicles containing carbomer by slit-lamp fluorophotometry in humans. Int J Pharm. 1984;20:187-202.
55. Rathore KS. In situ gelling ophthalmic drug delivery system: an overview. Int J Pharm Pharm Sci. 2010;2;Suppl 4:30-4.
56. Baranowski P, Karolewicz B, Gajda M, Pluta J. Ophthalmic drug dosage forms: characterization and research methods. Sci World J. 2014; 2014:1-14.
57. Lambert G, Guilatt RL. Current ocular drug delivery challenges. Drug dev report industry overview deals. 2005; 33:1-2.
58. Saettone MF, Giannaccini B, Guiducci A, Savigni P. Semisolid ophthalmic vehicles. III. An evaluation of four organic hydrogels containing pilocarpine. Int J Pharm. 1986;31(3):261-70. doi: 10.1016/0378-5173(86)90160-2.
59. Rajasekaran A, Kumaran KS, Preetha JP, Karthika K. A comparative review on conventional and advanced ocular drug delivery formulations. Int J PharmTech Res. 2010; 2:668-74.
60. Järvinen T, Järvinen K. Prodrugs for improved ocular drug delivery. Adv Drug Deliv Rev. 1996; 19(2):203-24. doi: 10.1016/0169-409X(95)00107-I.
61. Kaur IP, Garg A, Singla AK, Aggarwal D. Vesicular systems in ocular drug delivery: an overview. Int J Pharm. 2004;269(1):1-14. doi: 10.1016/j.ijpharm.2003.09.016, PMID 14698571.
62. Sasaki H, Igarashi Y, Nagano T, Yamamura K, Nishida K, Nakamura J. Improvement of the ocular bioavailability of timolol by sorbic acid. J Pharm Pharmacol. 1995;47:17-21.
63. Gaudana R, Jwala J, Boddu SH, Mitra AK. Recent perspectives in ocular drug delivery. Pharm Res. 2009;26(5):1197-216. doi: 10.1007/s11095-008-9694-0, PMID 18758924.
64. Rajasekaran A, Kumaran KS, Preetha JP, Karthika K. A comparative review on conventional and advanced ocular drug delivery formulations. Int J PharmTech Res. 2010;2:668-74.

65. Nanjawade BK, Manvi FV, Manjappa AS. In situ-forming hydrogels for sustained ophthalmic drug delivery. J Control Release. 2007;122(2):119-34. doi: 10.1016/j.jconrel.2007.07.009, PMID 17719120.

66. Tangri P, Khurana S. Basics of ocular drug delivery systems. Int J Res Pharm Biomed Sci. 2011;2:1541-52.

67. Sahoo SK, Dilnawaz F, Krishnakumar S. Nanotechnology in ocular drug delivery. Drug Discov Today. 2008;13(3-4):144-51. doi: 10.1016/j.drudis.2007.10.021, PMID 18275912.

68. Kaur IP, Garg A, Singla AK, Aggarwal D. Vesicular systems in ocular drug delivery: an overview. Int J Pharm. 2004;269(1):1-14. doi: 10.1016/j.ijpharm.2003.09.016, PMID 14698571.

69. Budai L, Hajdú M, Budai M, Gróf P, Béni S, Noszál B, et al. Gels and liposomes in optimized ocular drug delivery: studies on ciprofloxacin formulations. Int J Pharm. 2007; 343(1-2):34-40. doi: 10.1016/j.ijpharm.2007.04.013, PMID 17537601.

70. Kadian RE. Nanoparticles: a promising drug delivery approach. Asian J Pharm Clin Res. 2018; 11(1):30-5. doi: 10.22159/ajpcr.2017.v11i1.22035.

71. Jeencham R, Sutheerawattananonda M, Tiyaboonchai W. Preparation and characterization of chitosan/regenerated silk fibroin (cs/rsf) films as a biomaterial for contact lenses-based ophthalmic drug delivery system. Int J Appl Pharm. 2019; 11:275-84. doi: 10.22159/ijap.2019v11i4.33283.

72. Nisha S, Deepak K. An insight to ophthalmic drug delivery system. Int J Pharm Stud Res. 2012; 3:9-13.

73. Shivhare R, Pathak A, Shrivastava N, Singh C, Tiwari G, Goyal R. An update review on novel advanced ocular drug delivery system. World J Pharm Pharm Sci. 2012; 1:545-68.

74. Mudgil M, Gupta N, Nagpal M, Pawar PR. Nanotechnology: a new approach for ocular drug delivery system. Int J Pharm Pharm Sci. 2012; 4:105-12.

75. Alonso MJ, Calvo P, VilaJato JL, Lopez MI, Llorente J, Pastor JC. Increased ocular corneal uptake of drugs using polyε-caprolactone nanocapsules and nanoemulsions. In: 22nd International Symposium on Controlled Release Bioactive Materials; 1995.

76. Kayser O, Lemke A, Hernández-Trejo N. The impact of nanobiotechnology on the development of new drug delivery systems. Curr Pharm Biotechnol. 2005;6(1):3-5. doi: 10.2174/1389201053167158, PMID 15727551.

77. Morsi NA, Ghorab DA, Refai HA, Teba HO. Preparation and evaluation of alginate/chitosan nanodispersions for ocular delivery. Int J Pharm Pharm Sci. 2015;7:234-40.

78. Ansari MJ, Kohli K, Dixit N. Microemulsions as potential drug delivery systems: a review. PDA J Pharm Sci Technol. 2008;62(1):66-79. PMID 18402369.

79. Kambhampati SP, Kannan RM. Dendrimer nanoparticles for ocular drug delivery. J Ocul Pharmacol Ther. 2013;29(2):151-65. doi: 10.1089/jop.2012.0232, PMID 23410062.

80. Chaplot SP, Rupenthal ID. Dendrimers for gene delivery–a potential approach for ocular therapy? J Pharm Pharmacol. 2014;66(4):542-56. doi: 10.1111/jphp.12104, PMID 24635556.

81. Lopez AI, Reins RY, McDermott AM, Trautner BW, Cai C. Antibacterial activity and cytotoxicity of pegylated poly (amidoamine) dendrimers. Mol Biosyst. 2009;5(10):1148-56. doi: 10.1039/b904746h, PMID 19756304.

82. Bazzaz L, FY. Al-kotaji M. Opthalmic in-situ sustained gel of ciprofloxacin, preparation and evaluation study. Int J Appl Pharm. 2018;10:153-61.

83. Joshi A. Recent developments in ophthalmic drug delivery. J Ocul Pharmacol Ther. 1994;10:29-45.

84. Saettone MF, Salminen L. Polymers used in ocular dosage form and drug delivery systems. Adv Drug Deliv Rev. 1995;16(1):95-106. doi: 10.1016/0169-409X(95)00014-X.

85. Hashizoe M, Ogura Y, Takanashi T, Kunou N, Honda Y, Ikada Y. Biodegradable polymeric device for sustained intravitreal release of ganciclovir in rabbits. Curr Eye Res. 1997;16(7):633-9. doi: 10.1076/ceyr.16.7.633.5063, PMID 9222079.

86. Musch DC, Martin DF, Gordon JF, Davis MD, Kuppermann BD, Ganciclovir Implant Study Group. Treatment of cytomegalovirus retinitis with a sustained-release ganciclovir implant. The Ganciclovir Implant Study Group. N Engl J Med. 1997;337(2):83-90. doi: 10.1056/NEJM199707103370203, PMID 9211677.

87. Iyer MN, He F, Wensel TG, Mieler WF, Benz MS, Holz ER. Intravitreal clearance of moxifloxacin. Trans Am Ophthalmol Soc. 2005;103:76-81; discussion 81. PMID 17057790.

88. Hughes MS, Sang DN. Safety and efficacy of intravitreal bevacizumab followed by pegaptanib maintenance as a treatment regimen for age-related macular degeneration. OSLI Retina 2006;37:446-54.

89. Maurice D. Practical issues in intravitreal drug delivery. J Ocul Pharmacol Ther 2001;17:393-401.

90. Baum U, Peyman GA, Barza M. Intravitreal administration of antibiotic in the treatment of bacterial endophthalmitis. III. Consensus. Surv Ophthalmol 1982;26:204-6.

91. Myles ME, Neumann DM, Hill JM. Recent progress in ocular drug delivery for posterior segment disease: emphasis on transscleral iontophoresis. Adv Drug Deliv Rev. 2005;57(14):2063-79. doi: 10.1016/j.addr.2005.08.006, PMID 16310884.

92. Parkinson TM, Ferguson E, Febbraro S, Bakhtyari A, King M, Mundasad M. Tolerance of ocular iontophoresis in healthy volunteers. J Ocul Pharmacol Ther. 2003;19(2):145-51. doi: 10.1089/108076803321637672, PMID 12804059.

93. Frucht-Pery J, Raiskup F, Mechoulam H, Shapiro M, Eljarrat-Binstock E, Domb A. Iontophoretic treatment of experimental pseudomonas keratitis in rabbit eyes using gentamicin-loaded hydrogels. Cornea. 2006;25(10):1182-6. doi: 10.1097/01.ico.0000243959.14651.18, PMID 17172895.

94. Ebner R, Devoto MH, Weil D, Bordaberry M, Mir C, Martinez H, et al. Treatment of thyroid associated ophthalmopathy with periocular injections of triamcinolone. Br J Ophthalmol. 2004;88(11):1380-6. doi: 10.1136/bjo.2004.046193, PMID 15489477.

95. Canavan KS, Dark A, Garrioch MA. Sub-Tenon's administration of local anesthetic: a review of the technique. Br J Anaesth. 2003;90(6):787-93. doi: 10.1093/bja/aeg105, PMID 12765895.

96. Kim TW, Lindsey JD, Aihara M, Anthony TL, Weinreb RN. Intraocular distribution of 70-kDa dextran after subconjunctival injection in mice. Invest Ophthalmol Vis Sci. 2002;43(6):1809-16. PMID 12036983.

EXCERCISE

MULTIPLE CHOICE QUESTIONS

1. Which of the following organs includes in accessory organs of the eye?
   a. The eyebrows, eyelids, eyelashes
   b. The lacrimal apparatus
   c. The extrinsic muscles
   d. All the above
2. Which part of the eye is responsible for the function "Refracts light rays"?
   a. Sclera
   b. Cornea
   c. Pupil
   d. Choroid
3. Most common disadvantage of ocular solution is –
   a. Rapid precorneal elimination
   b. Non sustained action
   c. Both a and b
   d. Inconvenience

4. Most common disadvantage of ophthalmic ointments and gel is..........
   a. Bluring of vision
   b. Drug stability
   c. Drug choice flexibility
   d. All the above
5. In ocular drug delivery SODI stand for.......................
   a. Soft ocular drug inserts
   b. Superoxide dismutase
   c. Soluble ophthalmic drug inserts
   d. Soluble ocular drug implant
6. Which of the following is not includes in the basic components of tears?
   a. Plasma
   b. Proteins
   c. Mucins
   d. Water
7. The tears results from irritation of the eye by foreign particles
   a. Basal tears
   b. Emotional tears
   c. Reflex tears
   d. Psychic tears
8. The plasticizer used in ocular drug delivery system is
   a. HEC
   b. PEG
   c. PVP
   d. PAA
9. Example of nonerodible insert is –
   a. Lacriserts
   b. Minidisc
   c. SODI
   d. Ocusert
10. Following has branched structure-
    a. Nanosomes
    b. Niosomes
    c. Dendrimers
    d. Liposomes
11. Which is reservoir type ocular system?
    a. Ocusert
    b. Osmotic insert
    c. Both a and b
    d. Contact lenses
12. All are advantages of ocular drug delivery EXCEPT:
    a. Easy to administer.
    b. Low systemic side effects
    c. Accurate dosing
    d. Interference with vision

13. pH of the eye drop should be-
    a. 7.4
    b. 7.0
    c. 6.5
    d. 5.0
14. All are the parts of anterior segment of eye EXCEPT
    a. Aqueous humour
    b. Cornea
    c. Conjunctiva
    d. Retina
15. Which type of emulsion is generally used in ocular drug delivery.
    a. W/O
    b. O/W
    c. Both a and b
    d. None
16. Sclera drug permeability is dependent on the
    a. Molecular radius
    b. Ionic charge
    c. Particle size
    d. Both a and b
17. The rate of drug diffusion of Pio-40 is controlled by
    a. Polymer composition
    b. Membrane thickness
    c. Solubility of drug
    d. All of the above
18. Volume of cul-de-sac cavity is___________
    a. 20 μl
    b. 10 μl
    c. 30 μl
    d. 40 μl
19. Tear film is present on
    a. Sclera
    b. Retina
    c. Cornea
    d. Conjunctiva
20. Main rate limiting barrier for hydrophilic drug is –
    a. Corneal epithelium
    b. Stroma
    c. Basement membrane
    d. None of the above

SHORT ANSWER QUESTIONS

1. Write the advantages and disadvantages of ocuserts
2. Ophthalmic drug delivery systems.
3. What are the Barriers of drug permeation in occular drug delivery
4. Write a note on novel ocular formulations.

5. Discuss about the Approaches to improve ocular bioavailability
6. Write a note on liposomes and dendrimers
7. How nanoparticles improves the ocular bioavailability
8. Define implants and its types
9. What do you understand by the nanoparticles and microparticles
10. Write a note on *In situ* forming gel

LONG ANSWER QUESTIONS

1. Describe in detail ocular drug delivery system.
2. Describe the physiology of eye with its functions
3. Explain the barriers of drug permeation for ocular dosage forms.
4. Write the challenges in delivering drugs to the eye
5. Elaborate the methods to overcome the barriers for ocular drug delivery system.
6. Discuss about the Approaches for controlled and continuous ocular drug delivery
7. Explain the Approaches to improve ocular bioavailability and for posterior segment drug delivery

MCQ ANSWERS

1. (d)	2. (b)	3. (c)	4. (a)
5. (c)	6. (a)	7. (c)	8. (b)
9. (d)	10. (c)	11. (c)	12. (d)
13. (a)	14. (a)	15. (b)	16. (d)
17. (d)	18. (c)	19. (c)	20. (a)

CHAPTER - 8

Transdermal Drug Delivery Systems

Priya Namdev, Sakshi Tiwari, Dr. Sanjib Bahadur, Dr. Amber Vyas

Introduction, History of TDDS, Structure and Physiology of Skin, Preparation of TDDS[7], Evaluation Parameters of Transdermal Patches, Conclusion

INTRODUCTION

The oral approach has been the most common approach of drug delivery since decades and approximately 74 percent of drugs are ingested orally but are still not as successful as planned. Though oral dosing has a significant advantage in convenient administration, it even has major shortcomings, chiefly poor bioavailability owing to the hepatic metabolism and low solubility of drugs. There was a growing need to understand/develop new drug delivery route/system to resolve these hurdles; which can enhance the therapeutic effectiveness and safety of drugs by more precise spatial and temporal positioning within the body, thus reducing both the size and amount of doses and thus increasing their effectiveness with optimum dose concentrations. The transdermal delivery system of drug evolved to accomplish these goals and develop these characters.

On initial inspection, the skin is a not going direction for systemic drug administration. Evolution has supplied the mammalian organism with an external protecting, whose primary role of which is to serve as a barrier, mainly to the lack of tissue water. Suppose concerning this: the water concentration within the body of human is on the order of 50 M, although it is obviously much less in the atmosphere.

Definition

Transdermal delivery system of drug (TDDS) can be described as the topically administered medicines in self-contained, discrete dosage forms of patches that deliver the medication when applied to the skin at a predetermined and regulated rate over a prolonged period of time via the skin portals to the bloodstream circulation in order to increase therapeutic efficacy and minimize side effects of the product. TDDS retains drug concentration *within the therapeutic window after a long period of time ensuring drug levels do not fall below or exceed the maximum effective concentration*[1,2].

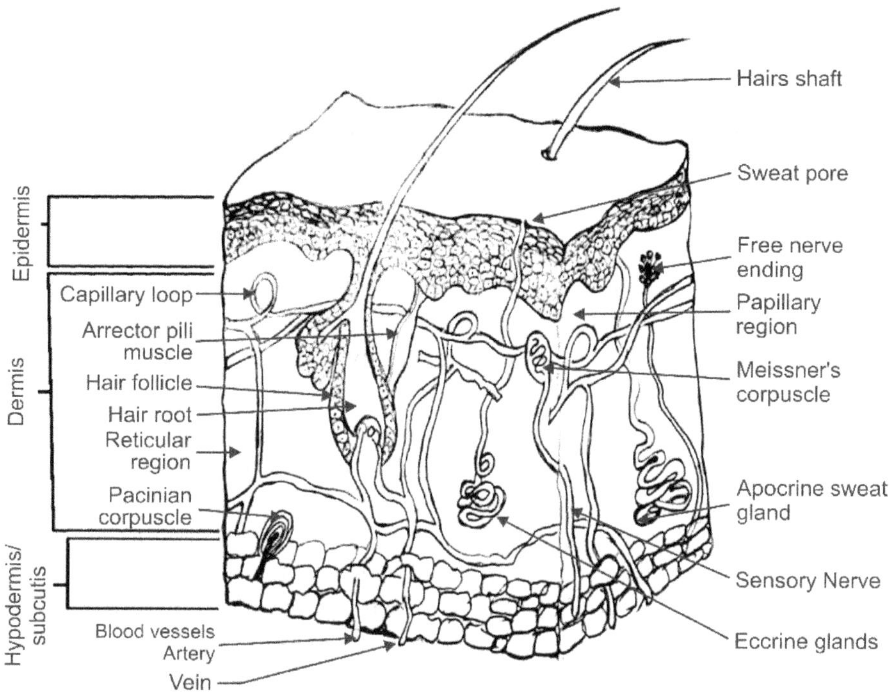

Fig. 8.1 Diagrammatic illustration of skin.

Moreover, pharmaceutical scientists have accepted the challenge of transdermal delivery of drug and, over the past 25 years, considerable progress and achievement have been recorded. So, in view of the formidable challenges faced by the stratum corneum, what led to the skin investigation as a possible route for the systemic input of drugs? Firstly, the skin offers a wide (1-2 m^2) and a very open drug delivery surface. Secondly, transdermal applications are very non-invasive compared to other pathways, requiring the easy adhesion of a "patch" much like a band-aid procedure. Thirdly, patient compliance is usually quite good - that is, people are generally very relaxed using a simple-looking patch (regardless of how complicated interior machinery is). And, fourth, with again a positive benefit for the patient, it is simple to withdraw a transdermal device either at the end of an application period or in the case continued delivery is contraindicated - except for intravenous infusions; no other delivery method provides this advantage.

While transdermal administration is currently limited to relatively few medications, compared with other "controlled release" technologies it has proven to be a significant commercial success. The estimated global transdermal systems demand is about $2 billion per annum. Overall, TDDS can be considered as a possible alternative to oral as well as other routes of drug administration in general with all of its beneficiary properties[4].

HISTORY OF TDDS

When the word TDDS has newly coined the awareness and history of transdermal drug use has been well known since ancient times. Several cultures have been known for using ointments, pastes, plasters and complex inunctions in the treatment of specific diseases. The mustard plaster can often be regarded as an example that has early been used in the natural remedy for serious chest congestion for quite a long time. Briefly in this process, crushed up mustard seed Brassica nigra (mustard seed) used to be mixed with hot water and residual paste was spread evenly over a flannel strip and applied to the patient's chest now with a cloth binding tightly wrapped well around body to maintain the plaster in place. Moisture and body warmth activated an enzyme (myrosin) that hydrolysed a glycoside (sinigrin) in the mustard, triggering the release of the pungent active ingredient allyl isothiocyanate (CH_2=$CHCH_2NCS$). The most notable version of modern transdermal medicine was Stronger Mercurial Ointment, which was used as a syphilis remedy. Fleischer announced in 1877 that the skin was absolutely impermeable and that it was a bold and drastic assertion that could not last for long. After nearly 80 years, collaborative experiments and innovative ideas began to emerge. Studies have been done to determine what caused the skin to have barrier properties which prevented molecular permeation.

In 1924, Rein suggested that a layer of cells connecting the skin's outermost layer-the stratum corneum (SC) - to the epidermis faced the greatest resistance to transdermal transport. Blank changed this hypothesis after removing sequential layers of SC layers from skin surface and showing a drastic increase in the rate of water loss from the skin once the SC was removed. In 1957, Monash proved to be an obstacle to penetration by a superficially positioned barrier in the skin. Finally, Scheuplein and colleagues showed that a passive process allowed transdermal permeation through the SC. In the 1970s, a new approach led to advances in the field of transdermal patches, resulting in the first patch approved by the US FDA in 1979 called Transderm-SCOP19, a three-day patch providing scopolamine against moving disease. Currently, there are a wide array of transdermal delivery systems used to administer various medications such as estradiol, morphine, lidocaine, and testosterone; hybrid patches covering almost over one contraceptive and hormone replacement drug; and iontophoretic and ultrasonic analgesic delivery systems. There has been as substantially increased in research & innovation in the formulation as well as clinical development with transdermal commercial products for heart disease / neurological problems such as Alzheimer's disease, Parkinson's disease, depression, anxiety, attention deficit hyperactivity dysfunction (ADHD) or cancer such as skin cancer or female cancer, postmenopausal bone loss, and urinary incontinence. Hence, TDDS appears to have significant potential as an appropriate and efficient route to the delivery of drugs[7].

STRUCTURE AND PHYSIOLOGY OF SKIN

To improvise the existing potential of TDDS, the very basic skin structure, physiology, and its function need to be understood. The skin is the body's largest organ, covering over 16 % of body weight, with a surface area of 1.8m^2. It has many roles, the most impactful here is to form a protective barrier to the atmosphere, enabling and restricting the passage of water, electrolytes and various substances in and out while defending against micro-organisms, ultraviolet radiation, poisonous agents and mechanical insults. The skin consists of three structural layers, macroscopically: the epidermis, the dermis, and hypodermis summarized in table 1[8].

Table 8.1 The skin layers.

Skin Layer	Specification
Epidermis	The outer layer consists mainly of keratinocyte layers but also includes Langerhans, melanocytes and Markel cells.
Basement membrane	The multilayered structure which forms the tissue area that joins the skin's epidermal and dermal layers.
Dermis	Deeper layer of strengthening connective tissue between epidermis as well as hypodermis: contains hair follicle roots, sweat gland, nerve cells, blood vessels, and lymph vessels
Hypodermis	Loose connective tissue layer, which is an essential fat deposit

A. Epidermis

- The outer epidermis layer is formed by stratified squamous epithelium. This layer acts as a chemical land physical barrier between the outside and the inside. The main cells of the epidermis, Keratinocytes, form the major cellular component (>90%) and synthesize keratin protein. The intercellular area consists mainly of lipids and desmosomes for cohesion between Keratinocytes[9]. The epidermis' four distinct layers shown in Fig.8.3 which move from the underside to the top are
- Stratum basale (Growing layer)
- Stratum spinosum (Prickly or spinous cell layer)

- Stratum Granulosum (Granular cell layer)
- Stratum lucidium
- Stratum corneum (Horny layer)

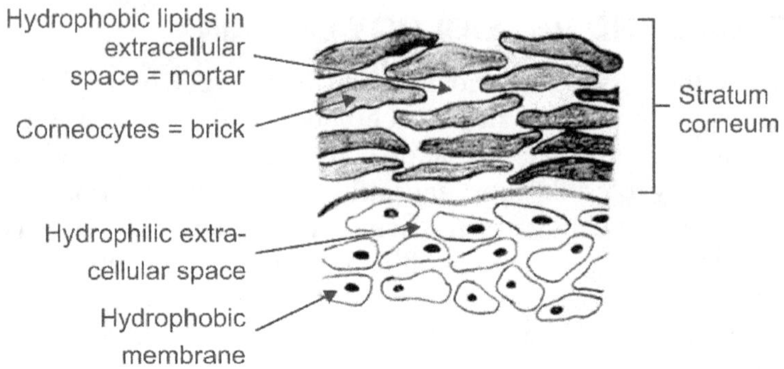

Fig.8.2 Diagrammatic representation of Brick and Motar.

This stratum lucidium layer is, however, a thin layer of translucent cells noticed on the palms and soles. It is a transformation from the stratum granulosum and stratum corneum typically this layer that is not evidently seen in the thin epidermis.

a) Stratum basale

Also called as Stratum germinativum. The innermost layer of the epidermis is adjacent to the dermis composed mainly of non-proliferating and proliferating keratinocytes bound by hemidesmosomes to the dermo-epidermal junction. A small amount of the basal cell making a group is the pigment (melanin) producing melanocytes. These melanocytes in this and many other strata are connected through dendrites to numerous keratinocytes. Merkel cells are often found in large numbers in touch -prone locations such as the fingertips and lips in the basal stratum. They are intimately related to skin nerves and prefer to be involved in the sensation of light contact.

b) Stratum spinosum

When basal cells divide and mature, they pass into the skin's outer layer, initially forming the spinosum stratum. Intercellular bridges, the desmosomes that appear at a microscopic level as 'prickles' and create lamellar bodies, from inside the Golgi, loaded with polar lipids, glycosphingolipids, phospholipids, natural sterols, and catabolic enzymes. Langerhans cells are dendritic, immunologically intense cells originating from the bone marrow as well as present on all epidermal surfaces but primarily in the center of this layer. Such cells play a significant part in the immune reactions of the skin by functioning as an antigen-presenting cell[10].

c) Stratum Granulosum

Ongoing their transition, cells of this surface tend to flatten, losing their nuclei, and cytoplasm which looks likely granular at this stage.

d) Stratum corneum

This the uppermost layer of dead keratinocytes. Keratinocyte maturation is located in the stratum corneum, which is composed of polyhedral, non-viable cornified cells known as corneocytes. There are 10-30 layers of stacked corneocytes, most of which are found in the skins, palms and sole.

Corneocyte contains a protein envelope (cornified protein envelope) under the plasma membrane and is filled with keratin protein retaining water. Constructively the stratum corneum is known to be a "brick wall," shown in fig.2 with the completely differentiated corneocytes forming the "bricks" embedded in the intercellular lipids "mortar". This brick wall appearance of skin structures makes the skin impermeable to foreign pathogens including irritants, allergens and micro-organisms. The intercellular matrices of stratum corneum, consisting of fatty acids and lipid cholesterol, is largely absent in an approximately equimolar mixture of ceramides, a unique characteristic of mammalian membrane[11]. On average the stratum corneum has about 20 layers each about 0.5 μm in thickness. The brick wall also prevents passive water loss (called transepidermal water loss) over the entire skin surface to just around 250 ml per day, so that a volume is quickly replaced to maintain homeostasis. The stratum corneum swells considerably when hydrated and can reach a thickness of up to 40 μm presenting a greater penetrability[12]

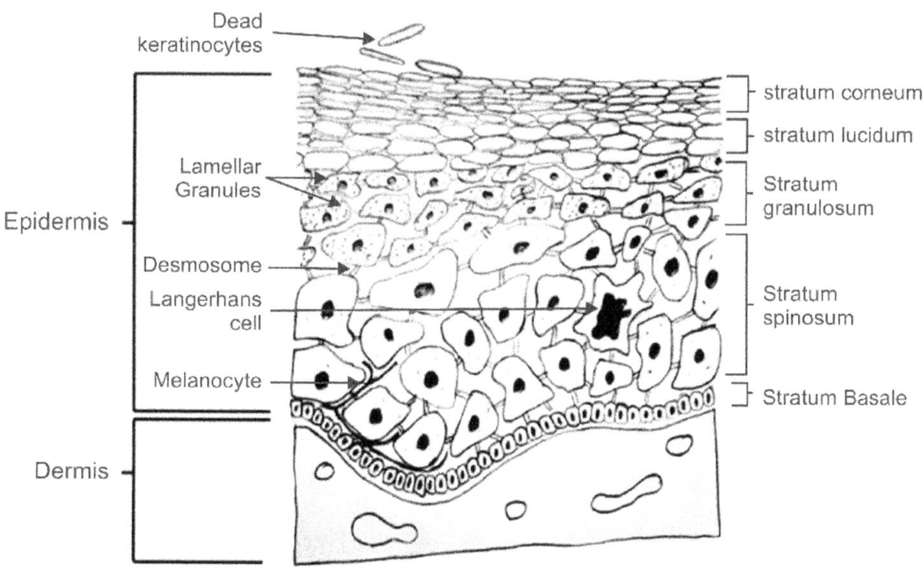

Fig.8.3 Layers of the epidermis.

Dermo-epidermal junction/ basement membrane

This is a complex two-layer structure, i.e. epidermis and dermis. The structures at the interface distinguish about their origin from epidermis and dermis: also the basal lamina is mainly of epidermal origin, the dermal anchoring fibrils[13]. The junction performs the following mechanisms:

1. Epidermal dermal adhesion
2. Mechanical strength for the epidermis, and
3. A barrier to cell exchange and some large molecules at the junction[14].

B. Dermis

The dermis is inner and larger (90% skin layer i.e. 3 to 5 mm thick). The dermis is a skin layer located between the epidermis and subcutaneous tissue. This layer consists essentially of connective tissue matrix. This is mainly divided among two parts; the portion adjacent to epidermis is called the papillary region and a lower, denser area known as reticular dermis. The papillary dermal layer is the top layer of dermis consisting of collagen fibbers' that are delicate and loosely structured.

The reticular dermis is the lower dermis layer located under the papillary dermis, composed of thick irregular connective tissue with tightly packed collagen fibers.

The reticular area is usually substantially thicker than the papillary dermis. Dermis includes blood and lymph channels, and ends of nerves. This layer also had an important role in controlling body temperature and supplying the skin with oxygen and nutrients, while further eliminating waste products and toxins.

C. Subcutaneous Layer

The subcutaneous layer or hypodermis, lower most skin layer in vertebrates is composed largely of fat and connective tissues that carry nerves and blood vessels and help to regulate body temperatures. In this layer the collagen and elastin fibers attach the dermis to the muscles and bones. Collagen fibers cover up 70 percent of dermis which gives it strength and toughness. Elastin holds normal flexibility and elasticity while the proteoglycans continue providing hydration and viscosity. Hypodermis layer thickness varies from person to person, and throughout the body. This layer also serves like an energy reserve, as it consists of adipose tissue[15].

Skin Appendages

Skin appendages are derived from the skin which includes sebaceous glands associated with the hair follicles, eccrine sweat glands, apocrine sweat glands, and nails.

Hairs

These skin appendages are derived from the epidermis and the dermis that are generally thick on the scalp and face. The hair follicles are evenly distributed on the human body surface except for the heel, hand palms, lips, and penis glans. Every follicle size changes somewhere in the range of 200 and 2000 μm in measurement and is lined by germinative cells creating melanocytes and keratin synthesizing pigments. The hair shaft is consisting of an outer cuticle, a keratinocyte cortex, and an inner medulla. The root sheath covering the hair bulb was located deep inside the dermal papilla. An errectorpilorum smooth muscle, attach with the hair shaft to the dermal tissue and contracting with cold, fear and emotions allows hair to erect, giving the skin 'goose-bumps'.

Sebaceous Glands

These glands are generated from epidermal cells and are firmly connected with hair follicles particularly those of the scalp, face, chest, and back, they are not found in hairless regions. They are small in babies, develop and then become active in adolescence, being delicate to androgens. By holocrine secretion, they produce oily sebum consisting of free fatty acids, triglycerides, and waxes, in which the cells separate and discharge their lipid cytoplasm. This sebum plays an important role in the following:

- Protects the skin and hair from UV radiation and lubricates
- keeping up the epidermal permeability membrane, structure, and distinction
- skin-specific hormonal signals
- delivers antioxidants to the skin surface

Sweat Glands

They are located within the lower dermis and are made of coiled tubes that discharge a watery residue into two unique types of eccrine and apocrine.

The eccrine glands are roughly 100 μm in diameter, have an absolute surface region of around 1/10,000 of the complete body surface. These glands are found particularly on the palms, soles, and axillae and forehead. It secretes watery fluid containing lactic acid, fatty acids, urea, glycoproteins, mucopolysaccharides, and salt dilution with a pH of about 5, which is activated by temperature-controlled determinants like the exercise and high ambient temperature, and maybe even emotional stress through the autonomous (sympathetic) nervous system.

The apocrine glands are confined to different body regions (such as axillae, anogenital region and areolar) and are around ten times larger in size than that of eccrine glands. These glands stretch out as low as the subcutaneous tissues and are linked by hair follicles. They get to be active in puberty, yielding an odorless protein-rich discharge which when followed up on by skin microbes gives out a characteristic smell. Those glands are regulated by sympathetic (adrenergic) nerve fibers.

Nails

Nails comprise of a sheet of keratinized flattened cells which are 0.3 and 0.5 mm thick. The nail iscomprised of a nail bed, nail matrix, and a nail plate. The nail matrix consists of keratinocyte that mature and keratinize into the plate of the nail. The nail bed lies under the nail plate. The nail plate looks likely pink because of adjacent dermal capillaries, and the white lunula at the lower part of the plate is the distal, visible portion of the matrix. The thickened epidermal tissue that immediately underlies the nail's free distal edge is termed the hyponychium. Fingernails grow to 0.1 mm daily; toenails grow more slowly. Fingernails effectively protect the fingertips and help grasp[16,17,18].

Functions of the skin

1. *Protection*: The skin protects the body's internal parts against external injuries. It imparts beauty and shape too. It also guards one against heat.
2. *Sensation*: It keeps us in touch with the outside environment by telling us about touch (tactile discrimination), temperature, pain, pressure, vibration, and stereognostic sensation.
3. *Temperature regulation*: It maintains the body temperature despite weather vibration and other conditions such as sweating, conductivity, convection, radiation, vasomotor mechanism, fats in the subcutis heat preserve, hair serves as a heat insulator and pilorum arrectores mechanism. Factors regulating temperature in human body is presented in Table 2.
4. *Secretion*: Sebum is secreted through sebaceous glands, an oily secretion. This keeps skin oily and prevents skin from drying out. Ceruminous ear secretion is waxy and foreign bodies or insects stick up there and thereby the eardrum is spared from damage. During pregnancy and lactation, milk is used as a source of nutrients to the baby, active breast secretion in women to feed the baby. Glands which secrete milk are modified by sebaceous glands. Nails and hairs are the defence and protection structures of skin respectively.
5. *Adsorption*: They absorbs oily substances through the skin.
6. *Storage*: They absorbs oily substances through the skin. Many substances are stored in the skin, such as: water, salt, particularly NaCL, Fats, Glucose etc.
7. *Consistency of pH*: The acidic sweat excretes toxins and thus helps preserve the blood's alkalinity.

8. *Synthesis of Vit. D*: Ergosterol present in the skin and subcutis is irradiated by ultraviolet rays of the sun. This synthesizes ergosterol into Vit. D_2- calciferol.
9. *Gaseous Exchange*: In some animals, the skin is an essential organ for O_2 and CO_2 exchange. But in humans, the skin excretes only negligible amounts of CO_2 during sweat excretion.
10. *Excretion*: Some salts such as NaCl and a metabolite, like urea, are excreted too. The major excretion is that of water by the visible sweat and more so by the continuous evaporation of the invisible preparation from throughout the skin[16,19].

Table 8.2 Factors regulating temperature in human body.

Factors Increasing heat loss	Factors Increasing heat production
Sweating	Exercise
Increase in skin blood circulation	Shivering
Cooler environment	Unconscious tension of muscles (muscle tone)
Decrease in clothing	Basal metabolism
Movement	Specific dynamic action of food, producing heat
Basal heat loss	Metabolism of carbohydrates, fats and proteins

Pathways for Drug Penetration:

There are three pathways for drug penetration such as:

- Transcellular Route
- Paracellular Route
- Transappendgeal Route

Transcellular Route: This is defined as movement of the drug through both keratinocytes as well as

- lipids (straight path to dermis).
- *Paracellular Route:* The Drug molecules' most widely known pathway of penetration. Drug continues to remain in lipid moiety in this kind of pathway and stays around just keratin (easy for lipid-soluble drug rather than protein)
- *Transappendgeal Route:* It serves to make channel for drug diffusion but because of the presence of hair follicles & sweat ducts it quickly affected[20].

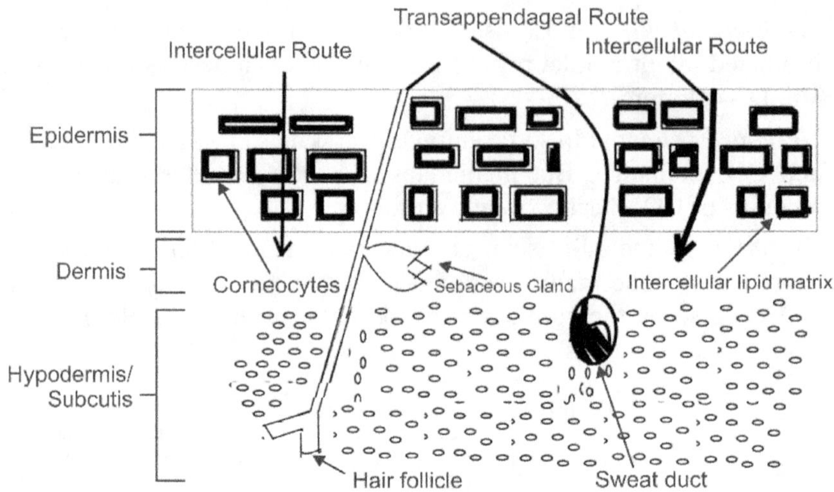

Fig.8.4 Schematic drug penetration pathways.

Mathematics of Skin Drug Penetrations[21]

For such a highly complicated multi-layered organ as the skin, & innumerable factors that affect transdermal delivery of drugs, the mathematical application seems daunting principles with the interpretation of such process. Simple mathematical principles can however be shown to explain the basic concepts of penetration across membranes, especially skin, and these help in the design of pharmaceutical formulations for transdermal and topical delivery of drug. If the diffusion rate of the solvent molecules is through the limit layer is the slowest step, the dissolution is said to be controlled by diffusion. In fact, Fick's first law, the most basic of the diffusion equations, has its roots here. Moving the solute molecules across the barrier layer will strictly follow the first law of Fick's diffusion. The law clearly states that, rate of change in dissolved substance concentration overtime will be directly proportional with the difference in concentration among both the two sides of a diffusion layer.

Fick's law of diffusion

Fick's first law of diffusion can describe, for simple passive diffusion, in which molecules move randomly through one region to another in the way of lowering concentration.

$$J \propto \frac{dC}{dx} \quad or \quad J = -D\frac{dC}{dx} \qquad .....(8.1)$$

Where,

D = diffusion coefficient, D is significantly impacted by temperature, concentration, solvent properties, pressure as well as chemical qualities of the diffuser. Therefore D is much more correctly referred to as a coefficient of diffusion rather than a constant.

J = Flux (mass flow rate at which material passes via the surface area of its unit)

C = concentration of diffusing substance,

x = space coordinate measured normal to the section

The negative sign shows that the molecular flux is within the direction of falling concentration. When an applied topical drug penetrates the skin, the diffusion gradient from outer surface more into tissue is generally assumed, i.e. is unidirectional.

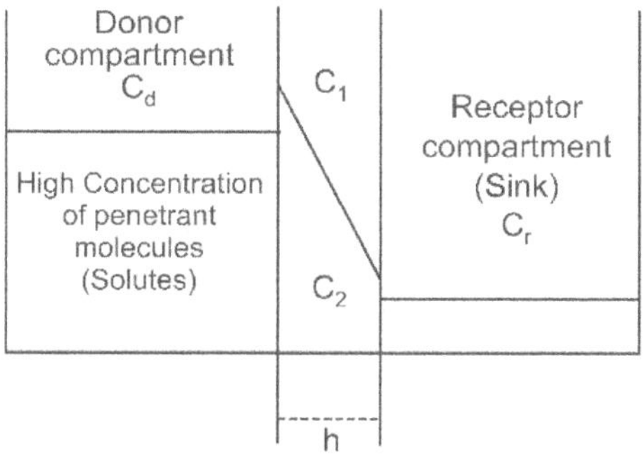

Fig.8.5 The concentration gradient of solute across the membrane. [C_1 and C_2, the concentration of drug in the membrane at donor and receptor of two sides, respectively. C_d and C_r, the concentration of drug in the donor and receptor of two sides, respectively and h is the thickness of the membrane].

According to the Fick's second law of diffusion the continues to give

$$\frac{dC}{dx} = -\frac{dJ}{dx} \qquad \text{.....(8.2)}$$

This equation (8.2) shows that the concentration of the diffuser with in volume element alters with time, i.e., $\Delta C/\Delta t$, because the flux or quantity diffusing alters with distance, i.e.$\Delta J / \Delta x$, in the direction x.

From equation (8.1) $\quad J = -D\frac{dC}{dx}$

or, $$-\frac{dJ}{dx} = D\frac{d^2C}{dx^2}$$

or, $$\frac{dC}{dx} = D\frac{d^2C}{dx^2}$$

Where,

J = flux (g/cm^2.sec)

D = diffusion coefficient of the drug in cm^2/sec

dC/ dx = concentration gradient

C = concentration (g/cm^3)

Factors affecting topical drug delivery[22]

Physiochemical properties of active moiety

- ***Partition coefficient:*** Drug possesses both hydrophilic and lipophilic solubility. Co-efficient partitioning determines the solubility or diffusion of the drug in lipids and aqueous systems. Ideal partition coefficient for intermediate topical delivery is log k 1-3. The drug candidate should have an optimum coefficient of partitioning. The partition coefficient of a drug may be modified by changing the solvent system or by chemical modification of the drug candidate's structure without affecting the drug's pharmacological activity. For highly lipophilic drug (log k >3), intracellular route is favorable, whereas for hydrophilic drugs (log k <1), it is permeated through transcellular route.
- ***Molecular size:*** Molecular size of the drug is inversely proportional to the transdermal flux. The ideal drug molecular size for topical delivery should be ≤ 400 Da. The absorption is higher when the molecular weight less. The size of drug molecules should therefore not be so large that absorption problems are generated.
- ***Solubility/Melting point:*** Most organic solutes have high melting point and low solubility at room temperature and pressure. Lipid soluble drug permeates faster than water soluble drug, but it should have aqueous solubility as needed in most of the topical formulation.
- ***Ionization:*** According to pH- partition hypothesis, unionized drug permeates through the skin.
- ***Drug Concentration:*** The flux is proportional to the barrier-wide concentration gradient, and if the drug concentration is more around the barrier, the concentration gradient would be greater. Hydrocortisones 1% and 2.5% were shown to be of similar potency in a cream formulation, as were triamcinolone acetonide 0.025%, 0.1%, and 0.5% creams. One of the big advances in formulating glucocorticoids, as first demonstrated with fluocinonide, came when it was discovered that adding propylene glycol to the vehicle could dissolve the drug entirely. As seen in the vasoconstrictor assay, this has contributed to corticosteroid products of greater potency. New medicines are now being evaluated during the phase of production to ensure that higher concentrations of drugs result in raising bioavailability.
- ***Temperature and pH*** - Drug permeation increases ten times, with a difference in temperature. The coefficient of diffusion reduces as the temperature decreases. Depending on the pH and pKa or pKb values weak acids and weak bases dissociate. The number of unionized drugs determines the concentration of the drug in the skin. Temperature and pH are therefore important factors which affect the penetration of drugs.

A. Physiological properties

- ***Anatomic site***

Dogma reports that skin absorption "varies widely from site to site on the body". There is variability but that's not greater than the normal inter-individual variability observed at a particular site across most of the surface. Some regions are considerably more permeable- the genitalia, particularly the scrotum, axilla, face, and post-auricular scalp. These high-permeability sites are actually, used to optimize a transdermal delivery of specific drugs, for example, the first testosterone patch was designed to be worn on the scrotum, and the scopolamine system is set behind the ear. There is space for maneuver, however, limited; most transdermal systems generally work equivalently at many different locations, and the recommended position mainly depends on convenience (e.g. choosing a discreet site for an estradiol system) and/or psychology (e.g. placing a nitroglycerin patch over the heart).

- ***Skin barrier functions in young children and neonates***

The neonatal skin surface is mildly hydrophobic, Compared to older ones fairly dry and rough newborns. Premature neonates, born before the age of 30 weeks of gestation, poorly developed barriers, including percutaneous toxicity due to inadvertent chemical absorption, are at risk for several problems.

- ***The effects of skin barriers in aged skin***

There is little change in trans-epidermal water loss rate across natural, intact skin from birth (assuming at the time) to early "late age". As the skin ages, it progressively becomes more fragile (and thus more sensitive, for example, to removing a well-adhered transdermal patch) and demands a gradually longer recovery period after injury. Therefore, care should be taken to monitor the chronic application of transdermal systems to elderly patients.

- ***Race***

It revealed that racial inequality between black and white skins have shown some structural and physiological elements of the skin. For black skin, the intracellular permeation is increased due to higher lipid content and greater electrical resistance to the skin levels compared to whites but that's not the difference on stripped skin found.

- ***Skin condition and disease***

Changes in barrier function due to skin disease generally result either from the alteration of the lipid/protein composition of the stratum corneum or from abnormal epidermal differentiation (e.g. in psoriasis). Interestingly, as concerning transdermal bioavailability, patches intended for systemic therapy are labelled for use only at "natural" skin locations, free of dermatological pathology[23].

Advantages of Transdermal Delivery System

The positive abilities of delivering the drug via the human skin for systemic effect are:

1. Avoid significant presystemic metabolism (such as that caused by degradation by liver or inside gastrointestinal tract), and therefore the need for a reduced daily dose.
2. Reduced interpatient and intrapatient variability — this is especially true in those situations where drug release through the transdermal patch is relatively slow than drug permeation among the stratum corneum.
3. Drug levels can be maintained for prolonged periods of time throughout the systemic circulation, in under the therapeutic window (— in other words just above minimum effective concentration and just below the point at which adverse effects become clearly visible).
4. Thus, the period of the drug action after a single drug administration can be extended, and the dosing frequency reduced.
5. Increasing patient compliance, as well as drug therapy feasibility.
6. Drug input can also simply be terminated by stripping away the patch.

Disadvantages of Transdermal Delivery System

The main drawback of this method is that these are limited just too potent drug molecules, usually those that require a daily dose of 10 mg or less. This usually translates into drugs to effective plasma concentrations within the (or lower) mg mL-1 range. However, if the medication is potent enough, it also must meet certain conditions to be widely considered a suitable candidate for transdermal delivery.

Firstly, its physicochemical characteristics should trigger its percutaneous absorption. This ensures that its molecular weight must be acceptable and that it should be adequately soluble in both lipophilic as well as aqueous conditions since the molecule should pass the stratum corneum (a lipidic barrier) and disburse via an even more aqueous-in-nature viable epidermis and the upper dermis to reach the dermal circulation of blood. Lack either of oil or water solubility would further limit effective drug absorption.

Second, the drug's pharmacokinetic & pharmacodynamic qualities must be so that the relatively prolonged and relatively slow input from the transdermal delivery makes perfect sense. For example, tolerance-inducing compounds are not a best idea for that kind of mode of delivery until suitable "wash-out" duration is designed into the dosing regimen. Drugs mostly with short biological half-lives, subject to sufficiently large first-pass metabolism, requiring inconvenient and frequent oral or parenteral dosage (with corresponding adverse effect issues including poor compliance), are promising candidates. But from the other hand, drugs which can be administered orally just once a day, mostly with reproducible bioavailability and that are well accepted by patient, do not demand a patch formulation.

Third, the medication should not be locally irritating, sensitizing as it most possibly prohibits its regulatory approval from triggering serious skin reactions under a transdermal delivery system.

Formulation of Transdermal Drug Delivery System:

An essential component of every transdermal drug delivery system is shown in Fig.8. 6.

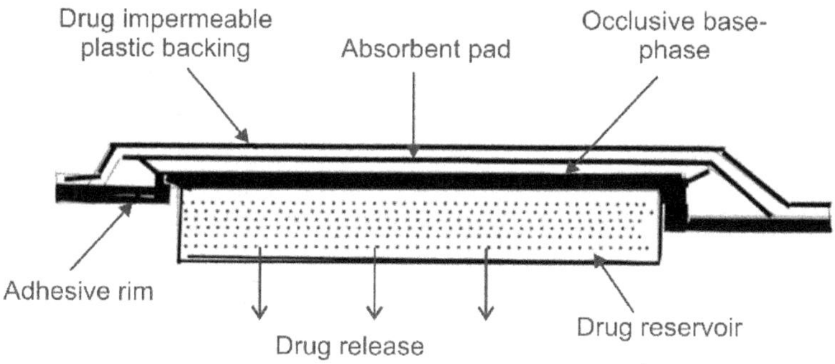

Fig.8.6 Schematic representation of basic components transdermal patch.

Polymer Matrix or Drug Reservoir

Polymers are the key component of TDDS, used in the skin preparation.

Selection and nature of the polymer are of vital importance in this formulation. Polymers used for the TDDS should be biocompatible and compatible with the drug and other system components such as penetration enhancers, and PSAs. Furthermore, they should provide consistent and successful delivery of the medication during the expected shelf-life of the product, which should be safe[24,25]. Considerations of the following properties for the need in transdermal delivery of polymers as shown in table 8.3. Polymers can be used in a flexible manner in TDDS including: Rate controller membranes, backing layers, adhesives (adhesives prone to pressure), and liner release. Mostly used polymers in the formulation of transdermal delivery systems are summarized in Table 8.4.

Table 8.3 Properties of the polymers.

Properties of the polymers
• Should remain stable, • Inexpensive • Specific drug diffusion • Non-reactive with the active ingredient • Simple to produce and to turn into desired product. • The polymer as well as its degradation products must also be non-toxic to the host • The polymer's mechanical properties do not deteriorate excessively when large amounts of active ingredients are introduced into it. • Biocompatibility and chemical compatibility with pharmaceutical products and Other system components.

Table 8.4 Examples of polymers used in formulation of transdermal delivery system.

Natural polymers	Synthetic elastomers	Synthetic polymers
Chitosan, Cellulose derivatives, gelatine, Shellac, zein, waxes, natural rubber, Proteins and their derivatives, starch, etc.	Hydrin rubber, Polybutadiene, silicone rubber, polysiloxane, nitrile, acrylonitrile, butyl rubber rubber, neoprene, etc.	Polyvinylchloride, Polyvinylalcohol, Polyacrylate, polyethylene, polypropylene, polyvinyl Pyrrolidone, hydroxy propyl cellulose, epoxy, ethyl cellulose, pyrrolidone, polymethyl ethacrylate, polyamide, etc

Rate-controlling membrane

The basic way to measure a drug's discharge is to disperse through inert polymer matrices. The product is physically mixed with polymeric powder (either lipophilic or hydrophilic) in this method and with a given area of surface and thickness controlled; a medicated polymer is then shaped in a medicated disk. However, an inverse relationship is observed between membrane thicknesses as well as release rate is observed. Moreover, these relationships were confirmed when boundary layer effects occurred in measurements of permeability. The permeation rate (J) of some cellular membrane synthesized from distinct A, B and C monomers (2-hydroxy-3-phenoxypropylacrylate, sec-butyl tiglate, 4-hydroxybutyl acrylate, respectively) was investigated at different membrane thicknesses (L), using clonidine as a single dose by considering the expression of Fick 's diffusion law[26]. Drug release levels are improved by adding a hydrophilic polymer, e.g. hydroxypropyl methylcellulose, to the rate control membrane. Drug movement across the membrane from the hydrophilic matrix can be seen to be regulated by the active substance partitioning from the matrices into a membrane. The diffusion qualities of the membrane are thus used to ensure accessibility of the drug and/or skin excipients[27,28].

Adhesives

The adhesive, a significant component, provides a strong bond between the conveyance systems with skin. TDDS adhesion is among the essential factors for the product's safety, effectiveness, and efficiency. It relates to the delivery of drugs and the therapeutic effect. This holds the substance which can be dispersed or dissolved throughout the matrix or the substance-containing compartment (solution or suspension) is isolated from the adhesive layer via a membrane regulating diffusion, the drug encompasses to hitting the skin through this adhesive membrane[29]. The strength of the bond among patch and skin is important since it reflects directly the performance of the drug delivered. Delivery of drug from patch decreases as a result of patch lifting, or falling apart, decreases contact surface area. To put it another way, weak adhesion results in inappropriate patient dosage. Secondly, patches that fail to adhere throughout their specified period of time need to be replaced more often, thereby increasing the expense of the patient. Thirdly, if the patch fails to adhere became a safety and performance issue. Potential hazards occur when exposed unintentionally (e.g. removal of a patch from an adult to a newborn baby while hugging, sitting or lying on the patch unintentionally)[30]. Considerations of the following properties for the need in transdermal delivery of Adhesives are shown in Table 8.5.

Table 8.5 Properties of the Adhesives.

Adhesives Properties
• Non-irritant • Easily removable • Inexpensive • Excellent skin contact • Compatibility with the drug and other excipients • No washable residue

***Pressure sensitive adhesives* (PSA)**

Until now, the fastening among all transdermal products to the skin can be achieved using a pressure-sensitive adhesive that can be placed on the device's face or in the device's back and extended peripherally. Silicones, polyacrylate, and polyisobutylene are the three most widely employed adhesives in TDD devices.

Recent innovations related to PSA

- The first strategy involves designing new polymers, including polyurethanes, and hydrogel hydrophilic polymers.
- The second strategy is to adjust PSAs chemistries physically or chemically in current use (such as silicones, PIBs, and acrylates). Physical alteration refers to the composition of a base adhesive with some special additives such that the effect, in combination with the medication and excipients in the formulation of the device, ensures increased drug availability and enhanced skin-adhesion properties. The chemical modification includes the chemical assimilation or implanting functional monomers used by traditional PSA polymers to improve drug supply rates[31].

Release liners

Before applying the patch, the patch is enclosed by just a protective liner which is removed during storage and disposed on skin. When this liner is in close contact well with transdermal patches the liner will have to be chemically inert. Release layer comprised of Teflon or silicone coating. Certain TDDS release liner materials include metalized laminate and polyester foil[32].

Backings

Backings are used for appearance, versatility and need for support. Therefore, during the design of the backing layer, the concern of the material's chemical resistance is important. Compatibility with the excipients should also be found because contact between the back layer is prolonged and excipients can start causing leaching out of the additives backing layer or can induce excipients, drugs or penetration enhancers to diffuse through the layer. The most convenient backing is the one that has the lowest module or greater flexibility, a high transmission rate of moisture vapour, and good oxygen transmission. Examples of backing items include vinyl, polyethylene, polyester films, aluminium vapour coated layer and polyolefin films[33].

Drug

Nowadays transdermal drug delivery has taken on an increase in popularity. The drug's diverse physicochemical, pharmacokinetic and pharmacological properties are considered for the production of TDS. Owing to the minimal permeability of the skin, drugs must be used transdermally delivered through the skin by passive diffusion and restricted by many serious constraints. The drug should be selected with a half-life of 10 h or less, poor oral bioavailability, low therapeutic index and non-sensitizing and non-irritating to the skin. Ideal Properties of drugs for TDDS have been shown in Table 8.6. Some examples of the drugs are: Tretinoin, Dexamethasone, Ketoprofen, Levosimenden, Primaquine.

Table 8.6 Physiochemical properties of drugs.

Ideal Properties of drugs for TDDS.	
Dose	Should be low (less than 20 mg/day)
Half-life	10 or less (h)
Molecular weight	<400 Da
Partition coefficient	Log P (octanol–water) between 1.0 and 4.0
Skin permeability coefficient	$>0.5 \times 10^{-3}$ cm/h
Lipohilicity	$10 < K\ o/w < 1000$
Oral bioavailability	Low
Therapeutic index	Low
Melting point	<200°C
pH	Between 5.0 and 9.0

Penetration enhancers

These are all compounds which boost permeability by modifying the skin as a pathway to the flux of a desired penetrator. In a formulation, penetration enhancers are added to increase the solubility and flux of medicine through the skin which would reversibly decrease the skin's barrier resistance. So allow the medicine to penetrate the viable tissues as well as reach the blood stream[34,35]. Desirable Penetration Enhancers Properties are given in table 8.7.

Table 8.7 Desirable Penetration Enhancers Properties.

Desirable Penetration Enhancers Properties
• Non-irritant • Non-phototoxic, non-sensitizing, and non-comedogenic • Ideally function faster and the response and time frame of effect should be both reproducible and predictable • Compatibility with the drug and other excipients • Do not have any pharmacological behaviour in someone's body — that is, Should not link with specific receptors; should act unidirectional. • Be colorless, tasteless, odorless, and cosmetically acceptable. • Have a desired parameter of solubility approximating that of skin.

Influence of penetration enhancers on the structure of the SC

A complex arrangement of lipid and protein materials, in which relatively distinct lipophilic and hydrophilic penetration pathways are formed, embodies the diffusional resistance known to exist in the SC. The SC's make-up and action in recent decades have resulted in wide collection of enhancers getting tested for their potential to boost improved skin portal permeation through co-administered a drugs[36]. The SC intercellular lipid matrices, the biochemical order, or the Corneocytes keratinized environment is changed to allow the compounds to the desired activity site at an appropriate rate. Barry worked on the possible interactions between penetration enhancers and the SC and put forward the lipid-protein partitioning (LPP) theory. The three main enhancement mechanisms as per this theory are: a) intercellular lipids interactions; b) intracellular keratin interactions; and c) The entry of large concentrations of co-solvents or enhancers into the SC, resulting in a higher dispersing capacity of the drug and/or co-enhancers barrier. A few examples of the frequently used conventional enhancers include water, amine acids, alcohol hydrocarbons, esters, amides, terpenoids, surfactant terpenes, and lipids essential oil, sulfoxides, and miscellaneous substances such as chitosan, cyclodextrin derivatives, etc[37-39]. Efficacy of some of the permeation enhancers is explored in TDDS and in Table 8.8.

Table 8.8 Some of the Permeation Enhancers.

S. No.	Chemical Classification	Enhancer
1.	Alcohols	Ethanol, Isopropyl alcohol
2.	Amides	Azone
3.	Esters	Ethyl acetate, Oleyl acetate, Isopropyl myristate, propylene glycol monocaprylate
4.	Fatty Acids	Lauric acid, Linoleic acid, oleic acid
5.	Glycols	Propylene glycol
6.	Pyrrolidone	N-methyl-2-pyrrolidones, 2-pyrrolidone
7.	Sulfoxides	Dimethyl sulphoxide
8.	Surfactants	Anionic surfactants, Sodium lauryl sulphate, Cationic surfactants Alkylpyridinium halide
9	Terpenes	Cineole, Eugenol, D-Limonene
10	Urea	Carbamide
11	Miscellaneous	Cyclodextrins, Water, Vitamin E, Phospholipids

Other excipients

Plasticizers

In many other formulations generally range from 5 to 20 per cent (w/w, dry basis) plasticizers were also used[40]. Along with the film's fragility and ductility, it is quite responsible for the film's adhesiveness with other surfaces or membranes, and improving film strength. Two of its sources are sorbitol or glycerol, with a dry base of 15%, phosphate esters, phthalate esters, fatty acid esters and derivatives of glycol such as PEG 400 and PEG 200. The choice and concentration of a suitable plasticizer has a significant impact on the permeation and the mechanical properties of the drugs[41,42].

Transdermal patch-types[43]

Five main forms of transdermal patches exist as follows

I) Adhesive dispersion system

The medication is used in this system directly inside the skin-contacting adhesive. The adhesive layer is responsible for releasing the drug in this form of a patch and helps to adhere multiple layers together with the whole framework to the surface. The adhesive coat is covered with a removable lining and a backing layer i.e. supporting layer.

$$\frac{dQ}{dt} = \frac{Cr}{1/Pm + 1/Pa} \quad .....(8.3)$$

Where,

Cr = drug concentration in a reservoir compartment,

Pm and Pa = the permeability coefficients of the rate controlling membrane and the adhesive layer

The sum of coefficients of permeability simultaneous permeation across t he pores and the polymeric material. The following concepts refer to Pa and Pm, respectively,

$$\text{Pm} = \frac{Km/r.Dm}{hm} \quad .....(8.4)$$

$$\text{Pa} = \frac{Ka/m.Da}{ha} \quad .....(8.5)$$

Ka/m and Km/r = are the partition coefficients for the interfacial partitioning of drug from the membrane to adhesive and from the reservoir to the membrane respectively;

D_m and D_a are the diffusion coefficients in the rate controlling membrane and adhesive layer, respectively; hm and ha are the thicknesses of the rate controlling membrane and adhesive layer, respectively[43].

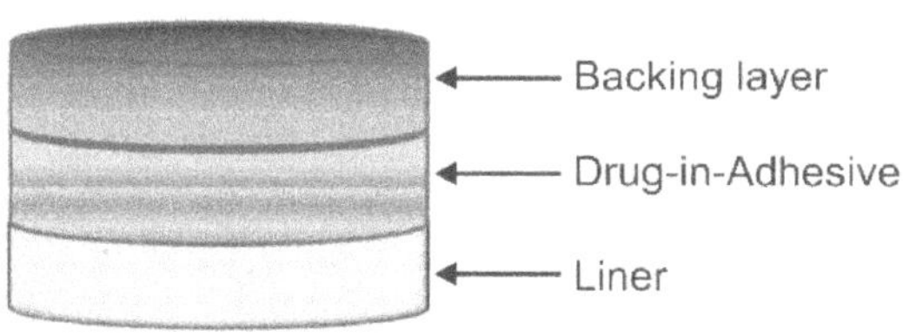

Fig.8.7 Diagrammatic representation of adhesive Dispersion system.

II) Multi-layer Drug-in-Adhesive[7]

The multi-layer drug-in-adhesive is identical to the single-layer drug in-adhesive since the drug is directly inserted into the adhesive. The multi-layer device adds another drug-in-adhesive sheet, which is normally divided by a membrane. This patch has a temporary liner-layer and a permanent backup safety as well. In this system, the drug which directly disperses the drug into the adhesive polymer and then spreads the medicated adhesive on the layer of the reservoir formulates reservoir. On this a layer of nonmedicated rate controlled adhesive polymer of constant thickness is applied. The rate of drug release:

$$dQ/dT = (Ka/r) \text{ X } Da \text{ X } CR/da$$

Where,

Ka/r = Partition co-efficient for interfacial partitioning of the drug form the reservoir layer to the adhesive layer.

Da = Diffusion co-efficient in the adhesive layer.

da = Thickness of adhesive layer.

CR = Drug concentration in reservoir compartment.

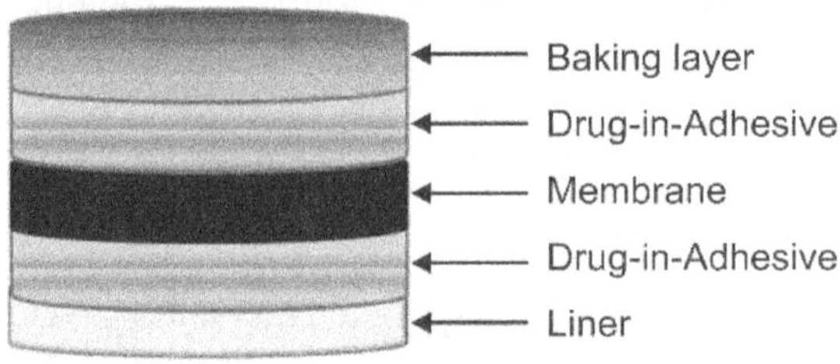

Fig.8.8 Diagrammatic representation of Multi-layer Drug-in-Adhesive.

Reservoir:[4]

The specification of the Reservoir Transdermal Device involves a liquid compartment that holds a medication solution or suspension isolated by adhesive and a partially-permeable membrane from its release liner. The product's adhesive portion may either be as a continuous layer seen between membrane and the release lining, or as a concentrate around the membrane. It involves (i) a covered drug reservoir (solution or suspension), (ii) a membrane controlled by a polymeric cons

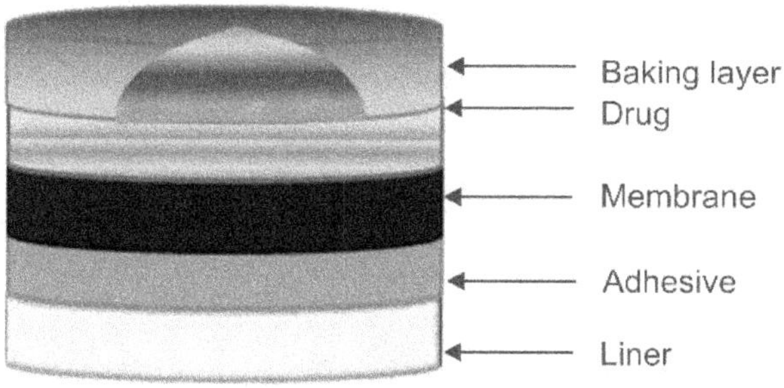

Fig.8.9 Diagrammatic representation of Reservoir.

III Vapour Patch[7]

The purpose of the adhesive layer in this form of patch just to serves to bind to the multiple layers together but and furthermore the market widely used to release essential oils during decongestion there Are also several many varieties of vapour patches on the market that are being used to improve sleep efficiency and minimize cigarette smoking conditions.

IV Matrix[7]

The Matrix system has such a semi-solid matrix drug layer which contains a drug suspension or solution which is directly in contact well with release liner. In this patch the layer of adhesive surrounds the drug sheet, partially superimposing it.

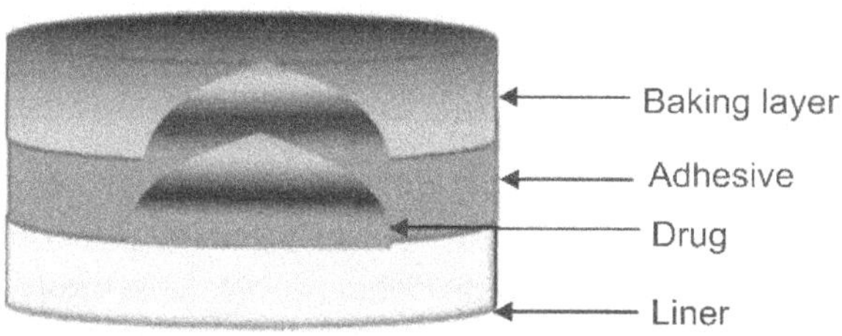

Fig.8.10 Diagrammatic representation of Matrix.

i. Drug-in-adhesive system

In this form, a drug reservoir is created by diffusing the drug into an adhesive polymer and thereafter spreading the adhesive polymer by melting or solvent casting on an impermeable layer of backing. For protection purposes unmediated layers of the adhesive polymer are supposed to apply top of the reservoir.

ii. Matrix-dispersion system

For this form the medication is homogeneously distributed in a matrix of hydrophilic or lipophilic polymers. This drug, which comprises a polymer disk, is placed upon an occlusive base plate in a container constructed from an impermeable back layer of medications. Instead of placing the adhesive upon this product reservoir's face, a piece of adhesive surface is placed together with the circumference to develop.

- More complex, different polymer compositions to provide drug containing matrix and adhesive
- Matrix may control drug release

The rate of drug release:

$$dQ/dT = (A \times Cp \times Dp/2t)^{1/2}$$

A = Initial drug loading dose dispersed in the polymer matrix,

Cp & Dp = Solubility and diffusivity of the drug in the polymer respectively.

iii. Micro reservoir system[7]

The delivery system of drug, in this type is mixture of a dispersal matrix and reservoir system. The drug reservoir is created by first storing the drug in an aqueous phase containing water soluble polymer and afterwards homogeneously dissolving the solution into that lipophilic polymer to form thousands of unattainable, tiny drug reservoir spheres. Such thermodynamically unstable dispersion becomes easily stabilised by using cross-linking agents to automatically cross-link to that polymer *in situ*. In mostly zero rate controlling membrane.

Approaches for boosting drug-permeation barriers[45, 46]

One current problem in approaching transdermal delivery system of drug is to conquer the formidable barrier feature of the skin. Many intense works in strategic growth is to improve production as well as promote molecular extraction for analysis and diagnostic purposes that are classified as active and passive. Both are based on two approaches: increasing the penetrability of a skin and/or giving driving force that works upon that drug.

A.) Technique for Boosting Passive Penetration[47]

Modern innovations under investigation range from chemical enhancements that both increase diffusiveness across the skin and even increase drug solubilisation with in skin[48]. Recent advanced approaches including the application of the principle to design of micro emulsion, super loaded formulations, and vesicular technologies[49]. The penetration enhancers can be used either individually or even the synergistic mixtures of molecular penetration enhancers that have proven their dominance in skin permeabilization capacity relative to specific chemicals can be used. Thus, the molecular simulation methodology and its appropriate applicability to the lipid barrier of a skin, choosing to focus on the diffusion of molecules through skin lipids and the mechanism of penetration modulation enhances the transport and breach the barrier of a skin have been observed recent[50].

1. **Microemulsion**

   The use of microemulsion vehicles in addition to cutaneous drug delivery has become increasingly popular due to their high solubilisation capacity both from hydrophilic and lipophilic drugs. This can be established by various constituents of oil, aqueous, co-surfactant, and surfactant[51]. Microemulsions have been found to act as an effective vehicle for the solubilisation with certain drugs and also as a protective medium for entrapped drugs against hydrolysis, degradation, and oxidation. Although the drug is toxic, it will also offer prolonged release of a drug & prevent irritation. Work by Chen and his colleague assessed the transdermal potential of triptolide from micro emulsions and the prepared formulations containing about tween 80 as a surfactant, propylene glycol as a co-surfactant, and oleic acid as an oil, concludes that triptolide-charged microemulsions began to show positive affect *in vitro* permeation via the skins of the mouse compared to an aqueous propylene glycol solution containing triptolide[52].

2. **Superloaded formulations**

   For convenient formulations and for including penetration enhancers, the drug penetration rate is necessary to be optimised. A successful prospect of improving drug permeability via the skin is just by increasing the dissolved drug concentration that will not harm the integrity of a SC in anyway. There is a relation among content and permeability of drug that ultimately leads to a higher drug flux with increase in drug thermodynamic activity[53]. When the dose released in the matrix is greater than its solubilisation in equilibrium, it reaches a super saturation state. Consequently, crystallization occurs shortly after storage in patches of super-saturated drug concentrations within that polymer adhesive. The amorphisation of drugs also becomes remarkable, as the main skill throughout the production of formulations aims to greatly boost bioavailability. Analysis studies of ibuprofen's solid-state amorphization showed improved bioavailability. Ma and colleagues showed that PEG 900 was a strong initiator of crystallization while PVP was observed to be a more effective crystallization inhibitor already for norethindrone acetate. Low molecular weight excipients like cholesterol, silicon dioxide, other steroidal molecules and macromolecules or surfactants, polyvinyl pyrrolidone, methacrylic acid copolymers (Eudragit ® RL 100 and Eudragit ® E 100) are just a few more great examples of crystallization inhibitors[54].

3. **Vesicles**

   Vesicle formulations which are used for skin delivery systems are amongst the most challenging approaches. There are several folds that explain the use of vesicles in dermal and transdermal delivery systems. Vesicles might (a) Function as drug carriers that carry entrapped molecules in/across the skin; (b) Function as penetration enhancers after penetration from the specific lipid components further into SC and subsequent modification of an intercellular lipid lamella inside the skin layer; (c) Beneficial as depot for the continuous release with dermally-active compounds; and (d) serve as a rate-limiting membrane barrier for the modulation of systemic absorption, hence providing a controlled transdermal delivery system[55,56]. Maheshwari and his coworker researched the vesicles of non-ionic surfactant mediated transcutaneous immunization for hepatitis B and discussed its merits in comparison with parenteral administration routes and came to the conclusion that the vesicles investigated are successful for topical vaccine delivery. Vesicles can be made out of different surfactants and lipids. They are most commonly used in the production of phospholipids/non-ionic surfactants (such as Spans 80) and are regarded to in ethosomes as phospholipids and niosomes and liposomes, and water and ethanol. Multiple studies of *in-vivo* and *in-vitro* transport studies recorded also that the liposomes increased rate of skin diffusion, with mostly significant reduction (or no effect) in percutaneous absorbtion or systemic absorption of hydrocortisone, other tretinoin, lidocaine, cyclosporine, corticosteroids, etc. These tests showed that liposomes are advantageous for the topical delivery of these medications and related work on clotrimazole (a bioactive fungal) suggests ethosomes as a competent dermal and transdermal carrier system[57] and a few studies also revealed the use of transfersomes for the formulation of antigens through transcutaneous immunization[58]. There were ultradeformable liposomes, created by the penetration of a surfactant into the lipid bilayers and also the action of hydration gradient throughout the SC forces those intact vesicles into viable epidermis[59].

4. **Inclusion complexes**

Cyclodextrins (Cyds) essentially affects the two pathways through percutaneous absorption. Initially, by solubilizing a drug thus increasing the accessibility just at absorption site and furthermore, by interacting with free lipids present with in SC[60]. Therefore, the medication is stabilized and irritation is also reduced. Survey results by Ventura with colleagues have shown that 6-di-O-methyl-cyclodextrin (DM-ß-Cyd) has the ability to contain celocoxibincluding both solid state as well as solution, which increases its solubility in water and drug release significantly. In the availability of only a hydroxypropyl-ß-Cyclodextrins (HP-ß-Cyd), stable dispersion is obtained and celecoxib interacts externally with this macrocycle in solution, forming the non-inclusion complex. The *in vitro* findings on percutaneous absorption of celocoxib, as well as the permissibility of SC and epidermis carrier, inspired scholars to use both modified cyclodextrins as possible transdermal delivery systems of drug for localized treatment of such articular diseases to achieve better compliance[61].

5. **Eutectic mixtures**

Conversion of solid drugs first into highly concentrated oily system under ambient temperatures showed higher skin penetration due to its higher thermodynamic activity within vehicle. A drug's melting point is inversely proportional to that lipid solubility and lipophilicity. The lowering of the melting point therefore exhibits improved transdermal permeation. Such systems are important because they serve two strategies which enhance the skin penetration of an active ingredients molecule through the skin. First, the low-melting mixture is formed with the drug is produced which improves its skin-wide partitioning. Second, the skin structure is directly disturbed and further facilitates drug permeation. This synergy can be exploited in the process by choosing the correct permeation enhancers or enhancer to just be paired with the drug[62].

6. **Nanoparticles**

Nanoparticles have inimitable properties that facilitate drug absorption, allow long-term drug release and protect the encapsulated material from chemical degradation so that they have the ability to distribute drugs effectively across the skin. Valenzuela and Simon recently highlighted using nanoparticles to cure transdermal hormonal treatment. Analyzing typical pads, sprays, lotions, and gels, estradiol emulsion of Micellar Nanoparticle (MNPEE), a moisturiser-like therapy, was found to be more beneficial due to low plasma estradiol concentration fluctuations, unpredictable skin-related harmful impacts and comfortable cosmetics-like moisturizing properties. This is also an alternative method that does not involve the permeability enhancers or even temporary absorption of the skin, all of which can increase discomfort potential. MNPEE's efficacy in treating menopause vasomotor symptoms was being proved also in a placebo randomised controlled study. FDA approved the medications to treat mild to extreme vasomotor symptoms. MNPEE was therefore considered safe and efficient for the thearpy of vasomotor symptoms that signifies the clinical validation of a transdermal application of estrogen treatment (ET) technology for post - menopausal women of vasomotor symptoms by Nanoparticles[63].

7. **Coacervation effect**

Coacervation is a type of ion pairing which aggregates the paired complexes to create a unique hydrophobic process. Ion pair transport through membranes was being examined to promote the diffusion of ionizable medicines[64]. Stott with his colleague researched that analysis of complex coacervates of certain tricyclic antidepressants (imipramine, amitriptyline, and doxepin) and sodium deoxycholate (NaD) and sodium cholate (NaC) and sodium lauryl sulfate (SLS) surfactant anionic bile salts. Such systems have been analyzed with the inference of enhanced AMI flux: NaD coacervates that deliver an 18-fold improvement, and AMI: SLS 22-fold compared to aqueous solution. Test results show that improved lipophilicity in the coacervate oil process will improve the transdermal diffusion of a charged species[65].

B) Technique for Boosting Active Penetration

1. Iontophoresis

Iontophoresis is the triggered movement of ions via a membrane underneath the impact of a small electrical signal applied externally (0.5 mA / cm2 or less), which has shown to increase the passage of the skin and the drug release rate of numerous drugs with low absorption/permeation profile i.e. non-ionic or ionic drugs are incorporated *in vivo* by potentially electrochemical gradient. The efficacy of iontophoresis relies upon that molecule's valency, polarity and mobility, including the electrical duration and composition containing the drug as shown in (Fig. 8.11)[66]. Transdermal iontophoresis mechanisms include electroosmosis (electric field solvent induced flow), electrophoresis (electrical field charge interaction), and electroporation (rising skin porosity due to electrical field)[67]. For several drugs, including oligonucleotides and peptides, the technique revealed improves its permeation several times, and this can extend the scope of transdermal controlled delivery of drugs of systemic medication. In addition, work on the transdermal iontophoretic transmission of [3H] SK&F 110679 (labeled at 5- and 7-position D-tryptophan residue) and [3H] GHRP (radio-labeled growth hormone-releasing peptide), via an iontophoretic patch delivery mechanism in rats, provides a conformational study for the delivery of programmable drug[68]. Since the drug is transmitted here in amount to the current that can be readily balanced. Unlike most other delivery systems, such dependence on the current makes drug absorption through iontophoresis less dependent entirely reliant biological variables. Compliance with would also be improved by providing electronic means to inform patients to change the dose if they wish[69].

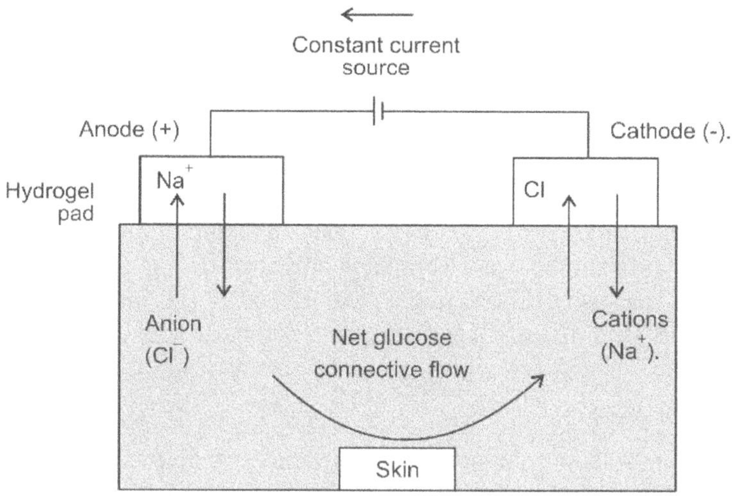

Fig.8.11 Diagrammatic representation of drug delivery through iontophoretic.

1. 'Sonophoresis

Ultrasound's applicability for the release of therapeutic compounds via the skin is usually referred to as sonophoresis (also termed as phonophoresis)[70]. The attention in the delivery of ultrasound molecules is thus focused on two considerations: (i) Capability to enhance the effectiveness of current transdermal formulations (e.g. non-steroidal anti-inflammatory medications and anesthetics) by optimizing the drug's topical action and (ii) Opportunities of sonophoresis to improve patient compliance through clinical fields which include psychiatry and diabetes and also in vaccine delivery[71]. Ultrasound Dermal therapy can include: (i) Cavitation (generation and oscillation of gas bubbles). (ii) Thermal effects (temperature increase) (iii) Induction of convective transport. (iv) Mechanical effects (occurrence of stresses due to pressure variation induced by ultrasound). Any of the above methodologies combined to appropriate physicochemical properties for optimizing transdermal delivery[72]are shown in (Fig. 6). For this technique, the drug is normally coupled with a coupling agent, but sometimes ointment or cream is used that passes ultrasonic energy from the strategy to the skin via this coupling agent[73]. Generally used sonophoresis frequencies are usually divided into two (i) Low frequency sonophoresis (LFS), that involves 20–100 kHz frequencies; and (ii) High frequency sonophoresis (HFS) involving 0.7–16 MHz frequencies (therapeutic as well as high frequency ultrasound ranges). Boucaud investigated the impact of sonication variables on the transdermal insulin delivery to hairless rats those are (i) Pulse length when the ultrasound would be on (ton), (ii) Intensity of the overall application time over the 'on' cycle (i) and (iii), i.e. the total of the time the ultrasound was 'on' during the exposure time (teff). The research showed that iontophoretic enhancement depends on the dose of energy and the length of the ultrasound pulse that would be consistent with such mechanism based on cavitation. Its most significant effect of reducing glycemia was achieved by following an ultrasound with <15 min and was closely related to subcutaneous insulin administration of a single dose 0.5 U with the result that insulin delivery was primarily due to sonication[74]. Zhang with Ye focused on the newer sonophoresis device with just a flat flex tensional transducer that was lightweight and durable as well as compact in size to deliver drugs efficiently[75]. That use of the safe physical enhancer for those transcutaneous immunizations and the delivery of genes seem to be another important research issue.

2. Electroporation

It's the very momentary structural disturbance of membranes of the lipid bilayer, resulting from the application of millisecond – microsecond high voltage pulses to improve the penetrability of the skin. Molecular movement by transient permeabilization of skin via electroporation results primarily from improved diffusion and electrophoresis. Transport efficiency based on the physicochemical properties and electrical parameters of the drugs[76]. The approach has been widely utilized to facilitate the permeability of compounds of varying lipophilicity and also size (i.e. proteins, small molecules, and oligonucleotides) besides biopharmaceuticals of molecular weight range higher than 7 KDa. The electrical pulses are described mostly by their own electrical parameters: voltage (50–1500 V), wave shape (exponential decay /square wave), pulse interval (just a seconds - a minute) and duration (only around μs - ms) [77]. Based on the procedure conditions and the clinical implementation of the electroporation, such electrical parameters could be optimized. Work by Mori indicated that time profile and electrical field of the voltage (or AUC of voltage against time) at the electroporation are quite important factors for improving the efficiency of the electroporation, and that only the output can be improved by the proper shape of the electrodes also in response to the electroporation application conditions[78,79].

3. Microneedles

Microneedles (MNs) comprise of small micron needles that interrupt the SC whenever applied to skin, to create micro-channels across the skin. Using these methods, drug can be administered through different modes[80, 81]. These different modes are: (a) Piercing through the skin of the variety of solid microneedles followed by placing a drug patch only at infected site (b) Coating drug on and injecting microneedles further across the skin for eventual dissolution of coated substance via the skin (c) Drug encapsulation inside biodegradable, polymeric microneedles accompanied by penetration via the skin for maintained drug release and (d) infusion of a drug by hollow microneedles[82-84]. The microchannels thereby provided help for topical delivery of drug molecules to cross the SC which is really the main barrier limiting transdermal permeability rate. In addition, microneedles seem to be completely painless and stress-free, while they do not penetrate the papillary dermis into which nerve endings are located. Peptides such as desmopressin and insulin, the material of genetics including oligonucleotides and plasmid DNA[85] disease-modifying antirheumatic drugs (DMARDs)[86], and anthrax, hepatitis B, as well as Japanese encephalitis[87]. Vaccines were shown to be administered *in vivo*. Besides that, MNs designed from silicone and insoluble metal are painless, although they have their own benefits and drawbacks respectively. Poor health, and also self-administration inconvenience. It might just be the main purpose why Mn-based TDDS has still not been commercialized[88]. A surprising result from S. Liu et al., shows that the novel MNs loaded with the insulin based primarily on hyaluronic acid (HA) has many advantages over previously prepared MNs, while it prevents severe skin damage[89].

4. Needleless jet injectors

Pain free delivery of protein as well as peptides is widely available as a device that delivers high-speed powders or liquid to the skin. In contrast to traditional injections, this delivery will provide a needleless alternative. They exist in two types, chiefly. Particles or liquid Biojector (Bioject) Vitajet and Medi-Jector systems and with their associated versions [Biojector — Cool SeroJet (Serono) and click; Medi-Jector — Zomajet (Ferring)] are some forms of jet injections with proteins in liquid state available. Additionally, these products are also currently running now being marketed for needleless insulin administration, ganirelix and recombinant human growth hormone (hGH). The pharmacokinetic characteristics are identical to those observed for needle injections[90].

5. Magnetophoresis

Magnetophoresis seems to be a method of expanding the penetration of drugs through biological barriers by applying magnetic field. A static magnetic field has been known to significantly, facilitate the transdermal penetration of drugs like salbutamol sulfate, benzoic acid, and terbutaline sulfate. Langer (2000) explored the fascinating concept of using magnetic or microchip-based systems to deliver pulsatile, controlled drugs[91]. There are quite a lot of publications about use of particulate systems incorporated by magnetite in delivery of drugs and imaging. The externally implemented magnetic field suggested that the systemically delivered nanoparticles or magneto-liposomes were driven to the target tissue. These substances have been extensively targeted as effective distribution vectors, leading to initiatives for use as agents for hyperthermic cancer therapy mediators, targeted therapies as well as nuclear magnetic resonance imaging (MRI)[92]. For this reason, the polymer matrix as a coating agent for para & super - paramagnetic particles must be composed of a biocompatible polymer. *In vivo* experiments involving porcine skin suggest that drugs are supplied by magnetophoretic patch systems at a higher rate than those of thermo-magnetic patch systems[93].

6. Photomechanical waves

Pressure waves propagated by intense laser radiation can permeabilize both the SC and the cell membrane and are widely recognized for about theirs precise control of a ablated skin depth and qualitative methods-definition of the ablated range[94]. These are essentially compression waves and hence exclude cavitation-induced biological effects. Its duration varies from nanoseconds from a few microseconds whereas the amplitude is within the hundreds of atmospheric conditions (bars). The pressure waves communicate with tissues and cells in ways distinct from ultrasonic waves. In 1999, Lee with his researchers discovered that whenever a solution of drug is mounted on the skin and protected by the a black polystyrene mark, a laser pulse is irradiated, which means that all these photomechanical waves are primarily responsible for further pressuring the horny layer and also enhancing the delivery of drugs. The PW aspects (peak pressure, time and duration) are based upon that laser parameters (wavelength, duration and fluency of the pulse) and the mechanical and optical properties of the mostly targeted material. The coupling coefficient can be used to measure the peak pressure. Drugs supplied through the epidermis can penetrate the vasculature and have a systemic effect. Therefore, pressure waves can be exerted for the rapid delivery of insulin and allergens- humans-aminolevulinic acid (ALA)[95].

7. Electron beam irradiation

Radiation has been reviewed as an effective method for polymer matrix synthesis for the immobilization of several drugs at ambient temperature as well as cold temperatures[96]. A new approach involving alpha particle irradiation was used to create microporous membranes of the nuclear line, which are used as TTS membranes monitoring drug release rate. Polymerization by radiation has unique qualities which include the final matrix, free of the any residual initiator. The process is performed in a wider temperature range and offers an opportunity for the product to be sterilized concurr ently, so polymerization of radiation is favored over thermochemical system. The activation energy within the radiation polymerization is 1/3 of a thermochemical cycle and thus it is somewhat more energy intensive. Kotiyan as well as his coworker designed a transdermal system with isosorbide dinitrate (ISDN) by using this method and also the solid state stability of its irradiation of drug was validated using enhanced skin penetration kinetics compared to an internationally marketed ISDN transdermal matrix system[97].

Newer combinational active penetration techniques

A highly specialized group of researchers from such diverse disciplines as the pharmaceutical, engineering, physics, biology, chemistry and medicine are working together to effectively, safely and practically lower the skin barrier. Numerous combinations were shown to compete synergistically, including chemical – ultrasound, chemical – electroporation, chemical – iontophoresis, and iontophoresis – ultrasound, electroporation – ultrasound, electroporation – iontophoresis & pressure wave's chemicals. These strategies have shown progress to a large amount of medications as well as macromolecules such as vaccines and insulin in increasing the penetrability of the skin[73].

PREPARATION OF TDDS[7]

A. Asymmetric TPX membrane method[22,98]

For this process thermal sealable polyester film with just a concave uniform diameter of 1 cm is then used as back membrane for manufactured patch. The sample of the drug is dispensed along into the concave thin membrane, completely covered by asymmetric membrane TPX {poly (4- methyl-1-pentene)}, and sealed together by an adhesive.

B. Circular Teflon mould method[22,98]

Solutions containing polymers are often used in the organic solvent in varying amounts. Calculated quantity of drug dissolves in half the amount of the same organic solvent. In another half of a organic solvent, permeation enhancers at different concentrations were being dissolved, and then added. Di-N-butyl phthalate was introduced to drug-polymer solution as a plasticizer. Stir the complete content for 12 hrs. Then in a circular Teflon mould, poured into this. For control solvent vaporization inside a laminar air flow jacket model through an air speed around 0.5 m / s, the moulds must be mounted on a levelled base and protected with inverted funnel. The solvent will evaporate within 24 hours. Prior to the actual evaluation, the dried films shall be stored at 25±0.5 ° C for another 24 hours in a desiccator usually contains silica gel to eliminate the aging effects. The films of its type shall be analyzed within a week of their final preparations.

C. Mercury substrate method[22,98]

In this method drug is dissolved in polymer solution along with plasticizer. The above solution is to be stirred for 10-15 minutes to produce a homogenous dispersion and poured in to a levelled mercury surface, covered with inverted funnel to control solvent evaporation.

D. IPM membranes method[22,98]

The drug required in this process is dispersed in such a solution of water & propylene glycol that included carbomer 940 polymers & shaken in magnetic stirrer yet for 12 hrs. The dispersion is now to be neutralized by addition of triethanolamine and further made viscous. Buffer of Phosphate with pH 7.4 is being used to produce solution gel when the solubility of drugs in aqueous solution is quite low. The formulated gel is injected into the IPM membrane.

E. EVAC membrane method[22,98]

Membranes will be used to formulate the target transdermal therapy system, 1 per cent carbopol reservoir gel, ethylene vinyl acetate copolymer (EVAC), polyethelene (PE) for the rate control membranes. When the drug isn't water-soluble, propylene glycol is being used to make a gel. In propylene glycol drug is dissolve; to the above solution, carbopol resin is applied and neutralized using sodium hydroxide solution of 5 percent w / w. The drug (present in gel form) was being mounted on a backing layer sheet that covers the specified area. The rate-controlling membrane is mounted upon on the gel and edges are heat sealed to get a device with leak proof.

F. Aluminium backed adhesive film method[22,98]

Transdermal delivery system of drug can develop unstable matrix if the dose of loading is higher than 10 mg. The adhesive film method backed by aluminium is an effective one. For the preparation of the same, chloroform should be solvent choice, because chloroform is soluble in most drugs and also adhesives. The drug was dissolved in chloroform, before applying and dissolving adhesive material to a drug solution. A former made of custom aluminium is lined most with aluminium foil and the edges are completely blanked off along with tightly fitted cork blocks.

G. Proliposomes Method[22,98,99]

The proliposomes are formulated employing film deposition technique through carrier method. Lecithin and Drug are often used as an efficient one in the proportion with 2.0 : 0.1. Proliposomes are prepared containing 5 mg of mannitol powder with a 100 ml of round bottom flask that is stored at a temperature of 60-70°C and rotating the flask in80-90 rpm and drying the mannitol at closed system for 30 minutes. Following drying the water bath, temperature is set to 20-30°C. Drug and lecithin are completely dissolved in an appropriate organic solvent mixture, an organic solution aliquot of 0.5ml was now introduced into a round bottom flask at 37°C, after proper drying of 2nd aliquots (0.5ml) of solution is added. After last loading, a lyophilizer connects the flask having proliposomes, and eventually drug-loaded mannitol powder proliposomes are allowed to place overnight in a desiccator, then sieved across 100 mesh. The powder collected is moved to a glass bottle and stored at freezing temperature until it is characterized.

H. Freefilm method[22,98]

The free cellulose acetate film is prepared by this method upon that surface of mercury. Utilizing chloroform, a 2 per cent w/w polymer solution should be formulated. Plasticizers will be used at a polymer weight concentration of 40 per cent w/w. 5 ml of a polymer solution must be poured into a glass ring that is placed among a glass Petri dish throughout the mercury surface. The solvent evaporation rate is to be maintained by putting an inverted funnel on over Petri platter. The formation of films is confirmed by observing the surface of mercury after the solvent has been completely evaporated. The dry film is separated and stored in desiccators between the wax paper sheets, until it is used. The dry film is separated and stored in desiccators between the wax paper sheets, until it is used. Free films of various thicknesses could be designed by adjusting the amount of just the polymer solution.

EVALUATION PARAMETERS OF TRANSDERMAL PATCHES[7, 22,98]

A. Physicochemical evaluation

B. *In vitro* evaluation

C. *In vivo* evaluation

A. Physicochemical Evaluation:

i. **Thickness:**

A thickness of the transdermal film is measured by the traveling microscope, screw gauge, dial gauge or micrometer at various film areas.

ii. **Uniformity of weight:**

Variation in weight is analyzed by weighing ten randomly selected patches individually and calculating the mean weight. The individual weight must not considerably deviate from those in the average weight.

iii. **Determination of surface pH**

Specific patch numbers are remained in contact to distilled water & excess water would be drained as well as pH by pH meter is recorded.

iv. **Drug content determination**

An accurately measured portion of the product (about 100 mg) was immersed in 100 mL with an appropriate solvent in which the product is soluble and now the solution is continuously shaken in the shaker incubator for 24 h. Then the entire solution is being sonicated. Active drug present in solution is predicted by measuring absorbance spectrophotometrically, after sonication as well as resultant filtration.

v. **Content uniformity test**

Randomly 10 nos. of patches are chosen, and the content of each patch is calculated. So when 9 in 10 patches provide content approximately 85% to 115% including its predetermined range but the other has content not quite around 75% to 125% within the predetermined range, then transdermal patches complete the content uniformity test. However, if 3 patches possess content ranging from 75% to 125%, 20 more patches will be tested also for drug content. As those 20 patches vary from 85% to almost 115%, the transdermal patches will pass the test. The samples so obtained are analyzed by HPLC or U.V. spectrophotometer.

vi. **Moisture content:**

The completely prepared films are individually weighed and further stored at room temperature now for 24h in a desiccators that contains calcium chloride. After that specified interval, the films are weighed up again until they exhibit a constant weight. The percentage of moisture is measured using the following formula.

$$\% \text{ Moisture content} = \frac{\text{Initial weight - Final weight}}{\text{Final weight}} \times 100$$

vii. **Moisture Uptake:**

Weighed films are stored in ambient temperature 24 h in desiccators. These are then removed and subjected in desiccators to 84 per cent moisture content utilizing saturated Potassium chloride solution until a constant weight is attained. The percent absorption of moisture is measured as shown below.

$$\% \text{ Moisture uptake} = \frac{\text{Final weight- Initial weight}}{\text{Initial weight}} \times 100$$

viii. **Flatness:**

A transdermal patch must have a smooth texture, and should never be time-bound. This can be proven with analysis of flatness. One stripe is cut from the center for flatness determination, and two of each side of patches. The length about each strip is evaluated, and the length variation is analyzed by percentage of constriction. Zero per cent constriction seems to be equivalent to flatness of 100 per cent.

% constriction = [I1 – I2] X 100

I2 = Final length of each strip

I1 = Initial length of each strip

ix. **Folding Endurance:**

Analysis of folding endurance aims to determine the folding capability of films that are subjected with frequent extreme folding conditions. Folding strength is determined by repetitive folding of the film to a certain place until this breaks. The couple of times a film might be folded around the same position without breaking are the value of endurance folding.

x. **Shear strength properties:**

This is the calculation of an adhesive polymer's cohesive strength. Adequate cohesive quality assurance methods of a device would further assume it won't fall on application and won't leave any residue when removed. It is estimated by calculating the time required to pull apart a stainless steel plate over adhesive coated tape when a given weight is hanged from the tape that pulls the tape in a parallel direction to the plate.

xi. **Tensile Strength:**

Polymer films are squished separately by the corked simple linear iron plates to just determine the tensile strength. Using an iron screen, one end of that film is fixed and another end is connected to a very freely movable thread across a pulley. The weights are slowly applied to the pan that is connected with the thread hanging end. A part of the thread-pointer is used to determine the film's elongation. It's reported the weight more than enough to break a film. The tensile force can be measured using the equation below.

$$\text{Tensile strength} = \frac{F}{a \times b}\left(1 + \frac{L}{l}\right)$$

F = force required to break;

a = width of film;

b = thickness of film;

L = length of film; and

l = elongation of film at break point.

xii. **Tack properties:**

It's the polymer's ability to adhere to just substrate with low contact force. Tack is highly dependent on the molecular weight and polymer composition, as well as the use of polymer tackling resins.

xiii. **Thumb tack test:**

A way of measuring of tack is the force needed to strip away thumb from the adhesive.

xiv. **Rolling ball test:**

This analysis involved measuring the distance travelling by ball of stainless steel along an adhesive facing upwards. The less the adhesive gets tacky, the further the ball travels.

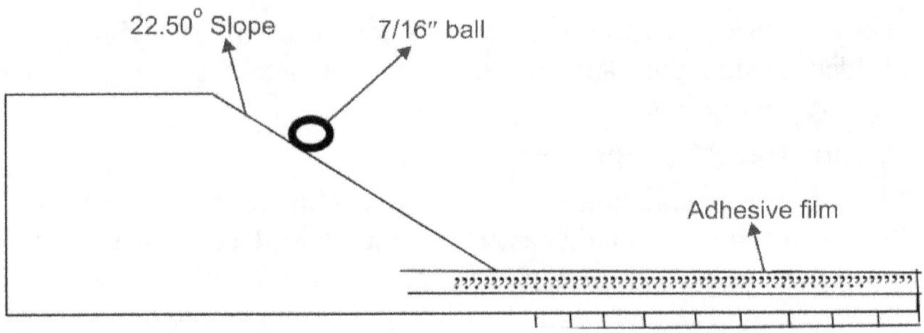

Fig.8.12 Diagrammatic representation of rolling ball test.

xv. Quick stick (Peel tack) test

The peel force necessary to break the bond among an adhesive and a substrate is determined by pulling the tape apart at a speed about 12 inches / min from the substrate material.

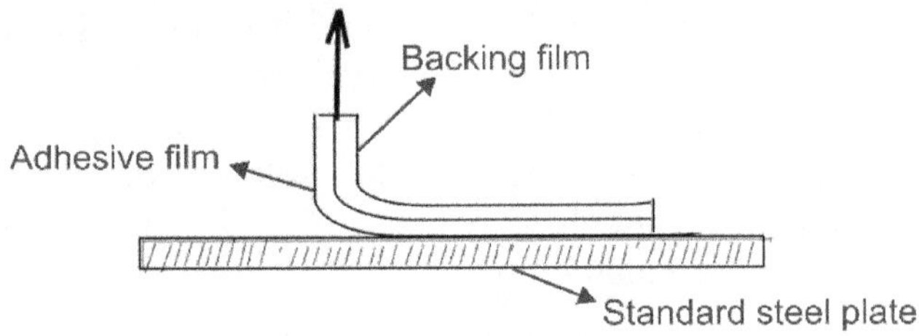

Fig.8.13 Diagrammatic representation of Quick stick (Peel tack) test.

xvi. Probe tack test:

Force needed to pull well a probe apart from a fixed rate adhesive is analyzed as a tack.

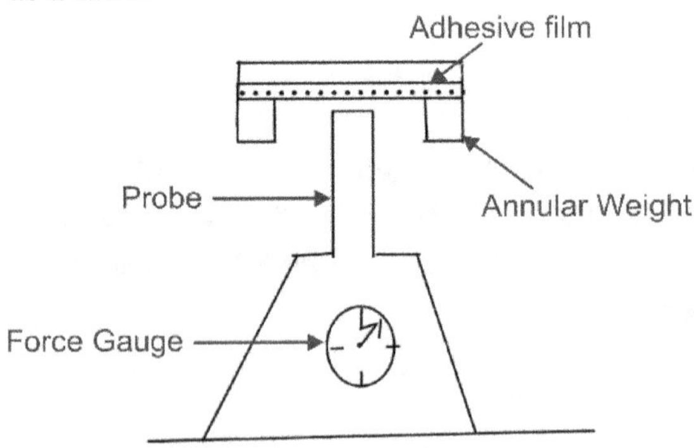

Fig.8.14 Diagrammatic representation of Probe tack test.

xvii. Peel adhesion properties

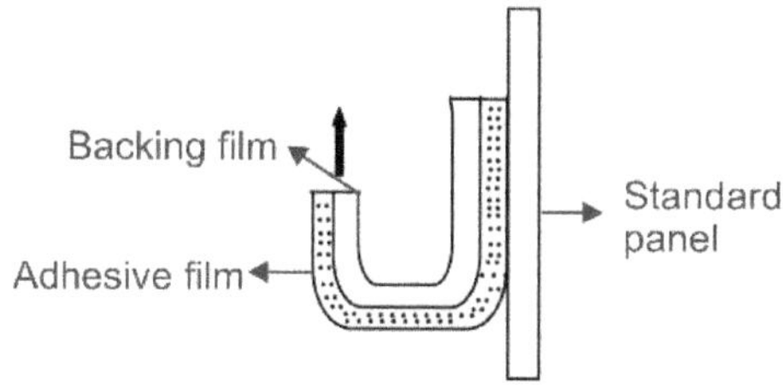

Fig.8.15 Diagrammatic representation of Peel adhesion properties.

Peel adhesion is just the force allowed to remove a test substance from an adhesive coating. It is measured by calculating the force needed for pulling the single coated tape, tried to apply at an angle of 180° to a material. It should not irritate the skin and should not cause any impurities to the skin.

xviii. Polariscope examination

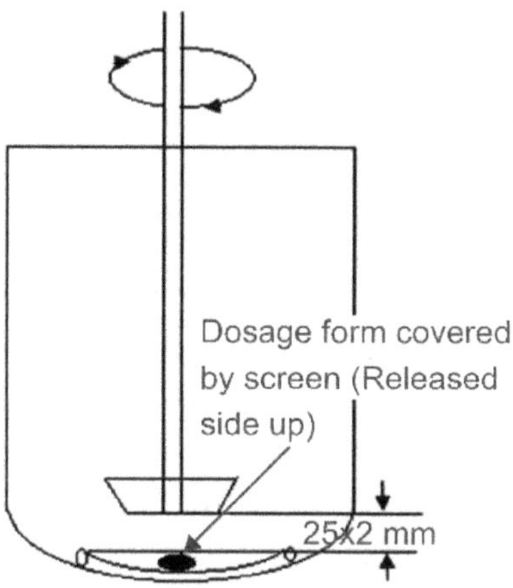

Fig.8.16 Diagrammatic representation of the Paddle over Disc.

This examination is to be carried out by polariscope to analyze the drug crystals through patch. A particular area of surface of the component shall be held on the material slide and the drug crystals shall be examined to assess whether the drug is present in the patch as a crystalline form or as an amorphous form.

xix. Percentage Elongation break test

The break in percentage elongation is to be measured by considering the extent just before break point, the break in percentage elongation can be calculated from the formula below.

Elongation percentage: $L_1 - L_2 \times 100$

Where, L_1 is the final length of each strip and L_2 is the initial length of each strip.

B. *In vitro* Evaluation:

i. The Paddle over Disc

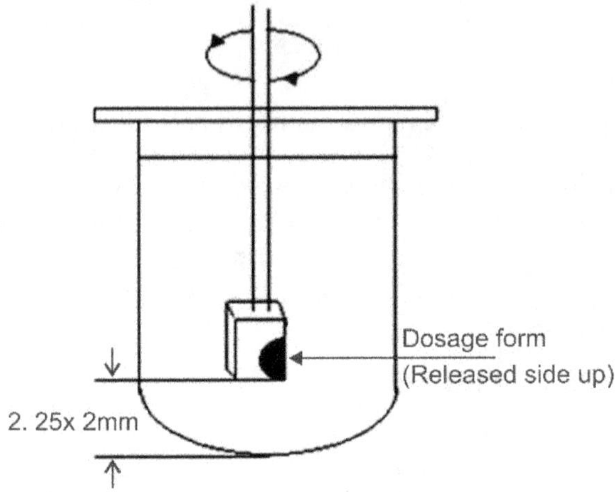

Fig.8.17 Diagrammatic representation of the Cylinder modified USP Basket.

This evaluation is identical to that of the USP paddle dissolution device, excluding that a transdermal system is held towards a disk/cell resting only at bottom of the container containing a medium at 32 ± 5°C.

ii. The Cylinder modified USP Basket

This analysis is related to the dissolution apparatus of USP basket type, except the device is mounted on the surface about a hollow cylinder submerged at 32 ±5°C in the water.

iii. The reciprocating disc

Patches connected to holders in this method will be oscillated in small amounts of medium, enabling the apparatus is also helpful though for systems delivering low drug concentration. Additionally it is possible to use paddle throughout extraction cell method.

C. *In vitro* Permeation Studies

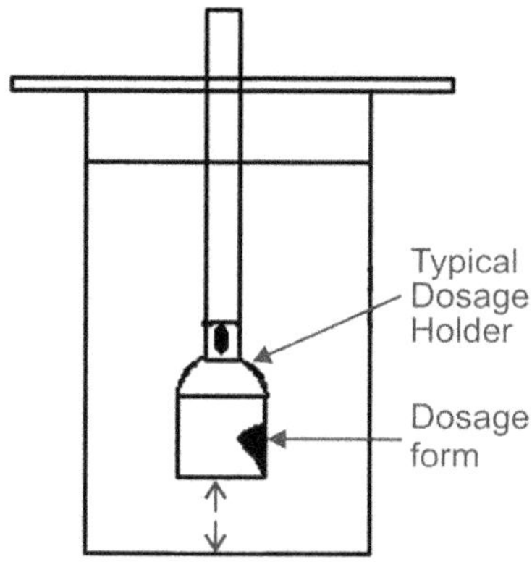

Fig.8.18 Diagrammatic representation of the reciprocating disc.

The amount of the drug freely accessible to absorb into the systemic pool is heavily dependent upon drug released from the transdermal polymeric films. The drug attained at the skin surface was further transported through penetration via the epidermis cells to just the dermal microcirculation, through skin appendages between the epidermis cells. Permeation studies are usually done by placing the manufactured transdermal patch with a somewhat vertical diffusion cell like Keshary-chien diffusion or Franz diffusion cell with rat skin/synthetic membrane between those receptor as well as donor compartment. The transdermal system can be applied to a hydrophilic side of a membrane, and then positioned in contact to receptor fluid within that diffusion cell with the lipophilic side. The receiver compartment is maintained at specific temperature (usually 32±5°C for skin) and is continuously stirred at a constant rate. The samples were taken in predetermined time intervals, where each time the same amount of buffer will be replaced. The samples are adequately diluted, and spectrophotometric absorbance was determined. Then through each time interval the amount of drug infused per centimetre square is measured. System design, skin surface area, patch size, temperature and skin thickness etc., are some conditions which can affect drug release. Thus, the study of permeation includes mounting of the skin upon its permeation cell, preparation of a skin, arrangement of experimental conditions such as stirring, temperature, sink conditions, withdrawal of samples with different time intervals, measurement of flux and examination of samples, i.e., permeated drug each cm^2 per sec.

iv. Horizontal-type skin permeation system:

This was commonly used in the analysis of drug permeation through the skin. For each compartment the cell is divided into receptor as well as donor compartments including a low volume of solution (3.5ml) and a small region of membrane ($0.64cm^2$). They are stirred continuously by matching set with star-head magnets, all of which are rotated to a maximum speed of 600rpm. The system is controlled by thermo-stated water through a water jacket surrounding the two compartments.

v. **Franz diffusion cell:**

The cell consisting of two chambers: donor as well as recipient. The receptor chamber has a 5-12 ml capacity, and an important 1-5 cm^2 surface area. The diffusion medium is stirred continuously by a magnetic bar at 600 rpm. The temperature in large proportion of the solution is managed to maintain by distributing thermo stated water via a water jacket covering the chamber of the receptor.

vi. **Flow-through diffusion cell:**

Circulation across diffusion cells has the advantage of being able to use them when the drug is less soluble in the receptor chamber. This cell can still be completely automated, and directly connected to HPLC.They also have wide donor chamber ensuring aloe adequate loading of the applicable drug, and then a small volume (0.3ml) recipient chamber to ensure fast penetrator removal at comparatively low pumping speeds.

C. In vivo Evaluation:

The true characterization of drug performance is *in-vivo* evaluations. The factors that cannot be considered in the course of *in vitro* studies can be thoroughly explored here during *in-vivo* studies. TDDS analysis may be conducted *in vivo* using animal studies and human volunteers.

i. **Animal models:**

The carrying out of human studies takes significant time and money, so animal models are favoured at a limited scale. Mouse, hairless dog, hairless rat, rabbit, guinea pig, hairless rhesus monkey, etc. are the main frequently reported animal species used for testing the transdermal delivery system of drug. Diverse experiments have helped to conclude that hairless animals are favoured to furry animals. Rhesus monkey is among the most reliable models for predicting transdermal delivery of drugs in man in vivo.

ii. **Human models:**

The final step of a TDDS production includes gathering pharmacokinetic and pharmacodynamic data after applying the patch to healthy volunteers. Clinical trials are undertaken to evaluate the effectiveness, the risk involved, compliance with patients, the side effects, etc. Step I studies were undertaken primarily to examine the health of volunteers, and step II clinical trials evaluate the safety of the patients in the short term and mainly the efficacy. Step III studies indicate the efficacy as well as safety of a huge number of patient human population and further Step IV post-marketing surveillance examinations is performed for patches marketed to also detect adverse reactions. Even if human studies demand significant resources, they are the safest to analyze the drug's effectiveness. Fieldman and Maibach reveal it for the very first time. That includes examination of percutaneous absorption going to follow topical application of the marked drug via an indirect ways of assessing radioactivity in excreta. 14C is commonly used for the radio labelling. Determining absorption after topical administration needs the investigator to calculate the quantity of radioactivity that has been retained with in body or more often excreted by normal routes. The percentage of the transdermal absorbed dose is estimated then as.

$$\% \text{ Close Absorbed} = \frac{\text{Total radioactivity after administering topically}}{\text{Total radioactivity exerted after intervenous administration}} \times 100$$

CONCLUSION

To solve the issues to the oral distribution route, transdermal drug delivery system are often used as complete alternatives route particularly focusing on functionality improvements, versatility in dosage and patient adherence. To deliver a drug through the skin successfully, we have to understand the different layers of skin and factors affecting the penetration. This type of delivery system of drug focuses on the role of ingredients such as polymer matrix, rate control membrane, adhesive, active ingredient, back layer, penetration enhancer, release liner, and excipients (Plasticizers). The huge advantage of TDDS is that it can be used in successful deliverable medicines for both hydrophobic and hydrophilic active substances. But to manage this drug release, more understanding between the different mechanism of biological activity and polymer is needed. Recent advancements have been achieved to enhance the efficiency of this delivery system including active and passive methods, without breaking the skin membranes. Such systems are continuously gaining popularity worldwide, as they bypass several problem that are concerned with low oral bioavailability, side effects or low compliance with regular dose intervals. The transdermal delivery system of drugs, statics and challenges will grow day by day and implementations of TDDS with the successful development of new strategies are expected to increase in the coming future.

REFERENCES

1. Van Brunt J. Novel drug delivery systems. Vol. 7, Bio/Technology.1989. 103 p.
2. Patil PM, Chaudhari PD, Patel JK, Kedar KA, Katolkar PP. Recent trends in challenges and opportunities of Transdermal drug delivery system. Int J Drug Dev Res. 2012;4(1):39–50.
3. Krug J. Kinetic pattern formation at solid surfaces. Collective Dynamics of Nonlinear and Disordered Systems. 2005. 5–37 p.
4. Naik A, Kalia YN, Guy RH. Transdermal drug delivery: Overcoming the skin's barrier function. Pharm Sci Technol Today. 2000;3(9):318–26.

5. Prausnitz MR, Langer R. Transdermal drug delivery. Nat Biotechnol. 2008;26(11):1261–8.
6. Pastore MN, Kalia YN, Horstmann M, Roberts MS. Transdermal patches: History, development and pharmacology. Br J Pharmacol. 2015;172(9):2179–209.
7. Bala P, Jathar S, Kale S, Pal K. Transdermal Drug Delivery System (TDDS) - A Multifaceted Approach For Drug Delivery. J Pharm Res [Internet]. 2014;8(12):1805–35.
8. Hadgraft J. Skin deep. Eur J Pharm Biopharm. 2004;58(2):291–9.
9. Proksch E, Brandner JM, Jensen JM. The skin: An indispensable barrier. Exp Dermatol. 2008;17(12):1063–72.
10. Shefler I, Salamon P, Y. Hershko A, A. Mekori Y. Mast Cells as Sources and Targets of Membrane Vesicles. Curr Pharm Des. 2011;17(34):3797–804.
11. Chen X, Kwak S, Lafleur M, Bloom M, Kitson N, Thewalt J. Fatty acids influence "Solid" phase formation in models of stratum corneum intercellular membranes. Langmuir. 2007;23(10):5548–56.
12. Wester RC, Maibach HI. Percutaneous absorption. Heal Risk Assess Dermal Inhal Expo Absorpt Toxicants. 2017;110:63–73.
13. Grams YY, Whitehead L, Lamers G, Sturmann N, Bouwstra JA. On-line diffusion profile of a lipophilic model dye in different depths of a hair follicle in human scalp skin. J Invest Dermatol. 2005;125(4):775–82.
14. R.-Briggaman_1975_The epidermal-dermal junction.pdf.
15. Alkilani AZ, McCrudden MTC, Donnelly RF. Transdermal drug delivery: Innovative pharmaceutical developments based on disruption of the barrier properties of the stratum corneum. Pharmaceutics. 2015;7(4):438–70.
16. Montagna W. The Structure and Function of Skin, The Pilary Apparatus. 1974;(1).
17. Honari G. Skin Structure and Function. Sensitive Ski Syndr. 2017;16–22.
18. Prausnitz MR, Elias PM, Franz TJ, Schmuth M, Tsai J-C, Menon GK, et al. Skin Barrier and Transdermal Drug Delivery STRUCTURE AND ORIGIN OF THE SKIN BARRIER Stratum Corneum Structure and Organization. Med Ther [Internet]. 2012;2065–73. Available from: http://drugdelivery.chbe.gatech.edu/Papers/2012/Prausnitz Derm Book Chapter 2012.pdf
19. Amidei C, Trese S. Neuroanatomy and physiology. Management of Adult Glioma in Nursing Practice. 2019. 1–20 p.
20. Marwah H, Garg T, Goyal AK, Rath G. Permeation enhancer strategies in transdermal drug delivery. Drug Deliv. 2016;23(2):564–78.
21. Watkinson AC, Brain KR. Basic mathematical principles in skin permeation. J Toxicol - Cutan Ocul Toxicol. 2002;21(4):371–402.
22. Rastogi V, Yadav P. Transdermal drug delivery system: An overview. Asian J Pharm. 2012;6(3):161–70.

23. Karande P, Jain A, Ergun K, Kispersky V, Mitragotri S. Design principles of chemical penetration enhancers for transdermal drug delivery. Proc Natl Acad Sci U S A. 2005;102(13):4688–93.
24. Valenta C, Auner BG. The use of polymers for dermal and transdermal delivery. Eur J Pharm Biopharm. 2004;58(2):279–89.
25. Preziosi P. Drug development. Compr Med Chem II. 2006;2:173–202.
26. Zhan X, Tang G, Chen S, Mao Z. A new copolymer membrane controlling clonidine linear release in a transdermal drug delivery system. Int J Pharm. 2006;322(1–2):1–5.
27. Iordanskii AL, Feldstein MM, Markin VS, Hadgraft J, Plate NA. Modeling of the drug delivery from a hydrophilic transdermal therapeutic system across polymer membrane. Eur J Pharm Biopharm. 2000;49(3):287–93.
28. Kandavilli S, Nair V, Panchagnula R. Polymers in transdermal drug delivery systems. Pharm Technol North Am. 2002;26(5):62–80.
29. Minghetti P, Cilurzo F, Montanari L. Evaluation of adhesive properties of patches based on acrylic matrices. Drug Dev Ind Pharm. 1999;25(1):1–6.
30. Cilurzo F, Gennari CGM, Minghetti P. Adhesive properties: A critical issue in transdermal patch development. Expert Opin Drug Deliv. 2012;9(1):33–45.
31. Tan HS, Pfister WR. Pressure-sensitive adhesives for transdermal drug delivery systems. Pharm Sci Technol Today. 1999;2(2):60–9.
32. Guy RH, Hadgraft J. Transdermal drug delivery: a simplified pharmacokinetic approach. Int J Pharm. 1985;24(2–3):267–74.
33. Raza R, Mittal A, Kumar P, Alam S, Prakash S, Chauhan N. Approaches and evaluation of Transdermal drug delivery system. Int J Drug Dev Res. 2015;7(1):222–33.
34. Williams AC, Barry BW. Penetration enhancers. Adv Drug Deliv Rev. 2004;56(5):603–18.
35. Chen Y, Quan P, Liu X, Wang M, Fang L. Novel chemical permeation enhancers for transdermal drug delivery. Asian J Pharm Sci [Internet]. 2014;9(2):51–64. Available from: http://dx.doi.org/10.1016/j.ajps.2014.01.001
36. Ochalek M, Podhaisky H, Ruettinger HH, Neubert RHH, Wohlrab J. SC lipid model membranes designed for studying impact of ceramide species on drug diffusion and permeation, Part III: Influence of penetration enhancer on diffusion and permeation of model drugs. Int J Pharm [Internet]. 2012;436(1–2):206–13. Available from: http://dx.doi.org/10.1016/j.ijpharm.2012.06.044
37. Soni S, Jain SK, Jain NK. Effect of penetration enhancers on transdermal delivery of timolol maleate. Drug Dev Ind Pharm. 1992;18(10):1127–35.
38. Sinha VR, Pal Kaur M. Permeation enhancers for transdermal drug delivery. Drug Dev Ind Pharm. 2000;26(11):1131–40.
39. Gupta R, Dwadasi BS, Rai B, Mitragotri S. Effect of Chemical Permeation Enhancers on Skin Permeability: In silico screening using Molecular Dynamics simulations. Sci Rep [Internet]. 2019;9(1):1–11. Available from: http://dx.doi.org/10.1038/s41598-018-37900-0

40. Amnuaikit C, Ikeuchi I, Ogawara KI, Higaki K, Kimura T. Skin permeation of propranolol from polymeric film containing terpene enhancers for transdermal use. Int J Pharm. 2005;289(1–2):167–78.

41. Pichayakorn W, Suksaeree J, Boonme P, Amnuaikit T, Taweepreda W, Ritthidej GC. Nicotine transdermal patches using polymeric natural rubber as the matrix controlling system: Effect of polymer and plasticizer blends. J Memb Sci [Internet]. 2012;411–412:81–90. Available from:
http://dx.doi.org/10.1016/j.memsci.2012.04.017

42. Crawford RR, Esmerian OK. Effect of plasticizers on some physical properties of cellulose acetate phthalate films. J Pharm Sci. 1971;60(2):312–4.

43. Arunachalam A, Karthikeyan M, Kumar DV, Prathap M, Sethuraman S, Ashutoshkumar S. Review Article Current Pharma Research Transdermal Drug Delivery System : A Review. Micro. 2010;1(1).

44. Hanumanaik M, Patil U, Kumar G, Patel K, Singh I, Jadatkar K. Design, Evaluation and Recent Trends in Transdermal Drug Delivery System: a Review. Ijpsr [Internet]. 2012;3(8):2393–406. Available from: www.ijpsr.com

45. Monika B, Amit R, Sanjib B, Alisha B, Mihir P, Dhanushram T. Transdermal drug delivery system with formulation and evaluation aspects: Overview. Res J Pharm Technol. 2012;5(9):1168–76.

46. Chauhan SB. Penetration Enhancement Techniques. J Appl Pharm. 2017;09(02):1–5.

47 Alexander A, Dwivedi S, Ajazuddin, Giri TK, Saraf S, Saraf S, et al. Approaches for breaking the barriers of drug permeation through transdermal drug delivery. J Control Release [Internet]. 2012;164(1):26–40. Available from: http://dx.doi.org/10.1016/j.jconrel.2012.09.017

48. Moser K, Kriwet K, Naik A, Kalia YN, Guy RH. Passive skin penetration enhancement and its quantification in vitro. Eur J Pharm Biopharm. 2001;52(2):103–12.

49. Zhao X, Liu JP, Zhang X, Li Y. Enhancement of transdermal delivery of theophylline using microemulsion vehicle. Int J Pharm. 2006;327(1–2):58–64.

50. Notman R, Anwar J. Breaching the skin barrier - Insights from molecular simulation of model membranes. Adv Drug Deliv Rev [Internet]. 2013;65(2):237–50. Available from:
http://dx.doi.org/10.1016/j.addr.2012.02.011

51. Kreilgaard M. Influence of microemulsions on cutaneous drug delivery. Adv Drug Deliv Rev. 2002;54(SUPPL.).

52. Kogan A, Garti N. Microemulsions as transdermal drug delivery vehicles. Adv Colloid Interface Sci. 2006;123–126(SPEC. ISS.):369–85.

53. Latsch S, Selzer T, Fink L, Kreuter J. Crystallisation of estradiol containing TDDS determined by isothermal microcalorimetry, X-ray diffraction, and optical microscopy. Eur J Pharm Biopharm. 2003;56(1):43–52.

54. Cilurzo F, Minghetti P, Casiraghi A, Tosi L, Pagani S, Montanari L. Polymethacrylates as crystallization inhibitors in monolayer transdermal patches containing ibuprofen. Eur J Pharm Biopharm. 2005;60(1):61–6.

55. Schreier H, Bouwstra J. Liposomes and niosomes as topical drug carriers: dermal and transdermal drug delivery. J Control Release. 1994;30(1):1–15.

56. Domaraju P. Vesicles - mechanism of transdermal permeation : A review Academic Sciences Asian Journal of Pharmaceutical and Clinical Research. 2020;(January 2012).

57. Maheshwari RGS, Tekade RK, Sharma PA, Darwhekar G, Tyagi A, Patel RP, et al. Ethosomes and ultradeformable liposomes for transdermal delivery of clotrimazole: A comparative assessment. Saudi Pharm J [Internet]. 2012;20(2):161–70. Available from: http://dx.doi.org/10.1016/j.jsps.2011.10.001

58. Drape RJ, Macklin MD, Barr LJ, Jones S, Haynes JR, Dean HJ. Epidermal DNA vaccine for influenza is immunogenic in humans. Vaccine. 2006;24(21): 4475–81.

59. Hussain A, Singh S, Sharma D, Webster TJ, Shafaat K, Faruk A. Elastic liposomes as novel carriers: Recent advances in drug delivery. Int J Nanomedicine. 2017;12:5087–108.

60. Carpentieri-Rodrigues LN, Zanluchi JM, Grebogi IH. Percutaneous absorption enhancers: Mechanisms and potential. Brazilian Arch Biol Technol. 2007;50(6):949–61.

61. Ventura CA, Tommasini S, Falcone A, Giannone I, Paolino D, Sdrafkakis V, et al. Influence of modified cyclodextrins on solubility and percutaneous absorption of celecoxib through human skin. Int J Pharm. 2006;314(1):37–45.

62. Stott PW, Williams AC, Barry BW. Transdermal delivery from eutectic systems: Enhanced permeation of a model drug, ibuprofen. J Control Release. 1998;50(1–3):297–308.

63. Valenzuela P, Simon JA. Nanoparticle delivery for transdermal HRT. Maturitas [Internet]. 2012;73(1):74–80.

64. Gasco MR, Trotta M, Carlotti ME, Carpignano R. Contribution of carboxylic acids to the permeability of imipramine. Int J Pharm. 1984;18(3):235–45.

65. Stott PW, Williams AC, Barry BW. Characterization of complex coacervates of some tricyclic antidepressants and evaluation of their potential for enhancing transdermal flux. J Control Release. 1996;41(3):215–27.

66. Dhal S, Gavara RR, Pal K, Banerjee I, Mishra M, Giri S. Facile transdermal delivery of upconversion nanoparticle by iontophoresis-responsive magneto-upconversion oleogel. Nano Express. 2020;1(1):010012.

67. Yan G, Li SK, Higuchi WI. Evaluation of constant current alternating current iontophoresis for transdermal drug delivery. J Control Release. 2005;110(1):141–50.

68. Green PG. Iontophoretic delivery of peptide drugs. J Control Release. 1996;41(1–2):33–48.

69. Kanikkannan N. Iontophoresis-based transdermal delivery systems. BioDrugs. 2002;16(5):339–47.

70. Park D, Park H, Seo J, Lee S. Sonophoresis in transdermal drug deliverys. Ultrasonics [Internet]. 2014;54(1):56–65. A

71. Polat BE, Hart D, Langer R, Blankschtein D. Ultrasound-mediated transdermal drug delivery: Mechanisms, scope, and emerging trends. J Control Release [Internet]. 2011;152(3):330–48.

72. Joshi A, Raje J. Sonicated transdermal drug transport. J Control Release. 2002;83(1):13–22.

73. Kumar R, Philip A. Modified Transdermal Technologies: Breaking the Barriers of Drug Permeation via the Skin. Trop J Pharm Res. 2007;6(1):633–44.

74. Boucaud A, Garrigue MA, Machet L, Vaillant L, Patat F. Effect of sonication parameters on transdermal delivery of insulin to hairless rats. J Control Release. 2002;81(1–2):113–9.

75. Zhang HY, Yeo SH. Design and fabrication of a sonophoresis device with a flat flextensional transducer for transdermal drug delivery. Sensors Actuators, A Phys. 2004;115(1):133–9.

76. Denet AR, Vanbever R, Préat V. Skin electroporation for transdermal and topical delivery. Adv Drug Deliv Rev. 2004;56(5):659–74.

77. Jadoul A, Bouwstra J, Préat V. Effects of iontophoresis and electroporation on the stratum corneum. Review of the biophysical studies. Adv Drug Deliv Rev. 1999;35(1):89–105.

78. Bolhassani A, Khavari A, Oraf Z. Electroporation – Advantages and Drawbacks for Delivery of Drug, Gene and Vaccine. Appl Nanotechnol Drug Deliv. 2014;

79. Neu WK, Neu JC. Theory of electroporation. Card Bioelectric Ther Mech Pract Implic. 2009;41:133–61.

80. Waghule T, Singhvi G, Dubey SK, Pandey MM, Gupta G, Singh M, et al. Microneedles: A smart approach and increasing potential for transdermal drug delivery system. Biomed Pharmacother [Internet]. 2019;109(July 2018):1249–58. Available from: https://doi.org/10.1016/j.biopha.2018.10.078

81. Liu GS, Kong Y, Wang Y, Luo Y, Fan X, Xie X, et al. Microneedles for transdermal diagnostics: Recent advances and new horizons. Biomaterials. 2020;232.

82. Henry S, McAllister D V., Allen MG, Prausnitz MR. Microfabricated microneedles: A novel approach to transdermal drug delivery. J Pharm Sci. 1998;87(8):922–5.

83. Saraf S, Gupta D, Kaur CD, Saraf S. Microneedles : From Micromachining To Transdermal Drug Delivery. Int J. 2011;1(2):80–7.

84. Sabri AH, Ogilvie J, Abdulhamid K, Shpadaruk V, McKenna J, Segal J, et al. Expanding the applications of microneedles in dermatology. Eur J Pharm Biopharm [Internet]. 2019;140(April):121–40.

85. Lin W, Cormier M, Samiee A, Griffin A, Johnson B, Teng CL, et al. Transdermal delivery of antisense oligonucleotides with microprojection patch (Macroflux®) technology. Pharm Res. 2001;18(12):1789–93.

86. Shah UU, Roberts M, Orlu Gul M, Tuleu C, Beresford MW. Needle-free and microneedle drug delivery in children: A case for disease-modifying antirheumatic drugs (DMARDs). Int J Pharm [Internet]. 2011;416(1):1–11.

87. Prausnitz MR, Avenue A, View M. Microneedle-Based Vaccines Vaccines for Pandemic Influenza. Adeno Assoc Virus Aav Vectors Gene Ther [Internet]. 2009;333(August):1–24.

88. Marshall S, Sahm LJ, Moore AC. The Success of Microneedle-Mediated Vaccine delivery into skin. Hum Vaccines Immunother. 2016;12(11):2975–83.

89. Liu S, Jin MN, Quan YS, Kamiyama F, Katsumi H, Sakane T, et al. The development and characteristics of novel microneedle arrays fabricated from hyaluronic acid, and their application in the transdermal delivery of insulin. J Control Release [Internet]. 2012;161(3):933–41.

90. Benson HAE, Namjoshi S. Proteins and peptides: Strategies for delivery to and across the skin. J Pharm Sci [Internet]. 2008;97(9):3591–610.

91. Webster JG, Zborowski M, Chalmers JJ. Magnetophoresis: Fundamentals and Applications. Wiley Encycl Electr Electron Eng. 2015;1–23.

92. Sensenig R, Sapir Y, MacDonald C, Cohen S, Polyak B. Magnetic nanoparticle-based approaches to locally target therapy and enhance tissue regeneration in vivo. Nanomedicine. 2012;7(9):1425–42.

93. Murthy SN, Sammeta SM, Bowers C. Magnetophoresis for enhancing transdermal drug delivery: Mechanistic studies and patch design. J Control Release [Internet]. 2010;148(2):197–203.

94. Lee S, McAuliffe DJ, Flotte TJ, Kollias N, Doukas AG. Photomechanical transdermal delivery: The effect of laser confinement. Lasers Surg Med. 2001;28(4):344–7.

95. Doukas AG, Kollias N. Transdermal drug delivery with a pressure wave. Adv Drug Deliv Rev. 2004;56(5):559–79.

96. Yoshida M, Kumakura M, Kaetsu I. Drug entrapment for controlled release in radiation-polymerized beads. J Pharm Sci. 1979;68(5):628–31.

97. Kotiyan PN, Vavia PR, Bhardwaj YK, Sabarwal S, Majali AB. Electron beam irradiation: A novel technology for the development of transdermal system of isosorbide dinitrate. Int J Pharm. 2004;270(1–2):47–54.

98. Singhal P, Singhal R, Kumar V, Goel K, Jangra A, Yadav R. Transdermal Drug Delivery System: a Novel Technique To Enhance Therapeutic Efficacy and Safety of Drugs. Am J PharmaTech Res. 2012;2(1):105–25.

99. Khan I, Yousaf S, Subramanian S, Korale O, Alhnan MA, Ahmed W, et al. Proliposome powders prepared using a slurry method for the generation of beclometasone dipropionate liposomes. Int J Pharm [Internet]. 2015;496(2):342–50.

EXCERCISE

MULTIPLE CHOICE QUESTIONS

1. ____________ is a self –contained discrete dosage form, which when applied to the intact skin, will deliver the drug at a controlled rate to the systemic circulation.
   a. Topical
   b. Implantable DDS
   c. Transdermal DDS
   d. Rectal DDS
2. An annual market of TDDS is around _________ billion worldwide.
   a. One b. Two
   c. Three d. Four
3. Transdermal drug delivery system reduces_________
   a. Dosing frequency b. Side effects of drug
   c. Daily doses d. All of the above
4. Surface area of the skin is________
   a. 1 meter square b. 2 meter square
   c. 3 meter square d. 4 meter square
5. The cellular content of the epidermis contains 95% ________
   a. Keratinocytes b. Melanocytes
   c. Langerhans cells d. Merkel cells
6. Skin appendages includes_________
   a. Sweat glands b. Hair follicles
   c. Sebaceous glands d. All of the above
7. Barrier properties of ___________ may be partly related to its very high density (1.4 g/cm^3 in the dry state) and its low hydration of 15%-20%.
   a. Stratum Lucidum b. Stratum Corneum
   c. Stratum Spinosum d. Stratum Granulosum
8. In transdermal permeation of drug, intercellular transport means
   a. Across lipid matrix b. Across keratinized cells
   c. Across hair follicles d. None of the above
9. In transdermal permeation of drug, intercellular transport means
   a. Across lipid matrix b. Across keratinized cells
   c. Across hair follicles d. None of the above

10. In TDDS, non polar drugs absorbed by_________ transport.
    a. Transappendageal
    b. Intracellular
    c. Intercellular
    d. None of the above
11. In TDDS, water soluble drugs are diffused through________ route
    a. Transappendageal
    b. Intracellular
    c. Intercellular
    d. None of the above
12. Lipophilic drug cumulates into _________ and acts as a depot from which drug is being released after detachment of patch
    a. Hypodermis
    b. Dermis
    c. Viable epidermis
    d. Stratum Corneum
13. The________ on the skin surface acts as a protective layer to prevent the removal of moisture from the skin and helps in maintaining the barrier function of stratum Corneum
    a. Water
    b. Lipid film
    c. Skin shedding
    d. None of the above
14. Which of the following excipients used for the hydration of skin
    a. Ethanol
    b. Methanol
    c. Humectants
    d. None of the above
15. Which of the following semisynthetic polymer used for the preparation of polymer matrix/reservoir
    a. HPMC
    b. Cellulose
    c. Zein
    d. PVA
16. __________ seals the backing to form a pocket to enclose the drug containing matrix or used as a single layer in the patch construction.
    a. Polymer matrix
    b. Polymer reservoir
    c. Rate controlling membrane
    d. Backing laminate
17. Transdermal permeation pathways for permeation enhancer________
    a. Polar
    b. Non-polar
    c. Polar/Non polar
    d. All of the above
18. Permeation enhancer acts by_________mechanism(s).
    a. Interaction with lipids
    b. Interaction with proteins
    c. Altering solvent nature of stratum Corneum
    d. All of the above

19. Which of the following membrane is used for appearance and flexibility
    a. Pressure sensitive adhesive
    b. Backing laminates
    c. Polymer matrix/reservoir
    d. Rate controlling membrane
20. Thickness of rate controlling membrane varies from___________
    a. 1-5 mm
    b. 1-7 mm
    b. 2-7 mm
    d. 2-9 mm

SHORT ANSWER QUESTIONS

1. What are the components of transdermal drug delivery systems?
2. Discuss in detail about methods to enhance drug permeation through transdermal route.
3. What do you understand by iontophoresis and how it enchance the penetration?
4. Write a note on adhesive dispersion system.
5. What are the Penetration enhancers? Give its examples.
6. What do you understand by fick's law of diffusion?
7. Evaluation of transdermal patches.
8. What are different pathways for drug penetration?
9. Permeature enhancement methods for transdermal permeation
10. Give the principle which affect skin also discuss the factors of drug absorption.

LONG ANSWER QUESTIONS

1. Enumerate the characteristics of drugs to be formulated as Transdermal Drug Delivery System.
2. Explain formulation and evaluation in detail of transdermal DDS.
3. Describe in detail the formulation aspects of transdermal DDS.
4. Write a note on evaluation tests of transdermal DDS.
5. Discuss about the physicochemical properties that affect the transdermal drug delivery.
6. Explain the various types of transdermal patches.
7. Define Transdermal drug delivery system (TDDS)? Describe various basic components of TDDS.
8. Enumerate about the techniques used for enhancing active penetration.

9. Discuss about the different preparation methods of TDDS.
10. Write a note on electroporation and microneedles.

MCQ ANSWERS

1. (c)	2. (b)	3. (d)	4. (b)
5. (a)	6. (d)	7. (b)	8. (a)
9. (b)	10. (c)	11. (a)	12. (d)
13. (b)	14. (c)	15. (a)	16. (c)
17. (d)	18. (d)	19. (b)	20. (c)

CHAPTER - 9

Protein and Pepide Delivery

Dr. Vishal Jain, Dr. Bina Gidwanim, Dr. Sanjib Bahadur and Dr. Kapil Agrawal

Introduction, Barriers to Peptide and Protein Delivery, Strategies for Protein Formulation, Evaluation, Depo-Foam Technology, Conclusion

INTRODUCTION

Protein and peptide delivery is one of the innovative strategies for drug delivery. Currently, successful delivery of protein and peptide drugs is becoming increasingly essential as biotechnology companies grow and started marketing their products[1]. That results in designing as well as research for novel means of protein and peptide drug delivery[2].

The most widely distributed component in the natural world & biological cells are protein and peptides. It functions as enzymes, hormones, structural components, and immunoglobulin. It also plays an active role in several biological activities, as well as in different metabolic processes and immunogenic protection. Berzelius first uses the word protein, originates from the Greek word "proteios" which means holding the first position[3]. The proteins mainly consist of one or more chains of polypeptides, and each polypeptide chain comprises of smaller units called amino acids. Proteins with high molecular weight comprise carbon, oxygen, sulphur, and nitrogen molecules. Proteins are molecules that are bound together by the covenant link called peptide bonds that have amino acids in the linear chain[4].

A short amino acid chain is a peptide which is the result of a condensation product of alpha-amino acids. When the carboxyl group of amino acids reacts to the amino acid group of another group, covalent chemical bonds are formed. In a peptide, the amino acids are bound to each other in a chain by the bond called peptide bonds[4]. Dipeptides are the shortest peptides formed when two amino acids attached by a single peptide bond, further by increasing the number of amino acids tripeptides, tetrapeptides etc. formed. The long, repeated, & unbranched peptide chain is a polypeptide[2, 5,6].

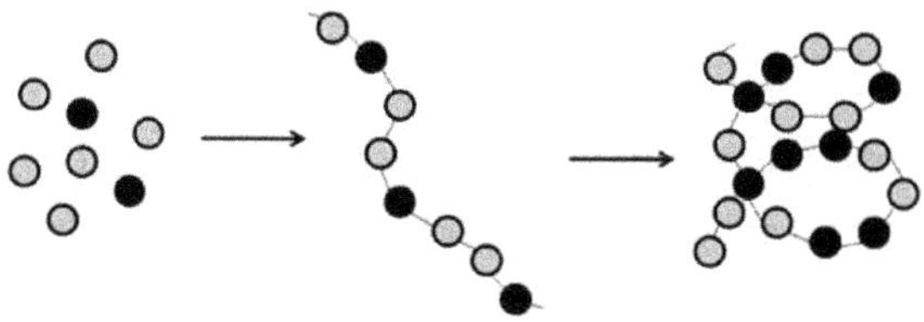

Fig.9.1 Diagrammatic representation of formation of Protein through amino acids.

The Necessity of the Protein and Peptide Drug Delivery System[5,7]

1. Proteins and peptides in organic molecules and biological cells are extremely essential.
2. Diabetes mellitus like disorders are caused due to insufficiency of protein and peptides.
3. Currently, R-DNA Technology, as well as hybridoma methods, is also involved in pharmaceuticals based on proteins and peptides.

The Role of the Protein and Peptide[8,9]

1. Transport of small molecules and biological molecules and their storage.
2. Coordinated activity through contraction of muscles.
3. The Regulation of hormone growth and differentiation.
4. Protection of the immune system via antibodies.
5. Nerve impulse generation and transmission.
6. The Fibrous protein support mechanically.
7. In biochemical reactions, enzymatic catalysis.

Benefits of the Protein and Peptide Drug Delivery System[10,5,9]

1. Erythropoietin is used primarily to producered blood cells.
2. For controlling the labor pain, oxytocin was a need.
3. Bradykinin enhances circulation in the periphery.
4. Insulin regulates the level of blood sugar.
5. The plasminogen activator of protein tissue is required for cardiac arrest, stroke.
6. Gastric ulcer bleeding is reduced by somatostatin.
7. The use of gonadotropin stimulates ovulation.

Challenges of the Protein and Peptide Drug Delivery System[11,9]

1. Quite large molecules and unstable ones[12].

2. By gastric juices & slightly mild storage conditions can quickly be destroyed[13].
3. Quickly eliminated/degraded by the body[14].
4. Difficult to procure in large quantities.

Properties of Protein and Peptide

Protein is water-soluble which can form a colloidal water solution. Protein and peptide are stable both physicochemically and metabolically. During the formulation of oral administration, multiple properties can affect the absorption rate of peptides and protein-drug-supply systems including particle size and molecular weight, solubility and lipophilicity, aggregation and hydrogen-bonding of active ingredients, metabolic breakdown by interacting with digestive enzymes and decreased membrane penetrability, conformational studies and three-dimensional space stereo specifications, immunological properties of drug molecules[15].

Routes of Administrations

Proteins and peptides for the oral administration of small therapeutic agents are negatively suited especially due to the enzymatic and gastrointestinal tract absorption barriers; hence, parenterally, subcutaneous or intramuscular injections are used for all protein/peptide drugs[16]. This route provides significant benefits such as quick and maximum absorption, avoids metabolism first-pass, in order to deliver protein and peptide these routes itself face difficulties such as poor patient compliance, the associated pain and discomfort and also it is an unsafe way to handle children[11,8,17]. The half-life of these parenterally administered medications is, however, is generally just a few hours, requiring more than one injection a week for the medicinal effect. Consequently, the rate of compliance for parenterally delivered medications is usually lower than those for oral dosage forms[18]. One approach to improve compliance and eliminate the discomfort of repeated injections is by the use and sustained release of the drug proteins and peptides with advanced parenteral delivery systems[19]. These benefits can also be obtained immediately or sustained delivery by non-parenteral routes such as the buccal[20], pulmonary[21], nasal, rectal[22], vaginal route[23,24] and in certain situations transdermal route via the bloodstream. Thus, for an essential aspect of the treatment of numerous diseases and disorders, advanced biopharmaceuticals started novel designing and delivering[21].

To face the challenges of protein and peptide delivery, a variety of strategies were also explored. One strategy involves the parenteral release of the medication in a controlled or continuous manner. For a well-defined pharmacokinetic profile to be achieved, controlled delivery requires the addition of one or more components to regulate the release of an active substance from the pharmaceutical formulations. The ability to modify the compound of the pharmaceutical formulations for having a specific releasing pattern is a significant benefit of controlled release formulations over traditional dosing types. One clear example is the prolonged delivery of synthetic analogues of gonadotropin in which a continuous drug serum concentration is potentially sufficient for therapeutic gain. A second important approach to delivery generally includes employing non-parenteral routes to release them immediately or continuously[25]. There are a wide variety of dosage formulations for the administration of conventional drug products i.e. small molecules drugs through non-parenteral routes. All non-parenteral routes of delivery, each has its significant benefits and drawbacks, depending on the site physiology. Special aspects must be considered when designing protein formulations for the development of proteins dosage forms via any of these pathways. The fragility and the need for effective processing and formulation methods to preserve the structure of proteins and achieve desirable release qualities is one of the primary reasons for the failure of new protein formulations[21,5,9].

Fig.9.2 Primary protein structure.

Structure of Protein[3]

The structure of protein divided in to four types

1. **Primary structure**

   The fundamental level of protein structure, the primary structure, is basically the polypeptide chain sequence of amino acids. For example, the insulin hormone contains two chains of polypeptides, A and B. (The insulin molecule here is cow insulin, but its composition is identical to human insulin). Each chain has its collection of amino acids, which formed in a specific order. For context, the sequencing of the A chain begins with glycine at the N-terminus and comes to an end with asparagine at the C-terminus, and is clearly distinct from the sequencing of the B chain.

Fig.9.3 Secondary protein structure.

2. **Secondary structure**

   The next phase of protein structure, secondary structure, means local folded structures that form in a polypeptide resulting from interactions among atoms of the backbone. (The backbone applies only to the polypeptide chain besides the R groups – so all we imply here is that the secondary structure does not include the R group atoms). The most widely known kind of secondary structures is α helix and the β pleated sheet. All these structures were formed by hydrogen bonds that form between the carbonyl O of one amino acid and the amino H of another.

3. **Tertiary structure**

   A polypeptide's three-dimensional structure is its tertiary structure. The tertiary structure possibly has to do with the relations that build up the protein between the amino acid R groups. R group interactions related to the tertiary system include hydrogen bonding, dipole-dipole interactions, ionic bonding, and dispersion forces in London – basically the entire spectrum of not-covalent bonds.

   This is a particular form of covalent bond that will support to the tertiary structure: the disulfide bond. Disulphide bonds are much stronger than other types of bond that lead to the tertiary structure than the sulfur-containing side chains of the cysteines. The polypeptide sections hold closely together, and are used as molecular "safety pins,"

4. **Quaternary structure**

   Many other proteins comprise of several chains of polypeptides also called subunits. When they unite, they give a quaternary structure for that protein. Haemoglobin: an example of a quaternary protein. Haemoglobin carries blood oxygen & consists of 4 subunits, 2 α and β, each.

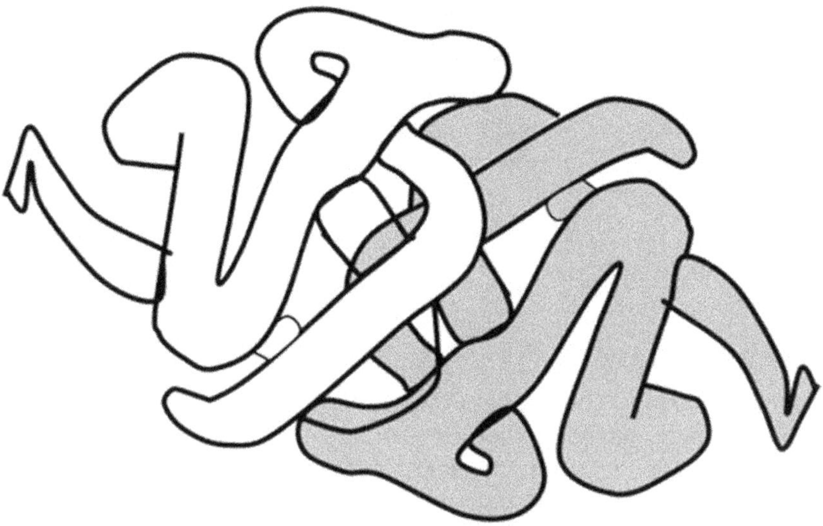

Fig.9.4 Quaternary Protein Structure.

The same interactions (mostly weak interactions such as London dispersion forces and hydrogen bonding) that lead to a tertiary structure also combine the subunits to create a quaternary structure.

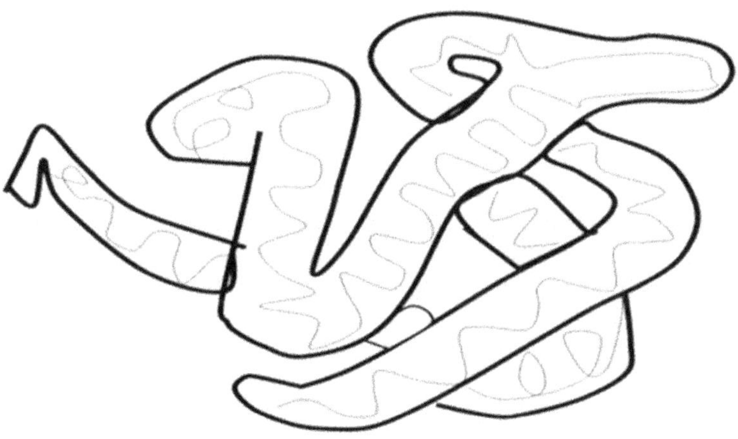

Fig.9.5 Tertiary Protein Structure.

Classification of Proteins[3,9]

Proteins are categorized according to their composition, structure and function.

Table 9.1 Classification of protein.

A) Based on Structure	B) Based on Composition	C) Based on Function
• Fibrous proteins • Globular proteins	• Simple Proteins • Conjugated Proteins	• Structural proteins, enzymes, hormones • Pigments, transport protein, contractile proteins • Storage proteins, toxins

A) Based on Structure

- Fibrous protein: The chains of the polypeptides are long and helically wound around an axis. They can be extracellular, are insoluble in water and act as a defensive factor Example - α keratin hair, silk fibroin, tendon collagen, skin elastin. Myosin and tropomyosin muscle cells may also be intracellular.
- Globular proteins: They are spherical and much more complex than the fibrous protein, but their biological processes are much more diverse.

They can serve roles as:

- Cell Adhesion Protein, Receptors, Carrier, Ion Channel.
- They can be soluble & plasma-like, albumin, protein hormones like LH, cytosolic proteins that circulate proteins like calmodulin.

B) Based on Composition

- *Simple Proteins or holoproteins*: These are of the globular form except for fibrous i.e, scleroproteins. This group comprises proteins which are structural components of amino acids only. These liberate the component amino acids when decomposed with acids. Examples - Protamines and histones, Albumins, Globulins, Glutelins, Prolamines, Scleroproteins or Albuminoids.
- *Conjugated Protein*: These are the proteins bound to a non-protein component known as a prosthetic group. The prosthetic category may be a metal or a compound. These release the constituent amino acids as well as the prosthetic group when decomposed with acids. For example, Chromoproteins, glycoproteins, phosphoproteins, and nucleo-proteins. (The terms chromoproteids, metalloproteids, etc., are often used instead of metalloproteins, chromoproteins, etc.)

C) Based on Function

- **Structure & support:** elastin, collagen, the membrane of glycoproteins.
- **The contraction:** myosin, actin.

- **Proteins for cell adhesion:** GAP junctions and proteins, including cadherin.
- **The reception signal:** insulin membrane receptors or steroid receptors.
- **A signal:** The molecule as growth factors (EGF) and follicular stimulating hormones can be helpful (FSH)
- **The immunity:** the function of immunoglobulin.
- **The Transportation:** for example hemoglobin (O_2) and transferrin (iron).
- **The Catalysis** - this is because proteins also play a part in metabolism, DNA transcript and replication, muscle contracture, cell signaling.

Protein and Peptide Stability Issues[26]

Due to the challenging nature of proteins and peptides, the processes involved in manufacturing-controlled drugs can damage the proteins, thereby reducing their biological activities or make the protein immunogenic.

Protein stabilization techniques are more challenging in sustainable delivery systems than those in the solution for protein for many reasons. First, the matrix the manufacturing process must withstand the protein. It must also continue to be biologically active for a longer period *in vivo* in the feed system where the protein can be exposed to the degradation conditions of pH, temperature, and concentration. In general, one of the main obstacles in putting these drugs on the market is to resolve the tendency for proteins to withstand degradation processes during its utilization in and after the injection into the body waiting for release. The processes of degradation and the effects of protein stability on biological activities should be understood, and formulation strategies developed for maintaining protein stability are therefore significant. An outline of protein degradation pathways and explores issues related to the stability of protein products manufactured and delivered in sustained-release systems. Based on this information, a variety of formulation approaches are proposed to develop reliable formulations for delivery systems[27].

Pathways of Protein Degradation[26,28]

The mechanisms for degradation of proteins can be divided into two categories, physical and chemical. Chemical degradation contributes to changes in the primary structure of the protein. When physically degraded, the protein's native structure can be altered by the changes in its higher-order structure, i.e., environmental conditions like pH, concentration, temperatures and the proximity of surfaces or chemically reactive groups can promote degradation.

1. Physical Instabilities

When physically degraded, the protein's native structure can be altered by the changes in its higher-order structure, i.e., environmental conditions like pH, concentration, temperatures and the proximity of surfaces or chemically reactive groups can promote degradation. In globular Protein's case, the hydrophobic residue is concealed in the interior and the hydrophilic residues. It interacts with the aqueous solvents. Protein molecules denaturation represents a loss or damaging of the globular protein molecular structure leads to the unfolding of the protein. Physical denaturation is often affected by changes in protein molecules' environment conditions like the pH, temperature, application of hydrophobic surfaces or by the addition of organic solvents to interfaces[29, 28,30].

2. Chemical Instabilities

Following four types of reactions, the chemical instability of protein and peptide will result.

1. Oxidation
2. Deamination
3. Hydrolysis of peptide bond
4. Exchange of disulphide

i. Oxidation

The oxidation of proteins and peptide molecules is the most common chemical instabilities. The amino acid side chain of a protein or peptide is prone to oxidation, the oxidation occurs through oxygen molecule in the atmosphere, different forms of ions such as copper or iron, many reagents like peroxides of hydrogen.

Example-In acidic conditions, the methionine residues are most likely to be oxidized with reagents such as hydrogen peroxide which produces methionine sulfoxide.

ii. Deamination

The hydrolysis of the amide side chain results in this kind of instability some residue of amino acids primarily includes Glutamine and asparagine, this is known as Deamination. Some conditions such as temperature variations and pH are generally seen as facilitated by biological therapeutic protein and peptides deamination process.

iii. Hydrolysis of peptide bond

Hydrolysis of the peptide bond process heats the aspartic acid residues at 90-1000 C, in pH 4 (acetate), and the loss of biological activity results from the hydrolysis of asp-X bands.

iv. **Exchange of disulphide**

Cysteine residues resulting from disulfide bonds contained in therapeutic proteins. These created bonds signify essential elements of the protein structural integrity. The inappropriate link of peptide bonds refers to alterations in the three-dimensional structure and biological activity of the protein molecules[31,26].

BARRIERS TO PEPTIDE AND PROTEIN DELIVERY[31]

Energy Barriers

There are primarily two methods by which enzymatic degradation occurs:

1. Hydrolytic break age of peptide bonds by enzymes such renin, angiotensin-converting enzymes, and insulin-degrading enzyme. Since proteolysis is an irreversible event, it could potentially harm peptide and protein drugs.
2. Chemical alteration of proteins, such as glucose oxidase, xanthine oxidase, or phosphorylation by kinases. It restricts protein medication absorption from the GI tract.

Barrier Intestinal Epithelial

Acts as a barrier to the passage of protein – containing medications over the intestinal epithelium. The transport of peptide and protein medicines over the intestinal epithelium is facilitated by a number of mechanisms, including-

A. Transport that is passive and carrier-mediated

B. Transcytosis and Endocytosis

C. Paracellular Motion.

A. Transport that is passive and carrier-mediated:

The primary mechanism appears to be active transport explains the large amount of di-and tripeptides absorbed from the small intestine

B. Transcytosis as well as endocytosis

The process of endocytosis allows for the cellular internalisation of peptides and proteins that are too big to be taken up via carrier-mediated transport. The Various Endocytosis Pathways Eating), involve cell pinocytosis (phagocytosis) (celldrinking)

C. Paracellular motion

The movement of medicines across the GI epithelial cells' junction. There are two mechanisms for medication absorption:

1. Permeation through epithelial cells' tight junctions (insulin)
2. Persorption The epithelial mucosa of the small intestine acts as a barrier against the penetration of macromolecules.

Endothelial Capillary Barrier

Peptides and proteins must either go via the spaces between the cells or, alternatively, traverse the endothelial cells themselves in order to cross the capillary endothelium. Cytoplasmic enzymes may modify or metabolise solutes that cross the endothelial cell membrane. Therefore, the endothelial passage presents an enzymatic or metabolic barrier to the passage of the solution.

Brain Blood Barrier (BBB)

A significant barrier to the transport of proteins to the brain compartment is the blood-brain barrier (BBB). There are various barriers, including the two that are the blood-brain barrier (BBB) and the blood-cerebrospinal fluid (blood-CSF) barrier that are well described.

The BBB is made up of a monolayer of cells at both locations, held together by tight junctions and equipped with additional mechanisms that preventors low the leaking of plasma into the CNS permits the passage of tiny, lipophilic, neutral gases and molecules. Proteins and otherlarge molecules have difficulty crossing the BBB.

STRATEGIES FOR PROTEIN FORMULATION[27]

The protein and the peptides have the following strategies.

1. Chemical Modification
2. Enzyme Inhibitors
3. Penetration Enhancers
4. Formulation Vehicle

1. Chemical Modification[32]

The chemical modification of peptide and protein drugs promotes their stability in enzymes and/or membrane penetration of peptides and proteins. It can also be preferred to minimize immunogenicity. The chemical modifications can be done in two different ways.

a. Amino acids Modifications
b. Hydrophobization

a. Amino acids Modifications

Modifications in the distinct amino acids, along with the substitution of another L-Amino acid with D-Amino Acids will alter the physiological properties significantly. Example: The two essential analogues of vasopressin are desmopressin and deaminovasospressin, formerly, deamination of first amino acid and last L-arginine D-arginine replacement to give Deaminovasopressin.

b. **Hydrophobization**

Increasing peptide or protein hydrophobicity by surface modification using lipophilic moieties can be beneficial to passive and active transcellular absorption through membrane penetration or bonding; or it can simply help increase protein stability. Palmitoylation is an example of hydrophobization to increase insulin lipophilicity. To facilitate the transfer of insulin across mucosal membranes in the large intestines, the Insulin molecule-conjugation with 1-3- dipalmitoyl-glycerol containing free amino acid glycine, phenylalanine, lysine to from Mono and dipalmitoyl insulin. Stability against enzyme degradation is necessary to improve.

2. **Enzyme Inhibitors**

The inhibitors of the enzyme (protease) are an enzymatic strategy of the delivery systems of protein and peptides. GIT and liver play an essential role in the metabolism of protein and Peptides, with the help of the variety of proteolytic Enzymes into smaller fragments of the two to ten amino acids. The CO- administered protein and peptide inhibitors of this Protease alter the atmosphere to suppress proteolytic activity for enzyme stability. The four types of enzyme protease inhibitors are Aspartic Proteases (Pepsin, Rennin), Cystinyl Proteases (Papain, Endopeptidase), Serinyl Proteases (Thrombin, Trypsin), and Metallo Proteases (Carboxy-peptidase)[33].

3. **Penetration Enhancers**

The formulation ingredients which temporarily punctuate the intestinal barrier increase the permeation of these drugs are penetration enhancers. As permeation enhancers most used groups of compounds include Surfactants (Polysorbate, SLS, Pluronic F-68), EDTA, Sodium carprate (fatty acids), Mucoadhesive polymeric systems (Thiomers, Cellulose derivatives), Phospholipids (PC). The principal process for enhancing penetration is that the compounds for detergents and surfactants improve the transport of the drug substances to interfere more efficiently with the structure of the lipid bilayer membrane. Another mechanism is that calcium chelates work on the complex formation of the calcium ions and moves through the tight junctions of the hydrophilic drug substance and make it simpler for Paracellular transport[34].

4. **Formulation Vehicle**

The Protein and Peptide Drug Delivery System is essential for the oral Delivery of Protein and Peptides can be effectively accomplished using different carrier systems.

a. Dry emulsion

b. Microspheres

c. Liposomes

d. Nanoparticles

a. Dry emulsion

It is essential to use multiple emulsions in drug delivery systems to prevent the instability of long-term storage. A new technique in which dry emulsions replaces the multiple emulsions. The Spray Drying, Evaporation and Lyophilization Techniques prepare the dry emulsion. The application of PH sensitive polymers such as HPMC in dry emulsion preparation is essential for the enteric-coated and site-specific emulsions[35, 36].

b. Microspheres

Microspheres are defined as the uniform distribution of drugs in oral drug delivery in the drug Protein and peptides. The pH-sensitive microspheres are generally used to protect the stomach against proteolytic degradation in oral delivery and protect the upper part of the small intestine from proteolytic degradation[35, 37].

c. Liposomes

Liposomes are tiny microscopic vesicles where the aqueous volume is surrounded by lipid molecules made up of the membrane. Insulin encapsulation with the sugar chain portion of mucin and PEG significantly prevented the degradation of insulin molecules in intestinal fluid via liposomes in the drug delivery system. The uncoated liposome type is suppressed by partially surface coating of the liposome molecules in PEG or mucin, which has acquired resistance to salt digestion and improved GI tract stability[39-41].

d. Nanoparticles

The colloidal structure of nano-sized nanoparticles is 10-1000 nm in size. The particles are absorbed without getting disturbed by the intestinal epithelium in the nanometric size range of the particles and are less susceptible to enzymatic degradation. The surface charges of particle sizes affect the absorption of the nanoparticle system in the GI tract[42, 43].

Techniques for formulating polymeric delivery system[26]

In the Protein and Peptide drug delivery system, the incorporation of drugs is subject to three techniques as follows.

1. Emulsification
2. Coacervation
3. Extrusion and spray drying

1. Emulsification

Water-soluble drugs are first dissolved in an aqueous solution (water solution) in this process and then solubilized in an organic solvent. With the required proportion to generate w/o emulsion, the two solutions are mixed.

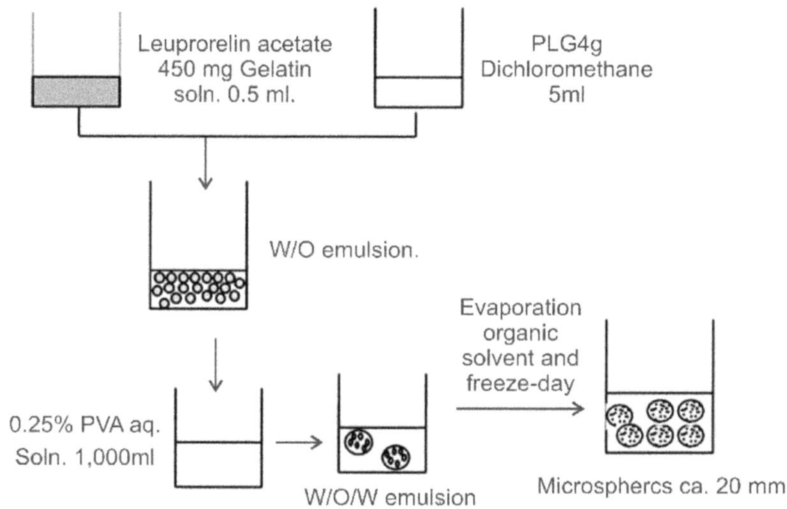

Fig.9.6 A Diagrammatic representation of Double emulsion method used for lupron depot manufacture.

This primary emulsion formulated is emulsified into an aqueous solution that included an emulsifier to create the emulsion w/o/w. Finally, by evaporating the solvent under minimal filtration pressure and raising the temperature, the organic solvent is gradually eliminated from the emulsion.

Double emulsion method is used for Lupron Depot Manufacture. The primary emulsion comprises of leuprorelin acetate dispersed in a solution of PLG in methylene chloride in an aqueous solution which contains gelatin. A solution of poly (vinyl alcohol) (surfactant and stabilizer) then emulsifies the water-in-oil emulsion (surfactant and stabilizer). The microspheres are formulated by methylene chloride evaporation, which is the continuous step of the primary emulsion.

2. Coacervation

In the case of simple coacervation, a protein-containing hydrocolloid was dissolved by the addition of another material (such as salt or alcohol) competing for a solvent due to its higher hydrophilicity, solubility, or concentration. The charge of the hydrocolloid is opposite to that of the competing material in complex coacervation[44-47]

Development of PLG microspheres using coacervation process is shown in figure 9.8 Silicone oil is a methylene chloride non-solvent; the primary emulsion can therefore be emulsified in silicone oil to obtain an emulsion of water-in-oil (methylene chloride)-in oil (silicone oil). The microspheres are developed from the primary emulsion droplets by extracting methylene chloride. This is accomplished by the addition of heptane, that is a methylene chloride solvent but a silicone oil non-solvent.

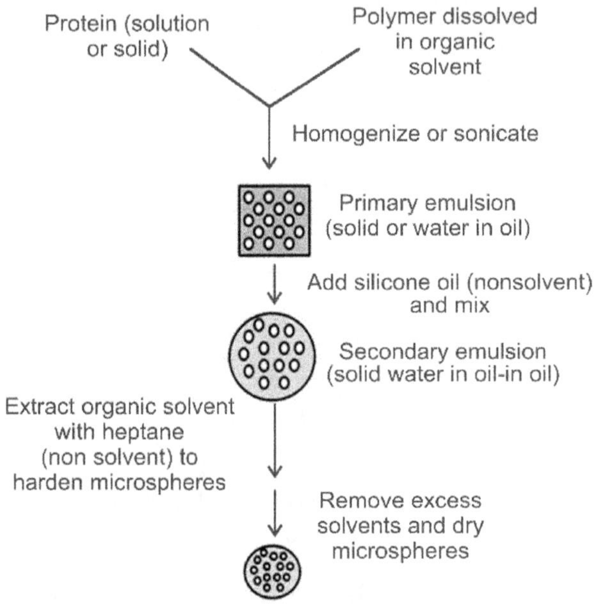

Fig.9.7 A Diagrammatic representation for development of PLG microspheres using coacervation process.

3. Extrusion and spray drying

The extrusion and spraying method are used to formulate microspheres and is primarily expelled from the orifice of fine tubes, syringe, or nozzles to microdroplets by the core material or matrix including drug, incorporated as a solution and the particulate. The size of the droplet depends primarily on the qualities of the liquid (Melt, solution, and suspension) and the diameter of the orifice to jet velocity[48-52].

Development of Prolease microsphere using Spray Drying Method is described in figure 9.9. First the solution of the PLG polymer, the protein formulation lyophilized is dispersed and then atomized into a vessel comprising frozen ethanol layered with the liquid nitrogen. As they pass through the cold nitrogen gas and liquid nitrogen, the droplets freeze and finally settle on the surface of the bed of frozen ethanol. When this ethanol melts, the methylene chloride (which is ethanol-mixable) was removed and the microspheres hardened[53].

EVALUATION[53]

Stability testing

The capacity of a certain formulation to maintain its physical, chemical, microbiological, toxicological, and protective specifications in a specific container or closure system. Evaluates the impact of environmental elements on a pharmacological substance's or a formulated product's quality in order to forecast its shelf life and determine the best conditions for storage.

Bioassay

Because proteins are complicated, bioassays are necessary to evaluate the formulation's efficacy. There are two types of bioassays: *in-vitro* and *in-vivo*. *In vitro* bioassays track the way that cells react to hormones and growth factors. The pharmacological reaction of animals to proteins is observed in *in vivo* bioassays. During instance, post-injection BSL in rabbits is measured for an insulin bioassay. UV spectroscopy can be used to identify proteins that contain aromatic amino acid residues like phenylalanine, tyrosine, and tryptophan. It is a method for analytical determination

Braford

This test is based on the idea that the coomassie brilliant blue G-250 dye's maximal absorptionalters when protein sarepresentinan acidic solution. The solution remains brown if there is no protein to bind to By usingVanderWaals forces, the dye forms a compound with the carboxyl terminus of proteins to create a blue-colored solution. A spectrophotometer can be used to measure the colour of the coloured solution and calculate the amount of protein present in the sample used as a method for examining temperature-dependent conformational changes and, more crucially, the impact of conceivable stabilising excipients in protein solutions. Used as a method for examining temperature-dependent conformational changes and, more crucially, the impact of conceivable stabilising excipients in protein solutions.

Chromatography

To study stability of proteins and peptides. Various modes used are

1. Normal Phase HPLC
2. Reverse Phase HPLC
3. Ion Exchange
4. Chromato-focusing.

Electrophoresis

Utilised SDS-PAGE, or sodium dodecylsulphate polyacrylamide gel electrophoresis. Boiling in the SDS solution causes proteins to become denatured. The negative charge of dodecyl Sulphate masks all charges on proteins. As a result, protein only moves on polyacrylamide gel based on the size of the protein molecule. This method can be used to calculate the Molecular weight of proteins. Silver nitrate and coomassie brilliant blue dye are the chemicals used to see the proteins on the gel.

Applications[5]

1. **Protein & peptides of CVS Acting Drugs**

   (Angiotensin 2 antagonist, Bradykinin, Captopril) is essential for the treatment of heart failure that lowers blood pressure and improves peripheral circulation[54].

2. **Active proteins and peptides in the CNS**

   (B-endorphin, Cholecystokinin) is necessary for appetite suppression and pain relief[55].

3. **GI-active Peptide and Protein**

   It is essential for the reduction of gastric acid secretion and digestive supplements. (pancreatic enzymes, Gastrin antagonist)[56]

4. **Protein and Peptide Immunomodulation**

   Peptides and peptides (Bursin, Cyclosporin, and Interferon) can act as immunomodulating agents either by inhibiting the immune system response or producing tolerance by stimulating the immune response[57].

5. **Protein and peptide regulation of metabolism**

   Vasopressin, Insulin is essential for the prevention and treatment of diabetes insipidus and diabetes mellitus[58,59].

Recent advances

PEGylation

PEGylation is a growing advancement in the delivery systems of protein and peptide drugs[60]. PEGylation is a method of linking the polymer PEG strands to most common fragments of peptides which can help resolve the protein and the obstacles of enhancing the purity and effectiveness of several therapeutic macromolecules such as peptides and proteins[61]. It is commonly used for protein and peptide modification, antibody fragments, & oligonucleotides. PEG is non-immunogenic and non-toxic, has defined hydrophilicity, and is highly versatile[62]. To increase bioavailability, PEGylation is vital, it applies to optimized pharmacokinetics, which is essential to prevent immunogenicity and for decreasing the frequency of administration. PEGylation is an effective mechanism to increase the molecular weight of the molecules, to increase the solubility of the drug and to protect against proteolytic degradation, to reduce the dosing frequency and to improve therapeutic activity[63].

Table 9.2 Marketed Preparation of PEGylation.

PEGylated Interferon alpha-2a	In Hepatitis B treatment
PEGylated Interferon alpha-2b	In Hepatitis A treatment
PEGylated liposome containing doxorubicin	In Cancer treatment

Depo-Foam TECHNOLOGY

Through IV or SC, therapeutic peptides and proteins are frequently delivered too rapidly for circulation and need to be administered to maintain their therapeutic blood level in the constant order of administration. Different kinds of liposomal formulations have been used as drug delivery carriers for the continuous release of proteins and peptides such as unilamellar or multilamellar vesicular systems, but some multilamellar liposomes were referred to as DepoFoam particles[64]. The DepoFoam technology can accommodate high drug loading and high drug material recovery, also has high efficiency of encapsulation, and is an important form of technique for the continuous delivery of macromolecular drugs. A distinctive feature of the DepoFoam system is that discontinuous internal aqueous chambers, enclosed by a continuous network of lipid membranes, produce a higher hydrophilic volume to lipid proportion and a much larger particle diameter than SUV's or MLV's within each DepoFoam particle[65,66].

Table 9.3 Marketed Preparation of DepoFoam technology.

Product	Formulation	Route	Indication
Acthar	Corticotropin	i.m, i.v, s.c.	Hormone Deficiency
Elspar	Asparginase	i.m, i.v.	Leukemia
Glucagon	Glucagon	i.m , i.v, s.c	Hypoglycemia
Pergonal	FSH and LH	i.m	Infertility
Metrodin	FSH 75 IU	i.m	Induction of ovulation

Some formulations of peptides and proteins marketed for sustained release[26]

Lupron Depot

Lupron Depot®, a sustained release formulation of leuprorelin acetate (Des-Gly-(d-Leu)-LH-RH ethyl amide acetate), was one of the first sustained-delivery products for peptides on the market. Leuprorelin acetate is a super agonist of LH-RH with a biological activity 10 times higher than that of native LH-RH. Depending on the dosage delivered the effects of LH-RH and its analogues on the gonads vary[67]. At acute concentrations, peptides enhance the pituitary glands production of gonadotropin and sex hormone production in the genitals. Okada explains the delivery issues related to oral and transmucosal (vaginal, nasal, and rectal). The issue was ineffective uptake and hence low bioavailability, that for transmucosal pathways varied from <0.1 to 1-5 %[68]. The bioavailability for nasal and vaginal delivery has increased to 5-10% in the involvement of absorption enhancers. Sustained doses of the hormone were found to have a greater castrating effect, indicating that therapeutic benefits could be provided by sustained-release preparations[69].

De-Capeptyl ® SR

A long-acting preparation of triptorelin, another LH-RH agonist, is De-capeptyl® SR. Triptorelin is the decapeptide that works like leuprorelin in a way. The preparation includes microspheres, along with mannitol, polysorbate 80, & carboxymethyl cellulose sodium, produced from this lactide-glycolide copolymer. The composition is reformulated for injection by using the vehicle that contains mannitol in water. It is necessary to deliver injections every 4 weeks, typically in the buttocks.

Posilac ®

The anterior pituitary gland secretes bovine somatotropin (bST), or bovine growth hormone, which has growth-stimulating activity by directly stimulating the receptors or by mediators like IGF-I. Posilac® is a recombinant bST, sometribove, sustained-release preparation and is developed by Monsanto to improve the production of milk in dairy cattle. The composition consists of zinc-complexed protein and an aluminium stearate (5 %w/w) oily base. The solid Zn-bST was dispersed in an aluminium stearate and sesame oil hydrophobic gel (semisolid at ambient temperature) matrix. Usually, oil-based formulations include vegetable oil, like sesame oil, a viscosity providing agent, and an anti-hydration agent. For drug particle stability and injectability, increased viscosity is needed, and the anti-hydration agent is needed to minimize the protein's moisture-induced degradation.

Other Macromolecule

A range of biological macromolecule-based drug release carriers has been described in recent years in a variety of dosage forms, including injectables, tablets, capsules, gels, hydrogels, beads, microparticles, nanoparticles, patches and films, fibers, liposomes, transferosomes, scaffolds, etc. The pharmacokinetics of loaded pharmaceuticals is improved by the use of biological macromolecule-based drug release carriers, which also have lower systemic toxicity and immunogenicity[70]. Synthetic fabrics like nylon, rayon, and spandex are prime examples of macromolecules, as are DNA, which is a genetic substance that comprises nucleic acids. The DNA is broken up during meiosis, and the nucleotides that are left are in charge of transmitting the genetic information to the gametes[71]. Certain other macromolecules, including mucins, can be utilized in maintaining the homeostasis of the airway surface liquid (ASL). ASL contains more than 130 proteins, including mucin glycoproteins, which are essential to the process in both the mucus and periciliary layer (PCL) gel phases[72]. L-amino acid oxidases, lysostaphin, metallo—lactamase-like lactonase, and chitosan are a few examples of macromolecules[73].

CONCLUSION

In the 1970s, sustained release of polymer peptides and proteins was first reported, that was feasible, and substantial progress occurred in this field. In today's world, tremendous advances have occurred with consideration to the suite of concepts and strategies involved in delivering peptides or proteins through the oral route. Several Sustained release formulations of peptides and proteins are now on or close to the market. The goal of this study was to understand the problems related to the preparation and development of the delivery system for protein and peptide drugs. The major challenges like properties that affect drug delivery, peptides and proteins degradation process, mechanism of release from the delivery system. These challenges in development are overcome by stabilizing the drug, obtaining desirable release kinetics to attain a target release profile. Through incorporation processes, such as emulsification and coacervation method, it is advantageous to incorporate protein into delivery systems in a solid and stable form, such as lyophilized powder. Some marketed examples are presented which shows that sustained protein and peptide delivery is commercially feasible and offers significant therapeutic advantages. The growth of peptide and protein-based pharmaceutical is indeed bright and rapidly become very important for therapeutic agents and are likely to replace many existing organic-based pharmaceuticals.

REFERENCES

1. Craik DJ, Fairlie DP, Liras S, Price D. The future of peptide-based drugs. Chem Biol Drug Des. 2013 Jan;81(1):136–47.
2. Nelson 1942- DL (David L. Lehninger principles of biochemistry [Internet]. Fourth edition. New York : W.H. Freeman, 2005.; 2005.
3. Schlick T. Protein Structure Introduction. In 2010. p. 77–104.
4. Book Reviews Biochemistry Third Edition The Retinoids : Biology , Chemistry and Medicine (Second Edition). 1994;22(1):1994.
5. Bruno BJ, Miller GD, Lim CS. Basics and recent advances in peptide and protein drug delivery. Ther Deliv. 2013 Nov;4(11):1443–67.
6. Florence A. Targeted and Controlled Drug Delivery: Novel Carrier Systems: S.P. Vyas, R.K, Khar, CBS Publishers, New Delhi, 2002, ISBN 81-239-0799-0. Int J Pharm. 2003;267:157.

7. Bhargav E. An over view: Protein and peptide based drug delivery. Int J Pharm Sci Rev Res. 2017;42(January):169–78.
8. Shaji J, Patole V. Protein and Peptide drug delivery: oral approaches. Indian J Pharm Sci. 2008;70(3):269–77.
9. Savale S. PROTEIN AND PEPTIDE DRUG DELIVERY SYSTEM. 2016;724–42.
10. Sanders LM. Drug delivery systems and routes of administration of peptide and protein drugs. Eur J Drug Metab Pharmacokinet. 1990;15(2):95–102.
11. Deb PK, Al-Attraqchi O, Chandrasekaran B, Paradkar A, Tekade RK. Chapter 16 - Protein/Peptide Drug Delivery Systems: Practical Considerations in Pharmaceutical Product Development. In: Tekade RK, editor. Basic Fundamentals of Drug Delivery [Internet]. Academic Press; 2019. p. 651–84. (Advances in Pharmaceutical Product Development and Research).
12. Persikov A V, Brodsky B. Unstable molecules form stable tissues. Proc Natl Acad Sci U S A. 2002 Feb;99(3):1101–3.
13. Dallas DC, Sanctuary MR, Qu Y, Khajavi SH, Van Zandt AE, Dyandra M, et al. Personalizing protein nourishment. Crit Rev Food Sci Nutr. 2017 Oct;57(15):3313–31.
14. Pickering AM, Davies KJA. Degradation of damaged proteins: the main function of the 20S proteasome. Prog Mol Biol Transl Sci. 2012;109:227–48.
15. Patel G, Misra A. 10 - Oral Delivery of Proteins and Peptides: Concepts and Applications. In: Misra A, editor. Challenges in Delivery of Therapeutic Genomics and Proteomics [Internet]. London: Elsevier; 2011. p. 481–529.
16. Physicians' Desk Reference. 50th Edition Medical Consultant: Ronald Arky. Medical Economics Co., Montvale, NJ. 1996. vi + 2879 pp. 23 × 28 cm. ISBN 1-56363-152-0. $69.95. J Med Chem [Internet]. 1996;39(11):2278.
17. Maher S, Brayden DJ. Overcoming poor permeability: translating permeation enhancers for oral peptide delivery. Drug Discov Today Technol [Internet]. 2012;9(2):e113–9.
18. Choonara BF, Choonara YE, Kumar P, Bijukumar D, du Toit LC, Pillay V. A review of advanced oral drug delivery technologies facilitating the protection and absorption of protein and peptide molecules. Biotechnol Adv. 2014 Nov;32(7):1269–82.
19. Patel A, Cholkar K, Mitra AK. Recent developments in protein and peptide parenteral delivery approaches. Ther Deliv. 2014 Mar;5(3): 337–65.

20. Muheem A, Shakeel F, Jahangir MA, Anwar M, Mallick N, Jain GK, et al. A review on the strategies for oral delivery of proteins and peptides and their clinical perspectives. Saudi Pharm J [Internet]. 2016;24(4): 413–28.
21. Ratnaparkhi MP, Chaudhari SP, Pandya V a. Peptides and proteins in pharmaceuticals. Int J Curr Pharm Res. 2011;3(2):1–9.
22. Zaman R, Othman I, Chowdhury EH. Carrier Mediated Systemic Delivery of Protein and Peptide Therapeutics. Curr Pharm Des. 2016;22(40):6167–91.
23. McBride JW, Malcolm RK, Dias N, Cameron D, Offord RE, Hartley O, et al. Development and pharmacokinetics of a combination vaginal ring for sustained release of dapivirine and the protein microbicide 5P12-RANTES. Int J Pharm. 2019 Jun;564:207–13.
24. McBride JW, Boyd P, Dias N, Cameron D, Offord RE, Hartley O, et al. Vaginal rings with exposed cores for sustained delivery of the HIV CCR5 inhibitor 5P12-RANTES. J Control Release. 2019 Mar;298:1–11.
25. Tamura T. Drug delivery system. 2004 2nd IEEE/EMBS International Summer School on Medical Devices and Biosensors, ISSS-MDBS 2004. 2004. 169–187 p.
26. Lee V. Encyclopedia of Controlled Drug Delivery, Volume 1 and 2. J Control Release - J Control RELEASE. 2001;71:353–4.
27. Kumar T, Soppimath K, Nachaegari S. Novel Delivery Technologies for Protein and Peptide Therapeutics. Curr Pharm Biotechnol. 2006 Sep 1;7:261–76.
28. Manning MC, Chou DK, Murphy BM, Payne RW, Katayama DS. Stability of protein pharmaceuticals: an update. Pharm Res. 2010 Apr;27(4):544–75.
29. Chi EY, Krishnan S, Randolph TW, Carpenter JF. Physical Stability of Proteins in Aqueous Solution: Mechanism and Driving Forces in Nonnative Protein Aggregation. Pharm Res [Internet]. 2003;20(9): 1325–36.
30. Zapadka KL, Becher FJ, Gomes Dos Santos AL, Jackson SE. Factors affecting the physical stability (aggregation) of peptide therapeutics. Interface Focus. 2017 Dec;7(6):20170030.
31. Reubsaet JL, Beijnen JH, Bult A, van Maanen RJ, Marchal JA, Underberg WJ. Analytical techniques used to study the degradation of proteins and peptides: chemical instability. J Pharm Biomed Anal. 1998 Sep;17(6–7):955–78.
32. Feeney RE, Yamasaki RB, Geoghegan KF. Chemical Modification of Proteins: An Overview. In: Modification of Proteins [Internet]. AMERICAN CHEMICAL SOCIETY; 1982. p. 1–3. (Advances in Chemistry; vol. 198).

33. Joseph D, Nadu T. Targeting The Enzyme - The New Tool for Drug Delivery Dhanish Joseph * and S. R. Suseem School of Advanced Sciences, Vellore Institute of Technology, Chennai - 600127, Tamil Nadu, India. 2019;10(2):489–93.

34. Williams AC, Barry BW. Penetration enhancers. Adv Drug Deliv Rev. 2004;56(5):603–18.

35. Barkat A, Khan B, Naveed A, Muhammad H, Khan HM shoaib, Waseem K, et al. Basics of pharmaceutical emulsions: A review. African J Pharm Pharmacol. 2011;525:2715–25.

36. Zhang L, Xu C, Mao J, Wang W, Han H, Pu Y, et al. Formulation and Characterization of Novel Dry Suspension and Dry Emulsion of 20(S)-Protopanaxadiol. AAPS PharmSciTech. 2019 Aug;20(7):275.

37. Berkland C, King M, Cox A, Kim K, Pack DW. Precise control of PLG microsphere size provides enhanced control of drug release rate. J Control Release. 2002 Jul;82(1):137–47.

38. Lengyel M, Kállai-Szabó N, Antal V, Laki AJ, Antal I. Microparticles, microspheres, and microcapsules for advanced drug delivery. Sci Pharm. 2019;87(3).

39. Zheng B, McClements DJ. Formulation of more efficacious curcumin delivery systems using colloid science: Enhanced solubility, stability, and bioavailability. Molecules. 2020;25(12):1–25.

40. Daraee H, Etemadi A, Kouhi M, Alimirzalu S, Akbarzadeh A. Application of liposomes in medicine and drug delivery. Artif Cells, Nanomedicine, Biotechnol [Internet]. 2016;44(1):381–91.

41. Chatin B, Mével M, Devallière J, Dallet L, Haudebourg T, Peuziat P, et al. Liposome-based Formulation for Intracellular Delivery of Functional Proteins. Mol Ther - Nucleic Acids [Internet]. 2015;4:e244.

42. Murthy SK. Nanoparticles in modern medicine: state of the art and future challenges. Int J Nanomedicine. 2007;2(2):129–41.

43. Jiang T, Jin K, Liu X, Pang Z. 8 - Nanoparticles for tumor targeting. In: Jana S, Maiti S, Jana S, editors. Biopolymer-Based Composites [Internet]. Woodhead Publishing; 2017. p. 221–67.

44. Sing CE, Perry SL. Recent progress in the science of complex coacervation. Soft Matter [Internet]. 2020;16(12):2885–914.

45. De Kruif CG (Kees), Weinbreck F, Vries. Complex Coacervation of Proteins and Anionic Polysaccharides. Curr Opin Colloid Interface Sci. 2004;9:5.

46. Comert F, Malanowski AJ, Azarikia F, Dubin PL. Coacervation and precipitation in polysaccharide-protein systems. Soft Matter. 2016 May;12(18):4154–61.

47. Weinbreck F, de Vries R, Schrooyen P, de Kruif CG. Complex Coacervation of Whey Proteins and Gum Arabic. Biomacromolecules [Internet]. 2003;4(2):293–303.
48. Haser A, Cao T, Lubach J, Listro T, Acquarulo L, Zhang F. Melt extrusion vs. spray drying: The effect of processing methods on crystalline content of naproxen-povidone formulations. Eur J Pharm Sci Off J Eur Fed Pharm Sci. 2017 May;102:115–25.
49. Guns S, Dereymaker A, Kayaert P, Mathot V, Martens JA, Van den Mooter G. Comparison between hot-melt extrusion and spray-drying for manufacturing solid dispersions of the graft copolymer of ethylene glycol and vinylalcohol. Pharm Res. 2011 Mar;28(3):673–82.
50. Surasarang S, Keen J, Huang S, Zhang F, McGinity J, Williams R. Hot Melt Extrusion versus Spray Drying: Hot Melt Extrusion Degrades Albendazole. Drug Dev Ind Pharm. 2016;43:1–51.
51. Wang Y, Selomulya C. Spray drying strategy for encapsulation of bioactive peptide powders for food applications. Adv Powder Technol. 2019;31.
52. Schmid K. Spray drying of protein precipitates and Evaluation of the Nano Spray Dryer B-90. PhD Thesis, Ludwig-Maximilians-University, Munich. 2011;
53. Costantino H, Firouzabadian L, Hogeland K, Wu CC, Beganski C, Carrasquillo K, et al. Protein Spray-Freeze Drying. Effect of Atomization Conditions on Particle Size and Stability. Pharm Res. 2000;17:1374–83.
54. Stern CS, Lebowitz J. Latest drug developments in the field of cardiovascular disease. Int J Angiol Off Publ Int Coll Angiol Inc. 2010;19(3):e100-5.
55. Zou L-L, Ma J-L, Wang T, Yang T-B, Liu C-B. Cell-penetrating Peptide-mediated therapeutic molecule delivery into the central nervous system. Curr Neuropharmacol. 2013 Mar;11(2):197–208.
56. Mora L, Aristoy M-C, Toldrá F. Bioactive Peptides. In: Melton L, Shahidi F, Varelis P, editors. Encyclopedia of Food Chemistry [Internet]. Oxford: Academic Press; 2019. p. 381–9.
57. Gokhale AS, Satyanarayanajois S. Peptides and peptidomimetics as immunomodulators. Immunotherapy. 2014;6(6):755–74.
58. Morrison CD, Laeger T. Protein-dependent regulation of feeding and metabolism. Trends Endocrinol Metab. 2015 May;26(5):256–62.
59. Khavinson VK, Tendler SM, Vanyushin BF, Kasyanenko NA, Kvetnoy IM, Linkova NS, et al. Peptide regulation of gene expression and protein synthesis in bronchial epithelium. Lung. 2014 Oct;192(5):781–91.

60. Veronese FM, Harris JM. Introduction and overview of peptide and protein pegylation. Adv Drug Deliv Rev. 2002 Jun;54(4):453–6.

61. Hoffman AS. The early days of PEG and PEGylation (1970s–1990s). Acta Biomater [Internet]. 2016;40:1–5.

62. Pisal DS, Kosloski MP, Balu-Iyer S V. Delivery of therapeutic proteins. J Pharm Sci. 2010 Jun;99(6):2557–75.

63. Bailon P, Berthold W. Polyethylene glycol-conjugated pharmaceutical proteins. Pharm Sci Technolo Today [Internet]. 1998;1(8):352–6.

64. Angst MS, Drover DR. Pharmacology of drugs formulated with DepoFoam: a sustained release drug delivery system for parenteral administration using multivesicular liposome technology. Clin Pharmacokinet. 2006;45(12):1153–76.

65. Ye Q, Asherman J, Stevenson M, Brownson E, Katre N V. DepoFoam technology: a vehicle for controlled delivery of protein and peptide drugs. J Control Release. 2000 Feb;64(1–3):155–66.

66. Mantripragada S. A lipid based depot (DepoFoam technology) for sustained release drug delivery. Prog Lipid Res. 2002 Sep;41(5):392–406.

67. Shore ND, Guerrero S, Sanahuja RM, Gambús G, Parente A. A New Sustained-release, 3-Month Leuprolide Acetate Formulation Achieves and Maintains Castrate Concentrations of Testosterone in Patients With Prostate Cancer. Clin Ther. 2019 Mar;41(3):412–25.

68. Jitendra, Sharma PK, Bansal S, Banik A. Noninvasive routes of proteins and peptides drug delivery. Indian J Pharm Sci. 2011 Jul;73(4):367–75.

69. Cox M, Scripture C, Figg W. Leuprolide acetate given by a subcutaneous extended-release injection: less of a pain? Expert Rev Anticancer Ther. 2005;5:605–11.

70. Jeevanandam J, Acquah C, Danquah MK. Biological macromolecules as antidiabetic agents. Biol Macromol Bioactivity Biomed Appl 2021:229–41. Cook AB, Bibic L. Macromolecules, Actually: From Plastics to DNA. Front Young Minds 2019;7.

71. Brody SL, Evans CM. Airway biology. Murray Nadel's Textb Respir Med 2022;12:49–65.

72. Sarah A, Tsze M, Teo YK, Cheng WT, Ban J, Tan L. Chapter 2 - Structure – activity relationship of biological macromolecules 2022:2022–3.

EXCERCISE

MULTIPLE CHOICE QUESTIONS

1. Peptide bond is a _________
   a. Covalent bond
   b. Ionic bond
   c. Metallic bond
   d. Hydrogen bond
2. The factor which does not affect pKa value of an amino acid is _________
   a. The loss of charge in the α-carboxyl and α-amino groups
   b. The interactions with other peptide R groups
   c. Other environmental factors
   d. Molecular weight
3. The repeating unit of proteins are-
   a. Glucose unit
   b. Amino acids
   c. Fatty acid
   d. Peptides
4. Unfolding of a protein can be termed as _________
   a. Renaturation
   b. Denaturation
   c. Oxidation
   d. Reduction
5. What are the following is not a factor responsible for the denaturation of proteins?
   a. pH change
   b. Organic solvents
   c. Heat
   d. Charge
6. Which type of the peptide absorbed in small intestine?
   a. Dipeptide
   b. Monopeptide
   c. Di peptide and mono peptide
   d. Dipeptide and Tripeptide
7. What are the barriers of PPDs-
   a. Enzymatic Barriers
   b. Intestinal Epithelial Barriers
   c. Capillary Endothelial barriers
   d. All of the Above
8. Hydrolytic breakage occupied bond is done by-
   a. Renin
   b. pancreatic amylase
   c. Glutamate dehydrogenase
   d. salivary amylase

9. Heamoglobin is an example of________protein
   a. Primary
   b. Secondary
   c. Tertiary structure
   d. Quaternary structure
10. Which route is best for administration of protein peptide drug-?
   a. Nasal route
   b. Parental Route
   c. Oculist route
   d. None of the above
11. Which modes are used to study stability of proteins and peptide drugs –
   a. Irreverse phase LMC
   b. Reverse phase HPLC
   c. High level HPLC
   d. None of the above
12. Mechanism involved in paracellular are-
   a. permeation
   b. Persorption
   b. Pre-assilation
   d. A+B
13. Which enzyme is most responsible for protein metabolism and degradation?
   a. Proteases
   b. Oxidases
   b. Kinases
   d. All of them
14. Enzymatic degradation of protein and peptide drug is by-
   a. Hydrolytic Cleavage
   b. Physical Modification
   c. GIT interaction
   d. none of these
15. Tertiary structure is maintained by
   a. Peptide bond
   b. Hydrogen bond
   c. Di sulphide bond
   d. All of the above
16. At a high temperature proteins are-
   a. In active
   b. Destroyed
   c. Denatured
   d. Both a and b
17. _________is a method of linking the polyethylene glycol strands to most common fragments of peptides which can protect the protein against proteolytic degradation
   a. Depo-foam technology
   b. PEGylation
   c. Both a and b
   d. None of the above
18. All are the factors responsible for denaturation of protein EXCEPT:
   a. pH Change
   b. Organic solvent
   c. Heat
   d. Charge

19. The most common secondary structure is-
    a. α-helix
    b. β-pleated sheet
    c. β-pleated sheet parallel
    d. β-pleated sheet non-parallel

SHORT ANSWER QUESTIONS

1. Write a note on protein.
2. What are the needs and challenges for formulation of protein and peptide delivery systems
3. Drug delivery systems for proteins.
4. Newer drug delivery systems for proteins.
5. Formulation approaches for protein and peptide parenteral delivery of drugs
6. What do you mean the process PEGylation?
7. Classify the types of protein.
8. What are the chemical instabilities associated with protein and peptide delivery?
9. Define the formulation vehicles for protein and peptide delivery systems
10. What are the barriers of for protein and peptide?

LONG ANSWER QUESTIONS

1. Describe the various formulation approaches for delivery of proteins and macromolecules.
2. Explain about formulation and evaluation of Protein and peptide Delivery system
3. Write a note on formulation strategies for protein and peptides-based drugs.
4. Discuss about the recent advance in Protein and peptide Delivery system.
5. Explain about the physical and chemical stability issue of protein and peptide Delivery system.
6. Classify the types of protein based on structures, composition and function.

MCQ ANSWERS

1. (a)	2. (d)	3. (b)	4. (b)
5. (a)	6. (d)	7. (d)	8. (d)
9. (a)	10. (d)	11. (b)	12. (b)
13. (d)	14. (d)	15. (a)	16. (d)
17. (d)	18. (b)	19. (d)	20. (a)

CHAPTER - 10

Vaccine Delivery Systems

Dr. Sanjib Bahadur, Dr. Deependra Singh, Dr. Manju Rawat Singh, and Dr. DK Tripathi

INTRODUCTION

Undoubtedly vaccination is the most successful strategy that can improve the public health for contagious diseases. There are currently more than 50 vaccine products currently on the market but there is still a strong global growing demand for the efficient vaccines as this reflects just a small fraction of all infective diseases[1]. Even the latest vaccines still necessisates to be improved. Although a wide range of drug pathogens have arrived, such as multidrug-resistant M. tuberculosis, and infections in which a truly appropriate treatment has not yet been discovered. Particularly, HIV requires intensified necessities for efficient prevention strategies[2].

The desired vaccine and the various characteristics of it should be attained, this has been defined by many researchers[3]. Most significantly, for the microorganism under consideration, an effective vaccine should have the potential to achieve the necessary immune system response. Serum antibodies induce immunity while intracellular microbes, including M. Tuberculosis, can effectively stop many viral and bacterial infections that may involve a response mediated by cells. An effective combination of both forms of immunity can effectively control several pathogens, like HIV. In the path of making the widely accepted consumption of the vaccine, it should be cost-effective. So that, a single dose of the vaccine can be conveniently administered, possibly near childhood, to promote safety because the people are highly susceptible, and circumstances of development should be well established and observable[2]. Without using a costly cold chain, the vaccines must be stable and effective enough to ensure immunogenicity till the administration[4]. The vaccine must be conveniently delivered in a single dose. So that, it permits the worldwide usage as commercially feasible vaccine [5]. All the criteria for the best suited vaccines are fulfilled by none of the currently available vaccines. Interestingly, the need for controlled-release technologies will make it possible to develop vaccines that can highlight most of these considerations[6], as indicated in Table 10.1

Table 10.1 Aspects of vaccine for the ideal formulation.

Biological factors	Economical factors
Lifelong immunity delivers	Given in a single dosing regimen
Never triggers illness	Reproducible standards for manufacturing
Minimal adverse reactions	Effective Without a Chain of Cold
Prenatally Delivered	Clinically qualified people aren't really necessary for the administration

Immunology on Vaccination

Early antibody response to the microbe that is induced by a prolonged remembering response with repeated exposure. It is normally indicated by an immune response to a natural infection. The body's immune response is observed after first antigen exposure by increasing serum antibody levels (within 14-28 days). This is accompanied by an extremely faster fall in antibody levels.[7] Interestingly, early exposure to the antigen boosts the body's ability to response, because of the multiplication of those lymphocytes specific to that antigen. The immune system becomes primed, and any subsequent exposure to the same antigen becomes generally greater, faster, and prolonged than the first one. Vaccines are expected to be introduced once at the initial dose and again in booster doses to maintain long-lasting complete immunity to ensure the advantage of these natural immune responses.

Accordingly, the incoming vaccines should merge initial immunization and boosts in a single shot / dose. The controlled-release technology has great potential to increase these figures, thus challenges brought by the immune system of the body[8]. Therefore, controlled-release technology can increase these figures with the advent of vaccines. These vaccines would combine the early immunization and boost in a single shot/dose.

Vaccine

The words vaccine and vaccination are originated from Variolaevaccine (cow's smallpox). In 1978, the first vaccine was developed by Edward Jenner for smallpox and coined this word to denote cowpox[9]. In 1985, vaccine for rabies was invented by Louis Pasteur. Vaccines can be prophylactic (for example, to prevent or improve the effects of any natural or "wild" pathogen of a future infection) or therapeutic (for example, cancer vaccines are now being investigated) [10]

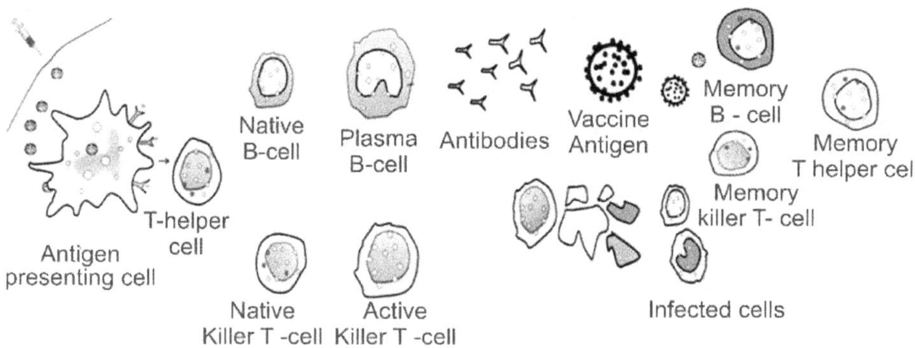

Fig.10.1 A Diagrammatic representation of work of a Vaccine.

By definition, *Vaccine is a biological formulation that activates the immune system of a person to develop immunity against a particular disease, protecting the individual from that disease*[11]. Typically a vaccine involves an agent that is like a microorganism-causing disease and is mostly made from the weakened or killed forms of the microbe, its toxins, or some of its surface proteins. The agent activates the immune system of the body to identify it, kill it, and keep a record of foreign threats. So that the immune system can easily recognize and kill most of the microorganisms if it is found later. Vaccines are typically delivered by injection, but they may also be given through the mouth (oral route) or sprayed into the nose (nasal route).

Need for a delivery system of vaccines

New vaccines, focusing the recombinant proteins and DNA are effective. But these are less immunogenic than conventional vaccines. Consequently, there is a high requirement to develop and produce potent and effective adjuvants as well as delivery systems. So that, these can be used in the latest generation of vaccines. Two types of adjuvants are available: (1) vaccine delivery systems (e.g., microparticles, emulsions, ISCOMs immunostimulating complexes, liposomes) and (2) immunostimulatory adjuvants (e.g., monophosphoryl lipid A, lipopolysaccharide, CpG DNA, or muramyl peptides) [12].

Types of vaccines

Live or inactivated species and subunits are among the different forms of vaccines.

1. Live attenuated vaccines

A vaccine developed from a weakened virus that does not activate the disease commonly triggered by the virus. A live attenuated vaccine allows the immune system of the body to identify and combat infections produced by the virus's non-weakened form. The smallpox vaccine of Edward Jenner was based on the cowpox virus (bovine vaccinia virus) in 1798, which did not cause severe disease in humans. But somewhat these are homologous to a human viral vaccine to develop immunity. Oral polio (OPV) vaccines, BCG (for tuberculosis) vaccines, the vaccine against chickenpox and measles, mumps, and rubella (MMR) are a few examples. Typically, the immune response is better, developing both humoral and cell-mediated responses. With a single dose, life - long immunity is also gained. There is also an exploration of live recombinant vaccines. Viral or Bacterial vectors are engineered genetically to show another organism's immunogenic protein. This recombinant vaccines will replicate and show the foreign antigen after the delivery to cause an immune response that of the protein[13].

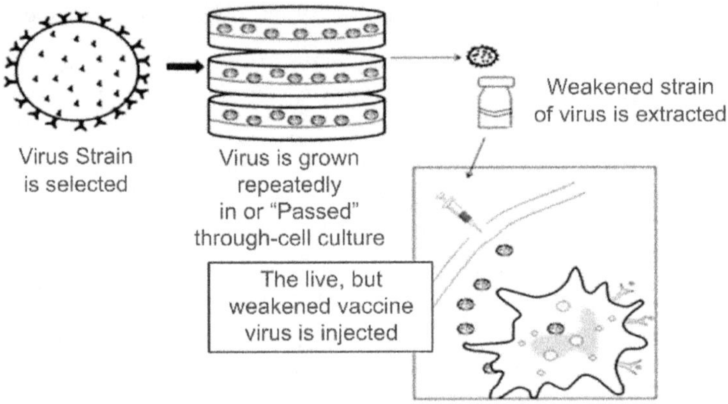

Fig.10.2 A Diagrammatic representation of Live Attenuated Vaccine.

2. Killed Vaccine

A killed or inactivated vaccine is also an option in contrast to attenuated vaccines. These vaccines are not contagious, that is, during the manufacture, all the pathogens are destroyed. Generally, the inactivation of pathogens occurs due to heat or chemical like formaldehyde or formalin, and thus usually, harmless. To make sure that all the infectious organisms are inactivated, the vaccine must be constantly monitored. The benefit of this kind of vaccine is that it has all the desired antigens, but immunogenicity was often decreased, contributing to the necessity for frequent boosters, for example, the vaccines killed are Polio (IPV) and Hepatitis A[14].

3. Subunit and Conjugate Vaccine

To produce subunit vaccines, only the sections of the germ that triggers an immune response are being used. Antigens ae referred to as these pieces of the germ. Subunit vaccines can produce 1 to 20 antigens. As this type of vaccine uses only the relevant, essential portions of the germ, the risk or adverse reactions is lower. The Hepatitis B vaccine, the Acellular pertussis vaccine, and the vaccine for influenza are examples of this type[15].

It is possible to develop another form of subunit vaccine through genetic engineering. This form of vaccine has remarkable advantages because the advancement of recombinant DNA technology will allow large and well quantities of the synthesis of preferred antigenic epitopes. A vaccine protein, the coding gene is incorporated into another virus, or into cultured producer cells. The vaccine protein is also produced whenever the carrier virus recreates or if the producer cell metabolizes. A recombinant vaccine is the product of this approach. The immune system will recognize the expressed protein and will provide potential defense against the targeted virus. The biggest challenge in the production of this kind of vaccine emerges in the identification of the epitopes with adequate antigenicity to obtain long immunity[16-18].

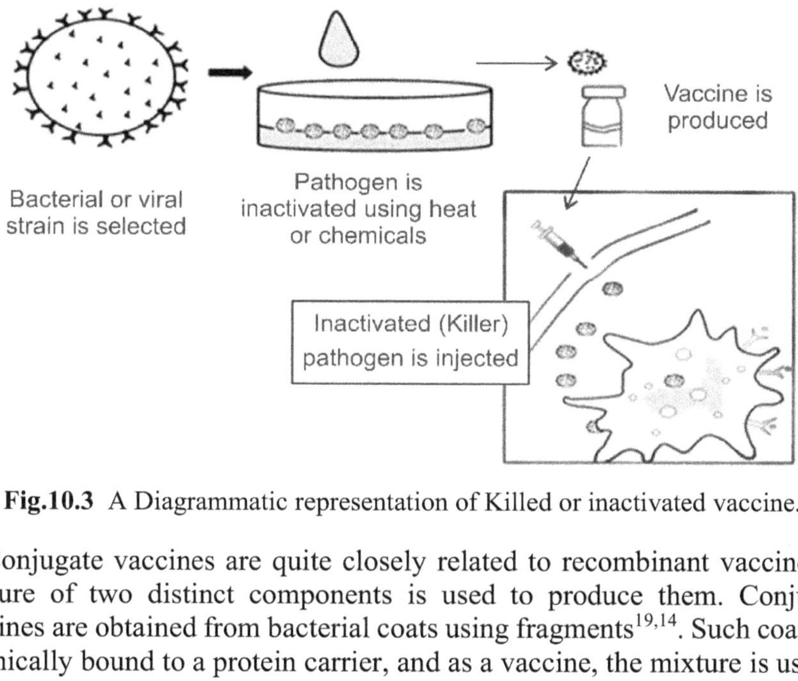

Fig.10.3 A Diagrammatic representation of Killed or inactivated vaccine.

Conjugate vaccines are quite closely related to recombinant vaccines. A mixture of two distinct components is used to produce them. Conjugate vaccines are obtained from bacterial coats using fragments[19,14]. Such coats are chemically bound to a protein carrier, and as a vaccine, the mixture is used.

Conjugate vaccines can be used to develop an effective synergistic immune response. Usually, the "part" of bacteria presented will not produce a significant immune response, whereas the protein carrier would obtain a positive immune response. The bacteria do not cause any infection, but it can create immunity against possible infection in combination with a carrier protein. This strategy is used to produce the vaccines which are currently in use for children for pneumococcal bacterial infections. The Pneumococcal Conjugate Vaccine (Prevnar®) and Hemophilus Influenza Conjugate Vaccine (Hib) are the examples[20].

4. Toxoid

The toxoid vaccines are produced from the toxins secreted by bacteria and are inactivated and used. Researchers have used a diluted chemical method that is formalin or even by use heat or any other strategy to inactivate the toxin. This inactivated toxin produced is termed as toxoid. These are harmless, for example, diphtheria and tetanus vaccines.

Toxoids may be inactivated or killed vaccines, but their category is often provided to highlight the concept. They involve an inactivated toxin rather than an inactivated type of bacteria.

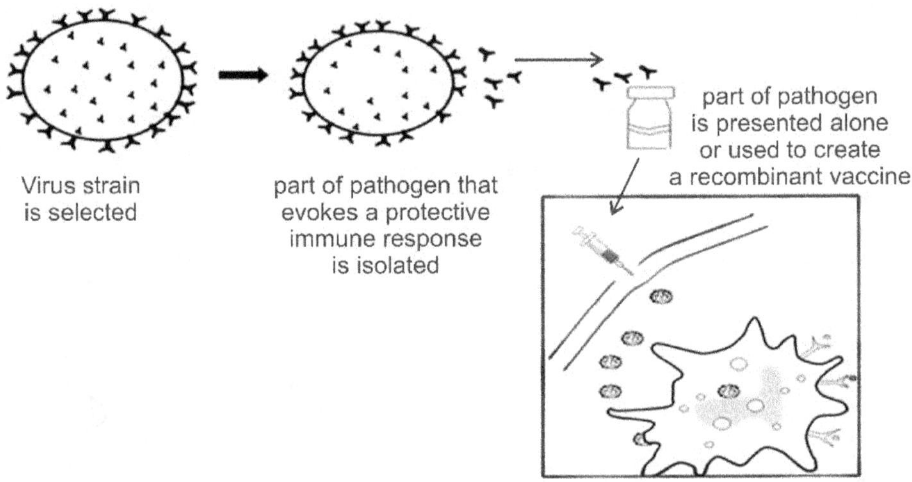

Fig.10.4 A Diagrammatic representation Subunit and Conjugate of Vaccine.

UPTAKE OF ANTIGENS

A toxin or other foreign substance which induces an immune response in the body, especially produces the antibodies is known as antigens. Vaccine contain weakened or inactive parts of a particular organism (antigen) that can trigger an immune response within the body[21,22].

The processing of vaccines can be done by:

1. Exogenous antigen processing
2. Endogenous antigen processing

1. *Exogenous Antigen Processing*

Exogenous pathway is utilized by specialized antigen-presenting cells to present peptides which are derived from proteins that are obtained from endocytosis of the cells.

Stages of exogenous antigen processing-

a. Uptake – access of native antigens and pathogens to intracellular pathway of degradation.
b. Degradation- limited proteolysis of antigens to peptides.
c. Antigen MHC complex- loading of peptides onto major histocompatiblity complex class-II.
d. Antigen presentation- transport and expression of peptide MHC complexes onto surface of the cells for recognition by T-Cells[23, 24].

2. ***Endogenous Antigen Processing***

It refers to the antigens produced from within the cell as a part of normal cell metabolized or when the cell is infected by bacteria or virus-

Stages of endogenous antigen processing-

a. Uptake –antigens/pathogens already present in cell.
b. Degradation- antigens synthesized in the cytoplasm undergo limited proteolytic degradation in the cytoplasm.
c. Antigen MHC complex formation - loading of peptides antigens onto major histocompatiblity complex class-I molecules.
d. Antigen presentation- transport and expression of antigens- MHC complexes onto surface of the cells[23, 24].

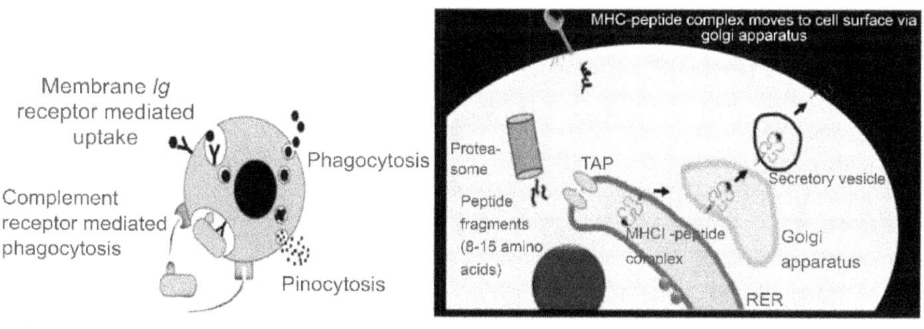

a) Exogenous antigen prcessing b) Endogenous antigen processing

Fig.10.5 Uptake of antigen.

THE SINGLE-SHOT VACCINE CONCEPT

The single-shot vaccine is a combination product of (abc), where (a) is a prime component—antigen with (b) an appropriate adjuvant—and (c) a microsphere component that encapsulates antigen and provides the booster immunizations by delayed release of the antigen. The Single shot vaccine provides patient protection effectively. In fact, many traditional vaccines require multiple injections, which results in a costly and inconvenient regimen. Single dose vaccines are given at a single contact point for preventing 4 to 6 disease. When creating such controlled release technology-based vaccines, following factors must be taken into account[25].

Important determinants for single-shot vaccine development:

- Biodegradation technology (the degradation of the materials into environmentally acceptable products such as water, CO_2, and biomass by the action of naturally available microorganisms under normal environmental conditions)
- Encapsulation efficiency (defined by the concentration of incorporated materials like API, excipients in formulation over the initial concentration used to make the formulation)
- Particle size distribution
- Preservation of bioactivity during formulation and release
- Scalable production process
- Effects of combination with various adjuvant
- Effects of different administration routes.

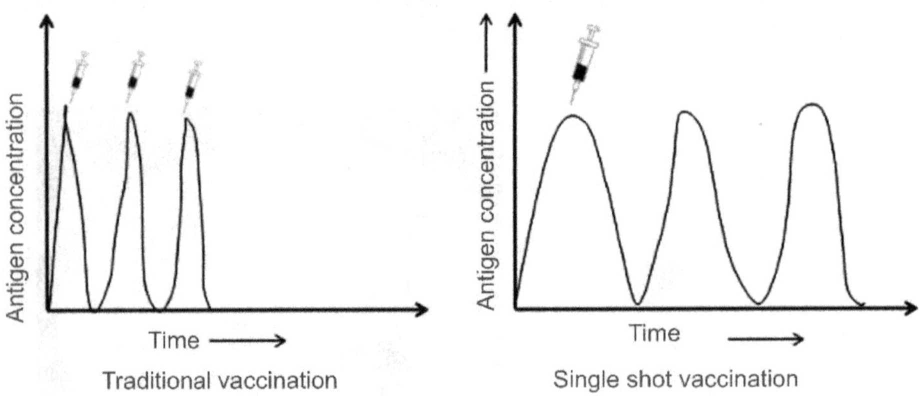

Fig.10.6 Traditional vaccination V/S Single Shot Vaccination.

MUCOSAL DELIVERY OF VACCINES

The delivery of vaccines via the mucosal routes allows antigens to interact with the mucosa- associated lymphoid tissue (MALT) to induce both mucosal and systemic immunity. The induced mucosal immunity can neutralize the pathogen on the mucosal surface before it can cause infection. Protective mucosal immune responses are most effectievely induced by mucosal immunization through oral, nasal, rectal or vaginal routes (but the vast majority of vaccines in use today are administered by injection. Mucosal vaccines are the future of vaccines derived immunity providing a faster, higher level and longer lasting immune response and disease protection to ensure a healthier, more productive animal.

Advantages

- Easy control of infection
- Effective control of non-invasive infections
- Widespread response

Disdvantages

- Antigen instability at mucosal sites
- Difficult to induce on Ig A response.

Particle absorption by the M cells of the intestine

The absorption of particles in the gut administered orally has been identified by several researchers. In past research from Sanders and Ashworth (1961), regular enterocytes in rats were able to consume smaller particulates of polystyrene (200 nm). The identified uptake sites and involved mechanisms differ among the authors. The intestinal macrophages, villus tips, ordinary enterocytes & the epithelium of the Peyer's patch were suggested as four alternate areas of use[26]. In 1977, Volkheimer reported that the large particles 'Persorption' (5-150 gm), usually starch grains, via villus tips were administered by in several species, including man. There is now a vast array of analysis wherein researchers aim to track the use of orally-fed particles, in particular M cells that are lining the Peyer's patches, to decide whether an orally-controlled release vaccine is feasible[27].

Microscopy was the most frequently used tool for monitoring the GI epithelial absorption of nanocarriers. Light microscopy in common has been popularly used. In this kind of study, the animal model used was the rabbit because they have comparatively numerous Peyer's patches in their GI tracts as compared to other mammals. The fluorescent translocation of polystyrene microparticles via intestinal walls of the rabbits was demonstrated by light microscopy in a particular sample. After intraluminal instillation, the temporal movement of these beads of 600 to 700nm all around the surface of epithelial of the FAE was recorded. Translocation took place within 10 minutes at the same time as soluble tracers will have to pass the epithelium. The intraluminal dose entered the FAE is 5% calculated by the authors. These findings suggest that thermoplastic microparticles were translocated quickly to Peyer's Patch and can be possibly used for the intake of vaccines. Certain approaches have also been used to identify or quantified microsphere, which include electron microscopy[28, 29], confocal microscopy[30], cytometry flow[31] and polymer extraction from the tissue through gel permeation chromatography quantification[32]. Similar findings came out in all these studies: Polymer microparticles with a diameter of <10/ m, sometimes within one hour of oral administration, may very well penetrate the GALT, and are promising as an antigen carrier in a sustained release vaccine[33].

Though the use of challenging & non-biodegradable microspheres has been illustrated, it is remarkable that the growth of a sustained-release system would be made quite successful by using biodegradable polymers. After an intraluminal instillation, polymer such as poly (D, L-lactic-co-glycolic acid) (PLGA), in the form of microspheres 1- to 10-//m, was also reported to be carried in rabbit Peyer's patches. The PLGA is biologically degradable and has been thoroughly researched and used as a carrier for a wide range of controlled release products compared to the other described system. Electron microscopy demonstrates that this copolymer's microspheres are translocated into the lymph tissue within one hour by M cells. This faster absorption of PLGA microspheres, as well as its biodegrading characteristics, has resulted in advanced work in vaccine applications with this polymer. Some degradable polymers exhibited penetration abilities, most prominently poly anhydrides[34].

Liposomal Uptake

The level of penetration of orally delivered liposomes was also investigated. Major uptake was shown in negative-loaded Liposomes greater than 374 nm and composed of at least 25 mol% Phosphatidylserine after intraluminal administering of a fluorescence marker 6-carboxyfluorescein. In contrast within the proximal small intestine, the absorption was primarily shown by the ileal patches of the Peyer in rats[35]. The studies revealed that these observations would thus allow such liposomes being used to treat the Peyer's patch specifically. To discuss the stability problems of the liposome in the extreme conditions in a gastrointestinal tract, the same authors showed that liposomes of dipalmatidyl diphaidylcholine, distearoyl phasphatidyl-choline, phosphatidylserine & cholesterol were not affected by the simulated gastric, bile & pancreatic fluids. These studies confirm the theory that these liposomes will succeed in providing antigens to the patch of Peyer and was shown to be entering the patch of Peyer after orally administered[36, 37].

Liposomes Based Vaccines

Vaccines can be administered by incorporating them into appropriate lipidic carrier via colloidal lipid-based delivery systems of the drug. The current development in the production of the vaccine involves micellar systems, triglyceride emulsions, self-emulsifying medicines (SEDDS) and solid lipid nanoparticles (SLNs). Liposomes are highly effective for systemic, mucosal, and transcutaneous immunization that is very efficient in the delivery of the vaccine. Water-soluble antigens encapsulation in the liposomes offers a controlled release profile over long periods[38, 39] Liposomes are also associated with the delivery of vaccine in the radical immunization of infection such as prostate cancer, colorectal carcinoma, influenza, malaria, hepatite A and HIV are increasingly studied, which leads to the rise in vaccines for an immune reaction like Lipid A (gram-negative bacteria polysaccharide) and mutamylic peptidase. Stimuvax is a nanoliposome vaccine currently developed for radical lung cancer vaccination. It is directed mainly at the mucin-1 cell surface protein, which exhibits satisfactory performance in initial phase III tests, concerning non-microscopic lung carcinoma[40].

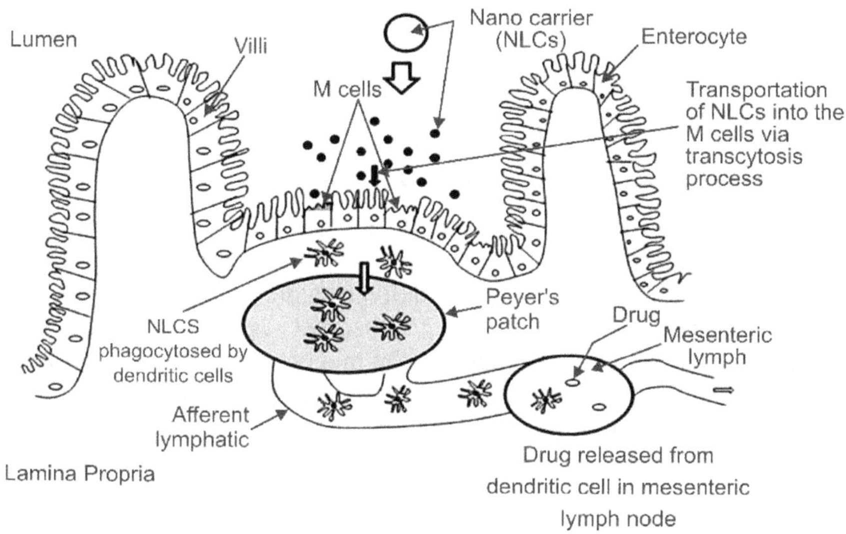

Fig.10.7 A Diagrammatic representation Particle absorption by the M cells of the Intestine.

Liposomal Vaccine Loading Antigen and Mechanism

Liposomes hold antigens in its inner micro-environment by surface adsorption or trapping. Consequently, liposomal preparations comprising antigens which are adsorbed on their surfaces produce significant immune reaction because of their lysosmotic way of entering cells, as they are easily fused into lipid bilayers so that they can be brought into the immune cells through endocytosis[41, 42]. These processes can easily be attached to T cells by covalent bonds, thus helping to increase the cell-mediated immunity of class I & II MHC[43, 44].

Factors that affect the Liposomal Vaccine Adjuvant Properties

The major factors that affect the liposomal support's adjuvant capacities are: (1) the ratio between phospholipid and protein, (2) surface charge, (3) particle-size and (4) phase transition temperature (Pt) of phospholipids. Lipid-to-protein ratio relates to the dry weight of solid proteins in lipids. Higher the ratio of lipid and protein reduces the stability of antigen by degradation in the vesicular structure[45, 46]. Phase transition temperature (Pt) is the overall temperature needed to alter the physical state of the lipid from the sol to gel. A shift in Pt induces the liposomal vaccine that changes antigenicity. It refers to the length of the chain and saturation degree of the phospholipid hydrocarbon chains and the electrostatic characteristics of the head unit. Increased Pt-value enhances the liposomes elasticity, which helps to improve the immune response for better permeation across biological barriers. As published, good antigen release profile is presented by phospholipids Pt from -32°C through 41.5°C. The release profile of antigen decreases eventually due to low permeation properties with increasing vesicle rigidity. In a similar manner, zeta potential is essential for the preservation of physical stability & improved liposome permeability[47].

Vaccine delivery applications of liposome

Liposomal vaccines were successful for delivering antigens against pathogenic microorganisms including pertussis, diphtheria, tetanus, and many others. For immunization, liposomes deliver against Yersinia Pestis, plague via the nasal pathway[48]. Moreover, liposomes coated in mucoadhesive polymers such as chitosan will increase the mucosal availability of diphtheria toxoid to deliver "polymer-coated liposomes". These systems also protect the gastric antigen trapped through the gastric fluid[49]. Using immunomodulators in tetanus-loaded liposomal vaccines also offers a substantial improvement in immune responses. Tetanus toxoid, for example, is ideally suited for the increase in the systemic and mucosal immune response through liposomes comprising co-adjuvants[50].

Latest literature reports the use of liposomes in the delivery of vaccines. Addition of the liposomal formulation inducer gives positive charge to its surface & improves permeability that helps increase the immune response[51]. The strategy in genetic DNA vaccines is especially advantageous. Generally, genetic materials have a negative charge on their surface, making it impossible for them to reach the cells. Cationic liposomes allow effective release in its internal microenvironment of genetic vaccines loaded[52].

Malignant tumor includes melanoma cells that show many immune-dominant epitopes on the membrane of cancerous cells referred to as antigens related to the tumors. Liposomes deliver cancer vaccines effectively that leads to antibody production and immune response, presumably by increasing biodistribution and cellular absorption of antigens by cells that recognize the immune system[53]. In a review, membrane fusogenic liposomes embodied with Sendai virus antigens have been found to conveniently deliver them directly through a fusing mechanism into the cytoplasm[54]. Lipovaxin™, Lipotek Inc. is a complex multidisciplinary vaccine designed to provoke cell-mediated immunity by passing antigens further into dendritic cells. Also, the vaccine has a tremendous ability to cause malaria and tuberculosis immunization[55]

Polymeric Nanoparticle Based Delivery System

The mucosa related lymphoid tissue is ideally absorbed by polymeric nanoparticles due to their size. The nasal and oral supply of vaccines is studied thoroughly. The successful immunization is caused by small antigen doses. Therefore, because of the ability of nanoparticles to release and defend proteins from enzyme degradation in GIT, the usage of antigens for oral delivery is optimal[34]. After an oral delivery of biodegradable PACA nanoparticles with ovalbumin in rats, secretory immune responses were shown to improve. The very slow degradation of PMMA nanoparticles (30-40 per cent annually) seems extremely effective for vaccination as prolonged interaction between antigen and immunocompetent cells promote sustained immunity. MAb precisely labelled nanoparticles in the M cells enhance the absorption level and thus the immune response of nanoparticular vaccines[56]. Metal chelating polymers like polyaminocarboxylic acids, including DTPA (diethylenetriamine-pentaacetic acid), and EDTA (ethylenediamine tetra-acetic acid) are non-covalent and useful in controlled in vivo delivery. The occurrence of a minimum of one histidine residue (for example, a protein or peptide antigen or a fusion build with its mark) at the amino or carboxyl terminus of a biological molecule is an essential significant contributing factor to the binding of the biological component into the polymer as it results in an optimized specificity of a metal ion bond in the metal affinity complex.

An efficient prophylactic gene expression (GXV) vaccine consists of at least four separate plasmid DNAs, coated with chitosan to form nanospheres and encoded correlating RSV antigens. Intra-nasal path in a murine RSV infection model, nanosphere inductions in the lung, cytotoxic T lymphocytes, nasal IgA antibodies, and the formation of IFN-gamma in the lung and splenocytes decreases viral titres. Certain forms of nanocarriers used as multivalent vaccine structures include polysaccharide-based spermine, metallic oxide particles, alginate capsules (natural polymers) and synthetic biocompatible and biodegradable poly (d,l-lactide co-glycolides) polymers[57].

Dendrimers Based Delivery System

Dendrimers with layered architecture which are branched and synthetic polymers which are promising for a range of biomedical systems. Improved understanding and recent growth in the design of biodegradable chemistry such as the role of Molecular weight and architecture *in vivo* dendrimer behavior, have allowed the use of these branched polymers as scaffolds for addressing the vaccine antigens[58]. Wright has developed a new system of adjuvant delivery with a range of material. A vaccine with an adjuvant starburst dendrimer was used in the present innovation. The popular influenza vaccine includes an appropriate quantity of an influenza antigen composition and a starburst dendrimer in a biologically compatible carrier. Use of starburst dendrimer allows adjuvant influenza to be developed without forming a harmful complex, as even a tiny proportion of dendrimer is an efficient adjuvant. A dendrimer is used as an adjuvant to make it easier to add a significantly small quantity of influenza antigen to achieve a compatible antigenic reaction if the antigen offered without the dendrimer[59]. Dendrimers are prioritized for the mid-generation and have elevated levels of titer antibody with lower antigen doses. Belledegraun et al., offers a highly efficient "vaccine" for an immune response aimed towards renal cell cancer, introduced a new approach to the cure the renal cell carcinomas using just a chimeric molecule comprised of a granulocyte-macrophage colony-stimulating (GM-CSF), which is attached to a G250 kidney cancer-specific antigen[60]. A preferred agent from the group comprising of a viral vector, a lipid, a cationic lipid, a dendrimer, and a liposome was used to transfect the cell. The benefits behind using smart segments & biodegradable multifunctional polymers were highlighted by Lowe et al[61]. Efficiently and effectively, the hydrophobic and hydrophilic portions were included in the biodegradable portion. The modifications include merging the polymeric multifunctional substance in a hydrophilic loading condition with a biologically active ingredient and delivering the formulation to a living subject as a drug delivery vehicle. Several structures include a hydrogel structure, dendritic structures, and certain structures, like micro and nanoparticulate, in the polymeric components present in the current technology. A dendritic structure revealed that involves a Poly (N-isopropyl acrylamide) segment or its derivative, a segment of Poly (L-lysine) and a segment Poly (lactic acid) and/or its derivatives[57].

ISCOMs-Immunostimulatory Complexes

In 1984, Morein and his team developed the immunostimulation complex (ISCOM) for the first time. To establish a vaccine delivery strategy that combines some factors of the virus particles like their surface protein size and orientation, further with effective immunostimulatory action of saponins[62]. ISCOMs are the complexes like open cages, usually of diameters of around 30-80 nm composed generally consists of proteins such as cholesterol, saponin, phospholipid and immunogen. In reference to other vaccine adjuvants, ISCOMs have proven themselves to facilitate a widespread immune reaction, encouraging elevated levels of antibodies and intense T- cell reactions, involving increased secretion of cytokine and cytotoxic T lymphocyte response activation in a range of animal experimentation models and have now proceeded to human trials Phase I & II[63, 64].

The authors Brunham and Murdin have a list of patents which provide teaching on two-step immunization mechanism against infection chlamydia by initial chlamydia protein administration, followed by the ISCOM chlamydia protein administration. Immunogenic compositions are useful in chlamydial vaccines and mentioned for diagnosis, including external membrane antigen extract of Chlamydia strain and ISCOM[65]. Additional ISCOM vaccines for Campylobacter infections, Moraxella and Helicobacter infections are also discovered[57, 66].

TRANSDERMAL DELIVERY OF VACCINES

Various administrations to the skin offer many advantages including advantages including ease of access, reduced spread of blood–bourne disease, a potential for generation of generation both systemic and mucosal immune response.

The skin has multiple barrier properties to minimize water loss from the body and prevent the permeation of environmental contaminants into the body. These barriers can be considered as physical, enzymatic and immunological.

i. ***Physical barrier***

   The epidermis is in a constant state of renewal, with formation of a new cell layer of keratinocytes at the stratum basale, loss of their nucleus and other organelles to form desiccated, proteinaceous corneocytes on their journey towards desquamation, which occurs from the skin surface, at the same rate as formation, in normal skin. The outermost layer, the stratum corneum, consists of a brick wall like structure of corneocytes in a matrix of intercellular lipids, with desmosomes acting as molecular rivets between the corneocytes. The stratum corneum presents an effective physical barrier to the permeation of large molecules such as vaccines. This is the first barrier property that must be overcome to provide effective transdermal vaccine delivery.

ii. ***Enzymatic barrier***

   The skin possesses many enzymes capable of hydrolyzing peptides and proteins. These are involved in the keratinocyte maturation and desquamation process[67], formation of natural moisturizing factor (NMF) and general homeostasis[68]. Their potential to degrade topically applied vaccine antigens should be considered.

iii. ***Immunological barrier***

   When the skin is damaged, environmental contaminants can access the epidermis to initiate an immunological response. This includes (i) epithelial defence as characterized by antimicrobial peptides (AMP) produced by keratinocytes – both constitutively expressed (e.g. human beta defensin 1 (hBD1), RNAse 7 and psoriasin) and inducible (e.g. hBD 2-4 and LL-37); (ii) innate-inflammatory immunity, involving expression of pro-inflammatory cytokines and interferons; and (iii) adaptive immunity based on antigen presenting cells, such as epidermal Langerhans and dendritic cells, mediating T-cell responses[69]. For example, Langerhans cells initiate specific immune responses by processing and presenting antigen fragments to naïve T cells in the lymph nodes[70]. This promotes the generation of both systemic (IgG and IgM) and mucosal (IgA) humoral immune responses[71]. Thus transdermal delivery targets the vaccine to the skin, thereby promoting its contact with Langerhans cells and potentially reducing the required dose of vaccine[72].

Many approaches have been investigated to overcome the skins barrier properties in order to deliver antigens via the skin.

A. Liquid-jet injection

B. Epidermal powder immunization

C. Colloidal carriers

D. Energy based approaches.

All methods aim to overcome the stratum corneum barrier and target vaccine to immune-responsive cells such as Langerhans cells.

a. Liquid-jet injection

Liquid jet injectors use a high-velocity jet (typically 100 to 200 m/s) to deliver molecules through the skin into the subcutaneous or intramuscular region. Jet injectors can be broadly classified into multi-use nozzle jet injectors (MUNJIs) and disposable cartridge jet injectors (DCJIs), depending on the number of injections carried out with a single device[73]. Commercially available liquid jet injector consists of a power source (compressed gas or spring), piston, drug or vaccine-loaded compartment and an application nozzle, with typical orifice size in the range of 150 to 300 μm[73]. Upon actuation the power source pushes the piston rapidly increases the pressure within the drug-loaded compartment, thereby forcing the drug solution through the orifice as a high velocity liquid jet. When the jet impacts on the skin it creates a hole through allowing the liquid to enter the skin. The process of hole formation and liquid jet deposition occurs within microseconds.

Applications of liquid-jet injectors have been focused on delivery of macromolecules that do not passively permeate the skin. Commercially available devices include the Antares Vision® and Choice® (Antares, Minneapolis) that deliver a variable dose of insulin; V-Go Mini-Ject system for insulin (Valeritas, Parsippany, NJ); Biojector 2000 (Bioject, Tualatin, OR); PenJet (PenJet Corp., Santa Monica, CA) for smallpox vaccination; Injex (HNS International, Anaheim, CA) for administration of insulin and human growth hormone; Zeneo (Crossject, Paris, France).

Despite the potential advantages of jet injectors, the uptake of the technology has been limited due to variable reactions, including pain and bruising, at the site of administration. In order to see future vaccine applications of the jet-injector approach, further technology development will be required to provide effective pain-free delivery at reasonable cost.

b. Epidermal powder immunization

Powder injectors were first used for DNA and RNA transfection into plants[74]. The technique has subsequently been investigated for transdermal protein delivery, gene therapy and vaccination[75-79]. The device design principles are similar to liquid injectors, with a powder compartment and compressed carrier gas, such as helium. Upon actuation, the particles are carried by the gas, to impact the skin surface at high velocity, puncturing micron-sized holes in the epidermis to facilitate skin deposition[80].

Powder injectors offer advantages over liquids in terms of formulation and stability issues. Initial safety studies suggest that the powder injectors are reasonably well tolerated, and the particle bombardment offers advantages with regard to Langerhans cell targeting and immune system activation. Research is continuing on technology development to better understand and optimize particle and formulation characteristics, and on clinical evaluation.

c. Topical application

In addition to the systems that bombard the skin with liquid or solid vaccines, a number of other methods have been investigated that can be applied to the skin, to reduce the stratum corneum barrier, and/or carry vaccine into the skin. Topical applications range from non-invasive formulation based approaches (e.g. colloidal carriers), energy based approaches (ultrasound or sonophoresis, and electroporation), stratum corneum ablation and minimally invasive approaches (such as microneedles).

REFERENCES

1. Offit PA, Davis RL, Gust D. Vaccine safety. Vaccines. 2008. p. 1629–50.
2. Shenoi S, Friedland G. Extensively drug-resistant tuberculosis: a new face to an old pathogen. Annu Rev Med. 2009;60:307–20.
3. Pisal DS, Kosloski MP, Balu-Iyer S V. Delivery of therapeutic proteins. J Pharm Sci. 2010 Jun;99(6):2557–75.
4. WHO. Vaccine-preventable diseases and vaccines-2017 update. International travel and health. 2012. 1–63 p.
5. Ventola CL. Immunization in the United States: Recommendations, Barriers, and Measures to Improve Compliance: Part 1: Childhood Vaccinations. P T. 2016 Jul;41(7):426–36.

6. Rauch S, Jasny E, Schmidt KE, Petsch B. New Vaccine Technologies to Combat Outbreak Situations. Front Immunol. 2018;9:1963.
7. Chaplin DD. Overview of the immune response. J Allergy Clin Immunol. 2010 Feb;125(2 Suppl 2):S3-23.
8. Zhao Z, Leong KW. Controlled delivery of antigens and adjuvants in vaccine development. J Pharm Sci. 1996 Dec;85(12):1261–70.
9. Riedel S. Edward Jenner and the history of smallpox and vaccination. Proc (Bayl Univ Med Cent). 2005 Jan;18(1):21–5.
10. Garbuglia AR, Lapa D, Sias C, Capobianchi MR, Del Porto P. The Use of Both Therapeutic and Prophylactic Vaccines in the Therapy of Papillomavirus Disease. Front Immunol. 2020;11:188.
11. Clem AS. Fundamentals of vaccine immunology. J Glob Infect Dis. 2011 Jan;3(1):73–8.
12. Nascimento IP, Leite LCC. Recombinant vaccines and the development of new vaccine strategies. Brazilian J Med Biol Res = Rev Bras Pesqui medicas e Biol. 2012 Dec;45(12):1102–11.
13. Minor PD. Live attenuated vaccines: Historical successes and current challenges. Virology [Internet]. 2015;479–480:379–92.
14. Bhardwaj S. Chapter 21 - Vaccines. In: Vohora D, Singh G, editors. Pharmaceutical Medicine and Translational Clinical Research [Internet]. Boston: Academic Press; 2018. p. 341–53.
15. Lidder P, Sonnino A. Chapter 1 - Biotechnologies for the Management of Genetic Resources for Food and Agriculture. In: Goodwin SF, Friedmann T, Dunlap JC, editors. Academic Press; 2012. p. 1–167. (Advances in Genetics; vol. 78).
16. Hansson M, Nygren PA, Ståhl S. Design and production of recombinant subunit vaccines. Biotechnol Appl Biochem. 2000 Oct;32(2):95–107.
17. FENNER F, BACHMANN PA, GIBBS EPJ, MURPHY FA, STUDDERT MJ, WHITE DO. CHAPTER 14 - Immunization against Viral Diseases. In: FENNER F, BACHMANN PA, GIBBS EPJ, MURPHY FA, STUDDERT MJ, WHITE DO, editors. Veterinary Virology [Internet]. Academic Press; 1987. p. 265–82.
18. Lee J, Arun Kumar S, Jhan YY, Bishop CJ. Engineering DNA vaccines against infectious diseases. Acta Biomater. 2018 Oct;80:31–47.
19. Goldblatt D. Conjugate vaccines. Vol. 119, Clinical and experimental immunology. 2000. p. 1–3.
20. Booy R, Hodgson S, Carpenter L, Mayon-White RT, Slack MP, Macfarlane JA, et al. Efficacy of Haemophilus influenzae type b conjugate vaccine PRP-T. Lancet (London, England). 1994 Aug;344(8919):362–6.
21. Blum JS, Wearsch PA, Cresswell P. Pathways of antigen processing. Annu Rev Immunol. 2013;31:443-73.
22. Roche PA, Furuta K. The ins and outs of MHC class II-mediated antigen processing and presentation. Nat Rev Immunol. 2015;15(4):203-16..

23. Janeway CA, Travers P, In WM Kenneth M, editor. Immunobiology. 8th ed. New York: Garland Publishing, Science, Taylor and Francis Group. LLC; 2012.
24. Watts C. The exogenous pathway for antigen presentation on major histocompatibility complex class II and CD1 molecules. Nat Immunol. 2004;5(7):685-92.
25. Roukema R, Kremer B, de Leede L. Advances in single-shot vaccine development; January 2, 2009.
26. Sanders E, Ashworth CT. A study of particulate intestinal absorption and hepatocellular uptake: Use of polystyrene latex particles. Exp Cell Res [Internet]. 1961;22:137–45.
27. LeFevre ME, Vanderhoff JW, Laissue JA, Joel DD. Accumulation of 2-μm latex particles in mouse Peyer's patches during chronic latex feeding. Experientia [Internet]. 1978;34(1):120–2.
28. Jepson MA, Clark MA, Simmons NL, Hirst BH. Epithelial M cells in the rabbit caecal lymphoid patch display distinctive surface characteristics. Histochemistry [Internet]. 1993;100(6):441–7.
29. Hodges GM, Carr EA, Hazzard RA, Carr KE. Uptake and translocation of microparticles in small intestine. Dig Dis Sci [Internet]. 1995;40(5):967–75.
30. Jenkins PG, Howard KA, Blackhall NW, Thomas NW, Davis SS, O'Hagan DT. The quantitation of the absorption of microparticles into the intestinal lymph of Wistar rats. Int J Pharm [Internet]. 1994;102(1):261–6.
31. Ebel JP. A Method for Quantifying Particle Absorption from the Small Intestine of the Mouse. Pharm Res [Internet]. 1990;7(8):848–51.
32. Jani P, Halbert GW, Langridge J, Florence AT. Nanoparticle uptake by the rat gastrointestinal mucosa: quantitation and particle size dependency. J Pharm Pharmacol. 1990 Dec;42(12):821–6.
33. Pappo J, Ermak TH. Uptake and translocation of fluorescent latex particles by rabbit Peyer's patch follicle epithelium: a quantitative model for M cell uptake. Clin Exp Immunol. 1989 Apr;76(1):144–8.
34. Lee V. Encyclopedia of Controlled Drug Delivery, Volume 1 and 2. J Control Release - J Control RELEASE. 2001;71:353–4.
35. Zhou F, Neutra MR. Antigen Delivery to Mucosa-Associated Lymphoid Tissues Using Liposomes as a Carrier. Biosci Rep [Internet]. 2002;22(2):355–69.
36. Harokopakis E, Hajishengallis G, Michalek SM. Effectiveness of liposomes possessing surface-linked recombinant B subunit of cholera toxin as an oral antigen delivery system. Infect Immun [Internet]. 1998 Sep;66(9):4299-4304.
37. Aramaki Y, Tomizawa H, Hara T, Yachi K, Kikuchi H, Tsuchiya S. Stability of Liposomes in Vitro and Their Uptake by Rat Peyer's Patches Following Oral Administration. Pharm Res [Internet]. 1993;10(8):1228–31.
38. Aramaki Y, Fujii Y, Yachi K, Kikuchi H, Tsuchiya S. Activation of systemic and mucosal immune response following nasal administration of liposomes. Vaccine [Internet]. 1994;12(13):1241–5.

39. Gregoriadis G, Gursel I, Gursel M, McCormack B. Liposomes as immunological adjuvants and vaccine carriers. J Control Release [Internet]. 1996;41(1):49–56.

40. Decoster L, Wauters I, Vansteenkiste JF. Vaccination therapy for non-small-cell lung cancer: Review of agents in phase III development. Ann Oncol. 2012;23(6):1387–93.

41. Reddy R, Zhou F, Huang L, Carbone F, Bevan M, Rouse BT. pH sensitive liposomes provide an efficient means of sensitizing target cells to class I restricted CTL recognition of a soluble protein. J Immunol Methods. 1991 Aug;141(2):157–63.

42. van Rooijen N, van Nieuwmegen R. Liposomes in immunology: evidence that their adjuvant effect results from surface exposition of the antigens. Cell Immunol. 1980 Feb;49(2):402–7.

43. Raphael L, Tom BH. Liposome facilitated xenogeneic approach for studying human colon cancer immunity: carrier and adjuvant effect of liposomes. Clin Exp Immunol. 1984 Jan;55(1):1–13.

44. Gregoriadis G, Davis D, Davies A. Liposomes as immunological adjuvants: antigen incorporation studies. Vaccine [Internet]. 1987;5(2):145–51. Available from: http://www.sciencedirect.com/science/article/pii/0264410X87900636

45. Bozzuto G, Molinari A. Liposomes as nanomedical devices. Int J Nanomedicine. 2015;10:975–99.

46. Alpar HO, Eyles JE, Williamson ED, Somavarapu S. Intranasal vaccination against plague, tetanus and diphtheria. Adv Drug Deliv Rev. 2001 Sep;51(1–3):173–201.

47. Martin C, Somavarapu S, Alpar HO. Mucosal delivery of diphtheria toxoid using polymer-coated-bioadhesive liposomes as vaccine carriers. J Drug Deliv Sci Technol [Internet]. 2005;15(4):301–6. Available from: http://www.sciencedirect.com/science/article/pii/S1773224705500534

48. Henriksen-Lacey M, Korsholm KS, Andersen P, Perrie Y, Christensen D. Liposomal vaccine delivery systems. Expert Opin Drug Deliv. 2011 Apr;8(4):505–19.

49. Rescia VC, Takata CS, de Araujo PS, Bueno da Costa MH. Dressing liposomal particles with chitosan and poly(vinylic alcohol) for oral vaccine delivery. J Liposome Res. 2011 Mar;21(1):38–45.

50. Tafaghodi M, Jaafari M-R, Sajadi Tabassi SA. Nasal immunization studies using liposomes loaded with tetanus toxoid and CpG-ODN. Eur J Pharm Biopharm [Internet]. 2006 Oct;64(2):138—145.

51. Christensen D, Korsholm KS, Andersen P, Agger EM. Cationic liposomes as vaccine adjuvants. Expert Rev Vaccines. 2011 Apr;10(4):513–21.

52. Christensen D, Agger EM, Andreasen LV, Kirby D, Andersen P, Perrie Y. Liposome-based cationic adjuvant formulations (CAF): past, present, and future. J Liposome Res. 2009;19(1):2–11.

53. Saupe A, McBurney W, Rades T, Hook S. Immunostimulatory colloidal delivery systems for cancer vaccines. Expert Opin Drug Deliv. 2006 May;3(3):345–54.
54. Qiang L, Yi J, Fu-De C. Melanoma vaccine based on the vector of membrane fusogenic liposomes. Pharmazie. 2004 Apr;59(4):263–7.
55. Gargett T, Abbas M, Rolan P, Price J, Gosling K, Ferrante A, et al. Phase I trial of Lipovaxin-MM, a novel dendritic cell-targeted liposomal vaccine for malignant melanoma. Cancer Immunol Immunother. 2018;67.
56. Lung P, Yang J, Li Q. Nanoparticle formulated vaccines: opportunities and challenges. Nanoscale [Internet]. 2020;12(10):5746–63.
57. Lakshmi P, Bhaskaran S, Saroja C. Recent trends in vaccine delivery systems: A review. Int J Pharm Investig. 2011;1(2):64.
58. Heegaard PMH, Boas U, Sorensen NS. Dendrimers for Vaccine and Immunostimulatory Uses. A Review. Bioconjug Chem [Internet]. 2010;21(3):405–18. Available from: https://doi.org/10.1021/bc900290d
59. Mhlwatika Z, Aderibigbe BA. Application of Dendrimers for the Treatment of Infectious Diseases. Molecules. 2018 Aug;23(9).
60. Gitlitz BJ, Belldegrun AS, Figlin RA. Vaccine and gene therapy of renal cell carcinoma. Semin Urol Oncol. 2001 May;19(2):141–7.
61. Finlay J, Roberts CM, Lowe G, Loeza J, Rossi JJ, Glackin CA. RNA-based TWIST1 inhibition via dendrimer complex to reduce breast cancer cell metastasis. Biomed Res Int. 2015;2015:382745.
62. Hu KF, Elvander M, Merza M, Akerblom L, Brandenburg A, Morein B. The immunostimulating complex (ISCOM) is an efficient mucosal delivery system for respiratory syncytial virus (RSV) envelope antigens inducing high local and systemic antibody responses. Clin Exp Immunol. 1998 Aug;113(2):235–43.
63. Morein B, Lövgren K, Höglund S, Sundquist B. The ISCOM: an immunostimulating complex. Immunol Today [Internet]. 1987;8(11):333–8.
64. Sjölander A, Cox J, Barr I. ISCOMs: An adjuvant with multiple functions. J Leukoc Biol. 1999;64:713–23.
65. Dong-Ji Z, Yang X, Shen C, Lu H, Murdin A, Brunham RC. Priming with Chlamydia trachomatis major outer membrane protein (MOMP) DNA followed by MOMP ISCOM boosting enhances protection and is associated with increased immunoglobulin A and Th1 cellular immune responses. Infect Immun. 2000 Jun;68(6):3074–8.
66. Vasilevsky S, Greub G, Nardelli-Haefliger D, Baud D. Genital Chlamydia trachomatis: understanding the roles of innate and adaptive immunity in vaccine research. Clin Microbiol Rev. 2014 Apr;27(2):346–70.
67. Zeeuwen PL. Epidermal differentiation: the role of proteases and their inhibitors. Eur J Cell Biol. 2004;83(11-12):761-73.

68. Hachem JP, Man MQ, Crumrine D, Uchida Y, Brown BE, Rogiers V et al. Sustained serine proteases activity by prolonged increase in pH leads to degradation of lipid processing enzymes and profound alterations of barrier function and stratum corneum integrity. J Invest Dermatol. 2005;125(3):510-20.

69. Meyer T. Stockfleth, E. and Chrstophers, E. Br J Dermatol. 2007Immune response profiles inhuman skin; 157:1-7

70. Romani N, Holzmann S, Tripp CH, Koch F, Stoitzner P. Langerhans cells - dendritic cells of the epidermis. APMIS. 2003;111(7-8):725-40.

71. Gockel CM, Bao S, Beagley KW. Transcutaneous immunization induces mucosal and systemic immunity: a potent method for targeting immunity to the female reproductive tract. Mol Immunol. 2000;37(9):537-44.

72. Babiuk S, Baca-Estrada M, Babiuk LA, Ewen C, Foldvari M. Cutaneous vaccination: the skin as an immunologically active tissue and the challenge of antigen delivery. J Control Release. 2000;66(2-3):199-214.

73. Mitragotri S. Current status and future prospects of needle-free liquid jet injectors. Nat Rev Dru g Discov. 2006;5(7):543-8.

74. Klein TM, Fromm M, Weissinger A, Tomes D, Schaaf S, Sletten M et al. Transfer of foreign genes into intact maize cells with highvelocity microprojectiles. Proc Natl Acad Sci U S A. 1988;85(12):4305-9.

75. Sartorelli P, Aprea C, Bussani R, Novelli MT, Orsi D, Sciarra G. In vitro percutaneous penetration of methyl-parathion from a commercial formulation through the human skin. Occup Environ Med. 1997;54(7):524-5.

76. Sarphie DF, Johnson B, Cormier M, Burkoth TL, Bellhouse BJ. Bioavailability following transdermal powdered delivery (TPD) of radiolabeled inulin to hairless guinea pigs. J Control Release. 1997;47(1):61-9.

77. Burkoth TL, Bellhouse BJ, Hewson G, Longridge DJ, Muddle AG, Sarphie DF. Transdermal and transmucosal powdered drug delivery. Crit Rev Ther Drug Carrier Syst. 1999;16(4):331-84.

78. Chen D, Endres RL, Erickson CA, Weis KF, McGregor MW, Kawaoka Y et al. Epidermal immunization by a needle-free powder delivery technology: immunogenicity of influenza vaccine and protection in mice. Nat Med. 2000;6(10):1187-90.

79. Chen D, Periwal SB, Larrivee K, Zuleger C, Erickson CA, Endres RL et al. Serum and mucosal immune responses to an inactivated influenza virus vaccine induced by epidermal powder immunization. J Virol. 2001a;75(17):7956-65.

80. Kendall M, Mitchell T, Wrighton-Smith P. Intradermal ballistic delivery of micro-particles into excised human skin for pharmaceutical applications. J Biomech. 2004;37(11):1733-41.

EXERCISE

MULTIPLE CHOICE QUESTIONS

1. A vaccine can be
   a. An antigenic protein
   b. Weakened pathogen
   c. Live attenuated pathogen
   d. All of the above
2. The term vaccine was interested by.
   a. Edward Jenner
   b. Robert Koch
   c. Louis Pasteur
   d. Von behring
3. Vaccines against viruses are usually,
   a. Given at birth
   b. Expensive
   c. Either live attenuated or killed
   d. Mainly polysaccharide
4. Antigen is an important constituent of the vaccines, to avoid contamination and increase the immune response, a component such as an adjuvant/stabilizer is added during the manufacturing process of a vaccine. Name the least commonly used adjuvant used in vaccine development.
   a. Formaldehyde
   b. Aluminum sulfate
   c. Potassium aluminum sulfate
   d. Aluminum hydroxide
5. Which of the following statement is Incorrect about the vaccine development process?
   a. A vaccine consists of live attenuated or killed germ cells,
   b. Aluminum can be used as an adjuvant in a vaccine,
   c. Animal trials are not necessary for vaccines before going to the human trial,
   d. An effective and safe vaccine production can take up to 10 to 15 years,
6. Which of the following is Not an example of a live attenuated vaccine?
   a. Tetanus vaccine
   b. MMR vaccine
   c. Varicella (chickenpox) vaccine
   d. Influenza vaccine
7. Subunit vaccine is all, Except
   a. A whole purified virus
   b. A purified part or pieces of the antigen
   c. An expensive type of vaccine
   d. A Hepatitis-B vaccine

8. The first scientificallyapproved vaccine was.....................................
   a. Oral polio vaccine
   b. Smallpox vaccine
   c. MMR vaccine (measles, mumps, and rubella)
   d. Tetanus vaccine
9. Which of the following statement is incorrect about the live attenuated vaccine?
   a. It is prepared using whole weakened living bacteria or virus.
   b. It can generate a long-term immune response with the administration of a single dose,
   c. Measles, MMR, and oral polio vaccine are live attenuated vaccines.
   d. It is stable at normal room temperature.
10. Which of the following statement is false regarding the important characteristics of the safe and effective vaccine?
    a. It must be safe and easy to use with low side effects in humans,
    b. It must provide immunity to at least 15% of the population,
    c. It must be available at a low cost,
    d. It must provide long-lasting immunity,
11. Select the incorrect statement regarding the inactivated type of vaccines:
    a. Prepared by using heat or radiation for the inactivation of toxins of the microbe,
    b. Most effective against bacterial pathogens but less on viral pathogens
    c. Poliovirus and Hepatitis A are common inactivated vaccines,
    d. Prepared by using heat or radiation for the inactivation of the microbe,
12. The vaccine which is administered as nasal spray is-
    a. Influenza   b. Measles
    c. Poliomyelitis   d. Rubella
13. Which form of influenza vaccine is live attenuated influenza vaccine
    a. Intramuscular injection   b. Nasal spray
    c. Intraosseous injection   d. Both a and c
14. Which one of the following is a kiiled vaccine
    a. Yellow fever   b. Rota virus
    c. Hepatitis A   d. Small pox

15. Toxoid vaccines are given against which of the following given disease:
    a. Diphtheria
    b. Chicken pox
    c. Tetanus
    d. Both a and b
16. The process of introduction of weakened pathogen into a human body is ________
    a. Immunization
    b. Vaccination
    c. Attenuation
    d. None of the above
17. Which type of vaccine uses attenuated form of the virus?
    a. Live vaccine
    b. Killed vaccine
    c. Inactivated vaccine
    d. None of the above
18. The first recombinant vaccine approved for human use is_____
    a. Hepatitis B vaccine
    b. DPT Vaccine
    c. MMR vaccine
    d. Tetanus vaccine
19. BCG Vaccine is a
    a. Killed vaccine.
    b. Live attenuated vaccine
    c. Inactivated vaccine
    d. Both a and c
20. Which type of vaccine is oral polio vaccine (OPV)
    a. Toxoid
    b. Live attenuated vaccine
    c. Killed vaccine.
    d. Inactivated vaccine

SHORT ANSWER QUESTIONS

1. Newer trends in delivery of vaccines.
2. Name the approaches used to enhance Transdermal delivery of vaccines.
3. Write a note on Uptake of antigens.
4. What is liquid jet injection system.
5. What do you understand by Single shot vaccines?
6. What are the barriers for transdermal delivery of vaccines.
7. What do you understand by Subunit and Conjugate Vaccine?
8. Write a note on Live attenuated vaccines and killed vaccine.
9. Explain the particle absorption by the M cells through intestine.
10. Write a short note on Polymeric Nanoparticle Based Delivery of vaccine through mucosa.

LONG ANSWER QUESTIONS

1. Describe in detail Vaccine delivery system.
2. Write a note on mucosal transdermal delivery of vaccines.
3. Define vaccines. Discuss in detail single shot vaccine.
4. Discuss the strategies used for mucosal and transdermal delivery of vaccines.
5. Describe the method used to enhance Transdermal delivery of vaccines.
6. Discuss about the various types of vaccine. Also, explain the uptake of antigen.
7. Explain about the mechanism and factors affecting formulation of liposome-based vaccine delivery.

MCQ ANSWERS

1. (d)	2. (a)	3. (c)	4. (a)
5. (c)	6. (a)	7. (a)	8. (b)
9. (d)	10. (b)	11. (a)	12. (a)
13. (b)	14. (c)	15. (d)	16. (b)
17. (a)	18. (a)	19. (b)	20. (b)